PRESIDENTS, PARLIAMENTS, AND POLICY

Advocates of parliamentary rule have been highly critical of presidentialism for dividing powers and providing the opportunity for gridlock between branches. Fixed executive terms can saddle publics with ineffectual leaders who are not easily removed. Yet the great theorists of presidential rule, beginning with the Federalists, saw very different qualities in the same institutions: a desirable combination of strong leadership with checks on executive discretion.

These diverse assessments arise because we have surprisingly little comparative work on how presidential democracies function. The introductory essays in this volume lay the theoretical groundwork for such comparative analysis. Drawing on detailed cases of economic policy making in Asia, Latin America, and Central Europe, this book shows the diversity of presidential systems and isolates the effects of presidentialism from other factors that influence public policy, such as party systems. In doing so, it casts doubt on the critique of presidential rule and underscores the continuing vitality of this particular form of democracy.

Stephan Haggard is a professor at the University of California, San Diego Graduate School of International Relations and Pacific Studies. He is the author of *Pathways from the Periphery: The Political Economy of Growth in the Newly Industrializing Countries, Developing Nations and the Politics of Global Integration*, and *The Political Economy of the Asian Financial Crisis* and coauthor with Robert Kaufman of *The Political Economy of Democratic Transitions*.

Mathew McCubbins is a professor of Political Science at the University of California, San Diego. He is coauthor of *The Democratic Dilemma, Legislative Leviathan*, and *The Logic of Delegation* and has coedited various books including *Elements of Reason, The Origins of Liberty: Structure and Policy in Japan and the United States*, and *Congress: Structure and Policy*. Professor McCubbins is the editor of the *Journal of Law, Economics, and Organization*.

POLITICAL ECONOMY OF INSTITUTIONS AND DECISIONS

Series Editors

Randall Calvert, *University of Rochester, New York*
Thrárinn Eggertsson, *Columbia University* and *University of Iceland*

Founding Editors

James E. Alt, *Harvard University*
Douglass C. North, *Washington University of St. Louis*

Other books in the series

Alesina and Howard Rosenthal, *Partisan Politics, Divided Government, and the Economy*
Lee J. Alston, Thrainn Eggertsson, and Douglass C. North, eds., *Empirical Studies in Institutional Change*
Lee J. Alston and Joseph P. Ferrie, *Southern Paternalism and the Rise of the American Welfare State: Economics, Politics, and Institutions, 1865–1965*
James E. Alt and Kenneth Shepsle, eds., *Perspectives on Positive Political Economy*
Jeffrey S. Banks and Eric A. Hanushek, eds., *Modern Political Economy: Old Topics, New Directions*
Yoram Barzel, *Economic Analysis of Property Rights, Second Edition*
Robert Bates, *Beyond the Miracle of the Market: The Political Economy of Agrarian Development in Kenya*
Peter Cowhey and Mathew McCubbins, eds., *Structure and Policy in Japan and the United States*
Gary W. Cox, *The Efficient Secret: The Cabinet and the Development of Political Parties in Victorian England*
Gary W. Cox, *Making Votes Count: Strategic Coordination in the World's Electoral System*
Jean Ensminger, *Making a Market: The Institutional Transformation of an African Society*
Kathryn Firmin-Sellers, *The Transformation of Property Rights in the Gold Coast: An Empirical Analysis Applying Rational Choice Theory*
Clark C. Gibson, *Politics and Poachers: The Political Economy of Wildlife Policy in Africa*
Ron Harris, *The Legal Framework of Business Organization: England 1720–1844*

Continued on page following index

PRESIDENTS, PARLIAMENTS, AND POLICY

Edited by

STEPHAN HAGGARD
University of California, San Diego

MATHEW D. MCCUBBINS
University of California, San Diego

CAMBRIDGE
UNIVERSITY PRESS

PUBLISHED BY THE PRESS SYNDICATE OF THE UNIVERSITY OF CAMBRIDGE
The Pitt Building, Trumpington Street, Cambridge, United Kingdom

CAMBRIDGE UNIVERSITY PRESS
The Edinburgh Building, Cambridge CB2 2RU, UK
40 West 20th Street, New York, NY 10011-4211, USA
10 Stamford Road, Oakleigh, VIC 3166, Australia
Ruiz de Alarcón 13, 28014 Madrid, Spain
Dock House, The Waterfront, Cape Town 8001, South Africa

http://www.cambridge.org

First published 2001

Printed in the United States of America

Typeface Sabon 10/13 pt.   *System* DeskTopPro$_{/UX}$ [BV]

A catalog record for this book is available from the British Library.

Library of Congress Cataloging in Publication Data
Presidents parliaments and policy / edited by Stephan Haggard Mathew D. McCubbins.
p.   cm. – (Political economy of institutions and decisions)
Includes bibliographical references.
ISBN 0-521-77304-0
1. Presidents. 2. Comparative government. 3. Economic policy. I. Haggard,
Stephan. II. McCubbins, Mathew D. (Mathew Daniel) 1956– III. Series.
JF255.P75 2000
                                                                330.9—dc21
00-029247

ISBN 0 521 77304 0 hardback
ISBN 0 521 77485 3 paperback

Contents

Contents

Tables and Figures

FIGURES

Contributors

Lisa Baldez	Washington University, St. Louis
John M. Carey	Washington University, St. Louis
Tun-jen Cheng	College of William and Mary
Gary W. Cox	University of California, San Diego
Stephan Haggard	University of California, San Diego
William B. Heller	University of Nebraska
Mark P. Jones	Michigan State University
Philip Keefer	The World Bank
Mathew D. McCubbins	University of California, San Diego
Gregory W. Noble	Australian National University
Mary Shirley	The World Bank
Matthew Soberg Shugart	University of California, San Diego

Acknowledgments

This project was sponsored by the World Bank, and we graciously acknowledge its support. We would also like to thank the Institute on Global Conflict and Cooperation for its institutional support. We further thank Paul Drake, Gary Jacobson, Rod Kiewiet, Brian Loveman, Skip Lupia, Roger Noll, Sam Popkin, and Barry Weingast for their participation in this project. We also thank Scott Basinger, Greg Bovitz, Andrea Campbell, Chris Den Hartog, Jamie Druckman, Shu Fan, Michael Ensley, and Jennifer Kuhn for their editorial and research assistance.

I

Introduction

Political Institutions and the Determinants of Public Policy

STEPHAN HAGGARD and MATHEW D. MCCUBBINS

INTRODUCTION

This volume is devoted to exploring the effects of political institutions on public policy. A generation of work has shown that institutions affect various political outcomes. For example, numerous scholars have shown that electoral systems shape the behavior of parties, candidates, and voters.[1] Other scholars have demonstrated that different constitutional structures, such as presidential or parliamentary systems, affect regime stability, accountability, responsiveness, and democratic durability.[2] Less is known about *how* and *when* institutions affect policy outcomes.[3]

---

[1] See Duverger 1954; Sartori 1968; Rae 1971; Riker 1982; Grofman and Lijphart 1986; Cain et al. 1987; Taagepera and Shugart 1989; Lijphart 1994; Ordeshook and Shvetsova 1994; Sartori 1994; McCubbins and Rosenbluth 1995; Cox and Shugart 1996; Cox 1997; and Cox and Amorim-Neto 1997.

[2] See Lijphart 1991, 1992; Shugart and Carey 1992; Stepan and Skach 1993; Linz 1994; Linz and Valenzuela 1994; and Shugart and Mainwaring 1997.

[3] There is some evidence that political institutions affect policy choice; see, for example, Shepsle 1979; Lancaster 1986; Brady and Morgan 1987; Abente 1990; Laver and Schofield 1990; North 1990; Kiewiet and McCubbins 1991; Cox and Mc-Cubbins 1991; Huber 1992; Shugart and Carey 1992; Root 1994; Strom et al. 1994; Ames 1995a, b; Cowhey and McCubbins 1995; Haggard and Kaufman 1995; Tsebelis 1995; Laver and Shepsle 1996; Levy and Spiller 1996; Tsebelis and Money 1997; Lupia and McCubbins 1998. It has been argued, for example, that single member district and single nontransferable vote electoral systems create incentives that lead legislators to demand particularistic policies – policies that provide private benefits to a district or constituency (Fiorina and Noll 1979; Weingast, Shepsle, and Johnsen 1981; Cain, Ferejohn, and Fiorina 1987; Ramseyer and Rosenbluth 1993). It has also been argued that bicameralism leads to greater budget deficits; and that separation of powers may produce gridlock and stalemate (Alesina and Tabellini 1990; McCubbins 1991; Alt and Lowry 1994; McCubbins and Rosenbluth 1995; Tsebelis 1995; Heller 1997; Tsebelis and Money 1997). While this evidence is often compelling, there are as many institutional hypotheses as there are observations.

For nearly 300 years, constitution writers and institutional designers have been cognizant that their choice of institutional structure affects political behavior. They have recognized that there is no single ideal form of democratic government, and that each choice involves tradeoffs. For example, if law-making authority is unified in a single place, whether it be in the legislature or the executive, then the likelihood that a single faction with a narrow purpose will seize control of government is greatly increased. At the extreme, tyranny results. If, by contrast, law making is so thoroughly separated that numerous competing factions each must consent to changes in law and policy, then government may be incapable of sustaining the public order.[4] The extreme form of this condition, decision by unanimity, can lead to paralysis and chaos. Every democracy, whether parliamentary or presidential, federal or unitary, treads this space between tyranny and anarchy.

To avoid the extremes of tyranny and anarchy, institutional designers must allocate power among officeholders and structure the incentives of these officeholders accordingly. To decrease the likelihood of tyranny, many democracies rely on a system of checks and balances to separate powers, so that the ability to change public policy is shared among many competing areas of government. Legislative power may be separated from executive power, and both are separated from judicial power. The focus of most research on democratic institutions has been on the creation, function, and effects of these institutional checks.[5]

According to one of America's early institutional engineers, James

Further, there are numerous counterexamples where institutions seem not to affect policy (Johnson 1982; Putnam 1993).

[4] By tyranny we mean, "The accumulation of all power, legislative executive, and judiciary, in the same hands, whether of one, a few, or many, and whether hereditary, self appointed, or elective . . ." (Madison, *Federalist* 47). By faction we mean, ". . . a number of citizens, whether amounting to a majority or a minority of the whole, who are united and actuated by some common impulse of passion, or of interest, adverse to the rights of other citizens, or to the permanent and aggregate interests of the community" (Madison, *Federalist* 10).

[5] Ibid., footnote 3. The recent, theoretical work that has most focused on the separation of powers is Tsebelis (1995). His focus is on how the number of veto gates in a political system, and the conflict of interest among the persons occupying those veto gates, affect legislative productivity. He shows in a cooperative game theoretic framework that an increase in either the number of veto gates or the diversity of veto players will reduce the likelihood of new laws passing. Thus his analysis emphasizes predominantly the checks in a system. Tsebelis's work on bicameralism, and especially on the navette system (see Tsebelis and Money 1997), looks at the balances between branches to a much greater extent, and therefore complements his work on vetoes and law production.

Madison, for a separation of powers to create effective checks and balances, each branch of government "should have a will of its own," and needs to be given "the necessary constitutional and personal means to resist encroachments."[6] In other words, beyond the separation of powers, there must also be a separation of *purpose* – so that different parts of the government are motivated to seek different goals. Failing this, the system of checks established by the separation of powers can be effectively disabled.

In general terms, a separation of powers can be thought of as the extent to which different components of government have the ability to exert influence through the exercise of a veto on the formation of public policy (for a more precise definition, see Cox and McCubbins's chapter in this volume). A separation of powers is the defining feature of presidential systems, but as Tsebelis (1995) points out, it can be found in parliamentary systems as well in the form of bicameral legislatures (Tsebelis and Money 1997), federal structures, or party systems that generate coalition governments (Laver and Shepsle 1996).

A separation of purpose, however, is orthogonal to a separation of powers; it can occur with or without a separation of powers. For instance, when a society has diverse interests, and its political institutions provide distinct channels for the representation of those interests, then a separation of purpose and power are both present. A unitary parliamentary regime, for example, lacks a formal separation of powers, but can also give rise to a separation of purpose in the form of a coalition government in which the goals of the different coalition members differ or through dominant parties that are internally divided, as in Japan.[7]

This discussion suggests the two-by-two typology of institutional regimes presented in Table 1.1. The diversity of country examples in the table illustrates an important point: Democratic institutions differ substantially with respect to separation of purpose and power, while many different institutional arrangements lie in between the extremes of tyranny and anarchy.

The central theme of this book is that these different institutional arrangements *also have systematic effects on policy making*. Although

---

[6] Madison, *Federalist* 51.
[7] For a discussion of the effects of coalition government on policy, see Huber (1998). In addition to coalition governments, minority governments can also be construed as examples of separation of purpose, to the extent that they must appease opposition parties in order to prevent the government from falling. See Strom (1990b).

Table 1.1. *Combinations of Separation of Purpose and Power*

		Power	
	Unified	Unified:	Separated:
		United Kingdom	Mexico
			Taiwan
Purpose			
	Separated	Japan	United States
		Czech Republic	Argentina
			Poland
			Chile

the relative merits and consequences of presidential and parliamentary systems have received substantial attention,[8] we argue that this distinction between macro institutions is inadequate; explaining political outcomes often requires greater focus on the details of institutional structure. How exactly is the separation of purpose established? What rules create a separation of purpose? How well does the separation of purpose match the separation of powers? In what ways do these institutions affect policy making?

To get a handle on these questions, our case studies look primarily at the right column in Table 1.1, examining the effects of variations among presidential regimes. While much of our theory is abstract enough to be applied to any political system, our emphasis on presidential systems means that many interesting questions about a separation of purpose in unified regimes remain outside the scope of this book.[9] At the same time, three advantages are derived from focusing on presidential systems. First, we can control basic constitutional arrangements – i.e., presidentialism and parliamentarism – in order to better isolate the effects of other institutions, such as bicameralism and electoral rules. Second, we can discuss how variations in important dimensions *within* presidential regimes affect gridlock, stalemate, responsiveness, stability, and accountability. Moreover, by doing fewer but more in-depth case studies, we may more closely analyze policy making and political outcomes than would be possible if we were to do more, shallower case studies.

---

[8] See, for example, Lijphart 1992; Shugart and Carey 1992; and Linz 1994.
[9] See Laver and Shepsle (1996) for more on unified regimes.

THE SEPARATION OF POWERS AND THE
SEPARATION OF PURPOSE

For this reason, that convention which passed the ordinance of government, laid its foundation on this basis, that the legislative, executive, and judiciary departments should be separate and distinct, so that no person should exercise the powers of more than one of them at a time. (James Madison, *Federalist* 48)

In order to lay a due foundation for that separate and distinct exercise of the different powers of government, which to a certain extent is admitted on all hands to be essential to the preservation of liberty, it is evident that each department should have a will of its own; and consequently should be so constituted that the members of each should have as little agency as possible in the appointment of the members of the others . . . Were the executive magistrate, or the judges, not independent of the legislature in this particular, their independence in every other would be merely nominal.

But the great security against a gradual concentration of the several powers in the same department, consists in giving to those who administer each department the necessary constitutional means and personal motives to resist encroachments of the others. (James Madison, *Federalist* 51)

There are nearly as many ways to separate power and purpose as there are democracies. The first part of this volume asks, what are the implications of each choice? To begin, we can measure the degree of separation of power in terms of the potential number of "veto players" in a political system.[10] In a pure dictatorship, a single individual holds the only veto, whereas in a system of unanimous rule, every person possesses a veto. The likelihood that a single individual or faction can control all of the vetoes in a system is expected to decrease, or at least not increase, with an expansion in the number of veto players. Alternatively, expanding the number of veto players is expected to increase, or at least not decrease, the number of different interests involved in political decision making. Therefore, this choice over the number of veto players is a crucial constitutional decision.

The number of veto players is only half of the story, however, because it ignores the effect of a separation of purpose. If power is separated, but purpose is unified, then the effective number of vetoes may be near one, as each separate institution is working toward a common goal, with jointly determined payoffs. By contrast, if each veto player's payoffs are

[10] A veto player is a person, group, or faction who, through their control of an office, post, or branch of government, can reject any proposed changes to existing policy.

independent from the others (e.g., their electoral fates are independent of one another), then the effective number of vetoes may be near the maximum number of vetoes.

In Chapter 2, Cox and McCubbins outline a general framework for understanding the separation of powers, of which presidentialism is an important variant, and the separation of purposes. They argue that the separations of power and purpose work together to establish two key tradeoffs with respect to policy outcomes. The first tradeoff is between a political system's *decisiveness* (i.e., its ability to make policy decisions) and its *resoluteness* (i.e., its ability to commit to established policy decisions). The authors contend that a polity's ability to change or to commit to policy depends heavily on what they call the *effective number of vetoes* in political decision making. Cox and McCubbins use this term to represent two salient aspects of the political process: the number of political actors that possess a veto over policy change, and the conflict of interest between those actors. In a polity in which the effective number of vetoes is large, changing policy will be difficult, but committing to policy will be relatively easier. The reverse will also be true. The fact that this tradeoff is determined jointly by the separations of power and purpose has been largely overlooked in the modern literature. However, the tradeoff between decisiveness and resoluteness is apparent from the definitions: a more decisive polity, possessing a greater ability to make or implement policy changes in the short run at least, must necessarily be less resolute, and thus less likely to be able to maintain the new status quo. By contrast, a more resolute polity must necessarily be less able to implement or even decide on policy changes, and hence must be considered less decisive. As Cox and McCubbins argue, each extreme along these dimensions has undesirable consequences. At one end, a polity that lacks decisiveness and is prone to gridlock will prove incapable of addressing pressing policy problems when they arise. At the other extreme, a polity that is irresolute will be threatened by policy instability.[11]

Cox and McCubbins further contend that a second tradeoff is implied by the separations of power and purpose, over the *public-* and *private-regardedness* of the policy produced. In other words, the extent to which the policies produced by a given system resemble public goods, improve allocative efficiency, and promote the general welfare versus funneling private benefits to individuals, factions, or regions, in the form of proj-

---

[11] See, e.g., North 1981, 1990; World Bank 1995; and Levy and Spiller 1996.

ects, subsidies, and tax loopholes depends at least in part on the country's choice of basic political institutions.[12] Cox and McCubbins argue that the greater the number of effective vetoes, the more private regarding will be the policies enacted; the reverse is also true. This outcome is a consequence of bargaining among veto players, where each veto player will be able to demand, and receive, side payments in the form of narrowly targeted policies. Thus, when the effective number of vetoes is great, even broad public policy will be packaged as a set of individual projects, or it will be packaged with narrowly targeted programs, tax relief, and so forth.

In Chapter 3, Shugart and Haggard extend this general theoretical exploration with their discussion of institutional variation among presidential systems.[13] Shugart and Haggard look at the relationship between key features of the structure of presidential democracies and the tradeoff between decisiveness and resoluteness. They divide the key presidential institutions first according to whether they affect the president's *reactive* (e.g., veto) versus *proactive* (e.g., decree authority) powers, and second according to how they influence the separation of purpose between the legislative and executive departments.

Shugart and Haggard then argue that the more reactive powers a president possesses, the more resolute (i.e., less decisive) will be the policy-making process; while the more proactive powers a president has, the more decisive (i.e., less resolute) will be the process. Although it is impossible to determine the sum effect of increasing both reactive and

---

[12] While usually regarded as corruption or inefficient side-payments by economists, Cox and McCubbins argue that the use of public policy for private gain, known in the literature as distributive policy, or colloquially as "pork," need not have negative consequences for a polity. Since an increase in transactions costs goes hand-in-hand with an increase in the effective number of veto players, it may in fact be the case that pork is the most efficient political currency with which to pay these transactions costs. Pork may then be the currency with which the "market" for policy change is completed. Furthermore, what may appear to be pork to some may be a collective good for some other faction that is simply indivisible. For example, if a port or a canal is needed to improve allocative efficiency, then the fact that it is built in one legislative district or province and not another does not imply that there is no social welfare gain; it only implies that some members of society gain disproportionately. But despite the inequality, the net improvement can be expected to be positive.

[13] Despite widespread academic enthusiasm for parliamentarism, many newly developing countries have opted for presidential rule. See, e.g., Shugart and Carey 1992; Mainwaring and Shugart 1997a.

proactive powers, it is clear that the *absence* of both implies that the legislature is essentially unchecked, in which case, the system will be less resolute. In addition, they observe that in presidential systems where the connection between voters and executive formation does not run through legislators, legislators themselves are likely to be less decisive (even when the presidency is proactive, and hence decisive). Legislators in presidential systems are less dependent on their party's national reputation than in parliamentary systems, in which the connection between voters and government runs through legislators.[14]

COMPARATIVE CASE STUDIES OF THE SEPARATIONS OF POWER AND PURPOSE IN PRESIDENTIAL SYSTEMS

In the second part of the book the contributors test a number of the hypotheses presented in the first part by Cox and McCubbins and Shugart and Haggard, concerning the relationship between institutional choices and policy outcomes. Specifically, the authors examine how institutional variations affect policy outputs in four countries: Argentina, Chile, Taiwan, and Poland. Argentina, Chile, and Taiwan are presidential systems; Poland is a premier-presidential system in which the president holds a veto. These case studies were chosen to allow the authors to compare them to one another while controlling for one crucial constitutional factor – the institutional separation of powers. These comparisons are particularly fruitful because there exists ample variation on other institutional dimensions, including the range of presidential powers and the electoral and party systems.[15] The choice of these countries also allows us to exploit temporal variations between authoritarian and newly democratic rule within each country. Thus, to some extent, the empirical studies follow Lijphart's (1971) most similar systems design enabling the authors to focus on specific institutional variations rather than resorting to broad claims about general country differences.[16] The goal of these studies is to test whether the evidence refutes or supports the hypotheses presented in the theoretical section.

---

[14] This feature applies only to pure presidential systems, and not to either parliamentary or premier-presidential systems, in which the connection between voters and government formation, indeed, does run through legislators.

[15] In Poland, the president has significant reactive (veto) power, but minimal proactive powers; in contrast, the presidents of Argentina, Chile, and Taiwan have strong reactive and proactive powers.

[16] See Przeworski and Teune 1970.

Despite the dominance of the case study approach in comparative politics, the utility of case studies for testing theories is by no means universally accepted. Because case studies do not generate sufficient amounts of data, they suffer from a fundamental "degrees of freedom" problem (Campbell 1975). Since such models often have more independent variables than observations, scholars such as King et al. (1994, 44) conclude that "as currently practiced, [case studies] often do not meet the standards for valid inference." This does not mean, however, that carefully designed and implemented case studies cannot be used to test theories. Indeed, medical researchers often study individual cases to investigate the efficacy of a new treatment. Evolutionary biologists test modern theories of evolution by examining a single, representative case. Moreover, case studies can be used, as we do in this volume, to develop and refine theory.

The problem, then, is not that case studies are antithetical to the scientific method. The problem is rather that case studies have not traditionally been used to test more general theories. In order to use a case study as a valid test, it is crucial first to state the theory's predictions in a manner that permits evaluation. Predictions often take one of two forms: They give us *sufficient* relationships between variables, in the form of "if A then B"; or they give us *necessary* relationships between variables of the form "B only when A." We must consider, however, that predictions from a theory may only be true within some context (i.e., only when other conditions are met). When this is the case, we must be careful to state and measure these conditional variables. Steps must also be taken to guarantee that the case being studied is a close analogy to the theory being evaluated. Thus, a case study serves as a critical test of a theory only when we have reliable measures for important variables, when specified contextual conditions are met, and when the case is a close analogy to our theory.

OUR VARIABLES

In using case studies as critical tests, we must be careful when we define and operationalize the variables of interest. This includes the independent institutional variables as well as the dependent policy variables. Indeed, to perform effective comparisons of institutional effects, we must move from the abstract institutional categories in the theoretical chapters to specific institutional arrangements. To do this, it is necessary to disaggregate both broad institutional characteristics and the key policy issues we believe institutional analysis can explain.

Dependent Variables

The case studies address three major policy issues: budgeting, privatization, and electricity regulation. Fiscal policy is clearly central to the conduct of national economic policy and has played a central role in recent efforts to achieve macroeconomic stability in developing countries. Privatization of state-owned enterprises is an important means for promoting economic growth and efficiency. Electricity regulation was chosen because it exemplifies the difficult nature of adopting market-oriented policies. It is increasingly recognized that privatization and marketization promise efficiency gains and higher growth, but only if accompanied by a credible and stable regulatory environment, both of which have their roots in the constitutional and political order.

In this volume, we address several questions about reform in each of these three policy areas. First, we ask why some governments implement reforms quickly and decisively, while other governments are marked by delay and indecision. Second, we ask why is policy making sometimes characterized by responsiveness to the median voter and to overall social welfare, while at other times it is characterized by responsiveness to narrow interests?[17] Finally we ask, what explains variation in the stability of policy once it is enacted (i.e., the resoluteness of policy)? Furthermore, once a government passes legislation, do agents and markets believe that it will persist, or do institutions send signals that policy is easily reversible?

As we will see, there are interesting tradeoffs among these dimensions of policy. Systems that are decisive need to develop other mechanisms for signaling that policy is stable, since the ability to change policy easily also implies that policy can be reversed. Conversely, systems where the policy status quo is hard to change are resolute, but they may prove dangerously indecisive, especially in the face of shocks or crises.

Independent Variables

In the empirical chapters, we divide the key institutional variables into four categories, each of which has some effect on both the separation of

---

[17] Examples of these interests are geographic constituencies, interest groups, and influential political supporters.

powers and the separation of purpose. Under each category heading below, we list the important questions that must be asked about each institutional arrangement in order to understand its incentive effects in the presidential systems we examine:

1. *The Powers of the President.*

    i. What specific powers does the president have over policy making? Does the president possess reactive powers, such as the authority to veto or delay legislation? Does the president possess a package or line-item veto?

    ii. What specific proactive powers does the president possess? In what areas does the president have the authority to take unilateral action – action that does not require legislative approval and is not subject to legislative control? Can the president issue decrees? Does the president require prior legislative direction, leave, or permission to do so? What is the president's authority over setting the budget? Does the president's budget become the reversionary outcome in the case of legislative impasse?

    iii. With respect to a separation of purpose *within* the executive, how much decision making is delegated to cabinet ministers? Are there independent agencies or consultative bodies other than the cabinet on which the president depends?

2. *Legislative Institutions.*

    i. Is the legislature unicameral or bicameral? If the legislature is bicameral, are the chambers coequal? Does one or do both chambers possess vetoes over policy proposals? What share of legislators are required to exercise this veto? Does one or do both have agenda power?

    ii. With respect to a separation of purpose within the legislature, if the legislature is bicameral, do the chambers have congruent or noncongruent constituencies?

3. *Federalism.*

    i. Does the national government determine the leadership of lower units of government, or is this leadership locally selected?

    ii. Do lower units of government have taxing and spending authority independent of the national government, or do they require explicit permission? Are state or local authorities able to check or resist policy initiatives from the national government? If so, by what means and to what extent can they resist?

4. *Electoral Rules and the Separation of Purpose.*

   i. How are legislators elected and reelected? Is the legislative electoral system organized around proportional representation or plurality rule? Is there intraparty preference voting? How many representatives are elected per district? How many electoral districts exist? How are they defined?

   ii. Where does the authority and responsibility for nominations lie? May legislators seek reelection? Do electoral rules govern political parties? How easy is it for a candidate to be included on the ballot?

   iii. How often do elections occur? Do they occur simultaneously for the separate branches?

   iv. Are the president's terms of office fixed? Can the president be renominated and/or reelected?

For some of these questions, the linkages with policy have been well developed in the literature and are surveyed in the chapters that follow. In these instances, our contribution is to place the accepted hypotheses within a unifying framework. This will allow us to address questions regarding when these institutional features are important and in what ways they are important. In some instances, we find, however, that the policy consequences of many institutions, and their interactions, have not been adequately theorized. We identify various institutional arrangements that occur frequently in developing countries and rarely in developed countries – such as combining fragmented party systems with presidents who possess strong reactive and proactive powers – and indicate some of their systematic effects on policy.

One important finding is that divided government need not lead to stalemate, gridlock, and indecisiveness. Rather, only when cross-institutional or cross-party coalition formation is difficult or costly will indecisiveness be the result of separated powers. When conditions favor coalition formation, even divided governments can act decisively. The consequence of the separation of powers and of divided government is then only to increase the distributive content of the policy produced. This will be shown to be the case for Argentina and Poland, and for the political system currently emerging in Taiwan.

The ability of separated institutions and the parties that control them to forge coalitions is, in part, a consequence of the institutions that affect the separation of purpose. The broader and more centrist the parties produced by the electoral system, the easier it will be for these parties to forge coalitions with other broad and centrist parties.

Unified government, by contrast, can be decisive but need not be. A unified government will act decisively only when its members prefer a policy change to the reversionary outcome. A new unified government may be more likely to attempt to change policy upon assuming office, but thereafter will be content to retain the reversionary policy that it created. As long as this party retains a veto over policy change, policy will be resolute.

THE COUNTRY CASES

The first three case studies evaluate the effects of the separation of powers and purpose on budgetary policy making. In Chapter 4, Baldez and Carey argue that many of the procedures defined in the Chilean Constitution of 1980 limit the discretion of elected officials and, to date, have marginalized the role of Congress. Consequently, legislative procedures serve to minimize the effective separation of powers regarding spending policy. One important example is the definition of reversionary spending levels, which are implemented when the Congress and president fail to pass a new budget. In this system, the president has tremendous proactive power, as his original proposal becomes law if the Congress and president fail to agree. This proactive presidential power clearly advantages the president in budgetary negotiations. In addition, the rules establishing the composition of the Senate (e.g., the block of *designados*, or appointed senators) have allowed Pinochet's party to retain a veto over policy changes proposed by the president and the lower house. The end product is budgetary resoluteness, with little in the way of policy innovation or change.

Baldez and Carey hypothesize that Chilean budget deficits should be small relative to other countries with alternative budgetary procedures, even after the transition to democracy. This is because it will be difficult to forge cross-institutional coalitions to create new spending programs. They also hypothesize that the share of the budget devoted to the military should decline with the transition to civilian rule, despite the fact that senators appointed by the outgoing military regime still hold a military party's veto in the Senate. Since the military no longer sets the agenda, it can protect the reversionary level of spending only with its veto. They test these hypotheses with data from 1985–1996, find strong support for their hypotheses, and conclude that rules of procedure appear to have substantial effects on policy making. They argue that the institutional legacy of Chile's authoritarian past will continue to generate fiscal restraint in the short run, but there are already signs that this tendency may not persist if the appointees of the military lose their veto in the Senate.

In Chapter 5, Jones analyzes the budget process in Argentina. He argues that the separation of powers under the Constitution, combined with the separation of purpose existing in Argentine society and enhanced by its electoral system, fostered chaos, conflict, and indecisiveness under divided government. Only under conditions of unified government was budgetary policy resolute. Jones identifies three critical institutions that contributed to this outcome: the president's procedural power; the separation of power among the two legislative chambers and the president; and the electoral laws that lead to strong party loyalty and, in this case, to separation of purpose.

The current budget-making procedure allows the president to amend the budget proposal unilaterally before it proceeds to the legislature as well as to veto certain legislative actions. In addition, the reversionary outcome in this system is defined as the previous year's budget. Jones finds that the consequences of divided government depend upon the ability of the president to forge coalitions with the majority parties or coalition members in the legislature. When coalition bargaining is difficult, budgets will be stable and incremental, as the reversionary outcome will be maintained. By contrast, when the president is forced into cross-party deals with Congress, the result is "explosive" budget policy with larger deficits and a great amount of particularistic policy – i.e., "pork." Under unified government, Jones expects to observe more stability and thus less variance in spending levels and deficits.

Jones tests these hypotheses using data from between 1983 and 1989, when President Alfonsin lacked a working majority in one or both houses of the legislature, and data from the period following 1991, when President Menem's party controlled both legislative chambers. Jones finds that the empirical tests strongly support his hypotheses, providing evidence for the assertions about the importance of the coincident separation of power and purpose. He suggests that in the event that divided government reappears, then the instability, gridlock, and fiscal crises of the 1980s may return as well.

Cheng and Haggard, in Chapter 6, argue that the introduction of electoral competition in the 1992 Taiwanese election also introduced a separation of purpose into a system of separated powers. This in turn forced the executive to accommodate the electoral interests of locally elected legislators in the Kuomintang (KMT) party. Given these developments, they expect the composition of spending to shift in favor of particularistic projects and away from national projects, such as military spending. The evidence largely confirms their expectations. Changes in fiscal policy have also been accompanied by a clear reassertion of legislative prerogatives in the budget *process* and by institutional reorganizations within the legislature, both of which have been responses to emerging collective action problems within the KMT. As electoral reforms increase competition, the separation of purpose within the Taiwanese government will increase. Consequently the existing separation of powers may lead to scenarios familiar in other presidential systems, including budget deficits and increased distributive content of policy.

Chapters 7 and 8 assess the effects of regulatory procedure on policy outcomes. Heller and McCubbins perform a comparative analysis of electricity regulation in Argentina and Chile, focusing on how national political institutions affect resoluteness in regulatory policy. They argue that the risk of investment depends on judgments about the resoluteness of regulatory processes and policy as well as on regime stability. In Argentina, where privatization developed erratically, regime instability has been an urgent concern. However, recent constitutional reforms have provided a somewhat firmer foundation for regime stability. The electrical power industries in Argentina have held most of the agenda power with respect to tariffs and prices, such that procedural power operates as a partial substitute for regime stability and offers a degree of resoluteness. By contrast, in Chile privatization developed steadily and without much threat of regime instability. The regulatory procedure established a profitable reversion for investors and a predictable process in which the regulators could control the agenda.

Haggard and Noble examine the evolution of electricity regulation in Taiwan. They show that Taiwan avoided the problems of extreme expropriation risk and distorted pricing due to America's influence through its aid mission (an effective veto). Little changed until the KMT began to liberalize the political system in recent years. Legislators began to face new electoral incentives, which placed them at odds with other branches of the Taiwanese government. The party has attempted to respond by reconfiguring its political support base and has begun to engage in distributive policy making, specifically by responding to so-called not-in-my-backyard (NIMBY) social movements against the expansion of nuclear power. Thus, while the transition to democracy has potentially improved efficiency by reducing the influence of cronies in regulatory policy making and by empowering the private sector, the candidate-centered single nontransferable vote (SNTV) electoral system and the distributive tendencies it engenders operate as a countervailing force against improved efficiency. Further, coalition formation is becoming increasingly expensive as emerging electoral competition has forged a separation of purpose among KMT legislators. This too should cause Taiwanese policy to become increasingly distributive. The long-run response to the recent changes remains to be seen, but decisions concerning pricing, allocation, and particularly privatization, are already yielding to distributive pressures within the KMT.

In Chapter 9, Keefer and Shirley study the reform of state-owned enterprises (SOEs) in Poland, a premier-presidential system. Their analysis illustrates the potential for separation of purpose to occur even when the president and the major government coalition partner share the same goal – in this case, privatization. SOE reform in Poland was handicapped by a decentralized system of control over the state-owned enterprises that were to be privatized, such that the enterprises themselves held vetoes over policy proposals. Their analysis compares the reform process in Poland to the reform process in neighboring Czechoslovakia – a parliamentary system similar to Poland's in many noninstitutional respects, but which followed a markedly different route to privatization. Because both nations achieved independence from Soviet control at approximately the same time, and because both countries sought to privatize their SOEs, the cases of Poland and the Czech Republic present a natural experiment in the effects of institutional variations. The goal of Keefer and Shirley's chapter is to explain how two nations in apparently similar situations could take such different avenues to liberalization and still end up with relatively similar results. The answer they suggest is that a unity of purpose that favored privatization existed in Czechoslovakia, but was absent in Poland.[18] Thus, while the Czechs pursued privatization with zeal, Poland was mired in indecisiveness. Interestingly, Poland's indecisiveness was resolved through a logroll that parceled out private goods at a public cost, in this case taking the form of subsidies to agriculture, an enterprise that had suffered under the existing policy. In Poland, then, decentralization and coalition politics, and not the separation of power or purpose between the president and legislature,

---

[18] Note that, in Table 1.1, the Czech Republic is listed as a "separation of purpose" country, because it is governed by coalition governments. The claim made here, and in Chapter 9, is that the Czech government enjoyed unity of purpose *with respect to the issue of privatization*. This distinction underscores the possibility that the degree to which purpose is unified may vary across issues, or over time.

appear to have been the key factors in the policy-making process. Thus the chapter by Keefer and Shirley expands the focus beyond the usual suspects, and also demonstrates how to incorporate information about the reversionary policy profitably, in order to discover how additional factors affect policy outcomes.

CONCLUSION

For too long, debate has focused on the question of whether institutions matter. In order to progress beyond this question, it is necessary to shift our focus from sweeping, general questions about institutions (such as presidentialism vs. parliamentarism), and to develop more fine-grained comparisons. It is important to delineate expectations more carefully and modestly. The chapters in this volume follow this strategy, by emphasizing the influence of various institutional arrangements that fall under the heading of "presidentialism."

In addition, a great deal of the literature on institutions focuses on dependent variables such as representativeness, efficiency, and governmental stability. All of these are important variables; ultimately, however, we are interested in them because of what they imply about the behavior of governments. One of the significant contributions of the works contained herein is their focus on institutions' impact on tangible government behavior – i.e., policy outputs.

This volume suggests as many new and interesting research questions as it answers. Indeed, we believe a focus on the interactions between separation of power, separation of purpose, and institutional detail, is a remarkably flexible and versatile analytic tool. It is general enough to apply across regime types, geographic regions, and substantive questions. Consequently, we hope this book stimulates the further development of this style of analysis.

PART I

Theory

2

The Institutional Determinants of Economic Policy Outcomes

GARY W. COX and MATHEW D. MCCUBBINS

INTRODUCTION

Why do some democracies choose economic policies that promote economic growth, while others seem incapable of prospering? Why are some polities able to provide the public goods that are necessary for economic growth, while others turn the machinery of government toward providing private goods? Why are some countries able to make long term credible policy commitments, while others cannot?[1]

In what follows, we present a theory that argues that the diversity of economic policies is rooted in the diversity of democratic institutions in each country. Each polity, according to the divisions and necessities of its society, chooses a set of democratic institutions to resolve its basic political problems. These institutions define a sequence of principal–agent relationships (Dahl 1967), commonly numbering at least three. First, the sovereign people delegate decision-making power (usually via a written constitution) to a national legislature and executive. The primary tools that the people retain in order to ensure appropriate behavior on the part of their representatives are two: the power to replace them at election time and the power to set the constitutional rules of the political game.

A second delegation of power occurs when the details of the internal organization of the legislature and executive are settled. This process entails the creation of ministerial positions, of committees, and of agenda control mechanisms. Here too constitutional regulations of the relation-

---

[1] See Schattschneider (1963); McConnell (1966); Krueger (1974); Peltzman (1976); Buchanan et al. (1980); North (1981, 1990); Olson (1982); Rogowski (1989).

ship between the legislature and the executive (is the legislature dissoluble? can cabinet ministers sit in the legislature?) come into play.

Third, the legislature and the executive delegate to various bureaus and agencies to execute the laws. In this delegation, administrative procedures and law set the terms of the delegation (McCubbins et al. 1987, 1989; Kiewiet and McCubbins 1991).[2]

To regulate these delegations, institutional arrangements are often employed to assure that delegation does not become abdication.[3] One key device is to separate power among a number of agents, and to separate the purposes of those agents, such that no single authority can control the outcome of delegation at any single stage. That is, by setting up ambition to counter ambition, the principals attempt to prevent their agents from taking advantage of their delegated authority. However, such arrangements are imperfect, as they entail certain tradeoffs. Our chapter studies these tradeoffs and the consequences, direct and indirect, of institutionally separating power and purpose. The structure of these constitutional principal–agent relationships affects the form of public policy.[4]

The separations of power and purpose together establish two key tradeoffs with respect to democratic outcomes. The first is between a political system's *decisiveness* and its *resoluteness.* The tradeoff that any country makes on this dimension – between having the ability to change policy and having the ability to commit to policy – depends heavily on the effective number of vetoes in the political system. Polities that choose to locate at either extreme will be ungovernable. At one end, a polity that lacks decisiveness will encounter gridlock and stalemate. At the

---

[2] Another important step in the process of delegation takes bureau chiefs as principals and their subordinates in the lower levels of the bureaucracy as agents. It is important, therefore, to recognize that even if politicians employ mechanisms to limit agency loss, the delegation can fail if top level bureaucrats cannot constrain *their* agents. This issue of internal delegation at the level of the administrative agency raises questions concerning the structure of incentives facing middle- and low-level bureaucrats.

[3] For an overview of such arrangements, see Chapter 2 of Kiewiet and McCubbins (1991).

[4] Economists have led the way in recognizing the link between political institutions and investment. Economic studies have shown, both theoretically and empirically, that institutional structure can stimulate investment by establishing a credible commitment to policy (North and Weingast 1989; North 1990; World Bank 1995; Guasch and Spiller 1996; Levy and Spiller 1996) or reducing transactions costs (Williamson 1975; Milgram, North, and Weingast 1990; North 1990).

other end, a polity that lacks resoluteness will be threatened by a lack of stability.[5] The second tradeoff implied by the separations of power and purpose in a political system is between the *private-* and *public-regardedness* of policy produced.

We begin by discussing in greater detail the two tradeoffs implied by the choice of institutions. We then perform a step-by-step analysis of the sequence of delegations of power from the citizenry to elected officials, looking first at the electoral and constitutional rules of the state and asking which rules seem to promote or hinder two *bêtes noires* of classical democratic theory: state "ungovernability" and the excessive influence of special interest groups. We next turn to the other delegations noted above, first that involving the internal organization of legislatures and executives, then that from legislatures to the bureaucracy. In the final section we derive implications for the case studies contained in Part II of the volume.

DEMOCRATIC TRADEOFFS

In exploring the consequences of separating power, it is essential to note that there are two distinct elements in any functioning separation-of-powers system. First, there is the legal separation of power itself – provisions that both houses of a bicameral legislature must approve legislation, for example.[6] Second, there are rules intended to ensure that a single interest does not gain control all the relevant offices or institutions, which would remove the effectiveness of the legal checks. That is, there must also be a separation of purpose.

It may be difficult to define the minimum separation of purpose – between, say, president and assembly – sufficiently to ensure that the separation of power in fact provides some insurance against tyranny. But the extreme cases are clear enough. On the one hand, we have

---

[5] See, e.g., North (1981, 1990), World Bank (1995), and Levy and Spiller (1996).

[6] The discussion above implicitly adopts a dichotomous view of the separation of power: Some systems separate power and some do not. As a first order approximation, this distinction is fair enough but as soon as one begins looking very hard, all sorts of shades and ambiguities appear. In what follows, we shall for the most part continue to use simple dichotomies – e.g., presidential/parliamentary or bicameral/unicameral – but return from time to time to the more ambiguous cases – e.g., premier-presidentialism (Shugart and Carey 1992) or asymmetric bicameralism (Lijphart 1984).

Mexico before the late 1990s, Taiwan before the late 1980s, or the U.S.S.R. as cases in which the unity of purpose provided by a single party was sufficiently great to defuse the political importance of parchment divisions of power. On the other hand, we have episodes of *divided government* in the United States or *cohabitation* in France in which those controlling different institutions clearly had different political preferences, in other words when the separation of power coincides with a separation of purpose.

Usually the term *divided government* refers just to presidential systems in which no single party controls both the assembly and the presidency. But here we extend the definition: *Government is divided when no single political party controls all separate powers*; otherwise, we shall say that *unified government* exists.[7] Divided government thus arises not just when the assembly and the presidency are in different partisan hands, but also when the two houses of a bicameral legislature are, or when the presidency and the courts are, and so forth.[8]

Counting the Number of Veto Actors

Although we use the term *divided government* to indicate a simple yes/no dichotomy, a finer-grained distinction can be made by counting the number of separate veto actors. Following Tsebelis (1995), we define a *veto actor* on a given issue dimension as the person, political party, or faction of a political party, that exercises a veto on that issue by itself.

The motivation behind this definition can be described as follows. First, a veto actor must be an actor, not just any collection of officeholders. If a single individual, such as a president, holds a veto over policy change, then that individual is a veto actor. But to exercise a veto held by a collectivity, such as an assembly or legislative committee, will re-

---

[7] The point is not that the separation of power will have no consequences if there is not a *partisan* division of purpose between institutions. Instead, the point is that an observable partisan division of purpose is the best proxy we have to measure the true underlying division of purpose (which is unobservable).

[8] As stated, our definition would also count a situation in which a coalition of parties controls all separate powers as "divided government." Possibly, of course, a coalition in one country may be as unitary as a catch-all party in another, so that the distinction between parties and coalitions fails to order the cases properly. Again, this is a measurement error problem. Conceptually, we would like to have a precise and continuous measure of how much purpose is separated between the coalitions/parties that control the various separate powers in a system. We simply use partisan divisions as the best available proxy.

quire collective action. The opportunity and transactions costs of collective action may be considerable, and are rarely overcome without a suitable organizational structure serving to mitigate these expenses (Olsen 1965; Williamson 1975; North 1990; Cox and McCubbins 1993).

Operationally, then, while we take all individuals to be actors, groups of individuals are actors only if they have some organizational basis – *de minimis*, recognized membership and leadership – that will facilitate their collective action. Thus, we do not count as veto actors all majority coalitions in a majority-rule legislature, because not all these coalitions have an organizational basis. Nor do we count as veto actors all majority coalitions within a committee that possess agenda power, because not all those coalitions have an organizational basis.

Our second criterion is that a veto actor must have a veto. Operationally, we look for subunits of the polity – legislative chambers, legislative committees, presidents – to which agenda power has been explicitly delegated. (If a party or faction controls this subunit, we say it has a veto.)

As the purpose of this definition is to make it possible to count the number of veto players in a system unambiguously, let us provide a few examples. In a unicameral parliamentary system such as New Zealand, were a faction-free party to secure a majority of seats in parliament, and were all policy made in cabinet, there would be just one veto player: the majority party. Were a three-party minimal winning coalition to form in such a system, how many veto players would there be? On an issue on which all three parties had very similar views, we might say there was still one veto player. On an issue in which each party had a distinct view, we would say there were three veto players: Any one of the three parties can "veto" a bill, and any party's veto carries weight because they can threaten to bring down the government if overridden. This is not as clear a veto as that exercised by a majority party because it simply refers to a party that has the power to impose a considerable cost (bringing down the government), if its "veto" is not respected, rather than to one that has the votes by itself to defeat a measure. One can object that the party seeking to veto a bill will also be out of government, so that its veto threat lacks credibility. In principle, the best course would be to count as a veto actor only those parties with credible veto threats; in practice, this may be very difficult and a workable second-best solution is to count all pivotal parties in a coalition as possessing a veto.

Consider now a bicameral, presidential system like the United States, with strong legislative committees. If the Democrats control the presidency and the House, while the Republicans control the Senate, the number of veto players on defense matters might be four: the Democratic president and House majority; the Republican Senate majority; the Senate Republicans on the Senate Armed Services Committee; and the House Democrats on the House Armed Services Committee. How can the Republican contingent on the Senate Armed Services Committee be counted as a faction? To qualify as a faction, they must both have distinctive preferences on defense issues and have an organizational basis for collective action. They do have an organizational basis for collective action: the committee caucus, with the chair of the committee as leader. Whether they do have distinctive preferences is an empirical matter that could be addressed in a similar fashion as Cox and McCubbins (1993).

In what follows, we shall consider the "typical" number of veto actors across all political issues, rather than take an issue-by-issue perspective. In taking this aggregate view, the issue of how to count subunit vetoes becomes more problematic – one would not wish to examine the preferences of all subunits – and so some shorthand rules must be adopted, such as counting as a veto actor any subset of a party that controls a veto, ignoring the issue of whether their preferences are distinctive, or if their preferences are not completely distinct from the remainder of the party, we may opt to count none of them.

In addition to referring to the number of veto actors, we shall also refer to the "effective number of vetoes" to emphasize that the veto points are held by actors with distinct preferences. At a constitutional level, the effective number of vetoes is thus determined by the interaction of two factors: (1) the institutional separation of powers; and (2) the separation of purpose, which depends *both* on the electoral code used to "filter" societal interests into seats in the national assembly (and other offices) *and* on the diversity of preference in society.

What are the policy consequences of increasing or decreasing the number of veto players? In the rest of this section, we consider how the effective number of vetoes affects two central democratic tradeoffs: those between decisiveness and resoluteness, and between public- and private-regarding policy.

Decisiveness v. Resoluteness

Decisiveness is the ability of a state to enact and implement policy change. Resoluteness is the ability of a state to commit to maintaining a given policy. How a state resolves this tradeoff is greatly influenced by the effective number of vetoes that the system typically generates.

As the effective number of vetoes increases, there is an increase in the transactions costs that must be overcome in order to change policy. As more actors must be taken into account in a policy logroll, it will become increasingly difficult to structure negotiations. As more interests are provided with vetoes, it becomes increasingly difficult to ensure that every party to the negotiations receives sufficient value to accept the deal. Hence changing policy becomes increasingly costly as the number of parties to a negotiation, or as the diversity of their preferences, increases. Costs hinder policy change, thus: *As the effective number of vetoes increases, the polity becomes more resolute, and less decisive.* The reverse is also true.[9]

We may see indecisiveness manifest itself as stalemate or gridlock, with few policy changes and more time-consuming negotiations required to pass legislation. We may see irresoluteness manifest itself as rapid or frequent policy change.

Our argument is similar to that of Buchanan and Tullock (1962), who, in their study of collective action, emphasized the costs that might arise from making a decision. In particular, they recognized the transactions costs that are incurred in negotiating an agreement, which they labeled *internal costs*. As the share of voters whose agreement is required rises, so do the internal costs of reaching a decision. So at one extreme,

---

[9] Debates over electoral structure use a slightly different language to describe the same institutional tradeoff. Methods of proportional representation (PR) make the legislature *representative* of popular wishes, by ensuring that even parties with modest vote shares gain a proportionate share of seats. These methods thus make it unlikely that a single party can gain control of the legislature; only fairly broad coalitions of parties can gain such control. In contrast, plurality rule and other so-called "strong" electoral systems tend to give large parties a sizable seat bonus, and therefore deprive small and middle-sized parties of any seats. Plurality rule thus makes single-party control more likely. To the extent that majority parties under plurality systems are less diverse than majority coalitions under PR, plurality rule leads to a greater possibility of control by a narrower range of interests. However, plurality rule also leads to more stable and decisive governments (cf. Powell 1982; Blais and Carty 1987). Governments in more proportional electoral systems tend to be less stable and hence policy is less decisive due to the complexity and fragility of multiparty coalitions. Thus, at the electoral stage the tradeoff is often framed as one between greater security (i.e., resoluteness) that only broad coalitions can act (ensured by PR) and greater stability in government (ensured by plurality rule), and hence decisiveness in policy making.

unanimous rules entail enormous internal costs, while at the other extreme, dictatorships create few internal costs.[10]

We can place various voting rules on a continuum, depending on the effective number of vetoes established by the decision rule, and map directly to the internal costs. For instance, a supermajority rule, requiring either sixty percent or two-thirds of an electorate, would impose greater internal costs than would a simple majority rule. We can thus restate our result: When internal costs are greater, the polity becomes more resolute and less decisive. The reverse is also true.

Public-regardedness versus Private-regardedness of Policy

The second tradeoff implied by the separations of power and purpose in a political system is between the *public-* and *private-regardedness* of policy produced. In other words, how much of the policy making is distributive in intent, and how much aims to provide public goods, improve allocative efficiency, and to promote the general welfare? The greater the number of effective vetoes, the more private regarding will be the policies enacted. This too is a consequence of bargaining among veto players, where each veto player will be able to demand, and receive, side payments in the form of narrowly targeted policies. Thus, when the effective number of vetoes is great, even broad public policy will be packaged as a set of individual projects, or it will be packaged with narrowly targeted programs, tax relief, and so forth.

STATE INDECISIVENESS AND IRRESOLUTENESS

A major theme of this essay is that state "ungovernability" – whether the inability to decide (indecisiveness), the inability to stick to a decision once made (irresoluteness), or the pursuit of inconsistent policies by different "subgovernments" (balkanization) – is typically a joint product of constitutional separations of power and electorally driven separations

---

[10] They also identified what they called *external costs*, which were the negative externalities imposed by not taking into account every individual's interests in a decision. A Pareto optimal decision would entail no external costs, but in the situation where no Pareto improvements are possible, because of diversity of preferences over the final outcome, external costs would be positive. Buchanan and Tullock theorized that the external costs of a decision rule increase as the effective number of veto players increases (to put it into our terms); thus, a unanimous rule would entail no external costs, while a dictatorship would entail the most.

of purpose. In this section, we consider the first two sources of ungovernability – indecisiveness and irresoluteness – in greater detail.

The Problem of Indecisiveness

Several branches of comparative research argue that dividing or separating power – creating veto points in the structure of the state – can lead
to state indecisiveness. When divided government occurs, as it has frequently in the United States and Latin America of late, a broad syndrome
of ill effects is said to arise. These problems include "institutional warfare" of varying intensity, unilateralism (where the executive and the
legislature attempt to circumvent each other in implementing policy),
various forms of gridlock, greater fiscal pork and rents, and a tendency
toward larger budget deficits.

An example of institutional warfare is the sequence of moves and
countermoves concerning impoundments taken by President Nixon and
the (Democratically controlled) Congress during the early 1970s. Nixon,
in an effort to stall or derail portions of the Great Society programs
enacted under his predecessor in office, Lyndon Baines Johnson, began
to impound funds for certain programs that had been duly authorized
and appropriated. In so doing, he was greatly expanding an executive
power of impoundment that previously had been used in a noncontro-
versial fashion. Had he not been challenged, the consequence would
have been a substantial shift in power to the executive, something along
the lines of a suspensory line item veto. In fact he was challenged.
Congress passed the Budget and Impoundment Control Act of 1974.
Among other things, this act spelled out the limits on the executive's
power of impoundment, reasserting congressional primacy in budgetary
matters (Schick 1980; Kiewiet and McCubbins 1991).

Unilateralism can be illustrated by the pursuit of separate foreign
policies regarding Nicaragua by the Reagan Administration and the
Wright Speakership. The Administration, knowing that it could not secure the assent of Congress for its hard-line policy, pursued this policy
anyway via covert action (the financial aspects of which came to light in
the Irangate scandal). The Speakership, knowing that it could not secure
the assent of the Administration for its conciliatory policy, pursued this
policy anyway via shuttle diplomacy centering on the office of the
Speaker. Such episodes have been rare in U.S. politics but unilateralism
by Latin American presidents is a more frequent occurrence. Collor, in
Brazil, to take a recent example, attempted to rule by decree, entirely

ignoring the statutory process and the legislature. Menem, in Argentina, has done this with greater success, as he was not impeached when he did so.

Gridlock is perhaps the most frequently diagnosed problem of divided government in presidential systems (cf. Linz 1990; Cox and Kernell 1991; Shugart and Carey 1992: 33; Mainwaring and Shugart 1997a). If neither side can pursue policy unilaterally, and neither will acquiesce in the policies of the other, then the result is stalemate. In some ways this is a natural consequence of the bargaining situation in which the parties find themselves. If two separate parties or coalitions each control one branch of government, and each has a veto, then they must come to some agreement for any new policy to be enacted via the ordinary constitutional process. But delay is one of the primary bargaining techniques in such situations: By refusing to agree, a party shows willingness to incur the costs of delay (which, in the case of budgetary politics, may include closure of portions of the government). Thus public wrangling and interminable delay are natural features of the politics of bargaining under divided government.

Finally, McCubbins (1991a, 1991b; see also, Jacobson 1990; Alesina and Carliner 1991, Kiewiet and McCubbins 1991, Fiorina 1992; Alt and Lowry 1994, Alesina and Rosenthal 1995) shows how the constitutional separation of powers in the United States can lead to dramatic increases in spending when one of the branches (i.e., the president, the Senate, or the House) is controlled by a different party from the other two. As each branch holds a veto over the others, successful legislation must accommodate each branch's policy preferences. So long as each branch prefers engaging in a logroll to get the spending *it* wants to acting as a blocker to ensure that the other branches don't get the spending *they* want, this provides a convincing explanation for the explosion of U.S. government deficits in recent years.[11] If, by contrast, at least one of the veto players

---

[11] The assumption that a political party will generally prefer to *get* the spending it prefers rather than to *deny* the spending that other parties prefer is fairly general when the budget constraint is soft. For, when budget constraints are soft, denying another party's spending confers a diffuse benefit on all taxpayers, and hence is not a concentrated benefit for one's constituents unless they pay all, or most, of the relevant taxes. In contrast, spending can typically be more highly targeted to the benefit of one's constituents. Nonetheless, there are conditions on the targetability of tax relief as opposed to spending that lead the same model to predict *lower* deficits. See Stewart 1989; 1991.

prefers to deny policy to the others, then the result will be a veto and, hence, no new policy at all.

The Problem of Irresoluteness

By contrast to indecisive polities, an irresolute state is one that finds it easy to make policy; in fact, it is *too* easy. Irresoluteness means that a country cannot sustain a policy once it has been decided. Irresoluteness may come about due to shifting coalitions in a multiparty system, or due to lack of cohesion in a majority party, but in either case there is a clear relationship with the absence of checks and balances. That is, irresoluteness arises when there are fewer effective vetoes.

One consequence of irresoluteness is the lack of *credible commitment* (Root 1994; World Bank 1995; Levy and Spiller 1996). This can mean a variety of things, from a country failing to uphold its promises to international investors or the International Monetary Fund (IMF),[12] to never carrying out a policy compromise. In the following section, we connect the tradeoff between indecisiveness and irresoluteness with the institutional choices that a country makes, paying particular attention to the institutions that govern the legislative and electoral processes.

SEPARATING POWER AND PURPOSE

If the tradeoff between indecisiveness and irresoluteness depends on the effective number of vetoes, the next question concerns how this number is determined. As indicated above, the effective number of vetoes increases when a polity has both many institutional veto points and political actors with diverse interests controlling those veto points. In this section, we consider the separation of power (multiplication of veto points) and purpose (increasing the diversity of preference of actors controlling veto points) further.

Separating Power

How exactly is the separation of powers achieved in reality? The best-known techniques of separating power are presidentialism (separating

---

[12] The essay by Heller and McCubbins discusses this problem, also known as "hold up."

the executive from the legislature), bicameralism (creating more than one house of the legislature), and federalism (by which separate spheres of action are created for national and subnational governments). In each case, a common observation in the literature is that separating power increases the difficulty of action. A long literature in the United States, dating back to the work of Ford (1898), views the separation of executive and legislative power in the U.S. federal government as inimical to "energetic" or "effective" governance. Although less often blamed for inaction, as Tsebelis (1995) has argued, bicameralism also can make policy changes more difficult (see also Tsebelis and Money 1997). And the veto power of state governors in Brazil (Mainwaring 1991) or of senators in the United States (Harris 1993) shows one way in which federalism too is seen as making policy change more difficult.

In the rest of this section, we discuss two lesser known species of separating power – judicial review, and regimes of exception – in a bit more detail. The main point is again that effective separations of power have often been identified as preventing departures from the status quo.

The judiciary may constitute another veto gate in the governmental process, if it is both independent and endowed with the power to judge the constitutionality of proposed or enacted legislation. In some countries, such as France, the judiciary's role is to interpret the constitution and reject legislative acts contrary to that interpretation (i.e., to declare acts null and void).[13] In other countries, while the judiciary cannot reject legislative acts outright, it can choose the amount of "force" employed in enforcing them. This ability gives the judiciary in countries such as Germany and Canada something akin to a power of judicial review (i.e., they can *de facto* nullify acts of the legislature, if not *de jure*). Further, in every country the judiciary is required to interpret statutes. This involves not only interpreting what the legislature wrote in a particular act, but also interpreting the act in light of the entire legal system, including other legislative enactments. Legislatures rarely provide enough detail in their enactments to deprive the judiciary of all interpretative discretion. Often too it is difficult to reconcile one statute with another, and the conflict between new and old statutes leaves the courts

---

[13] In the case of France, the Constitutional Council reviews legislation, judging its constitutionality, after it is passed by the legislature but before it is sent to the President for promulgation. A group of sixty National Assembly members is sufficient to refer a bill to the Constitutional Council. See Stone (1992) for a discussion of the French Constitutional Council as an additional veto gate in the system.

further discretion. The judiciary's interpretative discretion gives it a limited check on legislative authority. Courts in many countries also have a check on administrative and executive actions. Often special courts exist to hear appeals to administrative and executive decisions. In few countries, however, are the courts independent of the elected branches of government, and in very few countries do the courts have the means to enforce their decisions. For courts to be independent of the legislature and the executive, it must be difficult for the legislature and the executive to remove or sanction judges (e.g., judges have a fixed term of office, or life tenure, and the legislature must pass a bill of impeachment to remove a judge). While few countries have opted for an independent judiciary, such as in the United States, judges in many countries are partially insulated from political tampering.

If judges can veto policy, then any legislative project must clear one more hurdle before it becomes law. In principle, the existence of this additional hurdle might translate into gridlock – an inability to pass and sustain legislation. In practice, few states have a judiciary that is simultaneously independent and endowed with a strong power of judicial review of legislation, so that the importance of judicial review is less as a means to prevent legislation than as a means to continue the policy battle by other means after legislation is enacted.

Finally, the military constitutes an important veto gate in many countries, often defining the boundaries of acceptable policy change. The military and its supporters may have policy preferences on some issues, and may be willing to ensure its demands are met through force of arms. The military may also be given a constitutional role to protect the state against certain unwanted policy changes, and may, on its own accord, or at the behest of the national government, intervene to set policy right (Loveman 1993, 1998). Indeed, as Loveman argues, most of the military interventions in Latin America have been the result of constitutional actions by the military, or the government, under a regime of exception. As he shows, most constitutions contain provisions whereby, during times of war or crisis, the policy-making process defined by the constitution may be set aside. In each case the military uses its power to reject policy changes that it deems harmful.

The general point of this section is quite simply that the more powers are divided, the more likely is state resoluteness, and the less likely is state decisiveness. We recap this point in Table 2.1. We have illustrated this general point by five examples, concerning the separation of executive and legislative powers (presidentialism), the separation of

Table 2.1. *Institutional Rules and Policy Authority*

Institution	Structural Separation of Powers	Political Separation of Purpose	Possible Consequences
National Executive	Presidentialism Parliamentarism	Divided government See next section	• Institutional warfare (e.g., over the branches' respective powers to control expenditures) • Unilateralism (i.e., the prosecution of separate policies by different branches) • Gridlock (e.g., inability to pass budgets on time) • Budget deficits (e.g., those in the United States in the 1980s, see McCubbins 1991a,b) • Pork
National Legislature	Bicameralism Unicameralism	Divided partisan or factional control of houses See next section	• Gridlock (whenever the two houses cannot agree) • Budget Deficits (see Heller 1995) • Pork
Legal Relations Between National and Subnational Governments	Federal state Unitary state	Distinct regional preferences	The combination of federal government policy guidelines and state government policy making and implementation, by splitting up policy responsibility among different actors with different preferences, makes it very difficult to implement policies that do not enjoy widespread support. This means that any policy that ultimately is implemented is likely to be successful. It also means that reform policies often will be weak, as politicians focus on local constituencies in creating distributive, and often pork-barrel, policies.

National Judiciary	Independent with judicial review powers Subservient with no judicial review powers	Distinct judicial preferences	In principle, strong judiciaries may serve as just another veto gate. In practice, their role is more subtle. The existence of a relatively independent judiciary (e.g., the U.S. Supreme Court) enables reform-minded politicians to lock their preferences into legislation and guard against it being undermined in the implementation stage (McCubbins et al. 1987; 1989; McNollgast 1992).
Military	Independent military with exceptions to the Constitution Full civilian control of the military	Distinct military preferences	• Military interventions during political or economic crises. • Coups

35

legislative powers (bicameralism), the separation of governmental levels (federalism), the separation of legislative enactment and interpretation (judicial review), and regimes of exception. Madison argued that separating powers may be a risk-avoidance strategy, since it at very least keeps the government from harming the public, or acting tyrannically, by keeping it from doing much of anything. But stalemate could also be damaging if it keeps the state from effectively meeting its challenges.

Separating Purpose

Our goal in this section is to address the manner by which political actors with diverse preferences come to control separate vetoes within the legislative process. Our central variable is the party system, which we believe is shaped by a number of institutional factors, particularly the electoral system. Electoral systems as understood here are sets of rules – usually statutorily specified, but sometimes stemming from constitutional provisions or administrative decrees – that govern four broad aspects of elections: the structure of electoral districts, entry, voting, and the conversion of votes into seats. An electoral district is a geographically defined area within which votes are counted and seats allocated. A given electoral district can be characterized in terms of the rules that govern entry (who can get on the ballot?), voting (how are voters allowed to mark the ballot?), and the conversion of votes into seats within it. The last step – the conversion of marked ballots into an allocation of seats among the competing parties and candidates – is a purely mathematical one: Given any set of marked ballots, a set of rules conventionally known as the *electoral formula* specifies a unique allocation of seats. We will also use the term *district electoral system* to refer to the rules governing election within a particular district. The national electoral system can then be thought of as composed of a set of (variously interrelated) district electoral systems.[14]

---

[14] Sometimes electoral districts operate independently of one another, as for example they do in the United States. In such cases, votes cast in a given electoral district are never counted in any other district, nor do seats allocated to one district transfer to any other. Some systems, however, have complex districting schemes. In Belgium, for example, votes are initially cast in an *arrondissement*. Each party gets a number of seats from the *arrondissement* total equal to the number of "quotas" that its vote total contains. Votes that are not used to "buy" seats in the *arrondissement* are counted in a *province* (a collection of *arrondissements*) and can "buy" seats at that level; at the same time, seats that are not bought in the *arrondissements* transfer to the provincial level.

The general point here is that more individual politicians who control their own electoral fates, more factions, and more parties mean more independent participants in the legislative bargaining process that produces public policy, thus making it harder to initiate and sustain collective action in pursuit of public goods. We shall illustrate this tendency by considering some points raised in the literatures on governmental stability in parliamentary systems, divided government in presidential systems, and the nexus between personal votes, weak parties, and a polity's inability to provide public goods (cf. Haggard and Webb 1993, 150).

Personal Votes, Weak Parties, and Collective Action. The extent to which individual politicians cultivate a personal vote is an important characteristic of a political system, one whose consequences and correlates reach far beyond the electoral arena. Various scholars have argued that systems in which personal votes are large will promote, among other things, legislative rules that decentralize decision-making power to committees and away from party or government leaders (Mayhew 1974; Cain, Ferejohn, and Fiorina 1987, 224–228; Cox 1987b; Thies 1994; McCubbins and Rosenbluth 1995; Katz and Sala 1996), lower levels of party cohesion on legislative votes (Cooper, Brady, and Hurley 1977; Rose 1983, 39; Cain, Ferejohn, and Fiorina 1987, 12–15; Cox 1987b; Mainwaring 1991, 29), pluralist rather than corporatist patterns of interest group bargaining (Cain, Ferejohn, and Fiorina 1987, 18–21),[15] structural corruption (Reed 1994), and – naturally deriving from the foregoing tendencies – governmental paralysis, especially regarding the provision of collective goods (Fiorina 1980; Schick 1980; Burnham 1982; Mainwaring 1991; Cox and McCubbins 1993; Reed 1994). In a nutshell, large personal votes are linked to weak parties and weak parties mean that important collective goods go un- or undersupplied.

The key assumptions driving these results are that (1) individual legislators seek reelection (Mayhew 1974); and (2) in some electoral systems, cultivating a personal vote is an optimal reelection strategy (Fenno 1978; Weingast, Shepsle, and Johnsen 1981; Cox and Rosenbluth 1993;

---

[15] In some countries, particular groups are legally endowed with what are essentially "monopoly lobbying rights," typically along with the exclusive right to serve on various consultative and policy-setting boards and commissions. Such countries are commonly labeled "corporatist" in the literature (see Lehmbruch and Schmitter 1982). Pluralist countries, in contrast, do not regulate the process of lobbying in this fashion (see Truman 1951; Dahl 1956).

Carey and Shugart 1995; McCubbins and Rosenbluth 1995). When both assumptions obtain, it follows that legislators will seek to create a personal vote. There is considerable literature on what they might do to this end, and widespread agreement that the chief means are twofold: (1) provide private or local public goods and services to constituents; and (2) provide particularistic services and favors to special interest groups, in return for campaign contributions.[16]

We shall consider the exchange between legislators and interest groups at greater length later. Regarding the wooing of constituents, the reason for the dominance of targetable benefits in personal vote strategies is straightforward. Individual legislators cannot credibly claim much credit for changes in national public policy (Mayhew 1974; Fiorina and Noll 1979; Arnold 1990), but they can and do credibly claim credit for public works projects located in their district, for patronage appointments, and for other particularistic benefits they helped to deliver. Thus, when an electoral system creates incentives for legislators to cultivate a personal vote, legislators typically develop a "homestyle" (Fenno 1978) – a strategy for presenting themselves to their constituents – that features bringing "pork barrel" projects back to the district (Ferejohn 1974), providing ombudsmanlike services to constituents (Fiorina 1977), and so forth (Wilson 1987).[17]

Pursuit of the means by which to create a personal vote – that is, pursuit of a supply of goods from the public sector and rents for constit-

---

[16] The argument is not that individual reelection-seeking incentives are the *only* motivation for these activities. As Cain, Ferejohn, and Fiorina (1987, 221–24) have emphasized, to the extent that providing casework services produces votes, *parties* have an incentive to make sure that their members provide such services, even if there is no personal electoral incentive to do so. A particularly nice example of how this plays out is Costa Rica. There, legislators are limited to one consecutive term in the national assembly, and almost never serve nonconsecutively. They thus have no personal electoral incentive to provide casework and other local services for their constituents. Yet they do provide such services – because the Costa Rican parties provide them with nonelectoral incentives to do so (see Taylor 1960; Carey 1996).

[17] Weingast et al. (1981) show that these incentives to cultivate a personal vote lead legislators to oversupply particularistic benefits (see also McCubbins and Rosenbluth 1995). Tullock's well-known concept of "fiscal illusion" reflects how electoral incentives lead to certain tax policies, as reelection-seeking legislators' goals are better served by hidden taxes. These hidden taxes are less threatening to the legislators' reelection prospects because they reduce "traceability" (Arnold 1990) from the policy to the policymaker. These tendencies to oversupply particularistic goods, coupled with a propensity for low tax rates, lead to increasing budget deficits (Alesina and Tabellini 1990; McCubbins 1991a, b; Alt and Lowry 1994).

uents and special interests – affects the choice of legislative structure. To claim credit for goods and rents supplied by the public sector, it helps to be entrenched in a powerful committee that exercises differential control over a particular issue area – hence the legislative decentralization associated with personal vote systems (Cain, Ferejohn, and Fiorina 1987). If individual legislators and committees are powerful, then interest groups need only be large enough to influence these actors, hence the pluralist interest group structure associated with personal vote systems. Putting these features together, one gets parties that cannot control legislative decision-making, cannot command the loyalty of their own members, and cannot avoid being torn apart by the competing and unaggregated demands of their own allied interest groups. The ultimate consequence in terms of policy is the aforementioned governmental paralysis.

Electoral structures thus influence the extent to which individual politicians can create their own electoral power bases. For example, closed-list systems militate against the pursuit of purely personal electoral reputations. By contrast, systems that give voters a single vote that they must or can cast for an individual candidate (such as the United States, United Kingdom, Japan, Brazil, or Chile) make the pursuit of a personal vote – that is, a base of electoral support that derives from the candidate's own personal qualities and activities, rather than those of his or her party – potentially profitable. A mapping out of the incentives that different electoral systems present in this regard – whether to rely on broader party reputations or to craft distinctive individual reputations – has been attempted by Carey and Shugart (1995) and Myerson (1994).

Electoral Structure and the Number of Parties. If characteristics of the party system – especially the number of parties and factions and the degree of politicians' independence – affect the level of state indecisiveness in important ways, then the next question concerns how party systems come to be fractionated (or not) to begin with. Electoral systems can be classified in many different ways. For the purpose of predicting the number of political parties that will be viable in a given system – an intellectual task broadly similar to that faced in the industrial organization literature of predicting the number of firms that will be viable in a given industry – a key consideration concerns economies of scale. If one thinks of a political party as a firm engaged in the production of legislative seats, then economies of scale exist whenever two groups can garner more seats as an electoral alliance than they can as separate parties. If substantial economies of scale do exist, then groups interested in winning as many seats as possible will face a strong incentive to form electoral alliances (that, like the SDP/Liberal Alliance in the United Kingdom, or the CSU-CDU in Germany, may become permanent). Viewing the matter in this way, the pertinent questions are: How many more actual votes will be obtained (per unit of "support" in the electorate) in alliance than separately? How many more seats will be obtained (per vote) in alliance than separately? We shall deal with the latter question first, as anticipations of votes-to-seats translations condition the translation of "support" into votes.

Most electoral systems give large parties a more-than-proportional share of seats (i.e., seat shares that exceed their vote shares), while giving small parties a less-than-proportional share. The larger this big-party bias, the greater is the incentive to form electoral alliances. This incentive can be partly characterized, in terms of structural primitives of the electoral system, by examining the minimum viable size of a party under a given system.[18]

Political scientists use the term *threshold of exclusion* to refer to the largest vote share that a party can win in a given electoral district and still not be guaranteed a seat. In the U.S. system, for example, a party can win exactly half of the votes cast in a given district and not be guaranteed a seat (it might tie with another party that also wins half the seats and thus face a coin flip to see who wins the seat); but if a party wins any more than half the votes cast, then it is guaranteed to win. Thus, the threshold of exclusion in the U.S. system is fifty percent. The threshold of exclusion has been calculated for a wide range of electoral systems (see, e.g., Lijphart and Gibberd 1977; Laakso 1987) and its properties are well understood. This threshold is often taken as a rough estimate of the minimum viable size of a party, and taking its reciprocal accordingly gives a rough upper boundary on the number of viable parties in a given district.[19]

Because many electoral systems are composed of districts of varying

---

[18] One can also measure the big-party bias empirically. See, for example, Cox and Niou 1994.

[19] That the threshold of exclusion is a rough estimate can be seen as follows. It might be considered an overestimate of the minimum viable size because a party can win seats even if its seat share falls below the threshold. On the other hand, it might also be considered an underestimate because securing enough votes to win a seat gives a party some "revenue" but does not say at what cost. If there are fixed costs of advertising, for example, these may not be covered by winning a single seat in a multiseat district.

characteristics (not all are like the United States or Chile, in which every district returns the same number of members under the same rules), the upper boundaries on the number of viable parties may differ from district to district. Deriving a single upper boundary at the national level for complex systems is a difficult problem that the literature has not solved satisfactorily.[20] But for many systems a reasonable aggregate upper boundary can be computed simply by taking the median upper boundary across districts.

Voters who are instrumentally rational – that is, concerned solely with using their votes as instruments to affect the final seat allocation resulting from the election – will anticipate any big-party biases inherent in the translation of votes into seats. To the extent that their anticipations are accurate, they will not waste their votes on parties that are hopelessly out of the running, even if they prefer these parties to those in the running. Instead, instrumentally rational voters will vote for the most palatable of the parties that are on the margin between winning and losing, attempting to cast outcome-relevant votes. But the more voters who fear wasting their votes and so cast them strategically, the larger the potential gains to small parties or groups from combining their electoral resources, including their activists, attractive candidates, financial supporters, and so on. Strategic voting incentives thus act to put an upper bound on the number of viable parties in a system.[21]

A series of works have found that two key structural features drive the level of strategic voting in a given electoral system. The first is the *principle of seat allocation,* which summarizes some characteristics of the mathematical function that maps vote shares into seat shares. On the one hand, some systems award all the seats at stake to the party or candidate winning the most votes. We shall refer to these as employing a winner-take-all principle of seat allocation. In these systems there are

---

[20] The current state-of-the-art attempts can be found in Taagepera and Shugart (1989), Lijphart (1994), and Cox (1997).

[21] Do voters in fact vote strategically? There is substantial evidence that they have, in a variety of historical and electoral contexts: in post-World War II Britain (Spafford 1972; Lemieux 1977; Cain 1978; Johnston and Pattie 1991); in nineteenth-century Britain (Cox 1984, 1987a); in West Germany in 1953 (Bawn 1993) and the 1960s (Fisher 1974); in Canada in the late 1960s and early 1970s (Blais, Renaut, and Desrosiers 1974; Black 1978, 1980); in the 1968 U.S. presidential election (Brody and Page 1973; Bensel and Sanders 1979); in the 1988 presidential primaries (Abramson et. al. 1992); in post-1958 Venezuela (Shugart 1985); in the Spanish lower house elections of 1979 and 1982 (Gunther 1989); in post-World War II Japan (Cox 1994); and elsewhere.

substantial incentives for aspirants to office to coalesce. Parties have an incentive to coalesce because the largest coalition, or party, takes all. If, however, the parties do not get their act together – and present the voters with too many parties chasing too few votes – the voters have an incentive to continue the process of coalition via strategic voting. Although almost all winner-take-all systems employ single-seat districts, it is possible to use district magnitudes larger than one. In São Tomé and Príncipe, for example, parties present lists in multimember districts, with the list garnering the largest vote share winning all the seats at stake. Increasing the district magnitude, while holding constant the winner-take-all principle, merely increases the incentives to coalesce.

On the other hand, some systems attempt to approximate an ideal of *proportional representation* in which seat shares equal vote shares. These we shall refer to as employing a proportional principle. Systems that employ a proportional principle of seat allocation also present parties and voters with some incentives to coalesce, but these incentives become progressively weaker as the district magnitude increases. If the district magnitude is one, then – as it turns out – all commonly used PR methods reduce to simple plurality and the incentives to coalesce are the same as those described above. As the district magnitude increases, parties can guarantee themselves a seat with increasingly small percentages of the vote (see above). This makes smaller parties viable as stand-alone entities, means that they do not have to enter into alliances or submerge their identities within larger parties, and reduces the incentives to vote strategically (cf. Cox 1994).

The second key structural feature that affects the level of strategic voting in a system is the *district magnitude*, which is the number of seats to be filled in a given electoral district. In the United States, for example, the district magnitude equals one in all House districts, while in Israel the whole nation serves as the electoral district, from which all 120 members of the Knesset are elected.

Adopting the terminology of Sartori (1968), we can say that systems are *strong* when they provide substantial electoral incentives to coalesce, *feeble* when they provide little or no such incentives. Systems with low district magnitudes *or* winner-take-all seat allocation formulas are strong; systems with high district magnitudes *and* proportional seat allocations are feeble. Strong systems put a meaningful upper boundary on the number of parties, while feeble systems do not. Work by Duverger (1954), Sartori (1968), Cox (1987a, 1994, 1997), Palfrey (1989), Myerson and Weber (1993) and others provides some quantifications of these caps in idealized conditions (corresponding more or less to the friction-less inclines of physics):

1. Winner-take-all seat allocations cap the number of parties at two, regardless of district magnitude (Duverger 1954; Palfrey 1989; Cox 1994, 1997).
2. Proportional allocations in districts of magnitude M cap the number of parties at M+1 (Cox 1994, 1997; Cox and Shugart 1996).

Electoral Structure and Party Factionalization. Electoral structures can also affect the number of factions that arise in a polity (for present purposes, factions can be defined as organized groups within parties that compete for control of valued resources within those parties, such as nominations, party leadership posts, and campaign funds). In particular, systems that pit members of the same party against one another in direct electoral competition tend to promote factionalism.

The specific electoral features that create intraparty electoral competition are various. One example is the use of "open" lists in systems of proportional representation, as is done in Brazil, Chile, and Finland, for example. In a "closed" list system, voters are endowed with a single vote that they must cast for a particular party's list of candidates. Voters thus have no direct ability to affect which of the party's candidates actually represent them in the legislature – hence those candidates really cannot compete against one another. In an "open" list system, voters are endowed with a single vote that they must cast for an individual candidate.[22] Seats are allocated first to parties, based on the sum of the votes of all the candidates of that party. If a party wins x seats, then the top x vote-getting candidates from that party get those seats. Voters thus directly determine which of a party's candidates will represent them in the legislature – hence those candidates face substantial incentives to compete against one another. Because candidates from a given party can hardly compete against one another by identifying themselves with the party at large, they face incentives to form factions in an effort to differentiate themselves from their intraparty competitors.

This basic logic – that factions are especially likely to be created in systems that pit members of the same party against one another in electoral competition, because they then seek a basis other than party on

---

[22] In Brazil, voters may cast either a vote for a candidate or a vote for a list, although the vast majority choose to vote for a candidate.

which to win elections – can fuel the formation either of large factionalized parties (as in Japan, Italy, Uruguay, or Colombia), of atomized parties (as in Brazil), or of alliances of smaller parties (as in Chile). In all cases, the electoral system induces a more complex and less unitary structure to the component parties or alliances.

Summary. This section has reviewed the impact of electoral structure on the party system. Two main conceptual dimensions, along which electoral systems can be arrayed, have been identified. The first is the dimension ranging from *strong* to *feeble,* with the former providing strong incentives toward party and vote concentration, the latter feeble incentives. The second dimension orders electoral systems according to whether they induce *candidate-centered* elections and *personal votes* or *party-centered* elections and *party votes.*

Both of these dimensions reflect a variety of structural features, but the key features that drive each dimension can be described as follows. First, systems that use more proportional methods of seat allocation and have larger district magnitudes are feebler, while systems that allocate seats more on a winner-take-all basis and have low district magnitudes are stronger. Second, systems that allow or promote intraparty competition for votes and seats promote more candidate-or faction-based electoral politics, while systems that disallow or hinder intraparty competition for votes and seats promote more party-oriented elections. Together these two dimensions capture most of the institutional variation that is consequential for political performance. In Table 2.2, we summarize the expected impact of each kind of electoral system on the party system in a two-by-two matrix that interacts the effects of the two dimensions.

Table 2.2. *Electoral Rules and Their Party System Effects*

	Candidate-centered (e.g., SNTV, SMPR)	Party-centered (e.g., closed list PR)
Strong (e.g., SMPR)	Few decentralized parties (United States)	Least fragmented Few unitary parties (United Kingdom)
Feeble (e.g., PR)	Most fragmented Many decentralized parties (Brazil)	Many unitary parties (Netherlands)

Note: A unitary party is more hierarchically structured and approximates a unitary actor. A decentralized party is characterized by weak central leaders, factions, many mavericks, and so on.

The more feeble the electoral system, the more parties will tend to populate the electoral system (although this also depends on the number of cleavages in the society). The greater the number of parties, the more likely that policy enactment requires deals that cross party lines. Negotiation costs may be particularly high in such a case, because multiparty policy deals can have electoral consequences that differ across the members of the policy coalition. Thus, the more parties involved in a given deal, the more likely is delay and gridlock. Additionally, every time there is a shift in the governing coalition, for example, the deal may be renegotiated, which would have a destabilizing effect. So feeble electoral systems are expected to encounter more delay, gridlock, and election-induced instability.

Second, the more that individual politicians control their own electoral fates, the more parties, factions, and 'free-lance' politicians there will be. As a consequence, there will be more independent participants in the legislative bargaining process, and the transactions costs involved in policy making will increase substantially. The extent to which individual politicians cultivate a personal vote is an important characteristic of a political system, one whose consequences and correlates reach far beyond the electoral arena. Various scholars have argued that systems in which personal votes are large will promote legislative rules that decentralize decision-making power to committees and away from party or government leaders,[23] lower levels of party cohesion on legislative votes,[24] pluralist rather than corporatist patterns of interest group bargaining, structural corruption (Reed 1994), and – deriving from the foregoing tendencies – governmental paralysis, especially regarding the provision of collective goods.[25] In a nutshell, large personal votes are linked to weak parties and weak parties mean that important collective goods go undersupplied or unsupplied altogether.

Summary

A schematic representation of the topics covered in this section is presented in Figure 2.1. State ungovernability arises as a multiplicative

---

[23] See Mayhew 1974; Cain, Ferejohn, and Fiorina 1987, 224–28; Cox 1987b; Thies 1994; McCubbins and Rosenbluth 1995; Katz and Sala 1996.

[24] See Cooper, Brady and Hurley 1977; Rose 1983, 39; Cain, Ferejohn, and Fiorina 1987, 12–15; Cox 1987b; Mainwaring 1991, 29.

[25] See Fiorina 1980; Schick 1980; Burnham 1982; Mainwaring 1991; Cox and Mc-Cubbins 1993; Reed 1994.

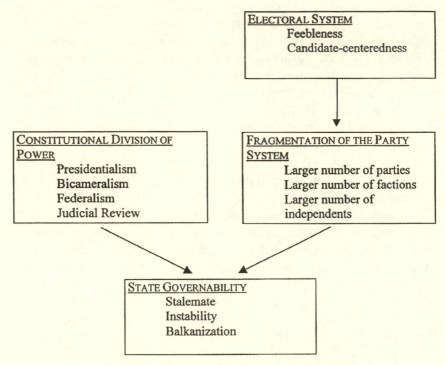

Figure 2.1. Summary of the Argument in Section 3

product of these two factors. A state with much constitutional separation of power may still be decisive if a single hierarchical party unifies the various separated powers. (Indeed, a standard argument about U.S. parties that one used to hear before the era of divided government is that they have served to make our highly divided system operable by just such a unification of interests across the branches of government; see American Political Science Association 1950; Fiorina 1980.) Similarly, a state faced with a fragmented party system may still be decisive if there is a single important office controlled by a single party (not that this would be desirable). It is only when there are many institutional veto points controlled by diverse interests that the problems of indecisiveness arise in full force.

To act decisively, an indecisive system uses private goods as the source of stability for public policy. That is, private goods become the basis of trades between politicians who join together to implement public policy. Because the flow of private goods continues only as long as the enacting coalition endures, the private goods enable politicians to forge a commitment and bond themselves to an agreement. In this case, then, pork should not be seen as inefficient, as it is essential for the implementation of public policy. Indeed, little public policy would be implemented in the United States, Japan, and Brazil without large amounts of private content. This is the subject of our next section.

PUBLIC- VERSUS PRIVATE-REGARDING POLICY

Having dealt with the issue of state governability at some length, we turn now to investigate another classical complaint about democratic governance: the tendency of some types of systems to produce private-regarding policies. This complaint can be seen as inherent in democratic accountability: If politicians can be held accountable at election time, they will be responsive to whomever controls the resources they need in order to win (re)election. Ideally, this means that they will be responsive to broad popular demands. In practice, however, it may also mean that they will be responsive to narrow and special demands, especially if these are backed up by a willingness to contribute large amounts of money to the relevant campaign funds. Thus, the following dilemma: In making politicians responsive at all, does one make them particularly responsive to special interests? If so, the polity will produce, not broadly gauged policy that addresses the supply of public goods, but rather narrowly targeted pork and rents that address the shoring up of political support.

We should note that we use the term *pork* in a broader-than-usual sense, one that includes two important subcategories. First, there is what might be called *fiscal pork,* referring to geographically targetable public expenditures whose incidence and location follow a political rather than an economic logic (even though the expenditures may produce goods that have some of the characteristics of public goods). This category includes classic pork-barrel projects such as dams, levies, and so forth (cf. Ferejohn 1974; Weingast et al. 1981). Often, projects in this category are called *morsels.* Broad national policy goals, such as cleaning the nation's water or building a better bomber to defend the nation's skies, take on the role of a carcass, with representatives cast as lions. The result is a metaphorical dismemberment or morselization of the policy goal – with sewage treatment plants or military subcontracts (the morsels) widely dispersed among the lions. In this case, the goods being provided may still qualify as public goods, or at least may have some of the features of public goods, but the means of producing and distributing these goods is politically determined, and may not be the least costly means of providing these goods to the society.

The second subcategory of pork embraces *rents,* as this term is used in the rent-seeking literature, referring to any of a wide array of subsidies, special tax provisions, regulatory exceptions, and so forth extracted from government (cf. Krueger 1974; Buchanan et al. 1980). The question then is: What institutions structure the social bargain so that fiscal pork and rent-seeking are minimized, and effective and responsible collective action can be undertaken?

This concern that pork and rents will be oversupplied and public policy undersupplied haunts many policy discussions (Ferejohn 1974; Weingast et al. 1981). Special interests seeking subsidies and rents not only pervert the meaning of democratic accountability, but they also create deadweight losses and distort economic incentives (Stigler 1971; Becker 1985). Thus the question arises: What constitutional regulation of the state and what electoral environment for politicians promote policy and hinder pork? Our argument, similar to the one in the previous section, is that the privatization of public policy emerges only when there is both a constitutional separation of powers and an electoral separation of purpose.

Electoral Structure and Legislators' Demands for Pork

Politicians can use particularistic benefits to good effect in winning elections. How effective such benefits are may depend on the structure of the society. For example, societies in which gift-giving at weddings and funerals is entrenched (e.g., Japan) may foster the expectation that legislators or members of Parliament (MPs) will give such gifts. More generally, pork may be more effective in more clientelistic societies.

The effectiveness of particularistic benefits in winning elections also depends on electoral structure. In particular, electoral systems that promote intraparty competition are widely believed to make the development of a personal vote – one that depends on something other than the candidate's party affiliation – more profitable (cf. Katz 1986; Myerson 1994; Carey and Shugart 1995; McCubbins and Rosenbluth 1995). The basic logic is quite simple. If more than one member of a given party runs for office in a given constituency, and voters have the option of supporting some but not all of these candidates, then candidates of the same party will need some way of differentiating themselves from one another. They cannot do so by emphasizing the party label, because they all share this label. Thus, they need to form factions or emphasize their personal qualities. Note that the effectiveness of particularistic benefits in winning elections also depends on the nature of campaign finance. If there are lax laws (as in Japan; see Rosenbluth 1989), special interests flourish as contributors. If there is public financing, and strict regulation of expenditure on mass media (as in the United Kingdom), special interests do not court the individual MP.

We can summarize the marginal impact of each kind of electoral system on the nature of policy formation. First, the more candidate-centered are elections (and the candidate selection process), the more politicians will seek focused policy benefits (e.g., pork) for their constituents. This is largely because individual legislators cannot credibly claim credit for improvements in the delivery of national public goods, but can credibly claim credit for more narrowly targeted private goods (Fiorina and Noll 1979). With their electoral fates riding primarily on their ability to deliver targeted benefits rather than public goods, public goods go undersupplied. The structure of the electoral system, in other words, creates a party system that is ill-suited to overcome the market failures that are thought to impede supply of public goods. More candidate-centered elections also mean that the number of agents that face separate electoral consequences from policy decisions, hence the number of agents that may need to be involved in any policy decisions, is larger. The consequence of this is that candidate-centered systems are less decisive, but more resolute, than party-centered systems.

In addition, having representation allocated on a geographical basis also adds a particular type of rent seeking, one in which the major interest groups are regional ones. The Clean Air Act of 1970 exemplifies how federalism may engender particular political compromises at the cost of effective policy. Instead of simply mandating national standards and leaving it to each industry to meet those standards in the most proficient manner, the political environment necessitated the adoption of one specific technological means for all industries to accomplish the statute's air quality goals. If straightforward national standards were adopted, the northeastern and midwestern senators (with enough votes to veto the legislation) were worried that key industries would relocate out of their states (Ackerman and Hassler 1981; McCubbins et al. 1987). As a result, Congress compromised on inefficient command-and-control intervention to achieve cleaner air.

Legislative and Executive Structure and the Supply of Pork

If politicians demand pork, they must find a supply of it. In order to extract pork from the state, one needs some leverage. One kind of leverage is the possession of a veto or the ability to delay significantly. This suggests that the more veto points there are, whether due to presidentialism, bicameralism, a malapportioned senate, or the decentralization of power within the legislature, the more pork will be attached to the passage of wealth-enhancing moves.

This point can be elaborated by considering a polity that has the opportunity to make a change in policy, possibly in response to changing conditions, that will enhance welfare by the Kaldor–Hicks criterion. By this criterion, it will be recalled, a policy change is judged welfare-enhancing if there exists a hypothetical package of lump-sum transfers such that, were the transfers costlessly made, all members of society would be better off. In the real world, how might Kaldor–Hicks improvements actually be made, given that even costless compensatory transfers are not in fact made, so that the envisioned policy changes will entail winners and losers?

One possibility is that groups within the polity are capable of making long-term trades of the form: "I'll let you have this Kaldor–Hicks improvement now, if you let me have one in the future that benefits me (and imposes costs on you)." Most polities lack the requisite level of trust between transacting parties to be able to conclude many such agreements on trust alone. And most also lack the wherewithal to allow parties to post long-term bonds. They thus have recourse to short-term methods of policy deal-making – i.e., those that do not require long-term trust (or bonding).

One such method consists of packaging a number of wealth-enhancing changes into an omnibus policy change that, on balance, benefits a large percentage of citizens. This of course requires that the Kaldor–Hicks improvements occur in clusters, with offsetting winners and losers.

If one imagines a situation in which all the available wealth-enhancing moves create similar winners and losers, then the only remaining technique for enacting such policies is to make actual side payments to those losers who are capable of vetoing the policy otherwise. These side payments will not, of course, be the costlessly transferred lump sum amounts envisioned in the Kaldor–Hicks scenario. They will be real-world subsidies, warts and all. In particular, real subsidies must be negotiated and delivered, entailing transaction costs, and their presence will typically produce deadweight efficiency losses. A recent example in the United States would be the 1986 Tax Reform Act. Generally thought to simplify tax rates, there were nonetheless a very large number of particularistic payoffs lodged in the transition rules (Birnbaum and Murray 1987).

The idea that more veto points will generally lead to more pork is distinct from any notion that more interest groups may lead to the same thing. More interest groups *can* be bad news, if these groups simply add to the burden of special demands weighing on the economy; but more interest groups can also be good news, if this means more competition, a leveler playing field for economic interests, and less egregious favoritism toward inefficient sectors. The tension here is similar to that between federalism as promoting inefficient regional balancing, and federalism as promoting healthy competition between the states.

Summary: Demand Meets Supply

The bottom line is as follows. A polity that both gives politicians a big electoral demand for pork and also gives them the ability in the legislature and/or the executive to control the allocation of pork produces a lot of pork. Some societies may be inherently more prone to distributive, particularistic, or clientelistic politics than others. But the electoral rules and legislative structure with which a society is endowed can help or hinder the impulse to particularism.

An outline of this argument is presented in Figure 2.2. When a state reduces the number of veto points and unifies previously diverse interests, it becomes more decisive. A decisive state means a centralized federal government that is less responsive to private interests. Policy becomes less distributive as the privatization and disbursement of public goods comes to an end. Ultimately, several policies and services may become nationalized. Education, for example, may become unified with a single national curriculum. Likewise, the central government may nationalize health care, the tax system (including sales and property taxes), and regulatory policy, thereby eliminating regional variation. These national policies endure as long as the enacting coalition remains in power; however, a change in the enacting coalition's constituency or an electoral shift that brings to power a new coalition could result in a transformation of these public policies.

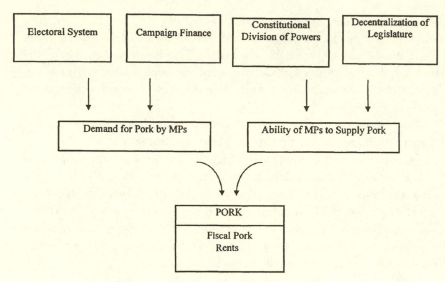

Figure 2.2.   Outline of the Argument in Section 5

MOVING DOWN A LEVEL: LEGISLATIVE BRANCH STRUCTURE

In previous sections, we examined how electoral and constitutional structures can affect the ability of states to address the variety of collective action problems that face their societies. Returning to the view of polities articulated at the outset of the chapter, according to which they can be seen as a sequence of delegations, in this section we move down a level in this sequence, considering the "internal" organization of the policy-making process. Many of the same themes reappear at this level of delegation. In particular, separation of power at the electoral and constitutional levels tends to be mirrored in legislative, administrative, and judicial procedures (McCubbins et al. 1987). The veto points at lower levels of delegation (e.g., legislative, administrative, and judicial), for example, reflect the veto points that exist at higher levels of delegation (e.g., electoral and constitutional). Separation of purpose is mirrored in a similar way, as individuals or groups who have access at the electoral and constitutional levels maintain similar access at the legislative, administrative, and judicial levels. Fragmentation at higher levels of delegation, thus, is mirrored at lower levels of delegation.

In this section, we describe how the structure of the legislature mirrors the decision-making environment of the larger political system. Divisions at the constitutional and electoral levels, for example, permeate down to the legislative level. When this happens, the resultant legislative decentralization (leading to subgovernments), like constitutional or electoral divisions of power, often produces a syndrome of ill effects ranging from stalemate to balkanization to instability. However, just as concentrating power in the hands of a responsible party is thought to avoid these constitutional and electoral difficulties, so it is sometimes argued that strong legislative parties provide a solution to the problems of legislative decentralization.

Special Interests and Subgovernments

The problem with legislative decentralization is that policy making gets parsed out to numerous, relatively small, self-interested actors. Instead of a coherent, majority making policy for the good of the nation – or at least for the good of the majority – this kind of atomistic policy making is thought to lead to fragmented, incoherent policy that usurps the majority will and transforms it into specialized benefits for multiple minorities. In the extreme, this kind of balkanization of politics can lead to the dominance of subgovernments in the policy process.

Subgovernments come in essentially three flavors. The most common form is pure committee government (Shepsle and Weingast 1987), in which legislative committees enjoy autonomy to make policy as they wish within their jurisdictions. While committee government is most identified with legislative committees in the U.S. House, scholars also have identified its trappings in Italy (D'Onofrio 1979; Della Sala 1993), within the LDP in Japan (Thies 1994), as well as in other European parliaments (von Beyme 1985). The principal concern in all these cases is that committee members are particularly interested in their committees' issue areas and are likely to seek policy outcomes different from what a majority of the legislature – not to mention the citizenry – would choose if given the opportunity. The noxious effects of committee government are exacerbated when committees ally themselves with the interest groups and executive agencies relevant to policy in their area, forming what the literature refers to as *iron triangles*.

In the case of the United States, many have argued that policy outcomes are controlled by these iron triangles (Freeman 1955; Schattschneider 1960; Bauer, Pool, and Dexter 1963; Ripley and Franklin 1976; Lowi 1979). These theorists argue that lobbyists for special interests, bureaucrats, and congressional committee members work together to usurp power from Congress and set their own policy agenda. The Chicago school models of regulation (Stigler 1971; Posner 1975; Peltzman 1976; Becker 1985) and the Public Choice school of rent seek examined interest group competition within the iron triangles framework, arguing that interest groups capture control over policy from legislators and redirect benefits toward themselves. The Chicago school models conclude, therefore, that interest groups deter the provision of public goods and spawn economic inefficiencies.

While an important addition to our understanding of policy formation, the Chicago school models fail to address many issues that arise in comparative studies of interest group influence. For example, why do the amounts and types of subsidies vary across countries? Agriculture is heavily subsidized in Europe and Japan but not in the United States (Calder 1988). We also observe variation between countries in levels of the provision of public health care, credit subsidies in small-business loans, and so forth. Another question from comparative political economy that is left unanswered by the Chicago school models is: "Why do some countries have protective regulations while others do not?"[26] When addressing these questions about interest group influence and differences in policy outcomes, it is important to determine whether policies are a by-product of capture by interest groups or the result of legislators following incentives that are created by institutions. More specifically, are legislators able to retain control over policy choice when pursuing their reelection strategy of cultivating a personal vote, or does the goal of reelection force them to relinquish policy control to special interests? Drawing this distinction can be important for developing a theory that specifies the institutional conditions under which interest groups can prevail. Only when we have such a theory in hand can we determine whether policy differences across countries result from different levels of interest group influence.

Noll (1989) also offers a critique of the Chicago school models, arguing not only that there is a lack of robust empirical evidence to corroborate their claims but also that "the relationship between the stakes of the group and their political strengths remains a mystery,

---

[26] Levy and Spiller (1996) address this previously unanswered question, concluding that the types of regulations that develop in a country are related to its political and social institutions. This study has important implications for understanding the degree to which institutions can signal a credible commitment to existing regulatory policy.

largely because in nearly all studies neither stakes nor gains in regulation are directly measured" (Noll 1989, 1277). Thus, we are left to conclude that while interest groups may be an instrumental part of legislators' efforts to cultivate a personal vote and pursue reelection, it does not necessarily follow that the appeasement of special interests always leads to capture of the policy agenda from politicians. Before attributing responsibility for policy outcomes to interest groups, Noll concludes, we must take into account that politicians will devise strategies designed to counter and minimize the influence of special interests within bureaucratic agencies and at the policy-making level. Furthermore, an understanding of politicians' incentives to cultivate a personal vote through the provision of particularistic goods to their constituents can help explain why special interest groups might *appear* to be capturing policy control. In other words, if a legislator's homestyle calls for the provision of particularistic goods to a certain segment of his or her constituency, then what may appear to be captured by interest groups is actually favoritism for a special interest that is *initiated by the legislator* without direct, organized pressure from that group that benefits.

The second flavor of subgovernment is similar to the first, but with parliamentary parties taking the place of committees. This particular form of party government, the converse of party government by responsible parties (see, e.g., Katz 1980), is perhaps most commonly identified with the postwar Italian parliament (Pasquino 1986). Though not far removed in essence from partisan consociationalism (Lijphart 1977), this multiparty "party government" is seen as resulting, not in well-thought-out compromises, but rather in a patchwork of policies for the benefit of numerous minorities to the detriment of the majority (cf. Dahl 1956). As with committees, parties also can ally themselves with extraparliamentary interest groups and sectors of the bureaucracy to move policy outcomes even more toward special interests and further away from the common good.

The third type of subgovernment that we identify is what might be called the dark side of corporatism. While corporatism often is seen as efficiency-enhancing, when peak labor and business association are brought into partnership with the state (e.g., Katzenstein 1985), absent such peak associations the corporatist delegation of policy-making power to private sector actors may produce a pattern similar to American-style subgovernments: Policies that affect specific issue areas are made by the actors most concerned with those issue areas; the legislature serves primarily to ratify decisions taken out of the plenum and the public eye; and interest groups are explicitly incorporated into the policy process (McConnell 1966; Lowi 1979).

In all cases where subgovernments dominate policy making, there is a profound risk that policy outcomes will thwart the majority will. This can occur in two ways. First, policy makers in each issue area agree to support each other's policy goals (Weingast 1979), resulting in an inchoate patchwork of disconnected, specialized policies. Or, second, policy makers refuse to support each other, leading to policy gridlock and a failure of the political system to produce new policy at all. Assuming that a majority desires something other than no new policy or an incomprehensible jumble of different policies, then subgovernments subvert the democratic process.

Legislative Parties and the Delegation of Power

In constitutional and electoral theory, political parties play a hero's role: They are viewed as (potentially) large enough to internalize many of the external effects that would be produced by an inchoate brew of special interest politics. Some see them playing a similar role in the narrower confines of legislative politics.

Cox and McCubbins (1993), for example, point out that if the committee government model did hold true – with separate committees, in alliance with relevant industry and executive agents, making policy without regard for the external costs thereby imposed – then there would necessarily be gains from trade between the committees. The committee government model itself suggests that a highly decentralized legislature would have great difficulty in capturing these potential gains from trade, because of credibility and commitment problems among the committees (cf. Weingast and Marshall 1988). Cox and McCubbins essentially agree with this point, and go on to argue that political parties arise as a vehicle or arena within which legislative trades can be transacted more reliably than on the floor of a decentralized legislature.

Specifically, Cox and McCubbins (1993, 109) assume that legislators are first and foremost motivated by the reelection goal (Mayhew 1974). They draw on voting research that suggests that party affiliation, personal characteristics, and ideology are the key components of voting behavior (and thus the keys to reelection). While personal characteristics and ideology are largely private goods that legislators pursue on their own (through pork barreling and casework), party reputation is a public good for all legislators in the party (Cox and McCubbins 1993, 123).

As is the case with most public goods, there exists an ensuing collective action problem. In order to assure positive benefits from the party label, the party must produce collective-benefits legislation where no single legislator can claim responsibility. That is, someone must ingest the costs of arranging complex logrolls that require searching or "integrative" bargaining (Bartos 1995). The collective action problem is overcome by the institutionalization of a central authority (i.e., party members delegate authority to the party leaders). Party leaders internalize the costs of providing collective benefits in exchange for internal advancement of the party in Congress (majority status) and internal advancement within the party. The leaders control various mechanisms to keep the party members in line such as committee appointment control and agenda setting.[27]

Because parties play such an important role in organizing the legislature, a change either in the identity of the majority party in the legislature or within the majority party itself often results in policy alterations. A new majority party, for example, is likely to emphasize policies associated with their party reputation. Similarly, a change in the internal structure of the majority party often transforms the nature of the logrolls that the party undertakes. Indeed, Kiewiet and McCubbins (1991, 205) show that "federal spending patterns clearly and consistently reflect the preferences of the majority parties in Congress as well as the party of the president." Cox and McCubbins (1993, 269) conclude that in general "what passes will . . . tend to have a partisan cast."

A similar line of reasoning applies to those models that see multiparty coalition governments as typically incapable of transacting, hence characterized by ministerial dictatorships or subgovernments (e.g., Laver and Shepsle 1990a). If such polities are indeed as characterized, then by definition substantial gains from trade could be had by anyone able to construct a stable alliance of parties, within which political deals could be made. This does not guarantee that the appropriate alliances will be forthcoming, because cooperation between parties is made especially difficult by the fact that they are typically in competition with one another for votes and seats, but it does suggest a standing prize for those able to solve the coalitional difficulties.

Finally, we have already noted that corporatist subgovernments may not be the parochial creatures that they are generally seen to be in the United States. The hero's role here falls to peak associations, that aggre-

---

[27] Of course, the party members maintain ultimate control over the party leaders, as the members are the principals and the leaders are their agents.

gate the competing and parochial demands of their constituent member organizations into something that better approximates an optimal policy for the country as a whole.

MOVING DOWN A LEVEL: EXECUTIVE BRANCH STRUCTURE

As we have discussed, certain institutions will engender an oversupply of goods by the public sector. We have argued that systems with greater fragmentation of authority, such as the constitutionally defined checks of bicameralism and federalism in the United States, increase the political need for accommodation of narrow demands as the number of veto players increases. In addition to the structural arrangements of power within a state, the rules by which the political game are played also fundamentally guide the type of policy the system will produce. For example, electoral rules that allow a more diverse party representation – in contrast to those that give rise to broadly based, two-party systems – will create an intragovernmental environment with a greater number of veto players and thus need for accommodation of narrow interests. The particularistic demands favored by these institutional arrangements are translated into policy outcomes through the principal–agent relationship between the enacting coalition and bureaucratic agency.

An agency's enacting coalition is composed of the relevant committee, or ministries, that drafted the legislation, the chamber majorities who approved the statute, and the president, or chief executive, who signed it into law. These players represent the set of veto gates the enabling statute must satisfy. The level of uncertainty and conflict in policy to be chosen determines the form this statute will take – whether the agency will be given broad or narrow latitude in picking its agenda, vaguely or specifically defined goals, limited or strict procedures, and so on (McCubbins 1985; McCubbins and Page 1987; Moe and Caldwell 1994).

Uncertainty applies to the costs and benefits of both the economic and political consequences involved in a new program. It will suffice here to say that, in general, uncertainty and conflict leads Congress to grant bureaucrats a broader scope of legislative authority and legal tools or instruments with more confining procedures. This allows legislators to guide policy in a particular direction without necessarily knowing the ramifications of every specific alternative or even what their interests might be (how it will affect their constituency).

Thus, legislators may not know what specific policies they prefer but they *do* know which interests ought to be represented. The problem becomes how to control the implementing agency so that it does not upset the policy compromises that were required to stitch together the coalition that forged the policy. Often it is impossible for policy makers to write specific policy guidelines for the implementing agency. The tools available to political actors for controlling administrative outcomes through process, rather than substantive guidance in legislation, are the procedural details, the relationship of the staff resources of an agency to its domain of authority, the amount of subsidy available to finance participation by underrepresented interests, and resources devoted to participation by one agency in the processes of another (Noll 1987). All else being equal, elaborate procedures with stiff evidentiary burdens for decisions and numerous opportunities for seeking judicial review before the final policy decision is reached will benefit constituents who have considerable resources for representation. Coupled with no budget for subsidizing other representation, or for independent staff analysis in the agency or in the other agencies that might participate in its proceedings, cumbersome procedures exemplify deck stacking in favor of well-organized, well-financed interests.

A prominent example of procedural deck stacking is offered by the regulation of consumer product hazards by the U.S. Consumer Product Safety Commission (CPSC). Although the CPSC was responsible for both identifying problems and proposing regulations, it was required to use an "offeror" process, whereby the actual rule writing was contracted out. Usually the budget available to the CPSC for obtaining a proposed regulation was substantially less than the cost of preparing it. Consequently, only groups willing to bear the cost of writing regulations became offerors, and these were the groups most interested in consumer safety: testing organizations sponsored by manufacturers or consumer organizations. Thus, this process effectively removed agenda control from the CPSC and gave considerable power to the entities most affected by its regulations (Cornell, Noll, and Weingast 1976). In 1981, Congress amended this process by requiring that trade associations be given the opportunity to develop voluntary standards in response to all identified problems, assuring that agenda control was never granted to consumer testing organizations.

The legislature can also make policy more representative to the politically relevant constituency by enhancing its role in agency procedures. The U.S. National Environmental Policy Act (NEPA) of 1969 provides an example of how this works. In the 1960s, environmental and conservation groups in the United States became substantially better organized and more relevant politically. By enacting NEPA, Congress imposed procedures that required all agencies to file environmental impact statements on proposed projects. This forced agencies to assess the environmental costs of their proposed activities. NEPA gave environmental actors a new, effective avenue of participation in agency decisions and enabled participation at a much earlier junction than previously had been possible. The requirements of the act also provided environmental groups with an increased ability to press suits against federal agencies.

In all agency decisions proof must be offered to support a proposal. The establishment of the burden of proof provides another example of how legislatures can stack the political deck in bureaucratic decision making. The burden of proof affects agency decisions most apparently when the problem that is before the agency is fraught with uncertainty. In such a circumstance, proving anything – either that a regulation is needed to solve a problem, or that it is unnecessary – can be difficult, if not impossible. Hence, assigning either advocates or opponents of regulation a rigorous burden of proof essentially guarantees that they cannot obtain their preferred policy outcome.

For example, the U.S. Federal Food, Drug, and Cosmetics Act, as amended, requires that before a pharmaceutical company can market a new drug, it must first prove that the drug is both safe and efficacious. By contrast, in the Toxic Substances Control Act of 1976, Congress required that the Environmental Protection Agency (EPA), before regulating a new chemical, must prove that the chemical is hazardous to human health or the environment. The reversionary outcome is that new chemicals are allowed to be marketed. The results of the differences in the burden of proof are stark: Few new drugs are marketed in the United States, while the EPA has managed to regulate none of the 50,000 chemicals in commerce under these provisions in the Toxic Substance Control Act.

Ultimately, the point of deck-stacking is not to preselect policy, but cope with uncertainty about the most desirable policy action by making certain that the winners in the political battle over the underlying legislation will also be the winners in the process of implementing the program. By enfranchising interests that are represented in the legislative majority, a legislature need not closely supervise the agency to ensure that it serve its interests, but can allow an agency to operate on "autopilot" (McCubbins et al. 1987, 271; McCubbins et al. 1989). Thus, policy can evolve without the need for new legislation to reflect future changes in the preferences of the enacting coalition's constituents. Likewise, in political systems with a separately elected executive, the executive will also undertake to mirror the political and electoral forces that he or she faces in the orders and rules imposed on the bureaucracy (Moe 1990; Macey 1992).

The courts also can play a role in the political control of the bureaucracy. Administrative procedures can affect an agency's policy agenda only if they are enforced, and their enforcement can be delegated by the legislature to the courts, in which case procedure can have an effect with minimal effort required on the part of politicians (Shapiro 1986; McCubbins et al. 1987). For supervision by the courts to serve this function, judicial remedy must be highly likely when the agency violates its rules. If so, the courts, and the constituents who bring suit, guarantee compliance with procedural constraints, which in turn guarantees that the agency choice will mirror political preferences without any need for political oversight (McCubbins and Schwartz 1984; Lupia and McCubbins 1994).

Legislatures can further limit the potential mischief of agency agenda control by carefully setting the reversionary policy in the enabling statute that established the agency. The clearest example is the creation of entitlements, whereby spending is specified by statute, and the agency has no discretion in how much, or to whom, it allocates funds. Another example is seen in the widespread use of "sunset" provisions, whereby an agency's legal authority expires unless the legislature passes a new law to renew the agency's mandate.

GENERAL SUMMARY

The thrust of our argument in this chapter, as summarized in Table 2.3, is that polities that combine institutional divisions of decision-making authority with political divisions of purpose will tend to be either inde-

Table 2.3. *Power, Purpose, and Decisiveness*

	Unified Power	Separated Power
Unified purpose	Decisive United Kingdom	Decisive Mexico, Taiwan prereform
Separated purpose	Decisive Japan, Czech Republic	Indecisive Argentina, Chile, Poland, United States

cisive or prone to morselizing public policy, or both. Institutional divisions of power can come in the form of presidentialism, bicameralism, federalism, provisions for judicial review, and so on. Political divisions of purpose can stem both from the inherent diversity of opinion within a nation's society and from the incentives that the electoral system presents to combine those diverse interests into many or few political organizations. Some electoral systems encourage the formation of a few hierarchical parties whose leaders internalize the costs and benefits of public policy as it affects a wide range of the population. Other electoral systems facilitate either large numbers of parties or decentralized (factionalized or atomized) parties.

When a polity combines institutional veto points with diverse political agents, the result is something like a multilateral veto game. In such games, one outcome is indecisiveness, when the various veto groups cannot agree on any action. Another is a kind of balkanization, when the various veto groups give up on arriving at a mutually acceptable policy and attempt to take unilateral action. A third possible outcome is that the veto groups trade control over some areas of policy, leading to subgovernments (another kind of balkanization). This kind of result is typically thought to lead to each subgovernment acting as a champion of particular kinds of subsidies and is most likely when the policy decisions made in one subgovernment have relatively small external impacts (other than budgetary) on political actors controlling other subgovernments (Cox and McCubbins 1993). This, of course, may lead to budget imbalances. When policy decisions must be made that affect virtually everyone in a consequential way, a fourth outcome is that policy is passed but takes a long time to negotiate and is laden with substantial side payments to the prospective losers.

We have expanded on this last point by considering hypothetical policies that represent Kaldor–Hicks but not Pareto improvements – that is, policies that improve net social welfare but make some actors worse off than they would be in the absence of reform. The more veto players there are, the more likely it is that the Kaldor–Hicks losers will have a voice somewhere in government that will enable them to block reforms that are pernicious to their own well-being, unless they are given what they deem appropriate compensation. Thus, distributive policy is not necessarily the product of perverse politicians, nor of perverse incentives. Sometimes, it is the currency that pays the cost of producing policy in polities that feature many and diverse veto groups. Without particularistic side payments, policy making in these multiactor systems would be much more difficult and, probably, much more rare.

Nonetheless, the morselization of public policy is never anyone's idea of the best solution. And the veto power that can be used to ensure that "appropriate" compensation is offered to Kaldor–Hicks, losers can also be used to extract "inappropriate" rents. What is clearest about systems with multiple and diverse veto groups is that they are indecisive and prone to heavy doses of private-regarding policy. Of course, locating at the other extreme of the continuum – having a highly irresolute state – could have negative consequences for a polity's governability as well. An irresolute polity may be plagued by chaos and instability. While it may not be as enslaved to particularism in its policy-making process, an irresolute policy will be unable to commit to its policy choices.

Thus we end where we began, with the idea that the choice of democratic institutions entails significant tradeoffs. While these tradeoffs might not have any consequences in a perfectly harmonious nation in which every individual possesses precisely the same preferences, in the presence of diversity the threat from locating too far at either extreme becomes potentially great. That is, as a society's heterogeneity increases, a system with a greater number of effective vetoes will see increasing risk of stalemate and gridlock, as well as an increasing costliness to a legislative strategy that emphasizes private-regarding policy. Likewise, as a society becomes more heterogeneous, if the polity has a very small number of effective vetoes the risk of inequality and underrepresentation will increase. Thus, the consequences of these institutional tradeoffs increase with social diversity, so understanding these consequences is crucially important.

3

Institutions and Public Policy in Presidential Systems

MATTHEW SOBERG SHUGART
and STEPHAN HAGGARD

In presidential regimes, policy making is by definition characterized by a separation of power; it is very often characterized as well by a separation of purpose. *Separation of power* refers to the independent authority of the executive and legislative branches. Separation of power arises from two defining features of presidentialism. First, the executive and legislature are elected separately; and, second, neither branch can act to shorten the term of the other.[1] Thus, the executive and the legislature are separate both in their origin and in their survival.

In addition to creating a separation of power, the first feature of presidentialism – the separate election of the two branches – also has the potential to generate a separation of purpose. *Separation of purpose* arises when separate elections result in different partisan groups controlling the two branches, a phenomenon often referred to as divided government. Separation of purpose may also emerge because presidents are typically elected by a national constituency whereas legislators are generally elected by much smaller subnational constituencies. Thus, presidents often tend to be preoccupied with national concerns whereas legislators tend to be much more interested in local issues. The degree to which presidents think nationally and legislators think locally depends upon a country's specific electoral rules.

The second constitutional feature of presidentialism – the independent tenure of the two branches – means that when separation of purpose arises, neither branch can replace the other; the two branches must either

---

[1] Presidents can, of course, be impeached and removed from office, but impeachment usually requires a lengthy procedure involving extraordinary majorities, and, in some countries, consent of judicial bodies. These onerous mechanisms are intended to prevent the majority of the day from deposing the executive for partisan reasons.

compromise to pass policy or face the consequences of gridlock. If parties are highly fragmented and poorly disciplined, or if the president's party is a minority in an ideologically polarized legislature, separation of purpose increases and, in turn, the potential for deadlock, instability, and balkanization also increases.[2] When compromise is used to ameliorate a separation of purpose among groups, presidentialism has the effect of expanding the range of interests that are consulted in the passage of new laws. New policies that do pass in such a system tend to be relatively stable because their enacting coalition consists of such disparate constituencies and so many veto gates that future change is likely to be quite costly.

However, if there is an extreme unity of purpose, that is, the president can count on a fully disciplined partisan majority in the legislature,[3] then presidentialism can be highly decisive. It can also become highly exclusive since interests outside the ruling party or coalition may be effectively ignored. Moreover, if there is an extreme unity of purpose, the potential for capricious policy change is great. We show that relatively few presidential systems are located at either of these extremes; nonetheless, their occurrence has fueled a substantial literature claiming that presidentialism is dysfunctional or even "perilous" (Valenzuela 1993; Linz 1994).

THE POLICY CHALLENGE

The goal of this chapter (as well as the entire volume) is to understand how institutions affect the ability of democratic systems to meet two fundamental policy challenges: initiating policy reforms and guaranteeing the stability and credibility of these reforms once enacted. In studying these two issues, we pay particular attention to why some constitutional designs favor the policy status quo. We highlight the tradeoffs actors must necessarily make between the decisiveness of their actions and the stability of their policy decisions (Cox and McCubbins, this volume). Additionally, we expect political institutions to affect the degree to which it is possible to overcome the rent-seeking and pork-barreling that

---

[2] Brazil and Colombia would provide examples of high separation of purpose stemming from particularistic legislatures (see, respectively, Mainwaring 1997; Archer and Shugart 1997). Chile in the 1970s, leading up to the coup that placed Pinochet in power, typifies extreme separation of purpose stemming from a polarized legislature in which the president's party is in the minority.

[3] Mexico from about the mid-1930s until at least the mid-1980s is an example of extreme unity of purpose. See Weldon (1997).

may characterize the policy status quo, especially in developing or ex-communist countries. We argue that systems in which politicians' incentives are to cater to narrow constituencies will be less capable of carrying out reforms than those in which politicians compete for the allegiance of the median voter by advocating broad, programmatic policy platforms.

A central theme of this chapter is that the separation of powers inherent in presidentialism has consequences for policy making even when it does not produce divergent partisan control of the assembly and executive. We argue that there is an irony in presidentialism in terms of its effects on the provision of national policy. While the president should be interested in providing public goods at the national level as a result of his nationwide constituency, legislators' separation from the executive typically makes them less interested in providing national policy than in parliamentary systems. Thus a separation of purpose remains a real possibility even when the assembly and the president are controlled by the same party.

In this chapter, we first provide a concise definition of presidentialism, contrasting it not only to parliamentarism but also with other less familiar regime types such as premier-presidentialism. We then turn to a more detailed discussion of separation of powers in presidential democracies, focusing particular attention on variations in the constitutional powers of presidents. Various powers allow presidents to affect legislation regardless of whether or not they enjoy copartisan legislative majorities. We classify these powers as reactive or proactive according to whether the power allows the president to defend the status quo or establish a new one. These powers vary substantially across cases.

We then examine the sources and consequences of separation of purpose. In particular, we analyze how the incentives of legislators are affected by the powers of the president and by the design of electoral institutions, and how various electoral institutions spawn a separation of purpose.

Finally, we show how the constitutional powers of presidents interact with institutions to promote either unity or separation of purpose. Constitutionally stronger presidencies are found in precisely those systems that are most prone to separation of purpose. This relationship is no accident; constitutional designers have granted these presidencies stronger powers in an effort to compensate partially for the absence of strong copartisan majorities. Nonetheless, extensive presidential powers are no substitute for strong and cohesive parties that enhance the unity of purpose between legislators and executives.

DEFINING REGIME TYPES

Democratic regimes can be defined along four dimensions: (1) whether the cabinet is accountable to parliament or to the president; (2) whether the president is popularly elected or is considered primarily ceremonial; (3) whether terms of office are fixed or controlled; and (4) whether the executive does or does not have veto power. In a "pure" *parliamentary system*, cabinets are accountable to the assembly majority, the assembly can be dissolved before the completion of a full term, and only the lower (or sole) house of parliament has veto power. If there is a president, he or she enjoys only ceremonial powers. By contrast, in a "pure" *presidential system*, cabinets are accountable to a popularly elected president who sits for a fixed term. While the president cannot dissolve the legislature, he or she typically possesses veto power. Each of these four elements of constitutional design is discussed in more detail in the following sections.

Cabinet Accountability

While the presidential – parliamentary dichotomy oversimplifies the actual range of democratic regimes in the world (Shugart and Carey 1992; see also Duverger 1980, Sartori 1994), it does capture a crucial variation among them, namely, their system of cabinet accountability. All democratic constitutions define a cabinet (i.e., the ministers who actually head the major governmental departments) and specify to whom it is accountable (i.e., who can remove the ministers from office). In no existing national democratic system do voters themselves elect or remove cabinet ministers.[4] Cabinet ministers typically serve either on the exclusive "confidence" of the assembly, in which case we have *parliamentary* cabinet accountability, or they are subject to the exclusive confidence of a popularly elected chief executive, in which case we have *presidential* cabinet accountability. In some cases, cabinets may need the simultaneous confidence of both the president and the parliamentary majority.[5]

---

[4] In some U.S. states, notably the two largest, California and Texas, some cabinet and regulatory officers – such as treasurer, superintendent of education, and insurance and railroad commissioners – are directly elected. Additionally, in some states such officials and governors may be "recalled" through an early election initiated by a collection of voter signatures.

[5] Such hybrids may be inherently unstable due to the lack of a clear principle of accountability (Shugart and Carey 1992). Variants of this hybrid accountability are

When we refer to parliamentary cabinet accountability, we exclude cases in which votes of no confidence must be approved by a supermajority, as, for example, was the case in Taiwan before 1997. In such cases, a party or coalition capable of passing legislation, which typically requires only a bare majority, is incapable of also controlling the composition of the cabinet. For our purposes, we view systems that require a supermajority to dismiss cabinet ministers as more akin to systems with presidential cabinet accountability.

By the definitions just developed, three of the countries examined in the case studies of this volume have presidential cabinet accountability (Argentina, Chile, and Taiwan before 1997), while two have parliamentary cabinet accountability (Czechoslovakia[6] and Poland). As a result of constitutional amendments in 1997, Taiwan has now established accountability of the cabinet to the majority in parliament. Only those cases with presidential cabinet accountability exhibit separate executive survival, meaning that the legislative majority cannot replace the head of government or cabinet ministers.

Election of Presidency

Separation of origin exists whenever the president is elected either directly by the voters or through an electoral college that is a completely separate body from the legislature. If the presidency is mostly ceremonial, and cabinets are formed mostly or entirely out of the legislature (as in parliamentary regimes), then we cannot speak of separate origin.[7] The

---

currently found in Armenia, Colombia, Ecuador, Peru, and Russia, among others. As Jones notes in his chapter, Argentina now has an institution of Cabinet Chief, subject to joint presidential and legislative confidence. However, this joint confidence does not extend to other ministers, who remain fully subordinated to the president; indeed, the real authority of the Cabinet Chief remains ambiguous.

    Another hybrid form is now used in Israel, in which the directly elected chief executive as well as the rest of the cabinet may be removed by a vote of confidence, which then brings about new assembly as well as executive elections. A variant on this latter idea was proposed in Bolivia in the early 1990s, but rejected (Linz 1994).

[6] Its two successor states, Czech Republic and Slovakia, have also been characterized by parliamentary cabinet accountability since 1993.

[7] Bulgaria and Slovenia are examples of countries with elected presidents but essentially a true parliamentary form of government, given the almost complete lack of discretion over cabinet formation accorded the presidency in each case. The French president has some discretion in selecting the premier, though given the two-bloc nature of the French party system, in practice such discretion has not meant much when the president's party was not part of the legislative majority (Shugart and Carey 1992, 123–24).

presence of an elected presidency is obviously a necessary condition for a regime to be presidential; however, it is not sufficient. Numerous regimes combine an elected presidency with exclusive accountability of the cabinet to parliament; the best known case of this is the French Fifth Republic. Given the cabinet's exclusive accountability to parliament, such a regime cannot be considered presidential. But again, provided that the presidency is not purely ceremonial, such a regime cannot be parliamentary either; thus, we call them *premier-presidential*. Presidents in such regimes have some authority in choosing the prime minister and possibly other cabinet ministers; once installed in office, however, only the assembly majority may dismiss them. The 1997 amendments in Taiwan appear to have established a premier-presidential system. However, there remains some ambiguity as to whether the president may also dismiss a cabinet that enjoys parliamentary confidence. If he or she can, then the system is what Shugart and Carey (1992) call president-parliamentary – implying a much stronger presidency and greater potential for interbranch conflict – instead of premier-presidential.

Of the countries examined in the case studies of this book, Argentina, Chile, Poland, and Taiwan have directly elected presidents.[8] The Czechoslovakian president is elected by parliament.

Fixed Terms

If the terms of the elected branches are fixed, then the survival of each branch is independent of the other; no branch can shorten the tenure of any other. Separation of survival may be weakened if the assembly can cast votes of no confidence in the cabinet or if the executive has the authority to dissolve the assembly and call for early elections.

In parliamentary systems, the cabinet and its head, the prime minister, can be dismissed at any time by the parliamentary majority. Usually, early elections can be called, although only in some parliamentary systems is dissolution of the assembly left to the discretion of the head of government.[9] Typically, the dissolution of power is formally exercised

[8] Argentina before 1995 and Taiwan before 1996 used electoral colleges, so election of the president was indirect. It was still separate, however, because legislators were not included within the electoral college.

[9] Even where the head of government has such discretion, he or she will exercise it only at electorally propitious times from the standpoint of the ruling party or coalition. It is often overlooked in the literature that separation of survival in office frequently applies partially to parliamentary systems as well. Obviously the term of the cabinet is not fixed in a parliamentary system, by definition – this feature is

by the head of state, such as the Czechoslovakian president. In premier-presidential systems, such as Poland, the cabinet and prime minister are subject to ongoing confidence of the parliamentary majority.[10] In most premier-presidential systems, the president has the power to dissolve the assembly, although such power is often restricted. In Poland, for example, dissolution can be exercised only in the event of the inability of parliament to invest its confidence in a new government after an election.[11] Thus, a parliament controlled by an effective majority coalition can never be dissolved. In Taiwan after 1997, the President has been granted the authority to dissolve the parliament, but only after a failed no-confidence vote.

Veto Gates

The basic concept of parliamentary sovereignty has been eloquently summarized by Linz (1994, 5), "In parliamentary systems, the only democratically legitimated institution is the parliament." If we overlook the issue of bicameralism,[12] parliamentary systems in their pure form contain only one veto gate: the assembly majority. Without other veto gates, the power of the assembly majority is unchecked.

captured by the variable of cabinet accountability. However, in many parliamentary systems there is no provision for dissolution of the assembly other than by a vote of the assembly itself (as in Israel before 1996, for example). Elsewhere, there may be no provision for dissolution at all, i.e., assembly terms are fixed (in the Netherlands and Norway, for example). In still other parliamentary systems, including Italy, only the (appointed) president has the authority to dissolve parliament. Of course, in established parliamentary republics as much as in constitutional monarchies, such authority is rarely if ever exercised except on the "advice" of the prime minister, but the head of state occasionally refuses a request for a dissolution.

[10] Only the lower house, the Sejm, holds this authority.

[11] Under the 1997 Constitution, the president is permitted to nominate a prime ministerial candidate, but if the nominee is rejected, parliament may attempt to select its own candidate. If this fails, and a subsequent nominee by the president is also rejected, then the president dissolves parliament. Once installed in office, a cabinet may be dismissed only on a constructive vote by parliament; i.e., the majority must elect a new cabinet at the same time it deposes the incumbent one.

[12] Even if an upper house is, of course, part of "parliament," the possibility of different majorities in the two houses raises the specter of disagreements and conflicts over who reflects the wishes of "the people," which is precisely the objection Linz has with presidentialism. We also leave aside the matter of veto power wielded by some appointed presidents in parliamentary systems, although this is an area that deserves more careful study.

Nearly all presidential systems establish the president as a veto gate;[13] the existence of multiple, separately elected veto gates is thus a central feature of presidential democracy. In contrast to parliamentary systems, legislative coalitions in most presidential democracies must either seek the president's support or else be able to assemble a supermajority that can bypass a presidential veto. The presidencies of Argentina, Poland, and Taiwan before 1997 have vetoes that can be overridden only by an extraordinary majority (a two-thirds supermajority is needed in all cases except Poland, which requires a three-fifths supermajority). Since 1997, a majority of parliament may override a presidential veto in Taiwan. Thus, all these presidencies except Taiwan after 1997 constitute veto gates: No bill can become law without either the president's assent or a legislative supermajority.

Conclusion

Four characteristics define presidential regimes and distinguish them from parliamentary and premier-presidential regimes: whether the cabinet is accountable to the president or the assembly, whether there is an elected presidency, whether terms are fixed, and whether the executive possesses veto power. All four factors affect the *degree* of separation of power within a regime, but all presidential systems exhibit some separation of powers (by definition). In the remainder of this chapter, we concentrate on the "pure" presidential systems, beginning with a discussion of variations in presidential powers before turning to the question of separation of purpose.[14]

PRESIDENTIAL POWERS

All presidents in pure presidential systems are in some sense "powerful" simply by virtue of being directly elected heads of government who

[13] It is theoretically possible to have a presidential system in which the president plays no formal role in shaping legislation. Such a president would be the executive in the strictest sense of the term: empowered to administer the law, but not to help make it. With minor exceptions, the presidential regimes in Benin and Venezuela are of this sort.

[14] Some of our findings are valid for premier-presidential systems, too, especially those such as Poland where the presidency has a strong veto. We shall indicate at times ways in which our findings can be extended to such a case. We shall also make periodic references to parliamentary systems, such as Czechoslovakia, even though our primary focus at all times is on the policy-making implications of separation of powers in presidential systems.

cannot be removed from office even when they run afoul of legislators' policy preferences. Nonetheless, there is tremendous variation in presidential powers across countries, and we expect these differences to have important consequences for policy making. Presidential powers are particularly significant in those crucial instances when presidential and legislative interests diverge, resulting in what we call a separation of purpose. The overall strength of presidents, defined as their ability to enact a policy agenda, varies with their legislative support, public approval ratings, and idiosyncratic factors such as personality and the ability to communicate effectively. Here we are concerned, however, strictly with those powers derived from the constitutional definition of the office. These powers determine the extent to which the president can function as an agenda setter and a veto player; they thereby affect the degree to which powers in a particular regime are separated.

Chief executives share a number of powers across presidential systems, including the ability to make diplomatic and administrative appointments and the authority to act as commander of the armed forces. With respect to law-making powers, however, presidential systems are characterized by tremendous variation. One way to think of the law-making powers of the president is to analyze their ability to affect the legislative status quo (Shugart 1998; Cox and McCubbins, this volume). We refer to powers that allow the president to establish, or attempt to establish, a new status quo as proactive powers. The best example of a proactive law-making power is decree power. We refer to those powers that only allow the president to defend the status quo against attempts by the legislative majority to change it as *reactive powers*. The most familiar reactive power is the veto power.

Decree Power

We focus on those decrees that have the force of law, and may possibly supersede existing law, *without prior consent of the assembly*. Thus we exclude from our definition those administrative and regulatory acts that are often called *decrees* but are issued within the confines of authorizing statutes.[15]

---

[15] Most of those legal instruments issued by presidents that are called decrees in government gazettes are of an administrative or regulatory nature and do not seek to change the legislative status quo. These are acts inherent to the executive in any country and would be called *executive orders* in the United States (Moe 1990a;

Few constitutions allow presidents to promulgate by decree *new legislation* without first gaining explicit authority to do so;[16] only Argentina, Brazil, Colombia, and Russia allow presidents the power to issue legislative decrees that take effect immediately and do not require prior authorization by statute. Those presidents who may enact laws by decree potentially can dominate the legislative agenda. Such decrees are more than mere agenda-setting because of their immediate legal force. Thus, the president can present congress and other actors with a *fait accompli*, forcing them either to tolerate the new status quo mandated by the decree or else pay what Power (1998), in reference to the Brazilian case, calls massive "clean-up costs." In other words, once a decree is issued, it becomes the reversionary policy, the point at which policy remains in the absence of successful legislative action to overturn it.

In some countries (e.g., Brazil), decrees are only temporary unless converted into regular legislation, but at least during that interim, presidential preferences prevail. Even when a majority can rescind a decree, and most assemblies possess such authority,[17] presidents can use decree powers strategically, attempting to discern a point in the policy space at which a congressional majority is indifferent between the status quo and the decree. Consequently, in emitting a decree, a president cannot be confident that it will survive in Congress; hence, decree power alone does not let the president dominate the legislative process. Decrees do, however, allow presidents to initiate policy change and obtain legislative outcomes that Congress on its own may not have passed (Carey and Shugart 1998, Shugart 1998).

Even using our narrow definition of decree as executive acts implementing new law not passed by the legislature, it is important to make

---

Sala 1998). If Latin American presidents appear to employ decree powers extensively in making policy (i.e., changing the status quo), it is partly because the closed nature of the economy typical of Latin America until recently puts more administrative powers in the hands of the executive.

[16] The distinction between laws and regulations is important and is made in all legal systems with which we are familiar. Courts or comptroller general offices typically are empowered to determine whether a regulatory decree in fact exceeds the authorization of existing legislation. Obviously the extent to which this oversight power is exercised depends on the degree of independence accorded to these agencies. This is an area in which much more research needs to be done. For a fuller discussion of these points, see Carey and Shugart (1998).

[17] Russia, under the 1993 constitution, is one of the few exceptions. Because a decree can be superseded only by a statute, and the president holds a veto requiring two-thirds majorities to override, the Russian president can effectively legislate even if no more than one-third of one house shares his policy preferences.

one further clarification concerning the source of decree authority. *Many decrees are issued under powers explicitly delegated by legislatures.* This point is of obvious importance in assessing the ultimate source of presidential power. If presidents issue legislative decrees under authority granted them by Congress – sometimes with tight restrictions on the range of acceptable policy choices and with strict reporting requirements – it is misleading to see those policies as simply reflecting presidential preferences. For example, in Argentina in 1989, newly inaugurated President Menem obtained authority from the outgoing Congress to issue new laws in policy areas defined as Reform of the State and Economic Emergency. Decree laws issued under this authority included privatization of a number of state-owned enterprises, a major departure from the status quo ante, but one that had been endorsed beforehand by an act of Congress.

Among the countries discussed in this book, only Argentina allows its presidents to issue decrees in a wide range of policy areas in the absence of a prior congressional delegation.[18] Because of the widespread use of "Need and Emergency Decrees" by President Carlos Menem (and, to a lesser degree, by his predecessor, Raul Alfonsin), Argentine democracy has been derided as a "delegative democracy" in which the president rules by decree without regard to formal congressional and judicial checks (O'Donnell 1994; see also Bresser Pereira et al. 1993). However, at least in the area of fiscal policy, Jones (this volume) shows that presidential decree power has proved unimportant, and Congress's role in the policy-making process has been institutionalized and effective. In other policy areas,[19] decree power has undoubtedly been more important (Jones 1997). Indeed, as Heller and McCubbins note in their chapter, the existence of such power is precisely why investors have been concerned about the long-run stability of regulatory policy in Argentina: A

---

[18] Elsewhere, including in Brazil, Colombia, and especially Russia, presidents have the constitutional authority to issue new laws by decree in a very wide range of policy areas. See Carey and Shugart (1998b). Among cases discussed in this book, there is a fiscal decree provision in the current constitution of Chile. The Chilean president may decree spending of up to two percent of the total annual expenditure in the event of "emergencies." However, Baldez and Carey note that this provision is generally agreed by all relevant actors in Chile to apply only to natural disasters, and not, as in Argentina, virtually any situation that the president deems to be of "need and urgency." Decree authority in Chile has not been used since the return to democracy.

[19] For example, Menem used decree power to create new taxes. The new Constitution prohibits decree power from being used in the area of taxation, however.

president who can change laws by decree can produce unpredictable policy results. Nonetheless, given restrictions on presidential decree power in the 1994 constitution (Jones 1997), it is likely to be of declining importance in Argentina.

Veto and Override

Whereas the ability to issue decrees is a proactive presidential power, veto power is a reactive power. A president with veto power may sign or veto a bill sent to his desk by the legislature. By signing it, he or she accepts the version passed by the legislature, assuming he or she cannot veto some parts of it and promulgate the rest, a possibility discussed below. If he or she must accept or veto the entire bill, he or she holds what is known as a *package* veto. When a president exercises a package veto on a bill, policy on all dimensions covered by the bill becomes the reversionary point (unless, of course, the veto is overridden). The reversionary point for bills relating to fiscal policy is typically defined either as zero spending or else as the current level of spending (with an inflation adjustment). In other issue areas, such as regulation, the reversionary point is often the status quo. Below, we discuss cases in which the president has the authority to set a different reversion point.

The veto is a *reactive* law-making power in that it allows the president to defend the status quo by reacting to the legislature's attempt to alter it. As a reactive power, the veto does not permit the president to get "more" of whatever policy the bill addresses; it is, rather, a conservative instrument that lets the president block change (Kiewiet and McCubbins 1988). For example, the veto is not an effective instrument for inducing more governmental spending on a particular item or for redesigning a particular regulation if Congress is happy with current spending levels or current regulations.[20] If, on the other hand, Congress wanted to spend more in some area than current policy mandated or if it wanted to alter the regulatory structure, a president who preferred the status quo could preserve current policy by exercising the veto.

The normative implications of the veto for economic policy making thus depend crucially on evaluations of the status quo. If the status quo is considered optimal in economic terms, the veto is a useful instrument for defending it against undesirable challenges; it can be used to secure

---

[20] We ignore for the moment the strategic use of the veto for the purpose of issue linkage.

desirable policy and prevent changes to it. However, the reactive nature of the veto makes it useless as an instrument for channeling policy in a new direction.

Provisions for overriding presidential vetoes vary considerably across the universe of presidential systems (Shugart and Carey 1992; Shugart and Mainwaring 1997), but in all the (pure) presidential systems in this book an override of the president's veto requires a two-thirds majority. In Poland's premier-presidential system, the S'amm constitution of 1992 also provided for a two-thirds override, but the constitution enacted in 1997 reduced the override threshold to three-fifths. In many other presidential and premier-presidential systems – for example in Brazil, Colombia, and Portugal – overrides require only a majority of all members, thereby obviously weakening the presidency's role as a veto gate. In still other constitutions, including France and Venezuela, the president either has no veto at all, or at best delaying power.

In a few constitutions, the president may veto specific provisions within a bill. In a full *item veto* – also known as a partial veto – the president may promulgate the items or articles of the bill with which he agrees while vetoing and returning to congress for reconsideration only the vetoed portions. While this power is not authorized in the constitutions of many countries, it is, in practice, sometimes used. Among Latin American and East Asian countries, only the Philippine constitution and, since 1995, the Argentine constitution, unambiguously permit the president to promulgate parts of a bill while vetoing others.[21] However, presidents have frequently asserted a right of partial veto with partial promulgation. For example, Jones details some cases in which this authority was exercised in Argentina before it was codified in the new constitution. Usually, Jones notes, item vetoes have been employed when the legislature has failed in its constitutional obligation to indicate a funding source for the spending increases it has already authorized.

Where the president can selectively veto parts of bills he objects to, he has the ability to "fine tune" legislation, thereby enhancing his authority relative to cases where the veto must pertain to an entire bill. In their chapter on Chile, Baldez and Carey offer a spatial model of item veto power in the area of budgeting that demonstrates this point formally. They conclude that the outcome under an item veto will be closer to the

[21] In the Philippines, partial vetoes apply only to spending and tariff bills.

president's ideal point than under a package veto for those dimensions of the bill on which the president prefers less spending than Congress.

Gatekeeping and Agenda-Setting Powers:
Exclusive Introduction of Bills

Some constitutions stipulate certain policy areas in which no bill can be considered by the assembly unless it is initiated by the president. This exclusive power – also known as *gatekeeping* – often extends to quite critical issues, most notably budgets, but also military policy, the creation of new bureaucratic agencies, and laws concerning taxation, trade, and credit policies. Akin to the veto, gatekeeping power is a reactive power because if the president prefers the reversionary policy to any outcome he or she deems likely to win the support of a veto-proof majority in Congress, he or she can prevent policy changes simply by not initiating a bill. For instance, Baldez and Carey note that recent Chilean tax policy has been very stable largely because the reversion point (a law enacted in 1990 and extended in 1993) is more progressive than Congress has subsequently preferred and because only the president can initiate tax policy.

The president's ability to set the agenda or to constrain Congress's agenda is made even stronger where there are restrictions on legislative amendments. Such agenda-setting powers are quite common in the area of budgetary laws. A number of constitutions, including those in South Korea, Taiwan, Brazil, Chile, Colombia, and Peru, limit Congress's authority to increase budgetary spending above the levels submitted by the president. Baldez and Carey show formally that such provisions enhance the capacity of the president to obtain outcomes closer to his preferences. In Chile, the reversionary outcome is the president's own proposal, further enhancing his authority and privileging whichever branch prefers the lower spending on any given item.

Despite the formal authority of the president to set the agenda through a prohibition against increased spending, Cheng and Haggard note that the influences on presidential preferences and the law of anticipated reaction must also be understood. In crafting the budget, the interests of those legislators who are needed to pass it must be taken into account. In Taiwan, Cheng and Haggard find that even though the president had quite extensive agenda-setting powers in the budget area, the increasing competitiveness of the political system led him to submit budgets that catered to legislators' interests.

Conclusion

By definition, all presidential systems entail separation of powers because the executive and legislative branches are each elected by voters (separate origin) for fixed terms (separate survival).[22] Despite these broad areas of similarity, there is considerable variation across presidential systems in the balance of powers between the elected branches. We have identified three principal law-making powers – decree power, veto power, and agenda-setting power – that presidents are often granted.

Table 3.1 summarizes the presidential powers of the three pure presidential systems that are covered by case studies in this volume. All three presidencies have strong vetoes that require extraordinary assembly majorities to be overridden. Such powers provide the president with a powerful instrument in defending the policy status quo. With respect to other types of presidential powers, there is somewhat more variation across our cases. In Argentina, Chile, and Taiwan before 1997 only the president may initiate the budget, and Congress cannot increase spending. In each case, however, different reversionary points affect how much leverage the president enjoys. In Chile, the reversionary point is typically current policy, but, in the case of spending, the reversionary point is the president's proposal. This contrasts with Taiwan, where the legislature may pass a temporary resolution, though the constitution prohibits the legislature from increasing spending over levels proposed by the executive. Finally, in Argentina, the authority to issue new laws by decree exists and has proven important in some reforms; it is not, however, as important as is frequently thought. By contrast, the president in Taiwan is usually considered quite powerful even though he does not have decree powers. As we will argue in more detail below, misperceptions about presidential powers stem from a lack of clarity about the sources of these powers. In Argentina, authority delegated from Congress proved to be the most important factor in most of Menem's reforms. In Taiwan, by

---

[22] Premier-presidential systems may exhibit partial separate origin to the extent that the president has authority to determine the composition of the cabinet, but such systems do not have separation of survival, because the cabinet can be dismissed through a parliamentary vote of no confidence.

Table 3.1. *Constitutional Powers of Presidents over Legislation: Argentina, Chile, and Taiwan*

	Argentina	Chile	Taiwan before 1997
Veto	Package and item; two-thirds override	Package; two-thirds override	Package; two-thirds override
Decree	In "need and urgency, as defined by executive, subject to restrictions (e.g., not in penal, tax, or electoral/party matters)	President may decree unauthorized spending of up to 2% of total budget (understood as applicable only in natural disasters)	No
Gatekeeping/ Agenda control	Only president may introduce budget bill; Congress may not increase spending without indicating a source for the revenue	Only president may introduce budget bill and bills on taxes creating public services and other matters; on budget Congress may not increase spending without indicating a source for the revenue and it may not increase estimates of revenue	Only president may introduce budget bill; Congress may not increase spending
Reversion	Current policy	Taxes: Current policy Budget: President's proposal	Congress may pass temporary resolution

Sources: Baldez and Carey this volume; Carey, Amorim-Neto, and Shugart 1997; Jones this volume.

contrast, presidential power came not from decree authority but from control over the party.

By surveying a larger number of presidential cases, we can better evaluate the similarities and differences between our case studies and other presidential regimes. Table 3.2 scores a number of presidential systems on each of the powers we have discussed, giving each a value of 0, 1, or 2. The higher the total score, the greater the constitutional prerogatives of the president in putting an independent stamp on legis-

Table 3.2. *An Index of Presidential Powers over Legislation*

Package veto
  0 No veto, or override by majority
  1 No veto on spending, but veto with extraordinary majority override on other bills
  2 Veto with extraordinary majority override on all bills
Item veto (with promulgation of vetoed items permitted)
  0 No item veto
  1 Item veto on some bills (usually spending), extraordinary majority override
  2 Item veto on all bills, extraordinary majority override
Decree (new legislation, absent prior delegation)
  0 No provision
  2 Provided
Exclusive authority to introduce bills in specified policy areas
  0 No provision, or applies only to budget bill with no major restrictions on amendment
  1 Provided also in nonbudgetary bills, but no major restrictions on amendment
  2 Provided, major restrictions on amendment (such as inability to increase spending on items)

	Index Value	Country	Package Veto	Item Veto	Decree	Exclusive Introduction
High powers	6	Argentina	2	2	2	0
	5	Russia	2	0	2	1
	4	Chile	2	0	0	2
		Colombia	0	0	2	2
		Georgia	2	0	0	2
		South Korea	2	0	0	2
		Peru	0	0	2	2
		Taiwan before 1997	2	0	0	2
	3	Brazil	0	0	2	1
		Ecuador	1	0	2	0
		Philippines	2	1	0	0
	2	Bolivia	2	0	0	0
		Dominican Republic	2	0	0	0
		El Salvador	2	0	0	0
		Guatemala	2	0	0	0
		United States	2	0	0	0
		Uruguay	0	0	0	2
	1	Costa Rica	1	0	0	0
		Honduras	1	0	0	0
		Mexico	1	0	0	0
Low powers	0	Nicaragua	0	0	0	0
		Paraguay	0	0	0	0
		Venezuela	0	0	0	0

lative output; countries are ranked from the weakest to the strongest. According to this scoring system, Argentina is one of the two strongest presidencies.[23] Several other Latin American systems with a reputation for "strong" presidencies vest practically no constitutional powers in the president; one of the most surprising of these cases is Mexico. The exercise in classifying presidents' constitutionally derived legislative powers allows us to isolate the actual sources of presidential authority and to make comparative-statics predictions about presidential power under changed conditions of partisan standing. The Mexican president's constitutional authority over legislation is minimal; his powers stem from strong majorities for the Institutional Revolutionary Party (PRI) within the legislature and extraordinary powers within the party itself. Without these advantages, Mexican presidents would be surprisingly weak in comparison to earlier periods and even in comparison to presidents in other systems (Shugart and Mainwaring 1997; Weldon 1997). Cheng and Haggard and Haggard and Noble tell similar stories about presidential power in Taiwan, a case that has a rather more moderate scoring than the image of a dominant, authoritarian president would imply.

SEPARATION OF PURPOSE IN PRESIDENTIAL SYSTEMS: LEGISLATIVE INCENTIVES

In the previous section, we discussed the separation of powers in presidential systems. We identified the institutional features that provide for a separately elected executive and we highlighted how the constitutional powers of the executive affect legislative outcomes. At many points throughout this discussion, we suggested that the ability of the president to achieve his or her legislative aims hinged not only on the Constitution but also on the unity or separation of purpose vis-a-vis the legislature. In this section, we ask, Under what conditions can we expect the separate institutions to have policy disagreements? Are there systematic features of presidential systems that affect separation or unity of purpose between the branches?

Most obviously, presidential systems permit the possibility of divided

---

[23] Arguably the Russian presidency is actually stronger, even though its index score is lower than Argentina's. The Argentine president has more means by which to influence policy outcomes, but the Russian president may issue decrees in nearly any policy area and attempts to rescind them are treated as ordinary legislative bills, unlike in Argentina, and hence are subject to the veto.

government by the assembly (or of at least one house of the assembly) and the executive to be controlled by different parties. Under divided government, a wider range of interests must necessarily be accommodated for policy to be enacted. As a result, the potential for stalemate increases, although much will depend on the nature of the party system and the polarization of the parties on key issues. Surveying the experience of 165 elections in presidential and premier-presidential systems, Shugart (1995) found that the president's party won a majority in just under sixty percent of the elections, and that no party held a majority in about a quarter of the cases; in less than one-fourth of the elections was there a single party or preelection coalition opposed to the president that held a majority. In a number of contemporary cases, a party or bloc of parties other than that of the president has controlled a majority in at least one house. Examples include Argentina under Alfonsín and in the last part of Menem's second term, Chile, since its return to democracy in 1989, and the first two years of Roh Tae Woo's presidency in Korea. In numerous other cases, including Brazil, since its return to democracy, no party has held a majority and the president's party may not even enjoy a plurality.

Divided government, however, is by no means the only, nor even the most important, source of separation of purpose in presidential systems. A fundamental fact of the policy-making process in presidential systems is that the president, elected in a nationwide constituency, confronts legislators who are typically elected from narrower (generally regional) constituencies (Geddes 1994; Moe and Caldwell 1994). This section examines how electoral institutions affect legislators' incentives and evaluates how these incentives affect separation of purpose. The underlying premise is that features of the electoral process that expand the degree to which legislators' incentives differ from presidents' incentives make policy gridlock more likely.

Presidential systems vary substantially in the extent to which the president's and legislators' electoral interests are aligned.[24] Two extreme scenarios are possible. In one case, legislators are responsive to the same national policy demands that voters weigh when assessing the perfor-

---

[24] This discussion assumes that there are meaningfully democratic elections for both branches such that legislators and the president must cater to voters' interests. That is, it leaves aside authoritarian cases like that of Mexico until the 1990s in which legislators are so dependent on the president (as leader of a hegemonic party) that they can essentially take voters' evaluations of them for granted. See Weldon (1997).

mance of the president. Individual legislators might disagree with the president on specific policy issues, particularly if they are from a different party, but both president and legislators are judged on the basis of their performance with respect to broad policy issues of national import. At the opposite extreme, voters reward or punish presidents and legislators on entirely different grounds. Voters might hold the president responsible for national policy but demand that legislators do little more than provide pork to their district.

Where any given system falls on this hypothetical continuum depends on several institutional factors. First, separation of survival (i.e., fixed terms) itself tends to produce a disjunction between national policy and legislative incentives. At least four additional institutional factors also impact a system's separation of purpose. First, we consider the nature of electoral rules and study how they structure the incentives facing legislators; we focus particularly on the incentives for legislators to align with the president. We then consider the effect of the timing of presidential and assembly elections as well as the staggering of the terms of assembly members. Whether legislators are all elected at the same time as presidents is likely to shape substantially the degree to which they see their electoral fates as being interconnected. Finally, we consider the degree of congruence between the constituency of congressmembers and the constituency of the president. We discuss each of these factors, with the aim of building an index that will allow us to rank presidential systems by their tendency to promote separation or unity of purpose.

Separate Survival and Legislative Incentives

Let us return to the comparison of presidential and parliamentary democracy. Because of the fusion of executive and legislative powers in parliamentary systems, the only source of executive authority is through partisan or coalitional support in the assembly.[25] Legislators in parliamentary systems band together in parties that seek to present a relatively coherent face to the electorate in the form of a party *label* that is identified with a basket of policy positions. They are encouraged to do so because the only way that they (or their voters) can influence the makeup of the executive branch is through their choice of party in legislative races. Voters tend to reward those legislators who have hewn closely to the party line, and therefore legislators have a powerful incen-

---

[25] The logic spelled out in this paragraph draws heavily on Shugart and Carey (1992).

tive to concern themselves with broad national policy. The composition of the executive cabinet, and thus the overall direction of policy, depends on the working majority of parliamentarians; a prime minister remains in office only so long as he enjoys the confidence of parliament. The cabinet and its head has little incentive or ability to stray from the preferences of their own party, and the preferences of rank-and-file legislators are powerfully shaped by national issues.

All of what has just been said about parliamentary systems should apply to premier-presidential systems since the cabinet in a premier-presidential system is also accountable to the assembly majority. Yet, in premier-presidential systems, the separate origin of executive and legislative authority, combined with the president's role as a veto player, is likely to reduce party discipline. The reason is that the presidential veto serves to undercut the usual parliamentary-style link between legislative campaigns and policy output and to encourage legislators to "cheat" more on the party label than they would in either a parliamentary system or in a premier-presidential system that lacks a presidential veto.[26] Moreover, in some premier-presidential systems, such as Poland, party discipline also suffers from open-list electoral rules.

Returning to the "pure" presidential cases, it should be clear that such systems generate very different incentives for legislators than those generated in parliamentary systems. The fully separate selection process of the executive and assembly and the lack of mutual dependence once in office permits voters and campaign contributors to demand different things of their executive and legislative candidates. As a result, voters need not demand that their legislators show loyalty to a party label. Since the executive is elected independently of the legislature, legislators can represent narrow interests without sacrificing the connection between voters and the executive. Although presidential systems give an official with a nationwide constituency a veto or other law-making powers, the very structure of presidentialism itself tends to reduce legislators' interest in providing public goods at the national level. Paradoxically, presidential systems may therefore be less attuned to broad national interests than parliamentary systems, other things being equal. The most

---

[26] This attribution of lapses in discipline to the presidential veto rather than open-list PR is strengthened by consideration of Finland, a premier-presidential system with a nearly identical electoral system, no presidential veto, and generally very strong party discipline.

important "other thing" is the nature of electoral procedures that might drive legislators in some systems toward a more national outlook.

Party-centered and Candidate-centered Electoral Formulas

Separation of survival may inherently reduce legislators' interest in representing voters' preferences on national policy issues, but the extent to which this is the case hinges crucially on the design of electoral systems, which in turn shapes parties and party systems. Most of the literature on electoral systems has been concerned with the effects of electoral laws on the number of parties and the proportionality of seats to votes (Lijphart 1984, 1994; Taagepera and Shugart 1989). These matters are important for policy making. For example, policy making in presidential systems is likely to be made more difficult to the extent that electoral laws foster multiparty systems in which presidents have difficulty forming legislative coalitions (Haggard and Kaufman 1995, ch. 5; Mainwaring and Shugart 1997b). We direct our attention here toward a second, and still largely neglected, way in which electoral laws affect parties: through the formula that determines which specific candidates take the seats won by their parties (see Carey and Shugart 1995).

One useful way of dividing electoral formulas is by the extent to which they encourage a party-centered or a candidate-centered vote. A party-centered electoral formula is one that encourages voters to emphasize their party preference more than their preference for specific candidates. Paramount among such rules is the closed-list form of proportional representation, in which parties present lists of candidates and voters are not permitted to alter the order of the names as presented by the party. Party-centered rules thus imply multiseat districts; otherwise the issue of rank is not relevant and does not confer authority on the party leaders who draw up lists of their candidates. However, vesting control over nominations in the hands of central party leaders (as opposed to primary elections or other decentralizing rules) may encourage even single-seat district (SSD) presidential systems to function in a party-centered manner.[27] Among most pure presidential systems, however,

---

[27] Also a prominent feature providing an increment of party centeredness even under a system of SSDs would be parliamentary cabinet accountability, for reasons noted above: Parliamentarism encourages voters to see the unit of representation as the party first and candidate second. However, because we are concerned in this section

single-member districts are far more likely to behave as candidate-centered electoral rules.

A candidate-centered electoral formula is one in which the voter is encouraged to focus on individual candidates rather than political parties. In presidential systems, single-member districts encourage candidate-centered elections. Candidate-centered elections are also fostered by those formulas that entail intraparty competition within multimember districts. In some multiseat election formulas, voters are permitted, or may even be required, to choose from among several candidates nominated by their preferred party. Examples are open-list proportional representation (PR), in which voters alone provide the rank order of candidates within a party list, and the single nontransferable vote (SNTV), in which party affiliation is not even a criterion in determining which candidates win seats.

Among cases covered in this volume, Argentina is the clearest case of party-centered rules, as it uses closed-list PR. Prior to the military coup in 1973, Chile had candidate-centered rules in the form of open-list PR, but in the present (post-1989) period, elections are much more party-centered. Despite the renewed use of open-list PR, there is no effective intraparty competition, because district magnitude has been reduced to two (in every district in each house) and each party regularly nominates at most one candidate per district. Although there is competition within interparty alliances, even this is muted by the practice of each alliance to nominate only one strong candidate in each district. In that way, as Baldez and Carey note in their chapter, parties that have full control over nominations can negotiate with their alliance partners and can virtually assure for themselves a certain distribution of seats prior to the election. Hence, we consider Chile to now have a relatively party-centered electoral formula, although no doubt less so than Argentina.

Taiwan arguably has the most candidate-centered formula of any presidential democracy.[28] Under the SNTV system, party is not even a criterion in the allocation of seats to candidates. Each candidate stands

---

only with pure presidential systems, we can leave the impact of parliamantarism on SSDs aside, and classify SSDs as candidate-centered.

[28] Its only rival for that title would be Colombia, which uses a system of multiple lists within parties with no pooling of the lists' votes at the level of the party. Moreover, most lists actually elect only one legislator, making the system essentially SNTV. See Cox and Shugart (1995).

alone, winning office (or failing to win office) entirely on the strength of his or her ability to collect personal votes. The formula provides centrifugal incentives to candidates who are only partly offset by the continuing ability of the once-dominant KMT to control candidate selection and to divide the vote efficiently. The increasing competitiveness of the electoral system and the gradual erosion of these powers has had predictable implications for policy, including a propensity to pork-barrel spending and the rise of "money politics" as politicians seek the funds required to differentiate themselves from their copartisans.

If we assume that the provision of public goods at the national level and responsiveness to the median voter constitute an ideal, we would want legislators to have incentives to discover what national policies voters wanted and to work on enacting such policies. Voters then would either reward (reelect) or punish (vote out of office) their representatives on the basis of their ability to pass desired national policies (Fiorina 1981).

The candidate-centered electoral formulas used in many presidential democracies give legislators the incentive to respond to far narrower interests. In extremely candidate-centered formulas, candidates have little incentive to cultivate a party reputation because they must appeal on some basis other than (or in addition to) party to survive intraparty competition; electoral incentives thus discourage campaigns that run on broad national public policy issues. Instead, legislative candidates tend to offer budgetary amendments of benefit to their own constituents, as Ames (1995a, b) has documented in Brazil. Near the middle of the century, Chile employed a candidate-centered electoral formula of this sort; open-list PR was used in districts with an average magnitude of around five. Legislators could initiate spending bills for pet projects to attract voter loyalty notwithstanding the restrictions on legislative increases in individual items in the annual budget bill (Baldez and Carey, this volume). This practice was subsequently abolished, but its abolition is partly responsible for increasing the stakes in executive-legislative conflict, conflict that ultimately led to the breakdown of the system (Valenzuela 1978; Shugart and Carey 1992). Legislators lost access to a principal means by which they had previously courted their voters and muted ideological disputes.

SNTV is even more candidate-centered than open-list PR, because votes for individual candidates are not pooled at the level of the party. In Taiwan, for example, parties must develop strategies to divide the vote relatively evenly among their candidates in any given district or else they risk winning fewer races than possible. Particularism is the most common strategy; individual legislators develop reputations as suppliers of targeted goods and services to specific blocs of voters. The two chapters in this volume on Taiwan provide examples of growing interest on the part of the ruling party in catering to particularistic constituencies as KMT majorities became less secure after 1992.

We would expect that legislators elected under more party-centered rules would tend to be more attentive to broader public goods types of interests than would those from candidate-centered rules, *ceteris paribus*. The reason is that party-centered rules give individual candidates less ability to "cheat" on the party label and thus to cater to local or sectoral interests that might conflict with national party priorities. However, even in extreme party-centered formulas, there is still the possibility that voters' preferences over policy issues might be relatively unimportant to individual legislators. Under such formulas, especially in systems with rather high district magnitudes, legislators have the incentive to curry favor with party leaders and lobby for higher list positions rather than to cultivate ties with voters. Therefore, while legislators are likely to exhibit greater policy responsiveness when they are elected under highly party-centered rules rather than highly candidate-centered rules, it is possible for parties to be *too* strong in the sense that they provide incentives to ignore constituent interests.[29]

Jones' chapter on Argentina demonstrates some of these problems, while also illustrating the significance of federalism as an intervening variable in determining the precise direction of intraparty accountability. The closed lists through which Argentine legislators are elected are drawn up primarily by party leaders *in the provinces*; as a result, Argentine presidents, even under unified government, face a party rank and file determined to increase transfers of revenues to provincial party leaders (see also Garman, Haggard, and Willis 1996).

While it is impossible to define an ideal balance of candidate-centered and party-centered electoral rules, generating the greatest responsiveness to voters' policy preferences rather than to either central party leaders or pork-seeking interests probably requires some intermediate types of electoral rules.

---

[29] This was the critique in Venezuela that led to a move from a fully closed-list PR system in fairly large districts to a mixed system in which about half of legislators are elected in SSDs (and the rest still in closed-list PR districts). See Shugart (1992); Crisp and Rey (2000).

Electoral Rules: Cycles, Staggering, and Proportionality

The cycle of elections in presidential systems has come to be recognized as an important feature of overall institutional design and one that plays a particularly strong role in bringing about either unity or separation of purpose between the elected branches. Divided government is an inherent possibility in systems that provide for separate origin. Electoral cycles that mandate midterm elections, as in Argentina, or that have presidential and assembly terms of different length, as in Chile since a constitutional amendment became effective in 1997, are far more likely to produce divided government than are other cycles. Shugart (1995) found that the later an assembly election occurs in a president's term, the more likely divided government was to result from that election.

Staggering refers to whether one or both houses are only partially renewed at each election. This feature increases the probability of separation of purpose by increasing the share of legislative seats that are held over from previous elections, even beyond what results from the nonconcurrence of presidential and assembly elections. Staggering is quite common in presidential systems, mainly in upper houses of federal systems. Often senators serve for longer terms than lower house deputies or even presidents, and only one-third or one-half are renewed at each election. In Argentina, even the lower house is staggered, with half being renewed every two years. Especially when combined with nonconcurrent elections, staggering of assembly terms increases the portion of the assembly that is elected at a time other than when the president is elected.

Our emphasis on the timing of elections may appear to overlook a characteristic of elections that appears even more basic: whether the assembly is elected by proportional representation or a majoritarian formula. At first blush it might seem that majoritarian formulas would encourage unity and PR separation. For parliamentary systems, such a statement would be unambiguously correct. However, in presidential systems, the direction of the effect depends on the other factors we have discussed here. With nonconcurrent (especially midterm) elections, a majoritarian formula is much more likely to promote divided government than is PR, which will tend to mitigate the normal electoral losses by the president's party in later term elections. Even with concurrent elections, a majoritarian formula actually increases the likelihood of divided government in those cases in which candidate-centered rules are used, because such rules make members of Congress less dependent on the national issues that typically motivate presidential campaigns (Shugart 1995). Moreover, it has been shown that the degree of proportionality of elections has much less – indeed, statistically insignificant – effect on the number of parties in presidential than in parliamentary systems (Shugart 1995; Mainwaring and Shugart 1997b).

Congruence of Presidential and Congressional Constituencies

A final, critical factor that affects the degree of separation of purpose is how "congruent" are the constituencies of the two branches. Assuming (as is currently the case in all pure presidential systems) that the presidency is directly elected, then, the president's constituency is a "district" that encompasses the entire electorate. The congruence of constituencies refers to the degree to which the districting arrangements in Congress correspond to this national constituency. Extreme congruence occurs when legislators are elected from a single nationwide district that is identical to the president's constituency. Single national constituencies for Congress are rare, but they are found in Peru and in elections for the upper house in Colombia and the Philippines.[30]

A chamber elected from districts – even single-member districts – could also be highly congruent with the president's constituency if each district constituency was a microcosm of the national constituency. Any divergence of purpose between houses in such a case would stem from other factors besides districting arrangements, such as from candidate-centered elections or different election timing. The greatest incongruence is to be found in chambers that, by design, overrepresent certain regions such that votes are not distributed equally across the country. This type of incongruence arises primarily in federal systems. Federalism itself increases separation of purpose "vertically" in that it creates separate national and subnational arenas in which politicians may pursue political careers and it creates subnational levels of government with autonomy over certain policy areas.[31] The impact of federalism on the national

---

[30] It is worth noting that even these chambers cannot be said to be fully congruent with the presidency, but the reason is to be found only in the electoral formula, not in districting arrangements: Presidents must win a plurality or majority of the votes, while members of Congress or their party contingents are typically seated with much smaller vote shares.

[31] One of the main policy dilemmas in federal systems concerns the transfer of revenues from the center to the states or provinces to fund their obligations, and the problems that ensue when purpose between levels of government is vertically divided. Jones's chapter deals extensively with this issue in the Argentine case.

legislative process is affected by how subnational interests are represented in the national level. Most federal systems, as well as a few nonfederal ones, have a powerful upper house that provides equal numbers of seats for each subnational unit regardless of population. A federalist upper house thus introduces a substantial element of malapportionment into the national legislature and creates high incongruence between the president's national constituency and that of at least one house of Congress.[32]

Institutions and Separation or Unity of Purpose

Given all of these factors, an index can be created measuring the degree to which institutions in any given separation of powers system promote unity or separation of purpose. Recall that we suggested earlier that presidential systems could be aligned along a continuum. One end of the continuum is characterized by systems that encourage legislative majorities to be responsive to national issues; in these systems, the president's party is likely to enjoy a majority or at least a substantial plurality. The other end of the continuum is characterized by legislators who respond to quite different, typically local, concerns; majority government is less likely to prevail in these systems.

Table 3.3 shows the construction of the index for twenty-two presidential systems. Some countries have dual entries due to major changes in electoral cycles or other variables. By showing many more cases than are discussed in detail in this volume, we can again see where our cases fit within a larger distribution of similar systems. The index values themselves have no cardinal meaning but serve only to identify ordinal rankings. The table shows that our cases are located in the middle range of the larger set of presidential systems. None promote unity of purpose to the degree of Costa Rica, the second oldest presidential democracy in the world, which combines concurrent elections, a unicameral Congress with no staggering elections, and a party-centered electoral formula. In fact, consistent with what our index predicts, Costa Rica's institutions have produced presidential majorities in every election except one since the restoration of democracy in 1948; moreover, these majorities have tended to be quite cohesive (Carey 1997).

---

[32] In fact, some lower houses are also significantly malapportioned, but bicameral systems rarely have two houses as malapportioned as the typical federal upper house.

Table 3.3. *An Index of Institutional Factors Favoring Unity or Separation of Purpose*

Coding
Electoral cycle
  0 Concurrent
  1 Mixed
  2 Nonconcurrent
Staggering of assembly elections
  0 All seats renewed at each election
  1 Staggering of terms of upper house
  2 Staggering of terms of both houses (or of sole house)
Electoral formula
  0 Party-centered
  1 Moderately candidate-centered (SMDs for most seats)
  2 Highly candidate-centered (open-list PR or SNTV)
Legislative congruence with president's constituency
  0 Highly congruent (nationwide legislative district or low malapportionment for sole house or both houses)
  1 Moderately incongruent
  2 Highly incongruent (at least one house highly malapportioned)

	Index Value	Country	Cycle	Staggering	Formula	Incongruence
High separation	7	Brazil I (1986–1990)	2	1	2	2
	6	Russia	2	1	1	2
	5	Argentina	1	2	0	2
		Brazil II (1994–)	0	1	2	2
		Colombia	2	0	2	1
		South Korea	2	0	1	2
		Taiwan before 1997	2	0	2	1
		United States	1	1	1	2
	4	Chile II (1997–)	2	1	0	1
		Dominican Rep. II (1998–)	2	0	0	2
		Georgia	2	0	1	1
		Mexico	1	1	0	2
		Philippines	1	1	1	1
	3	El Salvador	2	0	0	1
	2	Bolivia	0	0	0	2
		Chile I (1989–1993)	1	0	1	0
		Dominican Republic I (1966–)	0	0	0	2
		Peru	0	0	2	0
		Uruguay	0	0	2	0
		Venezuela	0	0	0	2
High unity	0	Costa Rica	0	0	0	0
		Guatemala	0	0	0	0
		Nicaragua	0	0	0	0
		Paraguay	0	0	0	0

On the other hand, none of the cases dealt with in detail in this volume has the degree of separation of purpose seen in Brazil, with its nonconcurrent electoral cycle (until 1994), federalist upper house with staggered terms, and extremely candidate-centered electoral formula. Indeed, Brazilian presidents have not had majorities since the return to full democracy in the late 1980s, and parties are notorious for their lack of discipline and national focus (Mainwaring 1997). In 1994, however, a constitutional amendment made elections concurrent. It is no accident, we would argue, that the first president elected under concurrent elections, Fernando Henrique Cardoso, has faced a somewhat more amiable Congress. Unlike his predecessors, Cardoso confronted a Congress in which most members (all of the lower house and one-third of the upper house) had been elected at the same time as the president. Separation of purpose should remain high, according to our index, but it should be somewhat lower than previously. Anecdotal evidence supports this expectation; while Cardoso has faced some difficulty with pension reform and privatization, he has succeeded in limiting the excessive transfer of resources to lower levels of government.

Among cases covered in this volume, Argentina is characterized by a relatively high degree of separation of purpose. Argentina employs a mixed electoral system with staggered elections in both houses, only portions of the legislature are elected concurrently with the president, and the upper house is malapportioned. The electoral formula is party-centered, however, which is one reason why Argentina does not rank as high as Brazil. Although the index is not sensitive enough to capture it, Argentina's recent constitutional reforms may have reduced the proclivity for separation of purpose to arise. The shortening of terms for both president (from six to four years) and Senate (from nine to six years) reduces somewhat both the amount of time any given president will face legislators elected before he was elected as well as the share of such holdover seats.[33]

By shortening the presidential terms from eight to six years but keeping congressional terms at four years (lower house) and eight years

---

[33] Also, the move from indirect to direct election of senators should encourage greater unity of purpose. Before senators only had to please provincial party leaders. Now they will have to please voters in their provinces, which may tend to broaden their interest in national issues to the extent that these matter to voters more than to provincial party leaders.

(upper house, which is staggered), Chile recently has moved toward institutions that will tend to promote greater separation of purpose.[34] If the appointed senators are abolished, however, the degree of incongruence between houses would be reduced and unity of purpose would be enhanced.

Taiwan has a moderate tendency toward separation of purpose now that there are competitive elections. This possibility may have been foreshadowed by the KMT's surprising decline to only forty-six percent of the vote in a late-term legislative election in 1995, although the party (barely) maintained a legislative majority.

To summarize, the institutional combination most conducive to unity of purpose is concurrent presidential and legislative elections, a party-centered electoral formula, a unicameral Congress elected congruently with the president's constituency, and full renewal of all legislative seats at each election. This institutional combination generates presidential majorities more so than other possible combinations (Shugart 1995). Even when there is no presidential majority, this format at least increases the likelihood that legislators are chosen out of a process in which the same national issues that dominate the presidential campaign are likely also to play a major role in their own election. The institutional combination most likely to produce a separation of purpose is nonconcurrent (especially all-midterm) legislative elections, a candidate-centered electoral formula, a federalist upper house, and staggered legislative elections. These institutions promote a separation of the electoral incentives of legislators from issues that dominate the presidential campaign. Presidents under such formats are unlikely to enjoy legislative majorities or are likely to enjoy them only through part of their terms.

It bears repeating that one very important factor that affects separation of purpose is the party system. All of the conditions facilitating unity of purpose can be undercut if the party system is too fragmented to deliver either unified government or at least stable legislative coalitions supporting a given president. However, while fragmented party

---

[34] This was probably not the motivation behind the change, whatever its results may be. The 1980 Constitution provided for eight-year terms for president and senate and four-year terms for deputies, with an exception that the first president, elected in 1989, would serve for only four years. The ruling Concertación coalition opposed the eight-year presidential term as too long, and so did the opposition, once it became clear that they would not come back and win in 1993. However, instead of four years, they settled on six, thus establishing nonconcurrent cycles.

systems occasionally arise in institutional settings that we predict would promote unity (e.g., Venezuela in 1993 and the Dominican Republic in 1996), the factors that we have listed here also tend to reduce the likelihood of divided government.[35]

Another party system factor worth noting is that the institutional features promoting separation of purpose can be overridden if a single dominant party exists that can control elections at all levels. Such parties existed until recently in Mexico and Taiwan, but democratization in both cases appears to be raising the likelihood of separation of purpose, just as we would expect. Mexico's ruling party lost its ability to control Congress in 1997, just as Taiwan's nearly did in 1992. Under fully competitive elections, it is unlikely that a single party could prevail and be so internally unified given an institutional structure that promotes a high separation of purpose.

THE INTERACTION OF SEPARATION OF POWERS AND PURPOSE IN POLICY MAKING

In this chapter we have shown how presidential systems differ from parliamentary and premier-presidential systems: They establish both the separation of origin and the separation of survival of executive and legislative power. Critics of presidentialism, typically drawing on a stylized comparison with parliamentary systems, have argued that these institutional conditions produce a number of generic problems, of which two are paramount. First, whenever a separately elected president possesses veto or other constitutional law-making authority – and this is true in nearly all pure presidential systems – the regime must incorporate a large range of actors in order to enact new laws. When coupled with the potential for separation of purpose, such systems can result in interbranch stalemate and indecisiveness. Second, the very frustrations that attend such indecisiveness can create unilateralism, in which presidents resort to decrees or Congresses attempt to impose their own preferences

---

[35] One caveat is that presidential systems in which the president is elected by the two-round majority formula are less likely to promote congressional majorities than are other formulas in use (Shugart and Mainwaring 1997). As it happens, the majority runoff system is frequently associated with other institutions that also promote separation of purpose, such as nonconcurrent elections, staggering, and incongruent bicameralism. Majority runoff is used for presidential elections in Brazil, Chile, Colombia, the Dominican Republic (since 1998), El Salvador, Peru, and Russia.

over the head of the president. In new and often fragile democracies, executive unilateralism runs the risk of reverting to authoritarian or "semidemocratic" rule.

In fact, parliamentarism can create similar problems for policy making, albeit by different means. For example, fragile and oversized multiparty coalitions can be equally prone to logrolls and stalemates. However, our central point is that while such criticisms are accurate with respect to some presidential systems, they are misguided because the policy-making process differs quite substantially across different presidential systems; it is these differences that we try to highlight.

Our interest is in explaining several general features of the policy-making process. In particular, we are concerned with the ability of governments to act decisively (particularly in enacting economic reform), the credibility and sustainability of policy choices once made, and the particularism of policy (i.e., how prone it is to exceptionalism, rent-seeking, and the distribution of pork). With respect to decisiveness, we predict that systems that tend to generate a unity of governmental purpose are likely to be most decisive. These include at least certain types of parliamentary systems, particularly Westminister ones, but also presidential governments that encourage the formation of stable legislative coalitions with incentives that are aligned with those of the president (Haggard and Kaufman 1995). There is no theoretical justification for the argument that parliamentary systems are, per se, more decisive than presidential ones. Any argument that makes such a claim is implicitly assuming that presidential democracies *must* fragment authority. As we have seen, presidential systems indeed have an inherent tendency to generate legislative incentives that differ from executive incentives, but the extent to which they actually do so is variable. Electoral institutions in some presidential systems promote unity of purpose and, therefore, decisiveness.

By contrast, we expect that governments that generate separation of purpose – not simply because of partisan differences but because of fundamentally different electoral incentives – will be less decisive. First, the wider the range of interests represented in the policy-making process, the more difficult it will be to change prevailing policy; we expect the policy process under a separation of purpose to be slower and less decisive. Second, because the legislative majority in a presidential system is forced to compromise with the president whenever the two are in disagreement, policy will be the outcome of public bargaining or transactions, which implies that the policy process is likely to be somewhat more *transparent*. Third, whenever such bargaining occurs and purposes are divided, there is the possibility that it can break down, resulting in interbranch stalemate.

As this discussion suggests, there is some tradeoff between the decisiveness of policy and its sustainability or credibility; governments that can act swiftly and with authority can also reverse what they have done. However, this problem may be somewhat *less* severe in presidential systems than in parliamentary systems. Unity of purpose is never complete in any presidential system, but this may be an advantage. The fact that any policy change must pass through at least two veto gates in a presidential system should serve, *ceteris paribus,* to increase its credibility; Heller and McCubbins make this argument most forcefully in their study of regulatory policy in Argentina.

One of the key objectives of our chapter has been to explore the interaction between divisions of power and purpose; it is therefore worthwhile to see how presidential systems compare along the two dimensions that we have explored in this chapter. The horizontal dimension of Table 3.4 shows the institutional tendency to promote a separation of purpose and the vertical dimension shows the strength of presidents according to their constitutional law-making. The cases are grouped into four categories on each dimension. Index values of 0 and 1 are considered very low, 2 is considered moderate, values of 3–5 are high, and 6 or more are very high. We consider presidencies with no veto or decree powers or with weak vetoes (those that can be overridden by a majority or that do not apply on spending bills) to be "potentially marginal" because a congressional majority that is opposed to the president can marginalize him or her by passing legislation that he or she cannot block (Mainwaring and Shugart 1997b). Moving up one category, "moderately" strong presidents are those who have only reactive powers such as a veto that takes an extraordinary majority to override or some gatekeeping powers. One level up are "strong" presidents who have either proactive powers or else a higher degree of reactive powers, such as an item veto or the ability to structure the congressional agenda (through restrictions on amendments on bills that only the president can introduce). Finally, the highest level contains presidents who have the potential to dominate even when they lack sympathetic legislative majorities because they have nearly the full range of constitutional powers over legislation.

What the Table 3.4 vividly shows is that there is an inverse correlation between the extent to which institutions promote a unity of purpose and

Table 3.4. *Comparison of Presidential Systems in Two Dimensions*

		Tendency to Promote Separation of Purpose			
	Index values	Very low 0,1	Low 2	High 3, 4, 5	Very high 6, 7, 8
Potentially dominant (reactive and proactive)	6, 7, 8			Argentina	Russia
Strong (high reactive or proactive powers)	3, 4, 5		Chile I Peru	Brazil II Chile II Colombia Ecuador Georgia South Korea Philippines Taiwan before 1997	Brazil I
Moderate (reactive only)	2	Guatemala	Bolivia Dominican Republic I Uruguay	Dominican Republic II El Salvador United States	
Potentially marginal (neither reactive nor proactive)	0, 1	Costa Rica Nicaragua Paraguay	Venezuela	Mexico	

the strength of the president. Systems in which presidential and legislative incentives are weakly aligned also tend to be characterized by strong presidents. Included here are federal systems with large disparities among the subunits in levels of development, such as Argentina, Brazil, and Russia, as well as three systems that, while not federal, have very strong regionalism: Colombia, South Korea, and the Philippines.

By contrast, systems that promote a unity of purpose have "weak" presidents, but again, only in the constitutional sense; presidents in the row labeled "potentially marginal" are unlikely to be marginal in practice because legislators within these systems are likely to share much of their outlook on policy. The upper left and lower right cells of the table are empty, although one surprising case is Mexico. Mexico has never been known for its marginal presidents, but as we have already noted, the reason for apparent presidential dominance has not been in the formal powers of the office, which are among the weakest of all presidential systems; rather, presidential dominance is attributable to leadership of a hegemonic party (Weldon 1997). With democratization, our expectation is that future presidents will have to be very effective coalition builders given the country's institutional tendencies toward separation of purpose and the dearth of presidential legislative powers.

The inverse relationship between unity of purpose and presidential powers is by now a robust finding that has held up against several related but different operationalizations, although none to date have considered the full range of factors that went into our index of separation of purpose.[36] A full explication of this finding goes beyond the scope of this chapter, but we offer the following hypothesis: In systems that are highly prone to divisions of purpose, presidents are granted powers to compensate precisely for the propensity to indecision, deadlock, and particularism that these systems may generate. Conversely, political systems that produce governments enjoying strong legislative backing do not require that the president have strong constitutional powers; more effective sources of strength lie in the fact that executive and legislative electoral incentives are aligned.

Does this mean that strong presidential powers can offset the divergence in executive and legislative incentives? Our answer is an emphatic no. With respect to decisiveness, it would appear that strong presidential powers are a substitute for the propensity to a high separation of purpose, but this is misleading. First, it is important to distinguish between the proactive and reactive powers of the president; decisiveness with respect to initiating new policies and undertaking reform is increased only by proactive powers, such as decree power. Yet in our cases, and in the broader literature, we find the following paradox: Decree powers

---

[36] Mainwaring and Shugart (1997) show that concurrent electoral cycles are associated with a higher tendency of presidents to have copartisan majorities, but electoral cycles are not part of their index of partisan powers; their index is based solely on observed tendencies toward majorities and party discipline (using electoral formula as a proxy). Moreover, Mainwaring and Shugart (1997) find that presidents with low constitutional powers are likely to enjoy high "partisan powers," defined as the likelihood of having copartisan majorities that are disciplined, and Shugart (1998) finds that "executive strength" (with proactive powers denoting strong executives) is inversely associated with party strength (defined as the incentive of legislators to cultivate a party vote) in new democracies.

appear most successful as a source of policy change precisely when they are used in support of some common purpose, either as a result of explicit delegation to the president by the legislature or in crisis settings when the legislature is willing implicitly to grant the president leeway. By contrast, when presidents and legislatures disagree strongly over policy, the use of decrees is likely to spur severe interbranch conflict not only over policy, as we saw in the early days of the Collor administration in Brazil, but over more fundamental constitutional issues, as has been the case in Russia during the Yeltsin presidency. Such conflict naturally calls into question both the decisiveness of government and the stability of the policy in question.

Thus, we expect that decree powers are likely to have a substantial effect only under a narrow range of circumstances. These would include when the preferences of the executive and legislature diverge but not to the extent that executive action will trigger a legislative response or when the exercise of proactive executive power has the effect of rapidly re-aligning executive and legislative incentives. An example of the latter would be executive initiation of a rapid macroeconomic adjustment program that is unpopular *ex ante* but serves rapidly to reduce inflation and thus becomes popular *ex post*.

With respect to the reactive powers of the president, these of course are of no use in changing the policy status quo; thus, they do not affect decisiveness. However, we did find that vetoes and exclusive introduction of bills are useful for increasing the stability and credibility of policy once it is made, and this might be of particular importance where there is a propensity for a separation of purpose. If the president prefers the reversionary policy to any outcome he deems likely to win the support of a veto-proof majority in Congress, he can prevent policy changes through vetoing or not initiating a bill. We would thus expect, *ceteris paribus*, that policy will be more stable and credible in countries with strong reactive presidential powers than in those where they are lacking; we would also expect that these powers would be particularly significant where divisions of purpose are high.

What about the relationship between presidential powers, separation of purpose, and particularism, the third dimension of policy in which we are interested? Again, it is tempting to believe that in systems with a high division of purpose, presidents would use their proactive powers to offset the tendency to particularism by focusing on programmatic issues and the provision of public goods. We do find instances, particularly in

Argentina, when proactive powers are deployed for these reasons. However, the increase in presidential discretion that expanded constitutional powers imply is not likely to be turned solely to programmatic policy making and the provision of public goods. In systems with a propensity toward a strong separation of purpose, the president himself will need to formulate policy with an eye to pleasing legislators; as Cheng and Haggard show in their discussion of Taiwan's budget policy, the president can also be a source of particularism. Economic policy making under Menem in Argentina is rife with corruption, some of which can be traced precisely to the exercise of discretionary powers.

Similar observations can be made with respect to the effect of reactive powers on particularism. Item vetoes, in particular, may appear useful for picking apart congressional logrolls and reducing the costs associated with them; in the United States, for example, arguments for a "line item" veto have been advanced as a way of reducing pork-barrel expenditure. However, these effects may be exaggerated since the president is not necessarily adverse to pork per se; he may simply use the item veto to cut pork extended to interests outside his own coalition. Other reactive powers, like the ability of the president to set ceilings on spending that Congress cannot exceed, can be salutary in cases in which the way Congress is elected (for example, by candidate-centered rules) gives it a strong propensity to seek pork for its constituents. We can hypothesize that strong reactive powers may permit the president to reduce the overall level of particularism from what it might be in the absence of such powers and that these powers permit the president to hold the line against congressional attempts to parcel out public goods reforms into morsels for narrow constituents.

We have already noted that presidential systems that provide for strong legislative backing provide the basis, at least in theory, for decisive, credible, and programmatic policy. However, we have conceded that certain forms of presidentialism appear to have some of the weaknesses its critics have noted. Would countries with institutions that foster a separation of purpose therefore be better off under parliamentarism? The answer is no. Parliamentary systems essentially force a compromise: Either one must accept separation of purpose and deal with large and possibly unstable coalitions or else one must manufacture majorities and thus leave minorities unrepresented in the policy-making process. Presidentialism with strong presidential powers, on the other hand, at least has the advantage of endowing the one actor elected in a nationwide constituency with powers to affect legislative outcomes, such as restraining spending through reactive powers or breaking legislative logjams through proactive powers.

Thus, it is not far-fetched to say that parliamentarism in societies characterized by marked regional disparities in wealth and levels of development may prove a worse form of government than the admittedly imperfect presidential ones they now have.[37] While the propensity to indecision, deadlock, and particularism may be higher as one moves toward the upper right of Table 3.4, this alone does not suggest that parliamentarism is superior. The reason takes us back to the central features of presidentialism: the expansion of enacting coalitions to include an actor elected separately and to a fixed term in a constituency that transcends the parochial constituencies of legislators. The following chapters explore how this institutional design functions in the specific cases of Argentina, Chile, and Taiwan, while another chapter explores the very different processes of a parliamentary (Czechoslovakia) and a premier-presidential system (Poland).

[37] Lijphart's (1977) model of consociational democracy implies that parliamentarism with grand coalitions is far more suitable for "divided societies" than is any form of presidentialism. However, the societal divisions of which he speaks are primarily ethnic, linguistic, and religious, and are expressed through strong cleavage-based political parties. The divided societies of which we are speaking, on the other hand, are divided more over regionalism and the clientelistic distribution of state goods and services. While exploring this distinction would take us far beyond the scope of this project, we would suggest that such divisions under parliamentarism may be far more prone to ineffective coalition government than the divisions in Lijphart's consociational democracies.

PART II

Budgetary Policy Cases

4

Budget Procedure and Fiscal Restraint in Posttransition Chile

LISA BALDEZ and JOHN M. CAREY

INTRODUCTION

Transitions to democracy are commonly expected to generate political pressures that can undermine efforts to maintain conservative fiscal policies. Budget cuts that hurt interests privileged under prior authoritarian regimes could undermine support for the new regime in at least some sectors, and could prompt authoritarian backlash. At the same time, new democracies must assimilate the distributive demands of groups that were excluded from policy bargaining prior to democratization, generating pressure toward deficit spending (Haggard and Kaufman 1995; Przeworski 1991). It is particularly remarkable then that Chile has run a fiscal surplus every year since its transition from military rule, averaging nearly two percent of gross domestic product in the first five posttransition budgets.

The Chilean case underscores the most important themes established in the introductory chapters of this volume: the separate effects of separation of powers and separation of purpose in presidential systems. This chapter illustrates the interaction between institutional arrangements that provide for separation of powers between the executive and legislative branch, versus those that encourage separation of purpose between branches – and within Congress itself. We develop hypotheses that illustrate the distinct impact of these two sets of institutional tensions on spending across various policy areas.

The contrast between Chile's current regime and the former military regime, as well as with the other large economies in the region, in the ten-year period from 1985 to 1994, is shown in Table 4.1. Not only does the new regime in Chile stand apart from the other new democracies, which tend toward larger deficits, but it is the only regime to generate regular surpluses. Indeed, the surpluses it produced in each of

Table 4.1. *Deficits/Surpluses in Latin American Democracies: 1985–1996*

Country	Mean Deficit/ Surplus as % of GDP	Mean Annual Rate of Real GDP Growth	Cuckierman Index of Central Bank Autonomy[a]
Chile (current regime)[b]	1.95%	7.47%	.46
Chile (military regime)	−0.07%	6.39%	NA[c]
Colombia[b]	−0.44%	4.30%	.27
Uruguay[b]	−1.04%	3.74%	.24
Peru (post-Fujigolpe)[b]	−1.17%	8.91%	.43
Venezuela	−1.30%	2.81%	.43
Argentina[d]	−2.22%	3.58%	.40
Costa Rica	−3.20%	4.13%	.42
Peru (pre-Fujigolpe)	−3.82%	−0.59%	.43
Brazil[d]	−9.41%	1.90%	.21

[a] Based on the index presented in Cuckierman (1992). Maxfield (1997) reports that Argentina, Colombia, and Venezuela enacted reforms in 1992 to increase the legal autonomy of their central banks.

[b] Data available through 1995.

[c] Formal central bank autonomy during the military regime was considerable, but existed "merely in name" according to Boylan (1998, fn36), who reports that restrictions on lending to the central government were routinely violated. Although we cannot provide a meaningful score on Cuckierman's scale, then, de facto central bank autonomy was probably lowest in Pinochet's Chile of all our cases.

[d] Data available through 1994.

Sources: Cuckierman 1992; *International Financial Statistics* 1990, 1992, 1996, 1997.

the first five years distinguish it from the authoritarian regime that preceded it, which was renowned for its fiscal austerity.

The budget process in Chile is a legacy of authoritarian rule because the rules governing budget making were created by the previous regime to limit the options available to elected civilian officials. Representative institutions such as the electoral system, bicameralism, and presidentialism interact with the budget process in such a way as to shape the range of possible policy outcomes, demonstrating the connection between budgetary procedure and fiscal restraint in Chile.

In the next section of the chapter, we present the constitutional provisions that most directly shape the budget process and offer a simple model of policy outcomes based on these provisions, from which we derive two general expectations about budget policy. Next, we discuss the Chilean military regime and its institutional legacy on the executive branch, Congress, and the current party system. Then we describe the process of drafting, amending, and passing the budget law, highlighting the extent to which procedural constraints shape bargaining. With this background established, we develop three hypotheses regarding the specific effects of procedure on various aspects of spending and evaluate how well data from the Chilean case supports these claims. The conclusion summarizes the implications of our findings for the long-term viability of authoritarian enclaves.

MODELING THE BUDGET PROCESS

Constitutional Provisions

Article 64 of the Chilean Constitution establishes the procedure for making government spending policy as follows:

> The Budgetary Law Bill must be submitted to the National Congress by the President of the Republic at least three months prior to the date on which it should become effective; should it not be passed by Congress within sixty days of its date of submittal, the proposal submitted by the President of the Republic shall enter into force.
>
> The National Congress may not increase or diminish the estimate of revenues; it may only reduce the expenditures contained in the Budgetary Law Bill, except for those established by permanent law.
>
> Estimation of the returns of resources stated in the Budgetary Law and other resources established by any other proposed law shall be the exclusive right of the President, following a report to be submitted by the respective technical agencies.[1]
>
> Congress may not approve additional expenditures by charging them to the funds of the Nation without indicating, at the same time, the sources of the funds needed to meet such expenditures.
>
> In case the source of funds granted by Congress were insufficient for financing any additional expenditures approved, the President of the Republic upon promulgating the law, subject to favorable report from the service or institution through which new returns are collected, countersigned by the Comptroller General of the Republic, must proportionately reduce all expenditures, regardless of their nature.

---

[1] Articles 16–19 of Organic Law 18,899 of 1975, which was inherited from the military regime, specify in further detail the exclusive control of the executive branch over how the data on which revenue estimates are based are to be collected.

The President's agenda control over fiscal policy, moreover, is not limited to the annual budget bill; it extends generally to all spending and tax policy. Article 62 states, in part:

The President of the Republic holds the exclusive initiative for proposals of law related to . . . the financial or budgetary administration of the State, amendments to the Budgetary Law included . . .

. . . The President of the Republic shall also hold the exclusive initiative for: Imposing, suppressing, reducing, or condoning taxes of any type or nature, establishing exemptions or amending those in effect and determining their form, proportionality, or progression . . .

. . . The National Congress may only accept, reduce or reject the services, employment, salaries, loans, benefits, expenditures, and other related proposals made by the President of the Republic.

The Chilean fiscal year is concurrent with the calendar year. Thus, under Article 64, the president proposes a budget to Congress by the end of September and Congress, in turn, must promulgate a budget law by November 30, one month before it is to take effect. The first public sector budget created under the current process was for 1991, and was passed by the newly elected president and Congress in 1990. For the seventeen years prior to that, the annual budget law, like all legislation, was decreed by the military government of General Augusto Pinochet.

The Model

The provisions above suggest that the Chilean procedures should restrain spending and give an advantage to the president relative to Congress in bargaining over budgets. These points are illustrated by comparing budgetary policy making under two alternative formats: the package veto and item veto. As shown in Figure 4.1, under the package veto format, Congress presents a budget law, which the president must either accept in its entirety or veto, in which case spending is set at some reversion point known to both players.[2] Under the item veto format, Congress presents a budget to the president, who has the option of vetoing specific spending provisions while promulgating the rest, with spending on those vetoed items set at the known reversion point.

Initially, we make some simplifying assumptions for the purpose of

---

[2] For a spatial model of negotiations between the U.S. House and Senate, and further between appropriations committees and other legislators in each chamber, see Kiewiet and McCubbins (1991, ch.6).

Package Veto

			accepts	Congress's proposal on X,Y implemented
Congress proposes on dimensions	X,Y	President		
			vetoes	Reversion policy on X,Y implemented

Item Veto

			accepts	Congress' proposal on X implemented
	X	President		
			vetoes	Reversion policy on X implemented
Congress proposes on dimensions				
			accepts	Congress' proposal on Y implemented
	Y	President		
			vetoes	Reversion policy on Y implemented

Chile

			accepts *OR* no action	President's proposal on X implemented
	X	Congress		
			amends	< President's proposal on X implemented
President proposes on dimensions				
			accepts *OR* no action	President's proposal on Y implemented
	Y	Congress		
			amends	< President's proposal on Y implemented

Figure 4.1. Three Budget Proposal Games

comparing these formats. First, we ignore veto overrides for now, in part to make the comparisons tractable and in part because the existence and implications of a veto on the budget law is subject to dispute in Chile – an issue discussed at length in the following paragraphs. Second, we assume that players have unique preferred policies. Thus, we assign an ideal point to the Congress and one to the president. Third, we assume the players know each other's most preferred policies and the reversion

Package Veto

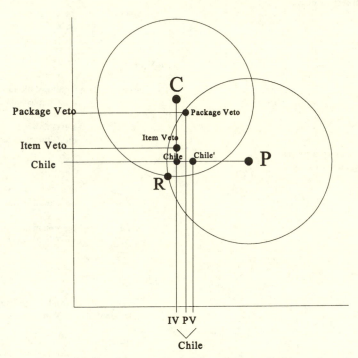

Figure 4.2. Expected Policy Outcomes Under Three Different Budgetary Procedures

point. Finally, for the two non-Chilean procedural formats, we assume that the spending reversion point is lower than the spending levels preferred by either Congress or the president on all dimensions.[3] These assumptions do not perfectly depict the complex nature of bargaining over the budget. Rather, the simplified model generates straightforward expectations about the outcomes of the budgetary process and is a good starting point for empirical analysis. In the subsequent empirical sections of this chapter we explore the ways in which the actual practice of

---

[3] Recall that Article 64 of the Chilean Constitution sets the reversion policy as the president's budget proposal. Even this apparently clear directive is the subject of disputing interpretations in Chile, the implications of which we discuss in the part titled *Appropriations for the Military*.

budget making relaxes these conditions somewhat, and evaluate the implications of these practices on policy outcomes.

One other aspect of the model warrants discussion. In Figure 4.2, we depict Congress and the president as differing across policy dimensions as to which prefers higher levels of spending. Thus, the president is the "high-spender" on dimension X and Congress on dimension Y. We choose this particular configuration of preferences for both empirical and theoretical reasons. In the context of Chile in the 1990s, for example, we might think of the Y-axis representing military spending – a priority of the conservative Senate – and the X-axis representing social welfare spending – a higher priority of center-left presidents. More generally, given the vast range of policy areas on which national budgets set policy, it is virtually inevitable that there will be some issues on which Congress wants more spending than the president and others on which the reverse holds. The configuration of preferences depicted in Figure 4.2 is also theoretically more interesting than the case in which one actor is the "high-demander" and the other the "low-demander" across all dimensions. Where Congress and the president differ across issues as to which prefers higher spending, bargaining (logrolling) over spending levels can potentially occur across various dimensions of policy. Because the rules of procedure on which we focus affect actors' abilities to realize such logrolls, this configuration of preferences most clearly illustrates the potential effects of procedure on policy. Finally, we point out that the conclusions we draw from our model are not dependent on the particular configuration of preferences depicted in Figure 4.2. We argue that the Chilean budget process generates spending restraint and favors presidential preferences relative to other standard procedures. Under other configurations of preferences (i.e., where one player or the other is always the low-demander), budget procedures other than Chile's may generate spending choices *as low as or higher than* Chile's, and outcomes *as far from the president's ideal point or further* – but not lower or nearer.

Consider the budget outcomes across two dimensions of spending under the package and item veto formats and the Chilean procedure. In Figure 4.2, the two axes represent levels of spending along dimensions X and Y. C and P represent the ideal points for Congress and the president, respectively. R is the reversion point if no spending bill is passed, and is less than either player prefers on either dimension. This is consistent with our empirical knowledge about comparative budget making. Where no spending bill is passed, spending generally either reverts to zero, or to the level of the previous year which, adjusted for inflation, is likely to be lower than current proposals. The circle centered on C and passing through R represents all the points to which Congress is indifferent to the reversion outcome; Congress prefers all policy points inside this circle to no agreement on a bill, and prefers no agreement to all points outside the circle. The same is true for the president with respect to the indifference curve passing through R and centered on P.

Under the package veto format, Congress should offer a bill setting spending on both dimensions as close to its own ideal point as possible constrained by the president's willingness to sign the bill rather than accept the reversion outcome. This policy is the point just inside the president's indifference curve labeled Package Veto in the figure, with the corresponding lines extending to the axes indicating the spending outcomes on each policy dimension.

Under the item veto format, the president has the ability to "unpack" congressional proposals, effectively considering each dimension independently. Congress, then, can think of itself as making two separate proposals – one on dimension X and the other on Y. On dimension X, the players' preferences are as shown in Figure 4.3. Congress should thus propose spending exactly at level C, given that the executive will prefer this to the reversion outcome. On dimension Y, the situation is somewhat different, as the president's ideal point is between R and C. Congress should propose a policy as close to C as possible, but one that the president marginally prefers to R.[4] This is labeled "Proposal" in Figure 4.4. In Figure 4.2, this point is identified in two dimensions as

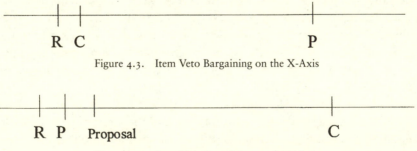

Figure 4.3. Item Veto Bargaining on the X-Axis

Figure 4.4. Item Veto Bargaining on the Y-Axis

[4] If the president's ideal point were between C and R, and were closer to C than to R, of course, Congress could simply propose its ideal point, C, on this dimension as well, and the president would accept.

Item Veto, with spending levels on both axes lower than under the package veto format.

Finally, consider the Chilean format. As outlined by the constitutional articles above, the president proposes an entire budget, Congress can amend specific items downward only, and if Congress does not pass a budget bill the president's proposed budget becomes law. Under the simplest interpretation, the president should simply propose point P. Congress accepts the president's preferred spending level on dimension Y, given that it prefers even more but cannot amend upward. On dimension X, Congress can use its amendment power to reduce spending to its own ideal level. The outcome would be spending at the level indicated by "Chile" on dimension Y and equal to the level under the item veto format on dimension X, reflecting the preferences of whichever branch, Congress or the executive, prefers less spending in each particular issue area.

What it means for Congress to "fail" to pass a budget law, however, is subject to some dispute, with corresponding ambiguity for whether the executive's initial budget proposal should serve as the reversion. We discuss this debate at length below. For now, the important point is that if Congress reduces proposed spending levels over executive objections, debate over whether these reductions would stand and, if not, over the location of the reversion point, has generated uncertainty in Chilean budgetary negotiations in the early 1990s that may allow the president to make proposals somewhat higher on dimension Y than Congress's ideal. We represent this range of uncertainty as that between the points marked "Chile" and "Chile' " in Figure 4.2.

Whichever interpretation of the Constitution ultimately holds in the event of a stand off, the Chilean process encourages low spending levels on both dimensions relative to other formats. Where the president wants low spending, he or she can secure his or her ideal due to his or her proposal power combined with Congress's inability to amend items upward. Where the president wants more than Congress, Congress may be able to impose its preferences in the event of conflict. Even if not, the president will be able secure higher spending only insofar as Congress prefers the newly proposed level to whatever reversionary point is specified by constitutional arbiters. Thus, spending in Chile should be lower under this format than it would be under a package veto format.[5] If the

---

[5] Technically, our model predicts that spending levels would be as low under the package veto format as under the Chilean format only if Congress preferred less spending than the president on all issue dimensions, and higher otherwise.

reversion point is, in fact, the president's initial proposal, spending should be lower than under the item veto format as well.[6] The implications of the constitutional dispute over the reversion point for spending policy are discussed at greater length later in this chapter. In all cases, outcomes across both dimensions are closer to the presidential ideal point than in either the package or item veto formats. Thus follow the two expectations stated above with respect to overall spending and presidential bargaining advantage.

INSTITUTIONAL BACKGROUND

Before introducing our specific hypotheses about the effect of Chilean procedures on spending policy, it is necessary to provide some background on the participants in the budget making process and their preferences, and to flesh out the mechanics of the budget process more thoroughly than do either the constitutional articles or the abstract model. We begin with the constitutional foundation of the executive and legislature.

A Strong Presidency

The Constitution of 1980, which includes Articles 62 and 64 establishing budgetary procedure, was adopted during the military dictatorship of General Pinochet (1973–1990). The Constitution reflects Pinochet's deep distrust of bargaining among politicians, and especially of Congress. Embodying the military regime's contempt for parties and for Congress as an institution, those who drafted the Constitution intentionally marginalized Congress in the fiscal policy-making process.

Pinochet's military regime was overtly antipolitical. The general believes[7] that the electoral aspirations of politicians, and of political parties as collective organizations, undermine their ability to identify and pursue the interests of the entire nation. In part, this opinion of partisan politics is driven by ideological contempt for Chile's period of "electoral social-

---

[6] Again, the item veto format could produce spending choices as low as Chile's only if Congress preferred less spending than the president on all dimensions.

[7] Pinochet remained commander of the Army until March 1998, at which point, as a former president, he became eligible for and assumed a lifetime seat in the Senate. His political beliefs, therefore, remain highly relevant to current Chilean politics.

ism" under Salvador Allende's Popular Unity government in the early 1970s. In part, it is drawn from the character of Chilean legislative politics prior to 1970, which depended heavily on distributive logrolls (Shugart and Carey 1992, ch.9). Pinochet's disdain, and that of his government more generally, for making government spending decisions according to political criteria was reinforced by the remarkable relationship between the regime and the Department of Economics at the University of Chicago. During the years of the Pinochet regime, more than 100 Chileans who received post-graduate degrees at Chicago went on to serve in government economic posts (Valdes 1995). The Chicago Boys, as they came to be known, were renowned for their free market orientation as well as for the enormous influence of their ideas within the government. For all these reasons, Pinochet's opinion of partisan politics did not soften over the years, particularly with respect to fiscal responsibility, so that in 1986 he remained vehement: "The politicians have never done anything for Chile, because they turned politics into a profitable business. They want to return because, having been out of the business for thirteen years, their pockets are empty" (Constable and Valenzuela 1991).

Philosophy aside, Pinochet had personal reasons for strong executive discretion over fiscal policy to be built into the Constitution. The general himself planned to serve as president under the 1980 charter. Although military rule remained intact for nearly ten years after the Constitution was originally ratified, Pinochet held open the possibility of restoring Congress during his tenure as president. Had he not suffered an unexpected loss in a 1988 plebiscite on his leadership, he likely would have continued in office at least through 1996. As it has turned out, of course, not only was Pinochet turned out of office as a result of losing a plebiscite in 1988, but the center-left *Concertación* coalition of parties, which orchestrated his 1988 defeat, ran successful candidates in the presidential elections of 1989 and 1993. Thus, since the 1980 Constitution has been effective, the presidency has been occupied exclusively by Pinochet's political opponents.

In sum, Pinochet and his advisors preferred a strong presidency, both due to their philosophy of government and because they fully expected Pinochet to occupy the office. These beliefs led them to design a Constitution in which powers over fiscal policy are divided between the executive and legislature, but in which this separation of powers heavily favors the executive. Specifically, they endowed the presidency with strong authorities to limit government spending, and prohibited Congress from increasing spending above these limits.[8]

The Current Congress

Congress is bicameral, with effectively identical powers for both chambers. Members of the Chamber of Deputies serve four-year terms, and senators eight.[9] Because Congress and the executive are elected separately, the Chilean system is characterized by some separation of purpose as well as of formal powers. The potential for separation of purpose has been especially pronounced since 1994 when, as a by-product of a constitutional reform shortening the presidential term from eight to six years, Chile moved to an electoral cycle in which presidents and legislators are more often than not elected nonconcurrently (Carey 1994). The most important factor contributing to separation of purpose in Chile, however, is the existence of, and appointment procedures for, nonelected members of the Senate.

District magnitude (M, the number of representatives elected in a district) in all Chilean legislative elections is two. The two-member electoral system is unique to Chile, and as with the 1980 Constitution, it is an institutional legacy that was strategically selected by the former military regime. Under the system, parties or coalitions present lists of two candidates, and voters indicate a preference for one candidate within one of the lists. The votes of both candidates on each list are totaled first, then the two seats are allocated. The first seat is awarded to the preferred candidate from the list with the most total votes, after which that list's vote total is divided by two. If this quotient is still higher than any other list's vote total, the second candidate gets the second seat. Otherwise, the second seat goes to the first candidate on the second-place list.

Two properties of the electoral system are critical from the perspective of the budget. The first is that, given the distribution of electoral support in Chile, M=2 elections systematically overrepresent the parties of the

---

[8] The authorities of the presidency were curtailed somewhat by a 1989 plebiscite negotiated by the outgoing military regime and the democratic opposition, but presidential budget power remained intact.

[9] The budget authorities of the two chambers are effectively identical. The annual budget law is submitted first to the Chamber, but is immediately forwarded to the Senate.

right – the heirs of the military regime, which are united in a formal coalition.[10] The system ensures that in every district, the top two coalition lists will win *equal* representation unless the top list *more than doubles* the vote total of the second place list. Before the M=2 system was adopted, based on the results of the 1988 plebiscite as well as previous elections, the military regime was well aware that its supporters were a minority in almost every region of the country, but that its support was consistently in the range of 30%–40% (Constable and Valenzuela 1989–1990). This was consistent with the level of support for Chile's rightist parties during the long period of democracy prior to the military regime (Scully 1995). The outgoing military regime knew that the parties of the center and left, which had united for the plebiscite campaign as the *Concertación*, had majority support and intended to sustain their coalition to ensure an opposition victory in the first free elections. Given this scenario, the M=2 system was a shrewd choice. It is unique in its tendency to overrepresent second-place finishers, and indeed, across the three posttransition legislative elections, the second-place coalition of the right has been overrepresented at a higher average rate than the first-place *Concertación* coalition (Carey 1998; Nohlen 1993; *El Mercurio* 1993).

The other important property of the M=2 system is that it encourages the formation of broad coalitions. Parties can win representation in Congress only if they are part of one of the two largest lists in a given district. Those parties on the radical left that have been unwilling or unwelcome to enter the *Concertación* coalition have been virtually disenfranchised, winning no seats (Nohlen 1993; *El Mercurio* 1993). The imperative to coalesce is formidable enough that Chile's traditional multiparty system now performs much like a two-party system. Although parties remain organizationally distinct and candidates bear party labels on ballots, these labels are superceded by coalition labels. Legislative seats are awarded on the basis of coalition – not party – vote totals. Moreover, coalition leaders negotiate candidate nominations jointly, divide legislative resources and committee assignments proportionally, and impose discipline in Congress on the members of all their constituent parties (Boeninger 1996; Godoy 1996). In allocating nominations for

---

[10] This coalition has been known as Democracia y Progreso (DP) for the 1989 election, Unión Por el Progreso (UPP) in 1993, and Unión Para Chile (1997), but it has been dominated by the same two major parties throughout.

congressional list positions, national leaders of all member parties in each coalition negotiate how many candidacies their copartisans will receive. Because each major coalition will almost certainly win one seat in each district, leaders can virtually guarantee a negotiated distribution of legislative seats within the coalition by placing one strong candidate and another lesser-known candidate on the coalition list in most districts (Rosales 1996). The authority of coalition leaders over nominations is effectively the authority to control the political careers of rank-and-file legislators. The result is that the Chilean Congress is organized around two major coalitions, the members of which regularly vote together on budgetary issues as well as broader platforms (Carey 1998).

The coalition of the right is composed primarily of two parties that were sympathetic to the Pinochet regime and, more importantly for the purposes of this chapter, that hold corresponding preferences on spending policy. They favor strong fiscal support for the military but an otherwise minimal public sector. The *Concertación* is more diverse, encompassing the centrist Christian Democrats and Radicals, as well as the Socialists and the newer Party for Democracy, composed largely of former Socialist politicians. Despite differences among *Concertación* parties, however, all share common preferences relative to members of the coalition of the right: They are less favorable toward the military but otherwise less committed to a minimal public sector. These key distinctions are important below.

Nonelected Senators

The $M=2$ electoral system applies to all 120 seats in the Chamber and the 38 elected seats in the Senate. Because the electoral systems are virtually identical for each chamber (except that senate districts are larger and turnover staggered) it is not surprising that the proportion of seats won by each coalition in both chambers is similar, as shown in Table 4.2. The Senate is distinct, however, in that it includes additional nonelected seats. There are nine appointed senators; and in addition, all former presidents who served at least six years in office are eligible for lifetime seats in the Senate.[11] The nine appointees are selected as follows:

---

[11] These nine senators are known as *designados* (designates) or *institucionales* (institutionals) because they represent various institutions within the polity. Originally, the 1980 Constitution called for twenty-six elected seats and nine appointed seats. As part of the agreement negotiated between the military regime and the opposition

Table 4.2. *Distribution of Seats Across Coalitions in Chilean Congress*

Chamber	Coalition	1989	1993	1997
Chamber of deputies	Concertación	58%	58%	58%
	Right	40%	42%	39%
	Independents	2%	0%	3%
Senate	Concertación	47%	47%	46%
	Right	34%	34%	30%
	Independents	0%	0%	2%
	Appointed	18%	18%	22%

- the Supreme Court selects three, two from among its former members and one former Comptroller General;
- the National Security Council (NSC) (half of whose members are drawn from the military) selects four – each a former commander-in-chief of a branch of the armed forces;
- the President selects two – one former university rector and one former cabinet minister (Constitution of 1980, Art. 45).

All nine appointed seats were filled just before the military government left power, so the terms of that initial cohort of appointed senators ran into March 1998.[12] Because the entire judiciary had been filled by Pinochet during his seventeen years as President and because the National Security Council was composed of officers appointed by him, senators in the first cohort reflected Pinochet's preferences. The second cohort of appointed senators was appointed in January, and inaugurated in March of 1998. Because two of them were appointed directly by an incumbent *Concertación* president, Eduardo Frei, and because the composition of the judiciary had changed somewhat during the first six years after the transition as civilian presidents nominated justices, these appointees might be expected to be less closely tied to Pinochet than their predecessors. Nevertheless, this trend is mitigated insofar as the four appointments by the NSC are constrained to a small set of retired military officers, all of whom rose through the ranks during Pinochet's regime; and the higher levels of the judicial system are still overwhelmingly

after the 1988 plebiscite, however, the 1989 plebiscite ratified a constitutional reform that increased the number of elected seats to thirty-eight.

[12] One appointed senator who died was not replaced, leaving eight nonelected senators throughout most of that period.

populated by Pinochet appointees. Finally, Pinochet's inauguration prompted widespread public protests and rekindled conflict between the coalitions over both the general's fitness to serve in an institution he suspended for more than sixteen years, and over the existence of nonelected senators generally. There has been sustained debate since before the military yielded power over whether the constitution should be reformed to abolish the nonelected seats. The *Concertación* has introduced amendments to eliminate these positions on at least four occasions since 1990. Amending the Constitution, however, requires supermajorities in both chambers of Congress, and opposition to reform by the first cohort of appointees, as well as by the coalition of the right, has blocked all reform attempts (Reuters 1996). Enough members of the Senate inaugurated in March 1998 support the institution of nonelected senators that there is no reason to expect such reforms to succeed in the immediate future.

Although the *Concertación* has won majorities in all legislative elections since the transition, the institution of nonelected senators has provided the coalition of the right with an effective majority in the Senate, thus ensuring that the separation of powers established in the Chilean Constitution is amplified by a substantial separation of purpose between the branches, and indeed, within the Congress itself. Without the nonelected seats, the coalition of parties that has controlled the presidency for the first ten years after the transition would have enjoyed majorities in both chambers of Congress. Separation of purpose under such circumstances would have been limited, given the extent to which national party and coalition leaders control the political fates of individual Chilean legislators. The existence of the nonelected senators has meant that any policy that requires legislative approval must be acceptable to the coalition of the right.

NEGOTIATING BUDGETS

In order to evaluate the effects of the budget process on specific policy choices, it is necessary to provide a more detailed account of the actual practice of proposals, congressional review and amendment, promulgation, and oversight, roughly sketched in Article 64.

Executive Proposal

The budget process formally begins each year when the Finance Ministry's Directory of the Budget (Dirección de Presupuesto, or *DiPres*) delivers the executive proposal to Congress. Estimates of revenues are based on the current year levels, adjusted for projections of economic growth from Finance Ministry analysts. *DiPres* tends to offer conservative estimates to preclude congressional budget cuts on the grounds of insufficient revenues. Based on estimated revenues, *DiPres* then provides a set of overall guidelines to the various executive ministries for their budget requests. Ministers, in turn, submit requests to *DiPres* with both technical and political rationales for cuts and increases. Any disagreements not reconciled between the ministries and *DiPres* are settled by the president.[13]

Congressional Action

Legislators and executive officials alike agree that legislators are more active in lobbying for changes during the sixty-day period between the proposal's submission to Congress and final passage than during preparation of the proposal itself. The proposal is sent to Congress by October 1 and is immediately referred to a Joint Budget Committee (JBC, or Comisión Mixta in Spanish). The JBC by law is composed of an equal number of members from both the Chamber and Senate. Chamber standing committees have thirteen members each, and the Chamber appoints all the members of its Finance Committee to the JBC. The Senate likewise sends its Finance Committee members, but as standing committees in the Senate have only five members, the Senate has another eight appointees as well, which have been divided more-or-less evenly between *Concertación* and opposition senators and ratified by floor vote. Within the Chamber, the *Concertación* assigns itself a majority of seats on all standing committees. Moreover, given the importance of the Finance Committee, it has provided itself an eight to five majority to ensure that it can move legislation even if a member or two are absent. Thus, the Chamber's contingent to the JBC gives a solid majority to the *Concertación*. In the Senate, committee assignments have been the sub-

[13] Personal interview with José Pablo Arellano. January 10, 1996. Santiago, Chile. Arellano is director of the budget bureau (Dirección de Presupuestos, or *DiPres*) within the Ministry of Finance since the reestablishment of civilian government in 1990. Arellano is the foremost official within the executive branch in charge of integrating ministry requests in establishing the executive's budget proposal and overseeing the execution of the budget. He is one of few high level executive officials to have maintained his post under both of the posttransition administrations.

ject of more contention because they are divided among the *Concertación*, the right, and the appointees, but the *Concertación*'s strong representation in the Senate has meant that its delegates to the JBC have always been split evenly enough that the overall committee has a *Concertación* majority (Palma 1996).

The JBC divides into five subcommittees of five members each, each of which reviews the executive spending proposals for a few ministries during six weeks of hearings. During this time, subcommittee members interpellate executive branch officials on specific spending programs and offer amendments. After six weeks, the JBC votes on the specific changes proposed by subcommittees, and returns the amended budget to the respective chambers. According to Palma, in four of the six years that the process has been in place, both chambers have ratified the JBC version without amendment. When floor amendments produce disparities between the budgets produced by each chamber, the JBC reconvenes to reconcile the differences. When this happens, time constraints quickly become important because by the time subcommittee work in the JBC is completed, only a few weeks remain before the budget must be promulgated.[14]

Amendments

Aggregate differences between executive budget proposals and final legislation illustrate two important points. First, the overall level of spending proposed has been altered by relatively miniscule amounts, if at all. In two of six budgets from 1991 to 1996, overall appropriations were exactly as proposed; and aggregate changes have never altered the proposal by more than 0.5%. Overall, these figures affirm the executive's ability to set the budgetary agenda. Second, in the four years in which overall spending was altered, it was *increased* twice, which would appear to contradict Article 64's prohibition on congressional amendments to increase spending.

Two factors are at play here – one having to do with budget estimates within the executive, and the other with interbranch bargaining. First, the executive proposal is originally submitted on October 1. During the

---

[14] There is no requirement that the conference committee named to reconcile these versions has to be the original JBC, but the JBC has served as conference committee in the only two instances of this (Palma 1996).

next sixty days, as fourth-quarter tax receipts and economic projections take shape, the executive itself inevitably wants to make changes to fine tune its budget projections (Boeninger 1996). Second, after October 1, legislators begin lobbying for increases as well, enlisting executive officials to sponsor the necessary amendments. Because no legislator can initiate such changes without executive sponsorship, the ministers and other executive officials who testify before the JBC subcommittees are influential brokers (Boeninger 1996; Arellano 1996). The selective ability of the executive to sponsor spending increases desired by legislators, in addition to accounting for a key element of executive bargaining power, explains how it is that amendments can inflate final budget appropriations over the level in the initial proposal despite the constitutional restriction on congressional spending increases.

With regard to spending cuts, Congress is in a somewhat stronger negotiating position, but still faces substantial constraints. One has to do with the difference between fixed and variable spending within the budget law itself. Most of the appropriations itemized within the budget are fixed by other permanent laws. This is true of most expenditures on personnel, which are constrained by contracts or entitlement laws. Pension rates and social security expenditures are two examples. Appropriations in such areas cannot be eliminated or reduced solely by congressional action on the budget law (Feliu 1996; Arellano 1996). According to Senator Olga Feliu, fixed spending accounts for roughly 85% of all appropriations (Feliu 1996). This leaves would-be budget cutters to focus on a relatively small subset of expenditures within the budget proposal.[15] Spending on capital investments and on goods and services is the main target because decisions to spend on these items can be deferred more easily than personnel spending (Feliu 1996; Arellano 1996). However, Senator Feliu, an appointee and ardent budget hawk, complains that it is difficult to line up legislative support to cut investments because investment generally implies spending on visible projects, which legislators prefer because they "can go back to their districts and wait with a little flag and some banners and say 'Look what I got you' " (Feliu 1996).

The extent to which final budget laws have reflected executive pro-

---

[15] Indeed, the aggregate impact of amendments, which has been up to .5%, does not appear so inconsequential when one considers that only 15% of appropriations are even on the table to begin with.

posals can be attributed primarily to procedural and bargaining obstacles that Congress faces in implementing cuts. Of 156 appropriations to specific ministries across the 6 years for which we have data,[16] only 72 (46%) show any changes in spending levels from executive proposals to final budget laws. The standard deviation across all 156 appropriations is a mere 1.81%, and only 3 of these spending levels were amended by as much as 10%. In short, executive proposals are amended, but the magnitude of amendments has been small overall. Given this limited scope, the role of our model in generating expectations about where we should observe conflict over spending levels is important. We review three exemplary cases below.

Promulgation, the Veto, and Reversion

Promulgation of the budget law requires the signatures of the president and the minister of finance. In all cases since the current process has been in place, the executive has approved the version of the budget passed by Congress. Negotiations on the 1996 budget, however, generated conflict between the executive and Congress over cuts proposed in the Senate. Although the branches reached a last-minute compromise agreement, there was debate over whether the president's veto power applied to the budget, and if so, what were the procedural implications.

The Chilean president is endowed with a veto over normal legislation that requires a two-thirds supermajority in both chambers of Congress to override (Article 70). Because the process for enacting the annual budget law is specified in a separate constitutional article, however, and because that article neither mentions the veto nor explicitly rules out its use, there is disagreement over whether and how the president might reject an amended version of the budget, and over what would be the corresponding reversion budget. Recall that Article 64 states, "should [the budget law] not be passed by Congress within 60 days of its date of submittal, the proposal submitted by the President of the Republic shall enter into force." What remains subject to debate, and perhaps to even-

---

[16] The statistics refer to appropriations in domestic currency, which account for around 90% of all appropriations. Appropriations in foreign currency are amended slightly less frequently and substantially. Also, it is important to note that the statistics refer to changes in spending at the ministerial level – the most detailed level at which executive budget proposals are published in the Chilean *Diario Oficial*. We are thus unable to examine rates of amendment below the ministry level comprehensively.

tual judicial interpretation, is whether the president's proposal would remain the reversion in the event that Congress passes an amended budget, which is in turn vetoed, and the veto is not overridden.

The sources of constitutional ambiguity here are whether the president is allowed to veto the budget law, and what the reversion policy should be if he or she can. Because Congress must approve a budget before it could be vetoed, it is not clear that the president's original proposal should serve as the reversion. Supporters of the coalition of the right, who have been shut out of the executive since the transition, hold that the language of Articles 62 and 64 implicitly preclude vetoes on the budget. Costa, the right-wing economist, acknowledges more constitutional ambiguity on the question:

One possible interpretation is that the part of the budget on which there is objection does not take effect. That is, the Ministry of Health has no budget – and it would be difficult to defend that as viable. Another interpretation is that the amount agreed to is the lower of the two figures.[17] A third interpretation, consistent with the precedent of the 1925 Constitution, is that the previous year's law remains in effect . . . This year [1996] the big unknown was what would happen. We didn't get an answer because at the last minute the executive and Congress reached an agreement, so we still don't know. There exists a fourth possibility – that the government instructs its legislators to prevent a quorum, and if there is no quorum there can be no approval of a law, and if there is no approval of the law, the president's original proposal takes effect. (Costa 1996)

Ultimately, Costa comes down against any interpretation of the veto that would allow the executive to secure spending levels higher than those approved by Congress:

Suppose the budget law were approved [by Congress] with cuts, then we're not in the situation of not having legislated on the matter. It was passed, and vetoed. If the president [vetoes], and the president's version takes effect – that's absurd. Better we don't have a budget law, because Congress can't say a thing about revenues – its only power is to cut appropriations. (Costa 1996)

DiPres Director Arellano, however, sees things differently:

[The veto] never has happened, but there are situations that are not very clear, but I would say that the president could veto . . . There are other mechanisms for reaching agreement – like the JBC – but if there were ultimately disagreement, the president could veto the budget bill. (Arellano 1996)

---

[17] This would appear, by definition, to be Congress's position on spending, given that, without executive approval, it can only reduce expenditures on specific items.

Even Arellano is ambiguous about what the reversion point would be in the case of a standoff: ". . . after 60 days the executive's proposal takes effect, but it isn't 100% clear what it means for Congress not to have approved the executive's proposal" (Arellano 1996).

A final ambiguity has to do with *which* proposal submitted by the president would enter into force in the event of budget process failure. Given that the executive updates its revenue and spending estimates over the course of the sixty-day period, adjusting its proposed bill accordingly, and even sponsoring some amendments at the behest of legislators during this time, it is possible to interpret Article 64 as referring to the version of the budget law supported by the executive as the sixty days elapses as the reversion policy (Boeninger 1996). According to Palma, however, the implication of Article 64 is that the original proposal would be implemented (Palma 1996).

If the president were to challenge Congress by declaring a veto, and the standoff were not resolved within the sixty-day limit, the expectation would be for judicial intervention. We are aware of no precedent suggesting how the courts would act, so we represent our uncertainty by the range of points between "Chile" and "Chile' " on the X-axis of Figure 4.1. Below, we suggest that this uncertainty contributed to the executive's ability to bargain for higher spending than Congress preferred on programs for women and children.

Oversight and Audit

The controller general oversees the execution of the budget. In Chile, the controller is a constitutional office, appointed by the president, subject to confirmation by the Senate, but then serving until the age of seventy-five and not subject to removal from office for any political reason. The controller handles the general accounting for public sector spending, and reviews all executive orders (*decretos*) that authorize expenditure or transfer of funds (Article 88).[18] Although the office has been highly politicized in earlier periods of Chilean history, in particular during the crisis of the early 1970s, our interview subjects agreed that, currently,

---

[18] Under the same article, the CG more generally reviews all executive decrees and is charged with "objecting to them whenever they should exceed or contravene the delegatory law or when contrary to the Constitution." This implies judicial authority for the CG to check executive initiatives, a power reserved for the courts in most systems.

the controller's oversight is juridical rather than substantive or political. The controller makes sure that ministries and agencies given funds for specific reasons actually spend those funds for the specified purposes. It does not, however, undertake evaluations of the efficiency with which funds are spent or the effectiveness of government programs (Boeninger 1996; Palma 1996). Thus, responsibility for budget oversight in Chile is constitutionally entrusted to an appointed agent responsible to neither Congress nor the executive.

HYPOTHESES

We derive three hypotheses on the basis of the model and the case material described above. The first hypothesis is that as long as there is any separation of purpose between Congress and the executive that drives different preferences on government spending, the low demander on spending is advantaged by the Chilean budget process. When the president is the low demander, his or her proposal establishes a maximum appropriation for each item. Where Congress is the low demander, its amendment authority allows it to set the appropriation at its preferred point. Because Congress cannot introduce new spending categories or move funds across existing categories, it is severely constrained in engineering logrolls that would expand the budget. The idea behind the first hypothesis is that politicians's appropriations decisions affect the fiscal balance, which implies that revenue policy does not vary systematically with appropriations decisions. The stability of revenue policy since the transition in Chile is addressed below.

The second hypothesis translates the general insight above to a specific policy area in which we expect separation of purpose – military spending – and in which we expect the executive to be the low demander, such that presidential agenda-setting powers should constrain spending levels. One clear expectation from our model is that when the executive wants less spending than Congress in a particular policy area, executive preferences should prevail. Since the transition to democracy in Chile, the executive has been controlled by a coalition that prefers higher spending in most policy areas than either the previous military regime or the Senate majority (Weyland 1997). Thus, the executive ceiling-setting authority should not be widely relevant. However, the *Concertación* was born out of opposition to the military regime. Many of its leaders personally suffered repression under the military government and all its parties endured the suspension of political and civil rights. If there is one area where the executive ceiling-setting authority should be relevant, then, it is on military spending. The hypothesis predicts relative, not outright, cuts in military spending, because the outgoing military regime established some guarantees of revenue flows to the armed services before turning over power. These details are discussed below.

Finally, the third hypothesis distinguishes in a finer manner between outcomes driven by institutional differences between the branches (pure separation of powers conflicts) versus differences between the major coalitions, as encapsulated in the separation of purpose between the executive and Congress as a whole. We expect congressional opposition to executive budget proposals to be strongest in the Senate, but conflict between majorities in each chamber means that the congressional position vis executive proposals will be subject to negotiation. When the coalitions themselves are internally divided, Congress will be hampered in bargaining with the president. When the interests of both coalitions in Congress are aligned, such that the separation of powers between branches coincides with separation of purpose, however, Congress will be in a stronger bargaining position, and better able to impose spending cuts. We examine these claims with regard to the Chilean case in the sections that follow.

SPENDING POLICY IN CHILE

Our first hypothesis holds that the spending restraint illustrated in our model of the budget process should translate into Chile's fiscal balance. Before examining the bottom line, however, it is necessary to clarify a couple of assumptions implicit in this hypothesis. One is the short-run stability of revenue policy, such that the main direct effect of legislation on fiscal performance is through spending decisions. Another is that the prohibition of logrolls established in Article 64 is effective in deterring agreements by policy makers to tolerate higher appropriations across various line items than preferred by item-by-item low demanders in an effort to reach a Pareto-superior overall outcome.

Tax Code

The assumption of short-run revenue policy stability is convenient, of course, given that our intent here is to analyze appropriations procedures, but is it unrealistic? We think there are both institutional and strategic reasons that it is reasonable. Constitutionally, the branches must pass a new budget bill each year; but there is no analogous requirement with respect to the tax code. Strategically, by giving the president exclusive proposal authority, Article 62 deters the president from offering any proposal that might be amended in a way that leaves him worse off than the status quo.

Are these expectations borne out empirically? There has been one significant reform of the Chilean tax code during the years examined in this study. In 1990, immediately after the transition to civilian government, President Aylwin's administration proposed an alteration of the income, corporate, and value-added tax structures, the main effect of which was to produce a more progressive system. The reform was passed over opposition in the Senate with support from the Renovación Nacional (RN) party within the coalition of the right with the stipulation that the reform would lapse after 1993. In 1993, the *Concertación* and RN again reached an accord, scaling back income tax rates and the value-added tax (VAT), and adding some exemptions while retaining the overall corporate tax structure (Weyland 1997). The overall result in 1993 was to codify the reform of 1990 as permanent law. There have been no major subsequent changes.

The bottom line on revenue policy, then, is that it has remained relatively stable since the transition. The original cross-coalitional agreement on reform was justified by its supporters in the coalition of the right on the grounds of avoiding conflict during the transition period and in the wake of an electoral defeat. Subsequent debate on the taxes has pitted the *Concertación* versus right coalitions. Given presidential gatekeeping authority, the divided Congress, and the empirical record, we believe the assumption in our model of short-run stability in the tax code is reasonable.

Legislative Logrolls

In our model, we emphasize the formal provision that restricts Congress to accept or reduce the executive's proposed appropriations. This constraint, however, would not have much bite if policy makers regularly engaged in logrolling, whereby the executive agrees to propose at levels sought by Congress in some policy areas if Congress agrees not to amend proposals downward where it is the low demander. Cooperation on deals like these presupposes repeated play among policy makers, which is not implausible given that the budget must be rewritten each year, and that the two branches communicate to each other through channels other than the formal proposal and amendment process depicted by our model. In fact, although Congress plays no formal role in drafting the executive budget proposal, there is some informal congressional input at this stage, especially for legislators from the *Concertación* coalition. As Andrés Palma, a Christian Democrat deputy, put it, "[Requests from legislators] are part of the negotiations that are outside the constitutional process, but that are part of political life; that is, all the legislators go to talk with the ministers" (Palma 1996). Nevertheless, it is less than clear that congressional lobbying has much impact on the final budget. According to *DiPres* Director Arellano:

> We listen generally to the opinions of the [*Concertación*] legislators, listen to their opinions, suggestions in terms of emphasis on priorities, but we don't have formal discussions with them nor with interest groups,

and later,

> [It's important] that we propose the budget in pretty general terms, not at the level of specific projects, we don't itemize every road in the law, but rather a global amount: investment in roads. The law doesn't say which roads we have to build. This is an administrative process, not subject to explanation or discussion . . . 'So we have less clientelism here because these decisions are not made in Congress, by law.' (Arellano 1996)

Former Minister of the Presidency Boeninger acknowledges somewhat more pressure from legislators who draw up lists of demands for expenditures in their districts and lobby for their inclusion in the budget in exchange for support for legislation the executive desires:

> Legislators form interest groups, of sorts, where a deputy from province A wants a particular road and so he forms an agreement with a deputy from province B who wants a dam or an electrical station, and they form a bloc and go to the Finance Ministry and propose: 'If you want to pass the budget law you need to include the road in province A, the station in province B, the fire station in province C, etc.'

But, Boeninger continues, *DiPres* manages to deflect such demands without compromising executive preferences:

> Then, normally, we had a means of reaching agreement with them . . . We started to make lists of projects we were going to fund in any case because they were already in our public works plan. Then when the legislators arrived they

would be offered: 'Look, Deputy So-and-so, this road in province such-and-such, why don't you ask for *this*, and then send a telegram to the province that you got it for them?' That way, he'd get the credit without altering the public works plan. (Boeninger 1996)

Given their backgrounds in the executive, one might expect that Arellano's and Boeninger's accounts overstate the degree to which executive budget negotiators are able to manipulate legislative requests. Their assessments, however, are supported both by the assessments of legislators and by the logic of the budget process. As Deputy Palma puts it, "We can't offer any proposals. I can't say, 'We're going to pave these streets.' No, what I have to say is, 'I'm going to speak with the minister to see if he'll provide the resources to pave these streets' " (Palma 1996).

Moreover, the executive's bargaining position in these negotiations is strengthened enormously by the provision in Article 64 holding that the president's proposed budget is implemented if Congress fails to pass a budget law within sixty days. Consider the difference from, for example, the Taiwanese case, in the incentives for executive negotiators to anticipate and accommodate the particularistic budget requests of legislators. In Taiwan, if the executive budget fails in the Legislative Yuan, the legislature can draft an entirely new document. In Chile, if the budget stalls, the default is the executive proposal. The credibility of legislative threats to block the budget in Chile, and the executive's need to appease congressional demands for higher spending, are minimal.

Strikingly, executive dominance in budget negotiations is applauded by at least some legislators, specifically because centralized budget authority reduces pressures for excessive spending. The following quotation is from *Concertación* Deputy Palma, but the sentiment in favor of central responsibility is echoed by coalition of the right Deputy Orpis as well:

You have to ask yourself, 'How is the system going to function best?' And the better I get to know legislators, the better I like this system. If we have an irresponsible president, we can control him. But to control one, and for him to assume responsibility, is better than to rest responsibility in 170, where it is completely divided. If we [legislators] had budgetary initiative power, we would have higher inflation, and everyone could blame everyone else for the inflation. Here the responsibility is with the executive, not Congress. And I think that's healthy. In a business, the boss is responsible for the bottom line, not the shareholders. (Orpis 1996; Palma 1996).

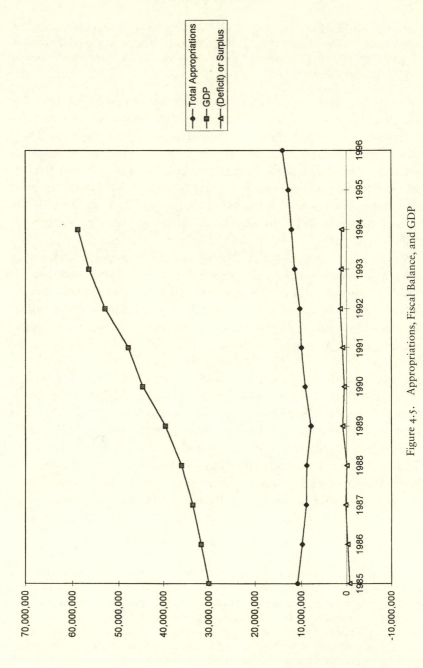

Figure 4.5. Appropriations, Fiscal Balance, and GDP

Deficits and Surpluses

Figure 4.5 plots total government appropriations, fiscal deficits/surpluses, and gross domestic product (GDP) since 1985.[19] Real spending actually declined 16% over the last six budgets decreed by the military government, and has risen 54% over the first six passed under the current process. The growth is not surprising, however, given the extraordinary economic growth Chile has experienced in the late 1980s and early 1990s. More relevant measures of fiscal restraint are spending relative to government revenues, and relative to the size of the economy, plotted through 1994 in Figure 4.6.

A couple of things are striking here. First, the military government ran deficits in three of its last six budgets, even in a context of strong economic growth. Moreover, in the late 1980s the Chilean public sector accounted for around 30% of GDP. Of the seven largest economies in South America – Argentina, Brazil, Chile, Colombia, Peru, Uruguay, and Venezuela – Chile's government expenditures accounted for the largest share of GDP through 1987, when surpassed by Brazil. It should be noted that the size of the public sector in the first years of the data set is not a mere holdover from a previous civilian government. By 1985, the Chilean military government had been in power for twelve years. Rather, it is a lagged effect of the devastating 1982–1983 recession in Chile, during which the government nationalized a number of failing banks which it subsequently privatized later in the decade (Stallings 1992). The military government's privatization of banks and other state-run corporations in the late 1980s, combined with strong economic growth, cut the public sector share of GDP dramatically and generated a fiscal surplus by 1989. Nevertheless, the overall size of the public sector is considerably smaller (and shows no sign of increasing) in the years since the current budget process was adopted than it was throughout most of the military regime. Moreover, under the current budget process the Chilean government ran

---

[19] All currency figures in this chapter are reported in thousands of 1995 US$. Spending and borrowing in Chilean pesos was adjusted for inflation to 1995 levels, then converted at the 1995 exchange rate. Spending and borrowing in foreign currency is always itemized in US$; these were adjusted for inflation (International Financial Statistics 1996). Data for this chapter are drawn from executive budget proposals and final budget laws from 1985 through 1996.

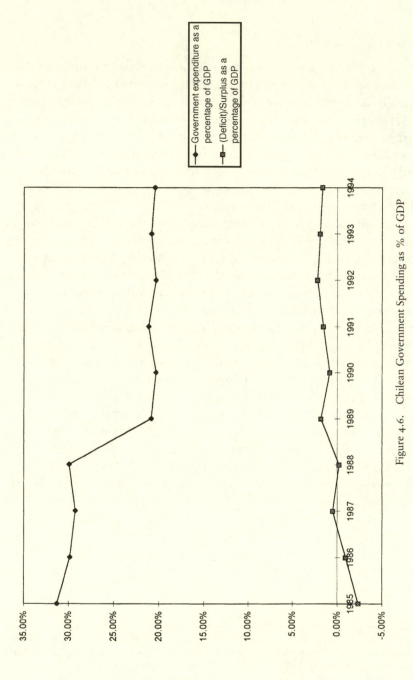

Figure 4.6. Chilean Government Spending as % of GDP

substantial fiscal surpluses – an average of 1.8% of GDP – in its first four years.[20]

At the beginning of this chapter, we presented data comparing Chile's deficit/surplus record with that of the other major economies in the region. The cross-national contrast was even more striking than that with the prior military regime. The new Chilean regime is the only one to run surpluses in the decade from 1985 to 1996 (see Table 4.1).

In sum, comparisons of aggregate spending levels with both the prior military government and with the other large economies in the region support the hypothesis that the Chilean budget process contributes to budget surpluses. Moreover, this conclusion is echoed in the assessments of Chilean politicians and observers. Although members of the *Concertación* and right coalitions differ in terms of fiscal policy, and although the right tends to criticize the government for preferring to overtax and overspend (Feliu 1996), politicians on both sides of the aisle concede both that the two *Concertación* administrations have spent cautiously, and that if an executive were to try to expand spending in a manner objectionable to Congress, Congress could and would block the move. As Rossana Costa, an economist with the Institute for Liberty and Development, an RN think tank, put it:

> Realistically, one has to recognize that on budget matters there are important areas of conflict, but that as long as we have a government that is cautious in public finance we don't have problems . . . Because today I'd prefer to spend 7 rather than 9 or 10, but as long as we have a surplus it's not going to produce a disaster.[21]

---

[20] Another critical cause of fiscal conservatism since 1990 is undoubtedly the prohibition on central bank lending to the central government, coupled with the insulation of central bank directors from political pressure, both of which are entailed in the organic law on central bank reform decreed by the Pinochet government in December 1989 (Boylan 1996, 27). Although the lending restrictions certainly deter deficits, the considerable size of surpluses in the early 1990s is still remarkable. At a broader level, the central bank reforms Boylan investigates and the budget procedures that are the subject of this paper are both part of a comprehensive package of institutional mechanisms crafted by the military regime aimed at reducing the discretion of subsequent civilian politicians over economic policy, and more specifically at guaranteeing both fiscal and monetary policy conservatism.

[21] Personal interview with Rossana Costa. January 5, 1996. Santiago, Chile. Costa is an economist with the Institute for Liberty and Development (Instituto Libertad y Desarrollo, ILD). The ILD was established by leaders of the RN party – one of the two main parties in the opposition coalition of the right. The ILD researches a range of policy issues, provides briefs and reports to legislators, and lobbies for the RN platform. Costa is the main budget analyst for ILD.

APPROPRIATIONS FOR THE MILITARY

Evaluating the second hypothesis requires a little more empirical detail than Article 64 provides. The most important complicating factors are the existence of two laws decreed by the Pinochet government in an effort to protect military funding levels from cuts at the hands of civilians: Law 13,196 (The Classified Copper Law) and Law 18,948, which establishes a minimum level of defense spending. Although Law 13,196's classified status prohibits its dissemination, it is common knowledge that the law requires that 10% of the national copper company's (CODELCO's) gross earnings are automatically transferred to the military's budget, outside of the conventional appropriations process (Palma 1996).[22] Article 96 of Law 18,948 stipulates that:

> Apart from expenditures on personnel, which are adjusted periodically according to norms that regulate these matters, the annual budget law must provide as a minimum for the rest of the Armed Forces a level of funding in national and foreign currency no less than that provided in the budget law of 1989, [corrected for inflation].

The intent of these laws was to limit civilian discretion over military budgets.[23] Indeed, it is due to these laws that the second hypothesis does not explicitly predict cuts in real military spending. Rather, the constraints imposed by Laws 13,196 and 18,948 suggest that the most austere option available to a *Concertación* president would be to maintain flat spending levels for the military while the rest of the budget grows. In fact, this is a fair description of what happened in the early 1990s. Table 4.3 shows that during the most severe years of general budget reductions under the military government in the late 1980s, the armed forces endured relatively light cuts, with their share of all appropriations never falling below 11.9%, and actually ballooning to 14.0% in 1989, the year in which Law 18,948 sets the floor for subsequent real spending levels. The first civilian budget in 1991, by contrast, immediately cut the military appropriation in both real[24] and relative terms.

---

[22] These transferred funds fall outside the regular appropriations itemized in the annual budget law, but are included in the total revenues and expenditures.

[23] Of course, the laws could be overturned, but not without Senate approval. The annual military windfall mandated by Law 13,196 helps explain CODELCO's survival as a nationalized industry even despite the privatizing zeal of the military government and, later, its allies on the right.

[24] There is a substantial cut below the 1990 appropriation, and even a slight cut relative to 1989. This is not in violation of Law 18,948, however; the law stipulates

Table 4.3. *Total Appropriations and Defense Appropriations*

Year	Total Appropriations	Defense Appropriations	Defense as % of Total
1985	10,839,012	1,335,256	12.3%
1986	9,772,377	1,158,334	11.9%
1987	8,891,724	1,084,299	12.2%
1988	8,812,723	1,130,811	12.8%
1989	7,825,566	1,091,925	14.0%
1990	9,122,265	1,107,538	12.1%
1991	9,978,047	1,083,458	10.9%
1992	10,323,436	1,165,808	11.3%
1993	11,424,932	1,221,256	10.7%
1994	12,084,794	1,205,927	10.0%
1995	12,798,289	1,246,576	9.7%
1996	14,015,367	1,349,582	9.6%

Source: Leyes de Presupuesto 1985–1996.

Moreover, although the military appropriation rose in real terms after 1991, it did so at a much slower rate than total appropriations such that by 1996 the armed forces accounted for only 9.6% of total appropriations. At the level of total expenditures, of course, copper revenues under Law 13,196 mitigated this relative loss somewhat,[25] so that the military's share of total government expenditures did not decline as precipitously as its share of appropriations. Still, the pattern is striking evidence of the military's relative loss of its budget share since the transition.

Law 18,948 indexes military personnel expenditures to other government personnel spending but fixes a floor for nonpersonnel spending in real terms. Assuming that the relative share of total government expenditures on personnel is steady over time, there is no reason to expect a change in the share of total expenditures devoted to defense personnel. But if nonpersonnel defense spending stays close to its legal floor in real

only that the government must *appropriate* (in Article 2 of the budget law) sufficient funds that *total expenditures* (in Article 1 of the budget law), which include transfers such as those provided for by Law 13,196, remain at or above the 1989 floor. Finally, the appropriation includes personnel spending, which is indexed according to a separate algorithm. This factor could contribute to minor discrepancies in the spending levels.

[25] In the years since 1992 for which we have data, the share of the military's total budget drawn from outside standard appropriations has risen from 15% to 18%.

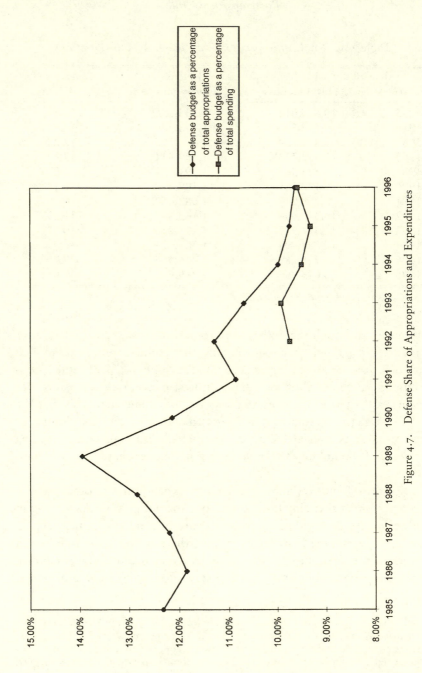

Figure 4.7. Defense Share of Appropriations and Expenditures

Legend:
◆—Defense budget as a percentage of total appropriations
☒—Defense budget as a percentage of total spending

terms while total expenditures grow, then nonpersonnel defense spending as a share of total expenditures should decline. This pattern is found
in Figures 4.7 and 4.8.

Accounts of the transition in Chile frequently, and accurately, criticize
the limitations on elected politicians, such as those on military budgets,
imposed by the Pinochet government's constitutional and legislative legacy (Constable and Valenzuela 1991; Valenzuela 1992; Zagorski 1992;
Aguero 1994; Casper 1995). What is not noted is that the budget floor
fixed by Law 18,948 has become moot as the rest of the budget (mirroring the larger economy) grows around it. Two *Concertación* presidents
have managed to reduce dramatically the share of appropriations allocated to the military, despite the "institutional hangover," simply by
pursuing a strategy of relative attrition. Given that defense is the only
major policy area in which *Concertación* presidents prefer lower spending levels than the divided Congress, the decline in the military's share
of the budget is compelling evidence of the executive's ability to restrain
spending through its constitutional proposal power.

CONGRESSIONAL REDUCTIONS OF EXECUTIVE PROPOSALS

Separation of Powers and Interbranch Conflict

The spending line in executive proposals most objectionable to legislators is one that lacks a clear policy objective when the budget is passed,
but serves to increase the general discretion of the executive over subsequent spending decisions. This is the Provisión para Financiamientos
Comprometidos (PFC, or Provision for Financial Obligations), located
within the appropriations to the Treasury for Operaciones Complemen-
tarias (Additional Operations). These funds are appropriated to the
Treasury, but are available for transfer, at the executive's discretion, to
programs administered by other ministries. First, they are used to cover
unforeseen expenses, such as infrastructure repairs above and beyond
regular maintenance but that do not constitute national emergencies.[26]
Second, they cover laws that will be passed over the course of the next

---

[26] The Constitution (Article 32:22) provides the president with the authority to decree
spending of up to 2% of the total annual budget in order to meet the needs of
national emergencies and disasters. This is generally understood to imply situations
such as earthquakes, floods, and blizzards. This authority has not been exercised
since the transition (Palma 1996).

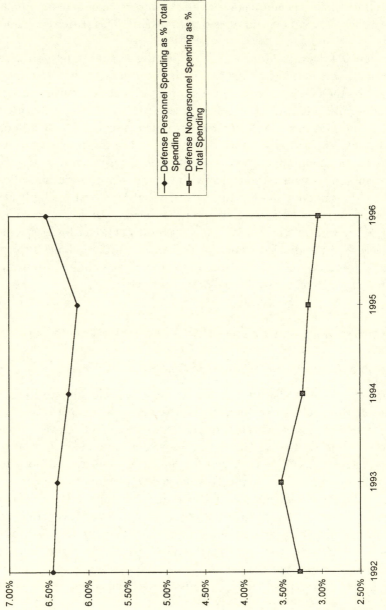

Figure 4.8. Defense Personnel/Nonpersonnel Spending as % of Total Spending

year authorizing expenditures, but for which specific funds will not be appropriated until the next year's budget (Palma 1996).

Article 21 of the Organic Law on the Financial Administration of the State (Law 18,899), yet another holdover from the military government that remains in effect, suggests a legal basis for this practice:

> The revenues and expenditures approved by laws sanctioned during the fiscal year, as well as those authorized by laws from prior years that were not included in the Budget Law, will be incorporated into the current budget. The location and classification within the budget of said revenues and expenditures will be determined by [executive] decree.

Yet Article 26 of the same law states that "transfers of funds between different Ministries and increases in funding for state enterprises can be authorized only by law." How can we explain these apparently contradictory provisions? Law 18,899 was issued in 1975. A budget line for appropriations directly to the Treasury was not created until 1977. The executive's position is that the Treasury is not technically a *ministry*, and therefore that transferring funds by decree from it to ministries does not violate Article 26's proscription of transfers *between different ministries* without legislative action, and is instead simply a matter of relocating and reclassifying funds to allow disbursal of funds authorized outside the current fiscal year's budget. The economist Rossana Costa describes the ambiguity as follows:

> [The law] says no funds can be transferred among *ministries* over the course of the year without legislative action. Back then [in 1975], we didn't have an appropriation to the Treasury. Now we do. But it's not a *ministry*. So the question is: 'Can the Treasury receive and give money during the year to ministries or not?' . . . It's an example of a hole in the law . . . The current interpretation is that of the government [executive] whether it can or cannot, but the system is immature. (Costa 1996)

Opponents in Congress object more sharply. Both of the opposition legislators interviewed for this project, Deputy Jaime Orpis (from the right-wing Independent Democratic Union party, UDI) and Senator Olga Feliu (*designada*) singled out the PFC as excessive (Feliu 1996; Orpis 1996).[27] Indeed, during the preparation of the 1995 budget law, Feliu

---

[27] Feliu's background is described above. Orpis (UDI) has been a member of the Chamber of Deputies, and a leading budget hawk within the opposition coalition, since 1990. He serves on the Chamber's Finance Committee, and therefore on all Joint Budget Committees as well.

prepared a report explicitly criticizing the transfer of funds through the Treasury to other ministries as a violation of the intent of Article 26 which, she holds, was clearly to prohibit executives from shifting budget allocations and altering priorities unilaterally:

> From a constitutional point of view, which demands that the national budget be approved by law and that all expenditures made by the executive have a basis in authorized law, it is not possible to interpret a legal norm by which transfers can be regulated by decree, so that through this mechanism – budget transfers – the executive could make expenditures not approved by Congress (Feliu 1994, 9).

The PFC continues to exist in the 1995 and 1996 budgets, but Feliu's objections clearly carry some weight with majorities in each chamber. The regulatory articles of the 1995 and 1996 budget laws themselves introduced new requirements that *DiPres* produce reports for the Finance Committees in each chamber of Congress that itemizes transfers and expenditures of PFC funds. Whereas *DiPres* provides regular reports on the execution of the budget at the level of programs, the PFC is the only item in the entire budget singled out for special reporting.[28] This stipulation increases legislative oversight over the PFC substantially.

Given the wide range of purposes to which the PFC is put, it is not surprisingly an enormous budget item. Its share of total domestic appropriations is shown in Figure 4.9. What is more remarkable about the PFC item is that it has shrunk both as a share of total appropriations (from 10.5% to 4.9%) and in real terms (from more than $US 1 billion to $US 684 million) over the last five budgets. We cannot document the extent to which PFC proposals have been amended down by Congress, because proposals itemized at this level of detail are not published. Individual legislators, however, have confirmed that the PFC has been the target of reduction amendments (Orpis 1996). In the aggregate, there is evidence that opponents of the PFC have been successful, either through amendments or by discouraging executive proposals. The bottom line here is that both the administration and the substance of the PFC are objectionable to legislators, that majorities have acted to con-

---

[28] The requirement reads as follows: "[*DiPres*] will send to the respective committees information on the semestral execution of spending on the items in this law, at the level of chapters and programs approved, including any information related to transfers under the item 'PFC' in the section on the Public Treasury." (1995, Article 25; 1996, Article 22)

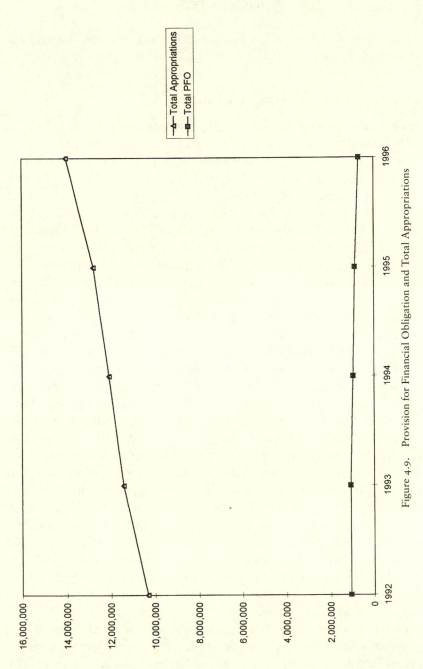

Figure 4.9. Provision for Financial Obligation and Total Appropriations

143

strain executive discretion in this area, and that the PFC has shrunk accordingly.

Separation of Purpose Across Coalitions

In 1995, the National Women's Service (Servicio Nacional de la Mujer), or SERNAM), the government's agency for women, attracted particularly virulent criticism from congressional opponents in the opposition coalition. Legislators from the RN and UDI, along with Catholic Church officials, condemned the platform SERNAM planned to present at the United Nations Fourth World Conference on Women, to be held in Beijing, China that September. The opposition characterized SERNAM's platform as representing the views of radical feminists and violating the Chilean national interest. In August, the Senate passed a resolution, with support from ten *Concertación* senators, censuring SERNAM's platform on the grounds that it supported the legalization of abortion, sanctioned homosexual marriages, and eroded the differences between men and women. Conservative adherents sustained their vehement objections to SERNAM's policy even after government officials acceded to these criticisms and changed the wording of its platform accordingly.

This assault on SERNAM continued beyond the UN Conference, extending to the budget proceedings. Three opposition deputies, Harry Jurgensen (RN), Carlos Kuschel (RN), and Jaime Orpis (UDI), proposed a series of cuts to SERNAM's budgets in the JBC. The JBC, in turn, rejected the cuts by a nine to five vote that fell precisely along coalition lines (Senado de Chile 1995, 2140–41). When the JBC's bill was returned to each chamber for final passage, however, opposition in the Senate raised objections again based on the level of funding for SERNAM. A series of negotiations ensued, in which the JBC met with representatives from the finance ministry to hammer out a compromise that could pass in both chambers of Congress before the executive's proposal automatically became law. At this point, opposition legislators reintroduced the Jurgensen–Kuschel–Orpis cuts, which enjoyed strong support in the conservative Senate. The maneuver was publicly denounced by SERNAM's Minister, Josefina Bilbao (La Epoca, 1995). Most of the opposition's proposed reductions were not approved, but some of them were reintegrated into the budget law at the precise levels initially requested by Deputies Jurgensen, Kuschel, and Orpis, as shown in Table 4.4.

Bargaining over appropriations for the National Youth Service (*Servicio Nacional de Menores*, SENAME) followed a similar pattern. Like

Table 4.4. *The Impact of Proposed Cuts to Women's and Youth Programs in the 1996 Budget*

Program	Item	Executive Proposal	J–K–O Proposal	Budget Law Appropriation	% Proposed Cut	% Actual Cut
SERNAM	01:21	4,000	3,646	3,646	8.85	8.85
SERNAM	01:25 (44-004)	476	.03	476	99.99	0.00
SERNAM	01:25 (44-005)	445	.03	445	99.99	0.00
SERNAM	03:21	226	96	226	57.56	0.00
SENAME	01:21	1,470	1,413	1,413	3.88	3.88
	Subtotals[a]	6,616	5,154	6,205	22.09	6.21
SERNAM	Total Budget	MD	MD	11,412	≤12.81	≤3.60
SERNAM	Total Budget	MD	MD	81,697	≤.07	≤.07

[a] The percentages in this row represent cuts to the specific items in the executive proposal targeted by the Jürgensen–Kuschel–Orpis amendments. To provide some perspective, the percentage of these specific cuts as shares of the entire final program budgets are reported below. Because comprehensive itemized data on the executive proposals for these programs were not available, nor were comprehensive records of all proposed cuts, we cannot be certain that the J–K–O cuts represent all congressional cuts to the programs. Thus, total cuts as percentages of final program budgets are at least those entailed in J–K–O, perhaps more.

Source: Senado de Chile 1995.

SERNAM, SENAME was the object of opposition criticism, although on administrative rather than ideological grounds, and a much smaller portion of its total budget was targeted. SENAME's mandate includes a program for juvenile offenders; SENAME administers part of this program directly, while contracting with private institutions to provide the rest. According to Senator Feliu, the dual administration of this program is both inefficient and juridically impermissible. In Senate debates, Feliu claimed that SENAME operates this program "at a cost 2.7 times greater than it pays the private centers for the same service." Furthermore, Feliu claimed, by so doing, SENAME is in violation of its own bylaws (Senado de Chile 1995, 2061–67). In accordance with Feliu's concerns, Deputies Jurgensen, Kuschel, and Orpis proposed a series of cuts to SENAME in the JBC, which were rejected by a coalition-line vote of nine to six. Nonetheless, as was the case with SERNAM, the opposition's recommended cuts to SENAME's budget were resuscitated during conferences with the executive and included in the final budget law.

The battles over SERNAM and SENAME show that Congress can

amend the executive's budget proposals downward, but they also illustrate the limitations on this ability, given the time constraints on the
budget process, when the majorities in each chamber are divided by a
separation of purpose. The cuts adopted to SERNAM's budget were
those originally proposed by Jurgensen, Kuschel, and Orpis. Second,
even with the amendments, overall appropriations to both SERNAM
and SENAME represented increases over 1995 spending levels – and
appropriations to these organizations grew at higher rates than the increase in the overall budget. This is particularly remarkable in the case
of SERNAM, where increases came despite the fact that some *Concertación* senators evidently sympathized with the right's objections to the
agency's activities at the Beijing Conference.

Budget hawks in Congress face a couple of key obstacles in cutting
executive proposals. In the first place, separation of purpose between
legislative majorities in each chamber throughout the 1990s has meant
that Congress does not confront the executive with a single voice. Moreover, in the event that the two branches cannot agree on a budget,
uncertainty over the reversion policy has encouraged compromise in
negotiations with executive officials. According to Deputy Orpis, "Ultimately, things were done at the last minute, and not everything turned
out well, but from my point of view there was a clear signal of austerity"
(Orpis 1996). Senator Feliu stated:

We [legislators] had accepted 98% of the budget, more or less, so that the
dispute was over a small amount. There was no lack of will on Congress's part,
just the rejection of certain expenditures. What the executive discussed was the
possibility of a veto. I'm not in agreement with this maneuver. All this was
discussed, and at the end of November the process was saved because the
executive accepted some things, Congress relented on some and a compromise
was produced. [Interviewer: But why did the executive wait until November 30?]
They didn't wait for anything. The period we have to review the budget law is
short, completely insufficient. The executive really didn't wait, [the effect] was
to produce a date such that it was very close to the end of the period. (Feliu
1996)

From the executive's side, *DiPres* Director Arellano:

[On the 1996 budget] the Senate had rejected what the Chamber and executive agreed to, and when there are such disagreements there is the JBC to resolve
them, and we did – finally. Why? [Because the disagreement was relatively small,
and because] after 60 days the executive's proposal takes effect, but it isn't 100%
clear what it means for Congress not to have approved the executive's proposal,
and we refused to get into a discussion about this. (Arellano, 1996)

The examples of the PFC and the battle over SERNAM and SENAME illustrate the difference between institutional and coalitional conflict in the ability of Congress to curtail executive spending requests. In the case of the PFC, conflict focuses on the institutional prerogatives of two branches, Congress has acted in a unified manner to impose constraints, and the item has been cut substantially in *real* terms even in the context of growing budgets. In the case of SERNAM and SENAME, some cuts to the executive proposal supported in the Senate were imposed, but the cuts were watered down considerably as the sixty-day timetable and uncertainty over the reversion policy in case of a veto both undermined the bargaining position of budget hawks in Congress.

CONCLUSION

The introductory chapters to this volume distinguish between the separation of powers and separation of purpose between branches in presidential systems. The former is generally established in presidential constitutions, whereas the latter results from the combination of voter choice and the various methods by which policy makers are selected. In this chapter, we illustrate these themes empirically, examining the complex division of spending powers between the branches, but also highlighting the manifestation of separation of purpose within Congress, rather than between the branches. The unique configuration of powers, combined with the clearly articulated differences in policy preferences among institutional actors, allow us to identify how separation of power and separation of purpose interact in shaping Chilean spending policy. We represent the key aspects of policy and institutional authority with a spatial model that suggests specific expectations about Chilean budgets – that they should be constrained (i.e., public regarded) overall, and that the executive should have a number of advantages over Congress in bargaining over appropriations. To evaluate these expectations, we summon data from Chilean budgets on fiscal balance, and on spending for the military, programs for women and minors, and discretionary spending by the executive. In all cases, the Chilean case supports the idea that procedures affect policy outcomes in the manner suggested by our model.

The designers of the 1980 Constitution exhibited remarkable faith in their ability to shape posttransition politics through institutional design, and insofar as they intended to ensure fiscal austerity, their confidence appears to have been justified. In this chapter, we do not engage in normative evaluations of budget surpluses, executive discretion over appropriations, or spending levels for particular programs. It is worth noting a couple of areas – the military's shrinking share of the budget despite decree laws aimed at guaranteeing its revenues, and the difficulties faced by the Senate in imposing cuts in social programs objectionable to its majority – in which policy has resisted the original intention of institutional engineers. The Chilean case illustrates both the potential and the limitations for procedures to affect policy outcomes.

5

Political Institutions and Public Policy in Argentina

An Overview of the Formation and Execution of the National Budget[1]

MARK P. JONES

INTRODUCTION

In recent years, many scholars (e.g., Bresser Pereira, Maravall, and Prze-worski 1993; O'Donnell 1994, 1996; Wynia 1995; Nino 1996) have discounted the political importance of the design of Argentina's democratic institutions, preferring instead to classify Argentina as an executive-dominated "Delegative Democracy" where concepts such as veto gates and veto players are of little relevance. Central to these critiques of Argentine democratic institutions is an underlying view that the Argentine Congress lacks any real ability to check the president, and is, for all intents and purposes, irrelevant to the policy process.

This study examines the political relevance of Argentine political institutions in general and of the Congress in particular via an analysis of the Argentine budget process. The goal of the study is twofold.

First, it provides the first comprehensive description of the rules governing the formation and execution of the national budget in Argentina. To properly analyze the impact of political institutions, one first has to understand how they are designed and the manner in which they function.

Second, it critically evaluates the thesis that Argentina is a "Delegative

[1] Stephan Haggard, Mathew McCubbins, Jim Granato, Robert Lowry, Scott Gates, Scott Desposato, and participants at the World Bank Conference on Administrative Procedure (La Jolla, CA, June 20–21, 1996) provided many helpful comments and suggestions. I am indebted to Alejandro Brocato, Alberto DiPeco, Marcela Durrieu, Alberto Föhrig, María Cristina Fra Amador, Guillermo Molinelli, María Teresa Pianzola, Rossana Surballe, Cristina Vallejos, the Oficina Nacional de Presupuesto, and many others for their assistance in the research portion of this project. Support for this research was provided by the World Bank and the National Science Foundation (Grant SBR-9709695).

Democracy." According to the "Delegative Democracy" perspective, power is delegated to the president via an election. The president, who enjoys both proactive and reactive powers, then faces few constraints on his or her ability to govern as he or she sees fit. Potential checks on the president's power such as the legislature, provinces, and other key players in the president's political party are conspicuously absent.

DELEGATIVE DEMOCRACY AND ARGENTINE
INSTITUTIONS: A BRIEF OVERVIEW

A "Delegative Democracy" view of Argentine political institutions does not recognize the separation of power that exists between the executive and legislative branches. This view ignores the powerful agenda-setting power of Congress: All legislation must past through Congress, and Congress has the ability to alter any legislation proposed by the executive branch. Further, in spite of President Carlos Saúl Menem's (1989–1995, 1995–1999) considerable use of decrees of urgent necessity, during his presidency the most important legislation (e.g., the budget and tax legislation) has been implemented via the normal legislative process (Eaton 1997).

Proponents of "Delegative Democracy" also neglect the strong separation of purpose that the Argentine electoral system creates for the president and legislators. While the president is public-regarding in that he or she responds to a national constituency, the legislators are private-regarding (due in large part to the rules employed for legislative elections) in that they respond primarily to the interests of their respective province. This separation of purpose results in different goals, vis-à-vis the distribution of national resources, between the president and his or her party's legislators, as well as among the members of the presidential party's legislative bloc.

The national budget is generally the most important piece of legislation adopted each year. A cursory review of the budget process reveals that during most of the presidency of Carlos Menem (Partido Justicialista [PJ]), the budget proposed by the executive branch has been approved by the PJ dominated legislature in a timely manner with only minor modifications, many of which have been successfully vetoed by Menem. This would appear to provide support for a "Delegative Democracy" vision of Argentine politics.

A more nuanced inspection of the budgetary process, which combines a theoretical understanding gleaned from the literature on the general study of political institutions (see Chapters 2–3) with an in-depth qualitative study of the Argentine budget process, suggests, however, that the Argentine Congress has played a prominent role in the budget process since the return to democracy in 1983. This review also suggests that the Argentine Congress has had an important influence on other areas of public policy.

This study demonstrates the prominent impact of Argentina's institutional rules on the policy process by providing some preliminary empirical evidence of the noteworthy effect of the Argentine Congress on the national budget during the Menem presidency. This is accomplished by testing three interrelated hypotheses: (1) that provinces benefit differentially in terms of the share of federal government transfers they receive depending on their proportional contribution to the presidential party's bloc in the legislature; (2) that the effect of this proportional contribution is affected by the size of the presidential party's legislative contingent, particularly whether or not the party has a legislative majority; and (3) that Congress has more influence on the budget when it is passed prior to the initiation of the budget year than when it is approved near the end of the budget year.

This analysis indicates that throughout the Menem presidency, especially beginning with the 1992 budget, the Argentine Congress has had a significant impact on the budget process. These findings suggest that in order to obtain the timely and relatively trouble-free passage of the budget bill the Menem administration has had to incorporate the interests of PJ legislators when drafting the budget. This and related findings are at odds with the common portrayal of the Argentine Congress as weak and inconsequential to the policy process. Combined with the recent work of a handful of other scholars (Mustapic and Ferretti 1995; Molinelli 1996a; Eaton 1997; Gibson and Calvo 1997), they suggest that Argentina has not been as executive-dominated as one might conclude based solely on a reading of the "Delegative Democracy" literature.

ARGENTINE POLITICAL INSTITUTIONS AND THE BUDGET

Argentina is a federal republic consisting of twenty-three provinces and a semiautonomous federal capital. It has a bicameral legislature, a relatively disciplined party system, and, since 1983, has represented one of Latin America's most vibrant and successful democracies. Currently, democratic politics is strongly entrenched in Argentina and there is little chance of reversion to military rule in the short or medium term.[2]

Executive Branch

Within the executive branch, three institutions are of particular importance to the budget process. They are: (1) the Presidency (Presidencia de la Nación), (2) the Ministry of Economy and Public Works and Services (Ministerio de Economía y Obras y Servicios Públicos), and (3) the Office of the Cabinet Chief (Jefatura de Gabinete de Ministros).

The Argentine president is directly elected via a modified version of the double complement rule.[3] The president is elected for a four-year term, and can seek reelection for one four-year term, after which he or she must wait four years prior to seeking a new term in office.[4] The Argentine Constitution provides the president with a number of important legislative powers, including the whole and partial (i.e., line item) veto as well as decree authority in selected areas. The current president (1995–1999) is Carlos Menem. Menem was elected originally in 1989 and reelected in 1995 following a 1994 constitutional reform in which the previous constitutional prohibition on immediate reelection was removed.

The head of the Ministry of Economy and Public Works and Services, henceforth referred to as the Ministry of Economy, is appointed by the president. Reporting to the minister of economy (and located within the Ministry of Economy) is the Department of Finance (Secretaría de Haci-

---

[2] The Argentine military is firmly under the control of the civilian government. The influence of the military on the budget process is comparable to (if not more marginal than) that of the U.S. military on the U.S. budget process. An important outside veto player, not discussed in this chapter, is the International Monetary Fund (IMF). The IMF is particularly important in regard to the issue of budget deficits, since government agreements with the IMF normally identify specific deficit ceilings, which place a restraint on both the drafting and execution of the budget.

[3] If in the first round no candidate receives either (1) over 45% of the valid vote, or (2) a minimum of 40% of the valid vote and at the same time is more than 10% ahead of the second place candidate, then a runoff is held between the top two candidates from the first round.

[4] In 1983 and 1989 the president was elected for a six-year term via an electoral college within which a majority of the votes was required for election. Electors were selected from 24 multimember districts ranging in size from 4 to 144 members using the same proportional representation (PR) formula and threshold utilized for the election of Chamber deputies. The president could seek reelection only after sitting out for one term.

enda), and under the Department of Finance, the National Budget Office (Oficina Nacional de Presupuesto). These latter two entities play a very prominent role in the budget process. Both report directly to the minister of economy, not to the president.

The institution of the Office of the Cabinet Chief is quite new. It was created during the 1994 constitutional reform and only came into existence with the start of the second Menem presidency in July of 1995. The cabinet chief possesses many powers previously exercised by the president. Like cabinet ministers and other executive officials the cabinet chief is named by the president and can be removed at the president's discretion. Unlike the case with all other executive officials, however, the cabinet chief can also be removed by the Congress (via a vote by an absolute majority of the members of both the Chamber of Deputies and the Senate). Constitutionally, the Office of Cabinet Chief could play a fundamental role in the budget process. At present, however, the role of the Office of the Cabinet Chief in the budget process is not particularly prominent.

Legislative Branch

Argentina has a bicameral legislature. The Chamber of Deputies has 257 members who are elected, using closed list PR, from multimember districts (the 23 provinces and the federal capital) for 4-year terms.[5] One-half (130 and 127) of the Chamber is renewed every 2 years, with every district renewing one-half of its legislators (or the closest equivalent).[6] Each of the 24 districts receives a number of deputies in proportion to its population, with the following restrictions: (1) that no district receive fewer than five deputies, and (2) that no district receive fewer deputies than it possessed in the previous democratic period (i.e., 1973–1976) (Gómez de la Fuente and Pérez Colman 1995). As a result of these rules the smallest provinces (i.e., Catamarca, La Pampa, La Rioja, Santa Cruz, Tierra del Fuego) are highly overrepresented (in proportion to their population) in the Chamber while the country's largest province (Buenos Aires) is highly underrepresented (see Table 5.1).[7]

---

[5] Before 1991 the Chamber had 254 deputies (3 were added after Tierra del Fuego achieved provincial status in 1990). In 1983 all 254 deputies were elected at the same time.

[6] No restrictions are placed on the reelection of either deputies or senators.

[7] If the 257 Chamber seats were allocated based purely on population (with every province receiving one seat at the minimum as in the United States), then the

Table 5.1. *Population and Representation in the Argentine Congress: 1992-1995* *

Province/District	Population Based on the 1991 Census	Number of Chamber Deputies	Population per Chamber Deputy	Number of Senators	Population per Senator
Buenos Aires	12538007	70	179114	2	6269004
Capital Federal	2960976	25	118439	2	1480488
Catamarca	264940	5	52988	2	132470
Córdoba	2764176	18	153565	2	1382088
Corrientes	780778	7	111540	2	390389
Chaco	799302	7	14186	2	399651
Chubut	356445	5	71289	2	178223
Entre Ríos	1021042	9	113449	2	510521
Formosa	363035	5	72607	2	181518
Jujuy	513213	6	85536	2	256607
La Pampa	260041	5	52008	2	130021
La Rioja	220910	5	44182	2	110455
Mendoza	1400142	10	140014	2	700071
Misiones	787514	7	112502	2	393757
Neuquén	385606	5	77121	2	192803
Río Negro	506314	5	101263	2	253157
Salta	863688	7	123384	2	431844
San Juan	526263	6	87711	2	263132
San Luis	286379	5	57276	2	143190
Santa Cruz	159726	5	31945	2	79863
Santa Fé	2782809	19	146464	2	1391405
Santiago del Estero	670388	7	95770	2	335194
Tucumán	1142321	9	126925	2	571161
Tierra del Fuego	69450	5	13890	2	34725
TOTAL	32423465	257	126161	48	675489

* The above distribution of deputies and senators is identical to that for the 1983-1995 period, with the exception that between 1983 and 1992 Tierra del Fuego had only two deputies and no senators. Since December 10, 1995 every province has had three senators.

Prior to the 1994 constitutional reform all of the country's twenty-two provinces (twenty-three after 1990) and its federal capital were represented by two senators.[8] Senators were elected indirectly for nine-

province of Buenos Aires would have 99 deputies instead of the 70 it currently possesses. This number is based on the 1991 Census. The current distribution of deputies is based on the 1980 Census.

[8] Tierra del Fuego's two senators did not assume office until 1992.

year terms by the provincial legislatures using the plurality formula, except in the federal capital where they were selected via an electoral college. By lottery two-thirds of the Senate began in 1983 with either three- or six-year initial terms, with no province having two senators on the same cycle.

Since 1995 the Senate has been composed of seventy-two members, with every province (and the federal capital) represented by three senators. Until 2001 these senators will continue to be elected indirectly by the provincial legislatures (with one-third of the Senate being renewed in 1998), with the stipulation that no one party can have more than two senators from a province. Where one party holds two seats, the third seat goes to the "first minority" in the provincial legislature.[9]

Table 5.1 displays the distribution of legislative seats in the Chamber of Deputies and Senate as well as provides information on every province's/district's population and number of deputies and senators per capita. The table makes clear the high degree of overrepresentation of the smaller provinces in both the Chamber and Senate.

As is the case in the U.S. Congress, the Argentine Chamber and Senate are divided into a large number of committees where a majority of the legislative work is conducted.[10] The Chamber Budget and Finance Committee is widely seen as the most important of the congressional committees due in large part to the ability of its members to influence the content of the budget (Durrieu 1996; Mustapic 1996; Surballe 1996).[11] The composition of the committee, as is the case with all congressional committees, reflects the proportion of seats held by the various parties in the Chamber. However, since the ultimate decision regarding the composition of committees rests with the house leadership (i.e., the president of the Chamber and the president of the Senate respectively), whichever party controls that office can (within certain limits) ensure that it has a majority on the Budget and Finance Committee. The Senate also has a

---

[9] Beginning in 2001 three senators will be directly elected at the same time from every province (and the federal capital) for six-year terms with two seats going to the plurality winner and one going to the second place finisher. These elections will be staggered (starting in 2003), with one-third of the provinces renewing their senators every two years.

[10] Unlike the U.S. Congress the Argentine Congress does not have subcommittees.

[11] This influence is mostly at the micro level, referring to the ability of committee members to obtain resources for constituent groups (both geographic and occupational), as well as to obtain resources that are placed under the direct control of Budget and Finance Committee members (e.g., the distribution of university scholarships) (Zublena 1996).

Mark P. Jones

Budget and Finance Committee, although its impact on the budget process is relatively minor compared to that of the Chamber Budget and Finance Committee.

Two points are of fundamental importance to understanding the role of the Congress in the budget process during recent years: (1) the presence of a PJ absolute majority in the Senate and near-majority or majority in the Chamber, and (2) the relatively disciplined nature of the Argentine political parties.

The current composition of the Chamber of Deputies and Senate is provided in Table 5.2. The composition of each house's respective Budget and Finance Committee is provided in Table 5.3. Dominant in both houses (and therefore in the committees as well) is the Partido Justici-

Table 5.2. *Actual Composition of the Argentine Congress by Party: 1996**

	Chamber		Senate	
Party	Seats	% Seats	Seats	% Seats
Partido Justicialista	133	51.8	40	55.6
Unión Cívica Radical	68	26.5	21	29.2
Frepaso (and allies)	29	11.3	1	1.4
Pacto Autonomista Liberal	4	1.6	2	2.8
Partido Renovador de Salta	3	1.2	1	1.4
Fuerza Republicana	2	0.8	1	1.4
Movimiento Popular Fueguino	2	0.8	2	2.8
Movimiento Popular Neuquino	2	0.8	2	2.8
Partido Bloquista	1	0.4	1	1.4
Cruzada Renovadora			1	1.4
Modín (and dissidents)	4	1.6		
Movimiento Popular Jujeño	2	0.8		
Partido Demócrata de Meadoza	2	0.8		
Partido Demócrata Progresista	2	0.8		
UCeDé	2	0.8		
Acción Chaqueña	1	0.4		
TOTAL	257	72		

* This table includes changes in the composition caused by defections and party switching. Included above are two senators from the province of Catamarca (1 PJ, 1 UCR) who have yet to assume office due to a legal/political dispute.

Source: Dirección de Información Parlamentaria 1996.

Table 5.3. *Composition of the Chamber and Senate Budget and Finance Committees by Party: 1996*

Party	Chamber Seats	Senate Seats
Partido Justicialista	19	13
Unión Cívica Radical	13	6
Frepaso	3	
Partido Bloquista	1	
Partido Demócrata de Mendoza	1	
Pacto Autonomista Liberal		1
TOTAL	37	20

alista. The principal opposition parties are the Unión Cívica Radical (UCR) and the Frente del País Solidario (Frepaso). In addition to these two opposition parties there are a large number of center-right provincial parties that tend to compete in only one province (where they are often the dominant or principal opposition party). Many of these parties often vote with the PJ in the legislature (frequently in exchange for benefits for their provinces), and on numerous occasions have been quite helpful when the PJ leadership has experienced difficulties with a select number of its legislators (particularly in the Chamber).[12]

A legislature with a large number of coreligionaries of the president, such as that enjoyed by President Menem, does not guarantee sufficient support for the president's policies. The degree of support also depends on the level of legislative party discipline and the general incentives for legislators to support the president. Mainwaring and Shugart (1997b) identify three important features of electoral laws that influence the level of party discipline in a country: (1) pooling of votes among a party's candidates, (2) control over who runs on the party label, and (3) control over the order in which members are elected from the party list.

Argentine Chamber deputies are elected via closed party lists using PR. The method of selection employed to create the party lists and choose Senate candidates ranges from a list or candidate of unity imposed by a district-level caudillo or the national party organization to competitive internal party primaries open to party affiliates, and increasingly (since 1993) independents (i.e., people who are not affiliated with

---

[12] Also important (especially in the past) has been the support of the center-right Unión del Centro Democrático (UCeDé) whose deputies generally have supported PJ initiatives in the Chamber (Gibson 1996).

any party). The provincial branches of the principal political parties (i.e., the PJ and UCR) normally enjoy a significant amount of autonomy in regard to activities such as the creation of party lists and the formation of electoral alliances at the district level. This is not to say that the national party is not an important actor in the electoral process at the district level. On balance, however, the provincial level party organizations are dominant.

Senators are elected by the provincial legislatures (the legislature essentially ratifies the winner of the intra-party election/selection). The single-member and indirect nature of the Senate elections signifies that votes for this office are not pooled, but the method of election has contributed to party control over the electoral process.

While interested in reelection, many deputies (and to a lesser extent senators) also actively aspire to positions in the national executive branch, their province's executive branch and (for deputies) the Senate. In either event, party loyalty (either to the national or district-level party organization) influences legislators' prospects for a political future either as a legislator or as a national or provincial government official. This factor, combined with the use of closed party lists/indirect election and a strong level of party control over the nomination process, has worked to maintain a relatively high level of party discipline in the Argentine Congress (Jones 1997).

THE BUDGETARY PROCESS

The budgetary process contains four key stages. The initial stage involves the drafting of the budget bill, and is followed by the treatment of the proposed budget in Congress. Once the budgetary bill becomes law, there remain two important stages: the execution of the budget and the subsequent control of this execution.

The Drafting of the Budget Estimates

Every governmental entity (e.g., ministries, decentralized organizations) creates its own draft budget on the basis of the budget ceilings provided by the National Budget Office.[13] These ceilings are based on revenue forecasts supplied by the Department of Finance's Office of Fiscal Anal-

---

[13] An entity is any public organization with independent legal status. There are three jurisdictions: the executive branch (which includes decentralized organizations), the legislative branch, and the judicial branch.

ysis (Oficina de Análisis Fiscal) and provide the entities with an important framework within which to organize their draft budgets. There is a strong tendency to utilize the previous year's budget as a base, normally increasing program percentages in line with the limits prescribed by the National Budget Office (Brocato 1996; Feo 1996).[14] Within an entity the separate units draft their own budgets which are then included (often with some revision) in the entity's budget. Decentralized organizations (e.g., many social security related entities) draft their own budgets.

Once the National Budget Office receives the draft budgets provided by the entities, it analyzes them, and then makes any modifications it deems necessary. In practice the National Budget Office normally cedes to the entity the responsibility of detailing the manner in which the funds will be spent, and instead focuses on the overall sum of expenditures that an entity will be allowed (Brocato 1996).

Budget estimates are provided for all programs – those that previously have existed, those based on a law previously approved by Congress, and (unlike in the United States) those that neither exist nor have congressional approval. If a program that previously did not exist has funds included for it in the budget bill, and the budget is passed with the allocation for the program intact, then as of January 1 (i.e., the start of the fiscal year) the program exists.

Ministries and other entities engage in lobbying at two principal stages in the budget process: (1) at the point where the entities receive their budget ceilings, and (2) at the point when a preliminary draft budget has been completed by the National Budget Office (López Murphy 1996; Molinelli 1996b; Surballe 1996). If the president wants to influence the budget he or she she can best do so at the same two stages. First, at the time when the National Budget Office provides the entities with their budget ceilings, the president can intervene to raise or lower the ceiling for a particular entity. Second, once the National Budget Office finishes the draft budget, the president can intervene in support of any of the numerous complaints by heads of entities that their budget is too low and so on.

Compared to the United States, there is not a considerable amount of lobbying during the budget process by private interests. However, similar to the behavior of ministries and others (including legislators and the

---

[14] The National Budget Office is currently trying to end this habit of incremental increases added to the previous year's budget by introducing a form of zero-base budgeting (Callieri 1996; Oficina Nacional de Presupuesto 1996).

provinces), the greatest amount of lobbying by business and related groups occurs at the formation stage of the budget process (i.e., at the entity level) (Callieri 1996; López Murphy 1996). That is, someone interested in the construction of hospitals in the province of Buenos Aires will lobby the Ministry of Health to include the construction of three hospitals in that province in its draft budget. Once details at that level of aggregation are in the budget, they normally stay. Of course, given varying levels of resources only two (instead of the requested three) hospitals may be constructed, but it is likely that if they are included in the initial request, they will receive funding at some level.[15]

The Proposed Budget and the Congress

Once the drafts submitted by the entities are analyzed and modified by the National Budget Office, the estimates are placed in an official budget proposal that is sent by the National Budget Office to the Office of the Cabinet Chief.[16] The Office of the Cabinet Chief, after reviewing the proposal received from the National Budget Office, then sends it to Congress.[17]

The Office of the Cabinet Chief delivers the proposed budget bill to the *mesa de entradas* (i.e., the clerk's office) of the Chamber of Deputies from which the proposed budget passes immediately to the Chamber Budget and Finance Committee. Under Article 52 (Article 44 prior to the 1994 constitutional reform) of the Argentine Constitution, the budget bill must enter via the Chamber (Dromi and Menem 1994; Grupo Sophia 1997).

[15] It is important to note that one of the biggest potential lobbying areas (public works) is under the control of the Minister of Economy and Public Works and Services whose overriding goal in the budget process is to keep expenditures as low as possible (with the goal of achieving a balanced budget, and where possible a surplus so as to reduce the principal on the country's foreign and domestic debt).

[16] A key point at this stage in the budget process is that while the entities submit detailed budget plans to the National Budget Office (i.e., detailing expenditures at a highly disaggregated level), the draft sent by the National Budget Office to the Office of the Cabinet Chief and then to the Congress contains expenditure data only at a very macro level (i.e., overall expenditures for programs and information on the number of people employed by the programs).

[17] The exact role of the Office of the Cabinet Chief in the budget process is still unclear. The first Cabinet Chief assumed office in July of 1995, and thus this institution participated in the drafting of only the 1996, 1997, and 1998 budgets. The Office of the Cabinet Chief can modify the budget proposed by the National Budget Office, although thus far it has not exercised this power in any noteworthy manner.

Approximately two weeks after the Cabinet Chief delivers the budget bill, the Chamber Budget and Finance Committee begins debate in a scheduled manner during which time all (or nearly all) entity heads (e.g., ministers, heads of decentralized organizations) appear before the committee to explain and justify their budgets and the program of activities that they are going to carry out (Pesce 1996; Surballe 1996). These presentations, and related interpellation by the members of the Chamber Budget and Finance Committee, represent the most important treatment of the budget in the Congress.

Once the presentations and interpellation are completed the Chamber Budget and Finance Committee votes on the budget bill, with the result being a majority ruling either to accept or reject the proposed budget (with modifications to the proposed budget submitted by the Office of the Cabinet Chief possible). There are also often one or more minority rulings (with or without modifications) to reject and/or accept the proposed budget. Roughly one week after this vote, when the ruling is published in the Orden del Dia, the budget bill arrives on the Chamber floor. Normally nothing of any great importance occurs at this point. There are, of course, a large number of speeches on the floor (most by members of the opposition) and normally the opposition offers alternative macrolevel plans. While the budget bill can be modified at any stage of the process (i.e., both in committee and when it is on the floor), relatively little modification of the budget proposed by the executive branch occurs at any time during the treatment of the budget bill in Congress.[18]

In late November or early December the budget bill most often is approved in the Chamber and is then sent to the Senate.[19] There the bill normally rapidly passes through the Senate Budget and Finance Committee and is sent to the floor. If the Senate approves the version of the budget bill previously sanctioned by the Chamber, then the bill is sent to the president. If the version of the budget bill previously approved by the Chamber is modified in any manner whatsoever by the Senate, it must return to the initiating house (i.e., the Chamber). When this occurs,

[18] Prior to the 1994 constitutional reform the legislative process was the same as that described above in terms of veto gates and agenda setting. The only salient difference is that the constitutional reform streamlined the legislative process by limiting the number of times that each house can vote on a bill to a greater extent than before (Sabsay and Onaindia 1994).

[19] Most bills (including the budget) require a plurality vote for approval. However, at the same time in order to hold session 50% + 1 of a house's members must be in attendance (i.e., 130 in the Chamber and 37 in the Senate).

the Chamber has two choices: (1) approve the budget bill in its modified form, in which case this revised version is sent to the president or (2) reject the modified version of the budget bill, in which case the original version is sent to the president.[20]

Once Congress sends the president the approved budget bill he or she can veto it in whole or in part (i.e., a line item veto). The use of the line item veto, while not explicitly mentioned in the Constitution prior to the 1994 constitutional reform, was nevertheless a de facto power exercised by presidents, particularly since the 1960s (Molinelli 1991; Mustapic and Ferretti 1995). Both Presidents Alfonsín and Menem employed the line item veto, although Menem has used the device to a far greater extent than Alfonsín (Mustapic and Ferretti 1995).

The line item veto can be utilized to remove any portion of the budget bill approved by Congress. President Menem often has employed it to remove amendments tacked on by members of Congress, particularly when those amendments have been included without adequately specifying the source of the funds needed to finance the expenditures resulting from the additions. For example, in 1994 Menem utilized a line item veto to remove 1.5 million pesos (1 peso equals 1 U.S. dollar) of funding for social development programs due to the failure of legislators to adequately identify the financing source of these expenditures (Poder Ejecutivo Nacional 1994). During this same year Menem also used a line item veto to remove 53 million pesos of expenditures in the area of education due to a lack of clarity regarding the objectives of the program to be financed (Poder Ejecutivo Nacional 1994). In 1995 one of the many line item vetoes made by the president removed an article that would have allocated 100% of the Special Tobacco Fund to the tobacco producing provinces. The rationale for this veto was the existence of a law limiting the producer provinces to only 80% of the Fund (Poder Ejecutivo Nacional 1995).[21] The line item veto also has been used to avoid the duplication of activities by two or more distinct entities.

---

[20] However, if the Senate approved the revised version with a two-thirds vote, then the Chamber (if it wishes to reject the revised version) must vote against it with a two-thirds vote. If two-thirds of the Chamber votes to reject the revised version, then the original version is sent to the president. If the Chamber fails to reject the revised version by a two-thirds vote, then the revised version of the budget bill that was passed by the Senate is sent to the president.

[21] One of the most notable lobbying efforts during the drafting of the 1996 budget was to maintain the Special Tobacco Fund, one of the few important subsidies that still exists (Vallejos 1996). For a discussion of the Fund, see Sawers (1996).

In the event of a presidential veto (whole or line item) the budget bill returns to the Chamber with the objections of the president listed. To override the president's veto requires a two-thirds vote in both the Chamber and the Senate. In the event that Congress fails to override the president's line item veto, the bill (absent the portion vetoed) becomes law.

If a legislator or legislative group wants to influence the content of the budget, it is easier to do so at the draft stage of the budget (via lobbying of the executive branch and decentralized organizations) than when the budget bill is under examination in Congress.[22] If, for example, a deputy or senator (or group of deputies and/or senators) is interested in obtaining financing for a specific program, ministry, or province, they are much more likely to obtain this financing at the draft budget stage via lobbying or vote/favor trading with the executive branch (or with a subsector of the executive branch such as the Ministry of Economy or Ministry of Interior) than during the period in which the budget bill is being discussed in Congress.[23] As a result of this practice, the budgets submitted by the Menem Administration to Congress have reflected the interests/requests of a large component of the PJ legislative bloc.

As a consequence of the norms discussed above, lobbyists do not have a notable presence in the Argentine Congress, especially when compared to the United States.[24] A minor exception is when they need to protect an expenditure (e.g., a specific program) that has been included by an

---

[22] A restriction that Congress faces when dealing with the budget bill is that wherever it increases expenditures (which is almost exclusively what it is interested in doing) it must at the same time identify the financing source for those new expenditures, either via new taxes, or cuts in other programs, etc. If Congress does not adequately identify the financing sources for these "new" expenditures which it adds to the budget sent by the executive branch, then in all likelihood these "additions" will be vetoed in whole or in part by the president. This restriction provides an added incentive for legislators to lobby at the entity level during the time period in which the entities are drafting their budgets.

[23] For example, a legislator (or group of legislators) may agree to back a controversial executive branch sponsored bill that will have a negative impact on her (or their) constituency in exchange for the executive's promise that in the upcoming year's budget there will be an increase in the amount of funding for a program that will benefit her (or their) constituency.

[24] Pion-Berlin (1997) provides an excellent example of the difference in lobbying in the two countries in his discussion of defense budgeting in Argentina and the United States. He contrasts the considerable amount of lobbying of members of Congress in the United States by military officials and defense contractors with the virtual absence of similar lobbying in Argentina.

entity in the event that Congress is considering eliminating that program (Molinelli 1996b).[25]

The result of the above behavior is that in recent years the budget's treatment in Congress has been relatively trouble free. This is a sharp contrast to the presidency of Raúl Alfonsín where, due in large part to the absence of a UCR congressional majority, the budget process was very conflictual.

Of course, there are still opposition critiques and counter proposals, but the twin factors of a working PJ legislative majority and relatively strong party discipline have ensured that the deals made between the executive branch and the legislative branch are, for the most part, respected. It would therefore be a mistake to infer from the relatively smooth passage of the president's budget in Congress that the budget process is extremely executive-dominated. Rather, the absence of conflict is explained by (1) a relatively disciplined PJ legislative majority that allows for bargaining over the budget to be conducted in an intraparty (and less public) manner and (2) the fact that normally most serious negotiation over the budget between legislators and the executive branch takes place prior to the formal submission of the budget bill to Congress.

In the event that no budget has been approved by the start of the new fiscal year (the Argentine fiscal year goes from January 1 through December 31), then until one is approved, the most recent budget law (normally from the previous year) is used. The executive branch is empowered to alter the previous budget to make it compatible in a rational manner with the reality of the new budget year (Ley de Administración Financiera 1992). That is, the executive branch is responsible for altering the financing specified in the previous budget so that it conforms with current financing levels and for altering expenditures, both to bring them in line with the current financial situation as well as to eliminate expenditures that are no longer relevant (e.g., money for a bridge that has been built or for a conference that has been held). The reversion to the previous year's budget combined with the strong role played by the executive branch in modifying and updating this

[25] There is, however, some lobbying of Congress aimed at increasing the amount of expenditures destined for specific groups. The groups that most actively lobby are pensioners, university students and faculty, and the provinces, the latter primarily via the governor's provincial delegation. Of course, many of the additions made as a result of this lobbying are often vetoed by the president, normally due to congressional failure to adequately identify the funding source.

budget provides the president with a considerable amount of power in the budget process.

The Execution of the Budget

Once the president signs the budget bill the National Budget Office drafts the administrative distribution of the budget. All expenditures for every entity are provided in a very detailed manner (i.e., down to the level of how much will be spent on paper for a specific program) such as was contained in the draft budgets submitted by the entities to the National Budget Office. Any necessary changes in these distributions, required due to modifications of the original plans submitted by the entities, are made by the National Budget Office. Where it makes changes to the original projects submitted by the entities, the National Budget Office normally does not directly alter expenditures at the detailed level, only at the macro level. Once completed, this administrative distribution is sent to the Office of the Cabinet Chief, which promulgates, via a decree, the detailed administrative distribution that the entities must follow in their expenditure patterns during the upcoming budget year.

The pay-as-you-go style rules governing the Argentine budget process are designed to avoid/attenuate budget deficits. While the process has not allowed Argentina to eliminate deficits altogether, it has helped to limit them. When a budget deficit occurs it must be covered either utilizing revenue from privatizations or domestic/international financing.[26]

In both the programming and execution of the Argentine budget, every expenditure must have a corresponding revenue source. Furthermore, given the uncertainty surrounding the forecasting of revenue, the amount of expenditures for every entity in the budget represents only the maximum that the entity may spend during the budget year. Most often, entities do not receive all of the credits included in their budget. The difference is usually the largest for expenditures based on financing from the National Treasury (Tesorería General de la Nación) and the smallest for expenditures based on external financing (e.g., from the World Bank) (Feo 1996).

---

[26] The Argentine currency regimen (the Law of Convertibility), which fixes the Argentine peso at par with the U.S. dollar, represents a strong restriction on resorting to any form of deficit financing.

The National Budget Office allocates the budget to entities based on a quarterly quota system (Feo 1996). Prior to the start of every quarter all entities submit a program of expenditures for the upcoming quarter to the National Budget Office. This program is divided into two parts: the contract (how much they can contract for, which is allocated at the quarterly level), and the disbursement (how much they can pay out, which is allocated at the monthly level). The National Budget Office analyzes these requests and makes changes (normally at the macro level) as it sees fit (Brocato 1996; Feo 1996).

If an entity wants to make any changes in its distribution of expenditures that were approved in the budget and then outlined in detail in the administrative distribution, it must officially request a change in the programming of its budget. Who approves the change depends upon the nature of the request (Jefe de Gabinete de Ministros 1996). In terms of hierarchy, the level of approval ranges from the passage of a law (e.g., to increase the number of workers listed in a budget item, change capital expenses to current expenses, increase the size of the budget) to the approval of a unit head (e.g., modifying the destination of expenses within a specific project). All changes are registered and coordinated with the National Budget Office.

Prior to June 30 the executive branch must provide the Congress with a detailed report on the execution of the previous year's budget. The National Budget Office prepares this report.

Control Over the Execution of the Budget

Control over the execution of the budget is carried out by three distinct entities. They are (1) the Office of the National Comptroller (Sindicatura General de la Nación [SIGEN]), (2) the National Audit Office (Auditoría General de la Nación), and (3) the National Budget Office.

Internal control is exercised by the SIGEN. The SIGEN is a component of the executive branch whose director (Síndico General de la Nación) and three assistant directors (Síndicos Generales Adjuntos) are named by the president.

External control is exercised by the National Audit Office (Auditoría). The Auditoría is a semiautonomous investigative branch of Congress.[27]

[27] As of 1995 the Auditoría had only 437 employees. By comparison, in 1995 the Finance Administration Program (where the National Budget Office is located) within the Department of Finance had 635 employees (Ley de Presupuesto 1995).

The Auditoría is governed by a president and a directorate and is responsible to the Joint Parliamentary Audit Committee (Comisión Parlamentaria Mixta Revisora de Cuentas) of the Argentine Congress. The Auditoría provides Congress with both a comprehensive evaluation of the execution of the previous year's budget as well as with specific audits and related investigative tasks requested by Congress (Rodríguez and Ventulle 1995; Merbilha 1996; Rodríguez 1996). Every year the Auditoría submits a "Plan of Action" to the Joint Parliamentary Audit Committee which the committee can approve, reject, or modify.

The Auditoría is run by seven auditor generals (elected for eight-year staggered terms). As a consequence of the 1994 constitutional reform, one of these auditor generals is designated as president of the Auditoría by the opposition party in Congress with the largest number of legislators. The remaining six auditors are designated by the Senate (three) and Chamber (three) in proportion to the number of seats held by the various parties in the two houses. As of 1997, two of the three Senate and Chamber appointed auditors are from the PJ while the remaining auditor appointed by each house is a member of the UCR. The president is a member of the UCR. All decisions of the Auditoría are made functioning as a collegial body, using majority rule for all votes. Thus, the PJ has effective control over the activities of the Auditoría.

The Joint Parliamentary Audit Committee is composed of six senators and six deputies, selected in the same manner as members of any regular congressional committee. That is, the membership is determined by the house's leadership, with the mandate that the composition be in proportion to each party's percentage of seats in the respective house. As of 1997, eight of the members (four senators and four deputies) are from the PJ with the remaining four (two senators and two deputies) belonging to the UCR. All committee decisions are made by a majority vote.

In addition to these two formal control mechanisms, the National Budget Office maintains a de facto control over the National Administration (Feo 1996; SIDIF Staff 1996). Integral to this control is the National Budget Office's Financial Information System (Sistema de Información Financiera [SIDIF]). SIDIF is a computer database that contains information at the level of disaggregation provided in the administrative distributions decree (i.e., the maximum amount of detail possible). The credits, contracts, and disbursements of every entity are monitored on a real-time basis using this system.

Primarily utilizing SIDIF, the National Budget Office watches all entities and is able to informally alert them if they are in violation of, or in danger of violating, the norms specified in the programming quotas. In the event that disciplinary action must be carried out, the National Budget Office informs the SIGEN which then takes over in the area of official sanctions/actions.

CONGRESS AND THE BUDGET PROCESS: AN EMPIRICAL ASSESSMENT

In the course of this description of the current functioning of the Argentine budget process I have asserted that in recent years the Argentine Congress has had a more substantial impact on the budget process than many readers might think due to both the relatively nonconflictual treatment of the budget in Congress as well as the academic and popular press portrayal of Carlos Menem's presidency as extremely executive-dominated (e.g., Bresser Pereira et al. 1993; O'Donnell 1994; *Página/12* 1994–97; Nino 1996; Wynia 1995). In this section I provide some initial evidence of a noteworthy level of congressional influence on the budget process during the 1990s by testing three interrelated hypotheses.

First, if Congress has a salient impact on the budget process then we would expect provinces to benefit differentially in terms of the proportion of federal government transfers they receive depending on their proportional contribution to the presidential party's bloc in the legislature (Atlas, Gilligan, Hendershott, and Zupan 1995; Porto and Sanguinetti 1996).[28] The greater the proportion of the presidential party legislative bloc (PRESIDENT'S PARTY) supplied by a province, the greater

---

[28] A large portion of the national transfers are not directly affected by the budget; nevertheless, a significant portion are. Furthermore, legislators and governors base their requests/demands for resources on the overall level of transfers allocated to the provinces. That is, when a group of PJ legislators from a province make their case for additional resources to the relevant executive branch officials, they base their demands on the distribution of the totality of national government resources that their province receives vis-à-vis those received by other provinces. They do not limit their comparison to those national transfers contained in the budget. Executive branch officials employ a similar calculus when making transfer related decisions. Future work should disaggregate federal transfers into different categories, with particular attention given to the ability of the legislature to influence different types of transfers in the short and medium term and to the direct and indirect effect of the budget process on these distinct types of transfers. Like most qualitative comparative static methods of analysis, this chapter makes the rather heroic assumption that all relevant factors other than those examined remain unchanged over time. In this instance, this is clearly not the case (e.g., changes in the Federal Tax-Sharing Agreement and global economy during the period under analysis).

the proportion of federal government transfers the province is likely to receive.

Second, the impact of PRESIDENT'S PARTY should be affected by the size of the presidential party's contingent in the legislature (Kiewiet and McCubbins 1991; Cox and McCubbins 1993). In particular we would expect the impact of PRESIDENT'S PARTY to be greater in those instances where the presidential party possesses an absolute majority in both houses than when the presidential party lacks such a majority and therefore, in order to obtain the passage of the budget, would need to gain the support of opposition legislators.

Third, we would expect Congress to have more influence on budgetary matters when a budget is passed by the Congress than in those budget years in which the president declines to submit a new budget, instead reverting to the previous year's budget. Thus, we would expect the impact of PRESIDENT'S PARTY to be greater for those budget years where a budget bill is passed prior to the initiation of the budget year than in those years where the president utilizes the previous year's budget to guide governmental spending.

Earlier, the manner in which members of the Argentine Congress influence the budget process was detailed. Under Menem, PJ deputies primarily influence the composition of the budget via the lobbying of the executive branch prior to the budget bill's submission to Congress. In order to achieve the passage of the budget in Congress, the Menem administration has had to satisfy the demands of PJ legislators to a greater extent than would have been the case had its plan been to merely revert to the previous year's budget. Of course, not passing the budget within the constitutionally mandated period entailed serious costs for Menem, both from the perspective of efficient planning but also because of the negative signal it would send to international investors, foreign governments, and the IMF.

Furthermore, even where the executive branch does not attempt to gain legislative approval of the budget prior to the initiation of the budget year, we would still expect some impact of the partisan "weight" of each province within the presidential party's legislative bloc on the budget allocation. This is because of the desire of the executive branch to reward party legislators and maintain their general allegiance for assistance in the passage of other legislation.[29]

---

[29] For reasons of space I do not discuss the issues surrounding the link between political institutions and particularism. For an excellent treatment of this topic the reader is directed to Chapters 2–4 of this volume.

Two factors are crucial to any discussion of the above hypotheses during Argentina's most recent democratic period (1983–).[30] First, it is necessary to have information on the size of the presidential party bloc in the legislature during each year, focusing in particular on whether or not the president's party had a majority in both houses. Second, it is vital to know the date on which the budget law was passed by Congress each year, with a special emphasis on whether or not is was passed prior to the initiation of the budget year or if it was approved after a large portion of the budget year had elapsed.

Presidential Party Legislative Bloc

A principal point upon which the presidencies of Raúl Alfonsín (1983–1989) and Carlos Menem (1989–1995, 1995–1999) contrast is the level of partisan support each president had in the legislature during their respective tenures in office (see Table 5.4). Between 1983 and 1989 President Alfonsín's UCR lacked a working majority in the Senate. Between 1987 and 1989 the UCR also lacked a working majority in the Chamber. Throughout his time in office, President Menem's PJ has possessed a working majority in both houses of Congress.[31]

While the PJ enjoyed a technical absolute/near-absolute Chamber majority throughout Menem's first term (1989–1995), two factors acted to reduce this majority slightly to a plurality between 1989 and 1991. First, in a few districts a small number of deputies elected on the PJ list were members of other political parties in alliance with the PJ and thus did

---

[30] Between 1984 and 1993 (i.e., the latter year being when the detailed process described in the previous sections was first used) the budget process was essentially the same as at present in terms of the principal veto gates and agenda setting. The president prepared the budget bill, and then submitted it to Congress. Both houses in Congress needed to approve the budget bill, which was then sent to the president who could sign the bill or veto it in whole or in part. In the event of a veto, the veto would stand unless overridden by a two-thirds vote in both houses. The reversionary outcome was the same as the present (i.e., employ the most recent budget law).

[31] Between Menem's early assumption of power on July 8, 1989 and December 10, 1989 the PJ lacked a plurality and majority of the seats in the Chamber and Senate respectively. However, as part of his deal with the UCR to assume office five months before the scheduled transfer date (due to the extreme crisis facing the nation in mid-1989) Menem received the UCR's commitment to not prevent him from implementing his key policies (Aramouni and Colombo 1992). The seat distribution discussion therefore does not incorporate data from this period.

Table 5.4. *Percentage of Seats Held in the Chamber of Deputies by Party: 1983–1997*

	1983–1985	1985–1987	1987–1989	1989–1991	1991–1993	1993–1995	1995–1997
Political Party							
Partido Justicialista	43.7	40.6	42.9	50.0	50.2	50.2	52.1
Unión Cívica Radical	50.8	51.2	46.1	37.0	33.1	32.7	26.9
UCeDé Center-Right	0.8	1.2	2.8	4.7	4.3	2.0	1.6
Provincial Parties	3.2	4.3	5.9	7.1	9.3	9.3	8.2
Center-Left and Left	1.6	2.8	2.4	1.2	2.0	3.1	9.7
MODIN					1.2	2.7	1.6
TOTAL	100.1	100.1	100.1	100	100.1	100	100
	254 seats	254 seats	254 seats	254 seats	257 seats	257 seats	257 seats
% Held by the largest 3rd party	1.2 PI	2.4 PI	2.8 UCeDé	4.7 UCeDé	4.3 UCeDé	2.7 MODIN	9.7 FREPASO

Percentage of Seats Held in the Senate by Party: 1983–1998

	1983–1986	1986–1989	1989–1992*	1992–1995	1995–1998
Political Party					
Partido Justicialista	45.6	45.6	54.4/54.2	62.5	55.6
Unión Cívica Radical	39.1	39.1	30.4/29.2	22.9	29.2
Center-Right	15.2	15.2	15.2/16.7	14.6	13.9
Center-Left and Left Party					1.4
TOTAL	99.99	99.99	100/100.1	100	100.1
	46 seats	46 seats	46/48 seats	48 seats	72 seats
% Held by largest 3rd party	4.4	4.4	4.4/4.2	4.2	2.8
	3 parties	3 parties	3 parties	2 parties	3 parties

* In 1990 the then national territory of Tierra del Fuego achieved provincial status. The province elected two senators in 1992.

Source: Jones 1997.

not consider themselves subject to PJ party discipline. Second, when Menem began his neoliberal economic program (which differed radically from both his campaign rhetoric and traditional Peronist policy) a few PJ deputies broke with the party (e.g., Grupo de los Ocho) while others who remained often clashed with the president, especially over legislation in the areas of economic and fiscal policy. Thus between 1989 and 1991, the PJ's working majority in the Chamber was much more precarious than that held after 1991. Nevertheless, throughout Menem's tenure in office the PJ contingent remained easily in the plurality, and with the support of the UCeDé and some center-right provincial parties, the PJ legislative bloc was able to provide President Menem in most (although certainly not all) instances with a relatively comfortable working majority in the Chamber.

Throughout Menem's tenure in office the PJ has had an absolute majority in the Senate. This contrasts starkly with the experience of the UCR which possessed neither an absolute majority nor a plurality of the seats in the Senate during the Alfonsín presidency. Between 1983 and 1989 the UCR held only 18 (39%) seats in the Senate. The PJ held 21 (46%) Senate seats, with the remainder divided among 4 minor parties, 3 with 2 seats (Movimiento Popular Neuquino [MPN], Pacto Autonomista Liberal [PAL], and Partido Bloquista [PB]) and 1 with 1 seat (Movimiento de Integración y Desarrollo [MID]).[32] The MID senator was elected with the support of PJ legislators in the province of Formosa and the MPN has historically had close ties with the PJ (Gibson 1996). In a related manner, the UCR's relations with the PB were complicated at times due to the strident opposition expressed by some UCR leaders and rank-and-file members in the province of San Juan (where the PB is based) to any type of special deals with the PB due to its role in the province during the 1976–1983 military dictatorship.[33]

The lack of a UCR Senate majority caused many problems for Alfonsín throughout his administration, and placed serious limitations on his ability to pass legislation (Jones 1994). The small UCR contingent in the

[32] The PAL is treated as a single party. It is an alliance between the Partido Autonomista (PA) and Partido Liberal (PL) in the province of Corrientes, to which smaller parties are often added. Since 1983 the PA and PL have each held one of the PAL's two Senate seats.

[33] It should be remembered that to hold session the Senate requires a quorum of 50% + 1 of its members (24 during the Alfonsín era). Thus, if a unified PJ opposed legislation the only way for the UCR to gain its passage was with the combined support of the MPN, PAL, and PB.

Senate was a product of the malapportionment of the seats of this legislative body discussed previously. The extremely malapportioned nature of the Senate, combined with an uneven distribution of UCR electoral support throughout the country, resulted in a weak UCR Senate contingent that contrasted sharply with the absolute majority of the popular vote won by Alfonsín in the 1983 presidential contest as well as the absolute majority of seats won by the UCR in the 1983 and 1985 Chamber elections (Jones 1995).

Passage of the Budget Law

Every year during the Alfonsín Administration the budget process was characterized by serious gridlock. Budget laws were passed in every year during Alfonsín's tenure. However, this legislative approval always occurred very late in the budget year. The budget laws were thus much more similar to approvals of accounts than actual budgets of spending priorities. While the high levels of inflation during the Alfonsín Administration certainly influenced the budget process, most observers attributed the delays to legislative gridlock, with Alfonsín presenting the budget bill to Congress at a very late date (often during the first of second quarter of the budget year) and the Congress most often delaying the bill once it arrived (Latin American Weekly Report 1984–1988; Economist Intelligence Unit 1989, 1990).[34]

The approval of the budget bill by Congress for the most part merely ratified the execution of the budget (which had been designed and executed by the executive branch via the use of executive decrees) to date. The budgets of the years 1984 through 1988 were on average approved during October (i.e., ten months into the budget year). During this period only one budget was passed prior to the last week of September and one was passed at the end of December.

Of the 67 months during which Alfonsín was president, only in 13 (19%) was the execution of the budget in accord with the budget approved by Congress for that year. During the remaining time period the previous budget law was used as a base by the president with modifications and revisions made through the use of executive decrees. The

---

[34] Of course, this legislative gridlock was in part responsible for Argentina's large budget deficits during the Alfonsín presidency, which in turn helped fuel the extremely high levels of inflation experienced during the mid- to late-1980s (Haggard and Kaufman 1995).

previous figure is in fact generous since it is based upon the date on which Congress approved the budget. Using the more official date of the budget law's publication in the *Boletín Oficial* (a law is not in force until published in the *Boletín Oficial*), only during 9 (13%) of the 67 months was the execution of the budget in accord with the budget approved by Congress for that year. The average budget law was published in the *Boletín Oficial* in November during the Alfonsín presidency.

In addition to causing gridlock, divided government also resulted in a high degree of unilateralism by the president in the area of budget policy. Evidence of this unilateralism is Alfonsín's failure to present a budget bill to Congress in the period specified by law, often presenting the bill late in the first or second quarter of the budget year already in progress.

During the Menem Administration, particularly starting in late 1991 with the assumption of office on December 10, 1991, of the one-half (130) of the Chamber deputies elected earlier that year, one finds a marked contrast to the Alfonsín Administration in regard to the date of the congressional passage of the budget law. Beginning with the 1992 budget all budget laws have been approved by Congress and published in the *Boletín Oficial* in December, prior to the initiation of the budget year. This is a sharp contrast to the budgetary process of the Alfonsín era during which time the average budget law was on average approved only in October and published in the *Boletín Oficial* in November of that budget year.

Faced with the absence of a UCR majority in Congress, President Raúl Alfonsín consistently opted to revert to the previous year's budget, with Congress relegated to the role of merely approving the accounts near the end of the budget year. While this latter approval did provide Congress with an opportunity to influence spending decisions to some extent, the general role of Congress in the budget process was quite limited. During Alfonsín's tenure in office we therefore would not expect a very strong relationship between the proportional contribution of the nation's provinces to the UCR legislative bloc and the proportion of national governmental transfers received by the provinces.[35]

---

[35] This does not imply that Congress did not indirectly influence the budget process by forcing Alfonsín to adapt to the absence of a UCR congressional majority by negotiating with provincial party and PJ legislators. This negotiation may in turn have resulted in these legislators' provinces receiving benefits in exchange for their support for legislation other than the budget. However, a set of analyses (not included for reasons of space and because the variables failed to have a significant

Conversely, during his entire term in office President Carlos Menem possessed a working PJ majority in both houses of Congress, a majority that was especially strong and reliable following the Chamber elections during the Spring (austral) of 1991. The majority PJ contingent in both the Chamber and Senate allowed President Menem to gain the passage of the budget law prior to the initiation of the budget year throughout most of his Administration. Under Menem, we would therefore expect the proportional distribution of the presidential party's legislative bloc in the Chamber of Deputies and Senate to have a much stronger and significant effect on the proportion of transfers received by the provinces than during the Alfonsín Administration. This should be particularly the case starting with the 1992 budget.

Statistical Analysis

To test the above hypotheses I employ (1) data on all federal government transfers to the provinces, (2) data on the composition of the presidential party's legislative bloc in the Chamber of Deputies and in the Senate, and (3) provincial population data.[36] Eleven budget years (1985–1996) are examined. I exclude the budget year of 1984 since the civilian government did not take power until December 10, 1983 and exclude the budget year of 1989 because of the divided control of the executive branch during that year. In the analysis, eleven separate regressions, using an Ordinary Least Squares (OLS) model, are conducted. The units

---

impact on transfers) indicate that neither the percentage of the national legislature comprised by a province's center-right provincial party legislators (the UCR's most likely parliamentary allies) nor whether or not a province had a provincial party governor had a noteworthy impact on the amount of transfers received by the provinces during the Alfonsín Administration. This suggests that the comparatively weak impact of PRESIDENT'S PARTY during the Alfonsín years is the result of the modest level of congressional influence on the budget, and not a consequence of significant budget transfers to select provinces made with the purpose of gaining the support of provincial party legislators for UCR sponsored legislation. The probability of deals between Alfonsín and individual PJ legislators (or more likely PJ *caudillos* from the interior provinces who controlled a small bloc of legislators) having a significant influence on the results is not very high, particularly in light of the weak effect of the provincial party variables.

[36] The federal government transfer and population data were provided by the Centro de Estudios para el Desarrollo Institucional (CEDI). The legislative seat composition data are from the Dirección de Información Parlamentaria of the Argentine Congress.

of analysis for all eleven years are Argentina's twenty-two Argentine provinces.[37]

The dependent variable is the proportion of all federal government transfers received by the twenty-two Argentine provinces (TRANSFERS). These transfers are carried out under a large number of different programs (e.g., fifteen in 1995), including the National Tax-Sharing Agreement (*Ley de Coparticipación Federal*), the National Housing Fund, the National Education Fund, the Fund for the Electrification of the Interior, a fund designed to alleviate poverty in the provincial portion of the Buenos Aires metropolitan region, and pension payments (Sawers 1996; Sanguinetti and Tommasi 1997).

The average Argentine province finances approximately three-quarters of its expenditures with these national transfers (Jones, Sanguinetti, and Tommasi 1998). This TRANSFERS variable is measured as the percentage of the total amount of federal government transfers (in April 1991 pesos; one April 1991 peso equals one April 1991 U.S. dollar) received by the twenty-two provinces during the budget year.[38]

Two independent variables are included in the analysis.[39] The focal independent variable is the proportion of the presidential party legislative bloc (PRESIDENT'S PARTY) provided by the twenty-two provinces during the year preceding the budget year. This variable was calculated as follows. First, every province's proportionate contribution to the presidential party's legislative bloc (i.e., the UCR bloc during the Alfonsín Administration and the PJ bloc during the Menem Administration), excluding legislators from Capital Federal and Tierra del Fuego, was calculated for the Chamber and Senate for the year prior to the budget year

[37] Capital Federal (i.e., the federal capital) and Tierra del Fuego are excluded from the analysis due to the different rules governing transfers for provinces and national territories (Porto and Sanguinetti 1996). For reasons of comparability Tierra del Fuego is also excluded during those years that it held provincial status.

[38] The percentage share of transfers received by the provinces is employed due to the greater ease in interpreting the independent variables' estimated coefficients. The analysis also was conducted using a logistic transformation of the TRANSFERS variable as the dependent variable. The results provided substantively similar results. Between 1985 and 1988 the variable PRESIDENT'S PARTY had no significant effect on the amount of transfers received by the provinces, while beginning in 1990, and particularly in 1992, PRESIDENT'S PARTY had a strong and significant effect on the amount of transfers received.

[39] For a discussion of the very marginal effect of demographic, economic, and fiscal variables on the amount of federal government transfers received by the provinces see Porto and Sanguinetti (1996). An excellent discussion of fiscal federalism in Argentina is Porto (1990).

in question (i.e., for the 1993 budget year the composition of the legislature in 1992 is employed). Next, the percentages contributed by each province in the two houses were summed and then divided by two. This final percentage, the province's proportion of the presidential party legislative bloc (PRESIDENT'S PARTY), is the key independent variable.

A province's population size should have a very strong impact on the amount of federal government transfers it receives (Porto and Sanguinetti 1996). A variable measuring the percentage of the national population, excluding Capital Federal and Tierra del Fuego, accounted for by a province in the year prior to the budget year is therefore included for control purposes. The relationship between this variable and the proportion of federal transfers received by the provinces should not be linear, however, since it is logical to expect that the impact of a province's share of the national population on the proportion of federal government transfers diminishes as the size of the population share increases. A brief review of the partial regression plots provides strong support for the superiority of the use of a logarithmic value for this population size variable. Therefore the logarithmic value is employed in the analysis.

Table 5.5 provides a review of the hypothesized impact of the key independent variable, PRESIDENT'S PARTY, on the proportional distribution of the federal government transfers to the twenty-two provinces

Table 5.5. *The Predicted Impact of President's Party on Transfers*

Budget Year	Presidential Legislative Majority	Budget Passed Prior to Budget Year	Predicted Impact of President's Party
1985	No	No	Weakest
1986	No	No	Weakest
1987	No	No	Weakest
1988	No	No	Weakest
1990	Yes	No	Intermediate
1991	Yes	No	Intermediate
1992	Yes	Yes	Strongest
1993	Yes	Yes	Strongest
1994	Yes	Yes	Strongest
1995	Yes	Yes	Strongest
1996	Yes	Yes	Strongest

between 1985 and 1996. The impact is expected to be weakest in those years where the presidential party lacked a majority in the legislature and where no budget law was approved prior to the initiation of the budget year (1985–1988). The impact is expected to be strongest in those budget years where the presidential party had a legislative majority and passed the budget law prior to the initiation of the budget year (1992–1996). Those years in which the president had a legislative majority, yet where no budget law was passed prior to the start of the budget year (1990–1991), should occupy an intermediate position.

Tables 5.6 and 5.7 provide the results of the statistical analysis. As expected, a province's proportionate contribution to the presidential party's legislative bloc has a positive, and in most cases significant, independent impact on the proportion of federal government transfers received by the province. For example, in the 1995 budget year (see Table 5.7) the PRESIDENT'S PARTY estimated coefficient of 0.819 indicates that a 1% increase in a province's contribution to the presidential party's legislative bloc would, *ceteris paribus*, result in a 0.819% (i.e., slightly more than four-fifths of 1%) increase in the proportion of federal government transfers received by the province. For 1995, this signifies that a 1% increase in a province's contribution to the presidential party bloc would result in a transfer increase of 121 million U.S. dollars (out of a national total, excluding Capital Federal and Tierra del Fuego, of 14.7 billion). However, of principal interest is the variance in

Table 5.6. *Determinants of Federal Government Transfers during the Alfonsín Presidency: 1985–1988*

Independent Variables	Budget Years			
	1985	1986	1987	1988
President's party	0.183[a]	0.219[c]	0.196	0.225
	[0.084]	[0.102]	[0.103]	[0.127]
Population size	1.651[a]	1.686[a]	1.968[a]	1.935[a]
	[0.370]	[0.414]	[0.431]	[0.466]
Constant	2.414[a]	2.181[a]	2.044[a]	1.982[b]
	[0.391]	[0.487]	[0.485]	[0.571]
R-square	.828	.795	.821	.775
N	22	22	22	22

Note: White standard errors are below the estimated coefficients in brackets.
[a] Significant at the .001 level for a two-tailed test.
[b] Significant at the .01 level for a two-tailed test.
[c] Significant at the .05 level for a two-tailed test.

Table 5.7. *Determinants of Federal Government Transfers During Menem Presidency: 1990–1996*

Independent Variables	Budget Years						
	1990	1991	1992	1993	1994	1995	1996
President's party	0.370[c]	0.493[b]	0.599[b]	0.672[a]	0.809[a]	0.819[a]	0.824[a]
	[0.135]	[0.130]	[0.164]	[0.164]	[0.165]	[0.160]	[0.167]
Population size	2.228[a]	2.329[a]	2.697[a]	2.704[a]	2.118[a]	1.863[a]	2.040[a]
	[0.250]	[0.292]	[0.364]	[0.360]	[0.313]	[0.310]	[0.375]
Constant	1.010	0.345	−0.451	−0.802	−0.872	−0.711	−0.690
	[0.748]	[0.685]	[0.862]	[0.858]	[0.759]	[0.730]	[0.743]
R-square	.830	.892	.880	.889	.902	.897	.895
N	22	22	22	22	22	22	22

Note: White standard errors are below the estimated coefficients in brackets.
[a] Significant at the .001 level for a two-tailed test.
[b] Significant at the .01 level for a two-tailed test.
[c] Significant at the .05 level for a two-tailed test.

the size and significance of the PRESIDENT'S PARTY estimated coefficient across the eleven budget years.

During the Alfonsín years (see Table 5.6) the PRESIDENT'S PARTY variable had on average a relatively weak independent impact on the proportion of federal government transfers received by a province. The size of the estimated coefficient ranged from 0.183 to 0.225, and was significant in only 2 of the 4 years (and even in those 2 only at the .05 level).

Conversely, the PRESIDENT'S PARTY variable had a significant effect on the proportion of the transfers received by the provinces during all seven of the Menem years (see Table 5.7).[40] The size of the variable's estimated coefficient as well as the significance of its impact was relatively modest for the 1990 budget year. The size of the PRESIDENT'S PARTY estimated coefficient increased steadily in the following years, paralleling both the increasing size and reliability (as the 1987 PJ cohort in the Chamber was replaced and the prominence of the 1989 PJ cohort diminished) of the PJ bloc in the legislature as well as (starting with the 1992 budget) the passage of the budget in the constitutionally mandated period (i.e., prior to the start of the budget year).

The variance over time in the size of the PRESIDENT'S PARTY

---

[40] This variable is capturing not just the effect of PRESIDENT'S PARTY on those transfers directly affected by the budget, but also the effect of the province's proportionate contribution to the presidential party bloc on all transfers.

variable's estimated coefficient is demonstrated quite clearly in Figure 5.1. During the Alfonsín years the coefficient was rather small, reflecting in part the comparatively modest role played by Congress in the budget process. Under Alfonsín the average size of the PRESIDENT'S PARTY variable's estimated coefficient was a mere 0.206 (the average standard error was 0.104). During the Menem Administration, particularly starting with the 1992 budget year, the PRESIDENT'S PARTY variable's estimated coefficient steadily increased in size.

Since the 1992 budget the executive branch has achieved the passage

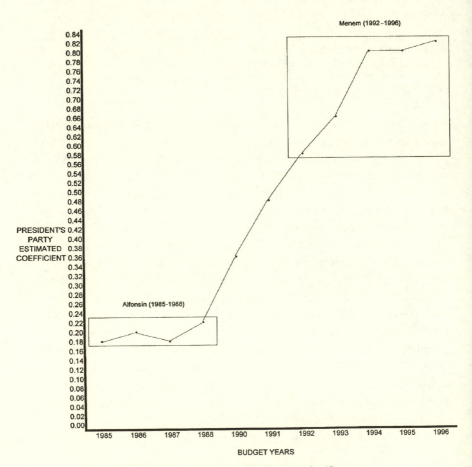

Note: For more information on the estimated coefficients see Tables 6 and 7.

Figure 5.1.   Changes in the Size of the President's Party Variable's Estimated Coefficient Between 1985 and 1996

of the budget in the constitutionally mandated period, but to do so it has had to take into account the wishes of Congress in drafting the budget to a much greater extent than was the case in those years in which the executive branch employed the previous year's budget (i.e., the reversionary option). During the five most recent budget years (i.e., 1992–1996), the average size of the PRESIDENT'S PARTY variable's estimated coefficient was 0.745. The estimated coefficient for this period is thus seven times greater than the average standard error for the PRESIDENT'S PARTY variable during the Alfonsín era. The difference in the size of the PRESIDENT'S PARTY variable's impact during the two time periods is very significant.

This analysis provides some initial support for the assertions in the previous sections of this chapter that during recent years Congress has had a significant impact on the Argentine budget. Since 1992 the budget process has been a relatively smooth affair. One explanation of this lack of conflict could be that Congress is a rubber stamp of the executive branch's wishes, and is thus a relatively ineffectual check on the president (i.e., the Delegative Democracy perspective). However, the findings presented here provide an alternative view of the Argentine budget process. Under this view, PJ legislators (both alone and in concert with their provincial copartisans) influence the composition of the budget during the draft stages, employing their proportional "weight" within the governing party coalition to extract benefits for their provinces. As noted previously, however, these deals are struck prior to the submission of the budget bill to Congress. Once the budget bill reaches Congress, the process is relatively conflict-free since in most (although not all) instances, PJ legislators' interests have been satisfied. The PJ then uses its legislative majority to pass the budget on time with the least amount of controversy possible.

Throughout his tenure in office, President Menem has had to take into account the wishes of PJ legislators in order to achieve the timely passage of the budget. This conclusion is contrary to the portrayal of Menem as an omnipotent leader ruling principally via decrees (*decretismo*) and of Congress as an inconsequential institution. This study suggests that the most important annual piece of legislation enacted during the Menem Administration was notably affected by the Argentine Congress.

CONCLUSION

This chapter has emphasized the prominent role played by political institutions in Argentina. Analysis of the Argentine budget process provides an excellent example of one of the many ways in which political institutions "matter" in Argentina.

The impressive theoretical arguments presented in Chapters 2–3 would lead us to expect Argentina's institutional rules to have an important impact on the country's policy process. Such a hypothesis is contrary to most recent scholarship on Argentine politics, which has consistently downplayed the influence of institutional structures in Argentina. Yet, the findings of this chapter provide strong support for the relevance of political institutions in Argentina. The correspondence between the theories articulated in Chapters 2–3 and this chapter's empirical findings increase our confidence in the global generalizability of these theories while at the same time raising some doubts regarding the accuracy of scholarship that discounts the importance of Argentina's political institutions.

6

Democracy and Deficits in Taiwan

The Politics of Fiscal Policy 1986–1996

TUN-JEN CHENG and STEPHAN HAGGARD[1]

Taiwan has long been noted for its conservative fiscal policy. For the three decades prior to 1990, tight fiscal policy typically yielded surpluses, and the country enjoyed one of the lowest debt/GDP ratios of any country in the world, developed or developing. Both orthodox interpretations of Taiwan's rapid growth that stress the role of market-oriented policies (Lundberg 1979) and their heterodox detractors who emphasize the positive role of state intervention (Wade 1990) have given substantial credit to the country's stable macroeconomic environment. Fiscal policy in Taiwan contributed to low and stable inflation, and it allowed the country to pursue an export-oriented exchange rate policy.

The gradual introduction of electoral reform beginning in the mid-1980s coincided with fundamental changes in Taiwan's fiscal policy. First, deficits began to emerge, with a concomitant growth of government debt (Table 6.1). From 1980 to 1988, the central government either enjoyed surpluses or else ran small deficits; only twice did the deficit exceed 1% of GNP. In 1989, spending surged and the deficit ballooned to more than 7% of GNP. Between 1989 and 1995, deficits averaged 4.5% of GNP. Regarding revenues, slower economic growth (which fell from 10% per annum in the early 1960s to 6–7% per annum in the mid-1980s), economic liberalization (which decreased government income from customs and monopoly sales), and tax cuts all reduced government revenue (Council on Economic Planning and Development [CEPD] 1993). But as Table 6.1 shows, revenue growth remained robust; it was simply outstripped by real spending growth.

[1] Our thanks to Greg Noble, Mathew McCubbins, Michael Munger, Matthew Shugart, and participants in a conference on Democratic Institutions in East Asia at Duke University for comments on earlier drafts. Chao-cheng Chen and Tonia Pizer provided excellent research assistance.

Table 6.1. *Fiscal Policy in Taiwan: 1980–1995*

	Budget Surplus GNP (%)	Central Government Spending GNP (%)	Real Revenue Growth (% change)	Real Expenditure Growth (% change)
1980	0.02	15.12	3.53	15.9
1981	−0.79	16.67	3.9	7.6
1982	−1.73	16.89	7.17	11.1
1983	−1.37	16.08	0.21	−0.9
1984	0.41	14.08	11.74	3.4
1985	−0.15	14.45	5.38	8.1
1986	−1.09	15.14	7.03	12.1
1987	0.03	13.36	10.62	3.6
1988	0.11	13.66	16.21	11.7
1989	−7.2	14.45	15.32	59.2
1990	−0.12	15.93	13.87	−12.7
1991	−4.67	17.35	−7.23	12.2
1992	−5.59	16.2	14.62	17.2
1993	−5.69	18.07	9.45	9.3
1994	−5.01	16.51	1.92	−0.1
1995	−3.21	14.86	−9.01	−13.4

Source: Compiled from Republic of China, Council on Economic Development and Planning, *Taiwan Statistical Data Book*, various years.

The *composition* of spending also changed during these years. Table 6.2 captures the major shifts. Increased government borrowing contributed to a rise of debt service, but the more striking change was the decline in defense spending. The military was at the core of the ruling Kuomintang's base of support and had long absorbed a large share of the budget. Yet beginning in 1991, the military's share of central government spending began to drop; by 1995, it was nearly 30% less than in 1990. The shifts in other categories seem less pronounced, but when placed in the context of the rapid growth of total government spending, they become more striking. Table 6.3 provides a detailed breakdown of governmental spending by functional category. Among the items experiencing particularly high growth are both broad programmatic initiatives, such as welfare spending and the environment, as well as classic pork-barrel spending on public works, such as transportation.

What accounts for these changes in fiscal policy? The null hypothesis is that the correlation between political and policy change is coinciden-

Table 6.2. *Central Government Expenditures: Shares by Broad Category (%)*

	1987	1988	1989	1990	1991	1992	1993	1994	1995
1. General administration	7.49	7.34	8.37	8.88	9.25	11.26	9.56	9.22	9.22
2. National defense	35.52	33.61	34.21	31.60	28.23	25.33	24.59	23.67	23.67
3. Education, science, and culture	13.22	12.82	13.79	14.53	14.98	15.63	15.22	15.48	15.48
4. Economic development	20.87	18.18	16.58	15.99	18.52	18.61	18.15	16.79	16.79
5. Social security	15.59	19.34	18.24	10.13	10.04	8.95	8.71	8.89	8.89
6. Community development and environment protection						1.96	2.57	2.85	2.85
7. Retirement pension				9.24	8.70	8.98	8.59	9.11	9.11
8. Debt service	4.10	4.92	5.53	6.72	6.49	5.55	8.95	10.42	10.42
9. Subsidies	1.91	2.60	2.23	2.14	3.25	3.23	3.22	3.12	3.12
10. Other	1.31	1.19	1.04	0.77	0.55	0.49	0.46	0.44	0.44
TOTAL	100.00	100.00	100.00	100.00	100.00	100.00	100.00	100.00	100.00

Source: Compiled from Republic of China, Executive Yuen. "Chung-yang chen-fu tsong yu-suan-an" [Central Government Budget Bills]. Taipei, various issues.

Table 6.3. *Central Government Budget Bill: Expenditures by Functional Category (% change from previous year)*

	FY1987	FY1988	FY1989	FY1990	FY1991	FY1992	FY1993	FY1994	FY1995	FY1996	FY1997
General administration	7.50	10.74	75.87	23.98	36.17	39.86	-3.94	5.49	-13.27	12.60	1.19
National assembly	-0.18	5.24	8.87	37.18	-12.25	-31.80	-78.84	238.16	-4.69	44.43	-3.81
State affairs (e.g., Office of the President)	3.35	6.31	9.23	12.08	17.37	-1.05	-0.28	10.71	3.20	-1.76	4.88
Executive yuan	2.20	11.00	6.62	14.64	40.74	30.01	4.72	-4.20	-52.35	-16.58	12.66
Legislative yuan	-0.23	13.44	14.38	13.35	28.89	17.44	47.75	568.70	-83.15	7.46	15.69
Judicial yuan	0.46	16.26	33.55	12.23	51.29	32.30	12.06	-7.73	-11.01	8.65	1.97
Examination yuan	-17.35	5.56	74.58	10.79	-16.29	32.67	53.11	-15.91	-9.02	20.93	11.22
Control yuan	6.18	12.63	30.41	6.95	47.33	9.85	-0.56	-12.75	-0.71	5.26	14.98
Civil affairs (e.g., elections)	33.06	0.34	163.49	69.44	35.12	95.52	-29.10	-0.43	12.64	26.99	-4.66
Fiscal affairs	20.74	8.61	83.94	20.39	34.22	20.74	15.34	-12.35	-4.10	1.53	4.34
Minority affairs	-6.19	17.27	34.25	12.15	58.69	1.93	7.22	7.47	22.84	3.59	-10.25
Overseas Chinese affairs	-18.33	14.13	10.49	39.29	14.29	10.90	5.55	-41.01	2.03	8.80	-17.88
Trust fund management	9.01	14.93									
Defense and foreign relations											
Defense and foreign affairs (1987–1988)	-0.58	9.72									
Defense (1989–)				11.25	9.64	6.87	4.50	-3.00	-4.30	2.12	3.29
Foreign relations (1989–)				3.95	34.15	12.06	-1.27	12.85	-5.08	10.86	5.79
Education, science, and cultural affairs	6.37	14.50	24.74	35.28	21.28	19.23	8.67	1.92	-4.00	6.13	6.19
Education	9.76	15.28	17.44	43.75	28.18	34.57	11.65	2.09	-1.88	2.51	4.88
Scientific research	2.61	13.58	18.92	22.89	13.83	-3.62	-1.17	-0.63	-4.19	15.15	4.14
Cultural activities	3.80	13.40	492.10	48.72	8.94	10.12	23.54	10.38	-22.30	8.61	29.55
Economic development and transportation/communication (1987–1988)	9.64	-3.29									

Economic construction	11.18	37.03								
Transportation	-2.18	22.27								
Trust management	18.29	3.38								
Compensatory and reparation outlays	-42.93	-90.26								
State owned enterprise fund and capital investment	23.20	-23.54								
Economic development (1989–)			26.38	23.56	18.05	6.55	0.24	671.84	-90.56	-11.47
Agricultural expenditures			20.48	48.19	17.59	11.91	7.28	0.30	-2.73	-2.54
Industrial expenditures			-8.45	-4.46	102.75	2.06	-4.06	-54.59	-17.07	-63.41
Transportation/communication expenditures			27.01	81.28	-3.15	4.52	-4.08	-32.87	-3.87	-16.52
Other expenses for economic services			63.52	-52.40	31.02	8.46	4.41	-4.52	-8.98	6.54
Social welfare (1987–1988)	6.67	18.98								
Social relief	4.25	20.53								
Pension and insurance outlays for public employees	9.31	17.66								
Health expenses	-18.34	31.44								
Social security (1989–1993)/Social welfare (1994–)			25.02	24.63	-31.58	9.86	-16.96	43.88	1.30	10.70
Social insurance			21.83	28.81	-69.09	11.38	-1.51	133.51	-6.86	-1.48
Social relief			81.83	40.31	58.80	-58.76	101.68	48.31	140.46	-18.35
Welfare services			47.06	18.16	12.08	8.42	11.40	1.06	-6.01	44.93
Employment			15.89	38.17	-14.84	12.64	30.61	-16.26	47.68	12.85
Public housing and community development			638.44	100.37	53.67	18.43				
Health and medical services			-28.28	24.46	35.15	-2.76	-4.12	-23.00	-18.99	-13.56
Environmental protection			26.99	-13.48	57.45	50.48				

(continued)

Table 6.3 *(continued)*

	FY1987	FY1988	FY1989	FY1990	FY1991	FY1992	FY1993	FY1994	FY1995	FY1996	FY1997
Community development and environmental protection (1994–)									−18.30	2.33	−26.75
Environmental protection								2.57	−33.52	49.55	−16.20
Community development							39.95	7.31	−46.88	−57.68	
Retirement and annuities (1992–)							2.33	3.62	1.88	15.17	29.66
Pension outlays							2.33	3.61	1.88	15.04	29.70
Administrative expenses							−11.85	21.60	2.47	239.35	2.65
Debt financing	42.93	33.88	31.20	58.96	14.92	−0.66	81.64	9.86	−14.23	56.73	10.62
Principal payments	39.31	41.28	29.55	64.00	25.94	−17.07	39.86	−2.23	−39.74	158.78	25.20
Interest payments	50.89	18.73	34.94	47.09	−13.89	61.45	163.53	22.62	6.89	9.30	−5.46
Administrative expenses	60.88	22.22	7.26	−71.34	1134.11	58.75	96.33	−12.70	−1.27	−17.46	−16.01
Subsidies to provincial and municipality governments (1987–1988)	−14.24	33.59									
Subsidies (1989–)				6.78	113.04	16.94	8.77	−3.80	−7.83	−0.62	28.15
Project grants				19.70	43.42	−9.41	−6.79	12.59	−18.64	1.83	−20.86
Budget balancing fund				−51.77	896.50	59.61	23.07	−15.21	2.39	−2.65	65.26
Other expenditures	5.24	7.28	83.50	8.01	12.22	17.57	1.61	−20.25	−3.32	−11.48	3.45
Other expenses	3.67	4.78	212.08	−7.79	757.04	−89.53	4.91	−1.22	−7.91	−28.71	19.76
Second reserve fund	6.06	985.71	−88.05	26.34	39.46	25.00	0.00	−30.00	0.00	0.00	−4.29
TOTAL	4.73	14.96	14.43	23.12	21.00	17.17	9.47	2.00	−5.05	8.55	6.16

Source: Compiled from Republic of China, Executive Yuan. "Chung-yang cheng-fu tsong yu-suan-an" [Central Government Budget Bills]. Taipei, various issues.

tal, and other factors bear primary responsibility for the change in fiscal stance. Given the collapse of the Soviet Union, one possible explanation is that Taiwan is enjoying a peace dividend similar to that in the United States. Yet, Taiwan's growing economic dependence on the mainland, uncertainty surrounding China's absorption of Hong Kong, and the threatening actions taken by Beijing prior to the 1996 presidential elections all suggest that the external environment remains equally if not more dangerous than in the past. There is certainly no improvement in Taiwan's security setting that would warrant such a dramatic shift in spending.

A second cluster of explanations focuses on economic factors rather than security factors. As Taiwan's extraordinary growth rates moderated somewhat during the 1980s, the government might have turned to a countercyclical fiscal policy stance. However, Taiwan had experienced much more substantial shocks in the past than it did in the 1980s – particularly at the time of the two oil shocks – and the government had explicitly eschewed countercyclical fiscal policy. Moreover, Taiwan's growth remained quite robust through the 1990s and there seemed little macroeconomic justification for larger deficits. Perhaps a more credible economic explanation is demographic. As the Taiwanese population increases in age and wealth, it is demanding more public goods, including additional spending on social welfare, infrastructure, and the environment (Cheng and Schive 1996; CEPD 1996). Yet even if these demographic factors are operating, they are clearly mediated by the institutional changes associated with democratization and electoral reform.

To trace the political influences on budgeting, it is important to distinguish between three phases of the transition to democratic rule. During the initial phase (1979–1986), the KMT tolerated informal opposition activity, but there was no fundamental change in political institutions or in the political rights extended to the opposition. The system remained constitutionally authoritarian with a strong unity of both powers and purpose. Our analysis begins with the transitional phase (1986–1991). The KMT government legalized opposition activity, but political institutions continued to be authoritarian in important respects. Not all legislative seats were fully contested and the president retained a number of extraordinary powers, both through the constitution and through his role as party chairman.

Yet, despite these apparent signs of executive dominance, several factors served to motivate the executive to appease legislators during the transition phase. Increasing competitiveness of the political system, the growing strength of opposition parties, and the entry of new political forces provided strong incentives for the ruling party to accommodate the budgetary interests of KMT legislators. During this period, there is an increasing separation of purpose between the executive and legislature. Given this division, we expect the composition of spending to shift, at the margin, away from the interests that had been pivotal to the KMT's reign during the authoritarian period and toward those interests that had either been taken for granted by the KMT (e.g., farmers) or underrepresented in the political system altogether (e.g., both business and labor).

A series of fundamental institutional reforms occurred in 1991–1992 (Tien 1996) that not only accelerated the division of purpose but also began a process of separating powers in a way characteristic of most presidential systems. President Chiang Ching-kuo lifted martial law in July 1987.[2] He died in January 1988, and his vice-president, Lee Teng-hui, was sworn in as president; he quickly lifted martial law. In March 1990, Lee was elected president by the KMT-dominated National Assembly under the constitution's indirect electoral procedures. Lee accelerated the process of institutional change by repealing the Temporary Provisions (1991), initiating constitutional revision (through the National Assembly, 1991–1992), undertaking internal reforms of the KMT, and, most significantly for our purposes, allowing the first direct and fully open election for all seats of both the National Assembly (December 1991) and the Legislative Yuan (December 1992). The KMT did not yield on the issue of the direct election of the president until 1995; thus, prior to Lee's reelection in March 1996 – when we close our account – the system was arguably still not fully democratic. Nonetheless, the direct election of the Legislative Yuan fundamentally changed the electoral context, not only for KMT legislators and aspirants for office but also for the president.

The institutional changes of the early 1990s lead us to make two sets of predictions, one focusing on the level and composition of spending and the other focusing directly on the budgetary institutions themselves. First, we expect the full election of the legislature under SNTV electoral rules to increase the incentives for spending of all sorts, but particularly

---

[2] That decision was quickly ratified by a unanimous vote of the KMT Central Standing Committee and five months later by Lee's formal election to the chairmanship of the KMT by the Thirteenth Party Congress, showing that the party was committed to observing constitutional procedure in this crucial element of the transition.

of the pork-barrel variety that is the hallmark of such an electoral system (Cox and McCubbins, ch. 2; Shugart and Haggard, ch. 3). Second, we expect the election of the legislature to lead to efforts on the part of legislators to reorganize the budget process with the goal of making it more directly responsive to their interests; we expect this reorganization to produce both a greater division of power as well as a greater division of purpose.

These expectations are confirmed in a number of important respects. There is clear evidence that the party leadership was responsive to changes in the competitiveness of the political system, even prior to full democratization. Deficits began to emerge in 1989, well before the constitutional changes of 1991–1992, but they were very likely implemented in anticipation of pending electoral reform. Changes in the composition of spending reflected a relative decline in the weight of those political forces at the core of the "old" KMT, particularly the military, and a rise of spending in categories that are of special electoral interest to the "new" KMT, particularly the urban middle classes, farmers, and Taiwanese business.

Although we see broad programmatic initiatives coming from the executive, the composition of spending also reflected the increasing separation of purpose arising from electoral rules and intraparty factionalism. The political logic of a single nontransferable vote (SNTV) system intensified intraparty competition and generated a struggle for campaign contributions. The electoral system contributed to the rise of money politics and the use of pork-barrel spending for political ends; construction and public works spending soared, particularly during 1988–1991. Both broader social cleavages and SNTV also contributed to a decrease in party cohesion and the exacerbation of factional conflicts *within* the ruling party. We show that these were yet another source of increased government spending, particularly during 1991–1993 when the president and premier were from contending factions within the KMT. Furthermore, we find that deficits were addressed only when this factional conflict was muted after 1993; the departure of many of the "nonmainstream" factions from the KMT and the formation of the New Party produced a new unity of purpose *within* the party and government.

Finally, we find clear evidence both of a reassertion of legislative prerogatives and of institutional changes in the budget process that reflected the gradual emergence of a separation of powers. To the extent that legislators faced collective action problems associated with the intraparty competition that SNTV fosters, we find evidence that they sought to solve those problems by empowering party leaders within the legislature (Kiewiet and McCubbins 1991; Cox and McCubbins 1993). Legislators have not fully succeeded in institutionalizing all of the changes they seek; nonetheless, the nature of those reforms provides unambiguous evidence of preferences that match our expectations.

To demonstrate these arguments, we begin with an outline of the institutional framework, beginning with the powers of the president before turning to the party and the electoral system. In the following two sections, we undertake an exercise in comparative statics, comparing the effects of political institutions before (pre-1986), during (1986–1991), and after (1992–1996) the transition to democratic rule. We focus on how the incentives of the president and legislators with respect to the budget are changed by increasing political competition, SNTV, and the rise of intraparty factionalism. We then examine some data on the composition of spending during the period and study the negotiation process associated with several particular budgets. Before concluding, we also show how changes in policies are matched by a reassertion of legislative prerogatives in the budgeting process and the emergence of a separation of powers.

PRESIDENTIALISM IN TAIWAN

Taiwan's democratic transition was controlled by the incumbent authoritarian leadership (Cheng and Haggard 1992; Leng and Lin 1993; Moody 1992; Haggard and Kaufman 1995, ch. 8; Huong 1995); consequently, the transition process unfolded rather slowly. Important constitutional changes were initiated not by newly elected governments, as in Argentina, Brazil, the Philippines, and Poland, but by an incumbent executive and ruling party initially shielded from direct electoral competition. The president naturally had a strong interest in limiting any reduction of his powers, and was able to constrain the growing separation of purpose that resulted from electoral reform and a more competitive political system.

On the surface, Taiwan's constitution is characteristic of a premier-presidential or mixed system. Prior to 1996, the president was elected indirectly by the National Assembly. The president, in turn, appointed a premier. Formally, the president's role was to act as an arbiter and coordinator of the country's complicated five branch (*yuan*) structure.[3] The premier ran the government, appointed the cabinet, and was formally accountable to the Legislative Yuan.

In fact, the Taiwanese system was presidential. The president had no power to dissolve the Legislative Yuan and the legislature had no way of holding the cabinet directly accountable. The premier could refer a bill back to the legislature for reconsideration; but, if the legislature passed it with a two-thirds vote, the premier was required to accept the bill or resign. The premier, however, was not forced to resign on a vote of no-confidence; thus, there was no way for the legislature to replace the executive.

The power of the president to appoint the premier and the inability of the legislature to remove him is sufficient to define the system as presidential.[4] But a number of "metaconstitutional" powers made the president's influence greater than his formal constitutional authority would suggest. At the outset of the transition, the control the president exercised with respect to the electoral chances and career paths of both legislators and other politicians called into question the very separation of powers and purpose that is the hallmark of most presidential systems. Yet, even after the transition to more democratic rule, the president remained incredibly powerful; indeed, as chairman of the ruling party, his authority was augmented.[5] As political competition both outside and

---

[3] See Article 44 on the Constitution.

[4] Both the opposition and minority factions within the ruling party favored revising the Constitution in a parliamentary direction during the constitutional reform of 1991–1992. Such reforms would expand the power of the legislature and guarantee wider representation in the cabinet. Not only were these reforms defeated by the party hierarchy, but the president even *enhanced* his already substantial appointment powers by eliminating a previous provision that required the premier to cosign a number of executive appointments. The president nominates, and with the consent of National Assembly appoints, the president and members of the Control Yuan and Examination Yuan; as we will see below, the checks in National Assembly consent are attenuated precisely by presidential control over those appointments. The president also appoints the grand justices of the Judiciary Yuan; though they have a tenure of ten years, other members of the judiciary can be sacked by the president at any time.

[5] As commander-in-chief, the president also controlled the military hierarchy, and continues to do so (Constitution, Article 36). He thus makes decisions on promotion and demotion of generals; these decisions do not require ratification by any other branch of government. An important component of the president's martial law powers was the centralization of de facto decision making in a National Security Council directly under his control.

inside the party increased, however, it became increasingly clear that the apparent strength of the executive *ultimately rested on the capacity of the party to maintain ruling majorities in the National Assembly and particularly in the Legislative Yuan.* After 1992 that capacity was increasingly in doubt.

To understand the strength of the presidency during the transition requires some understanding of the hierarchical structure of the KMT (Tien 1989; Huang 1996). The Central Standing Committee (CSC) is the governing body of the KMT; it is elected every year by the Central Committee, which in turn is formally accountable to the larger Party Congress; the Congress meets every four years and elects the chairman. However, as in Communist systems of "reciprocal accountability" (Shirk 1993), the party leadership plays a large role in controlling who participates in the Party Congress. The CSC has thirty-one members, fifteen of whom are appointed by the president in his capacity as party chairman. The remaining sixteen are elected from among and by members of the Central Committee, but the president exercises a powerful influence even over these elected slots.[6] Thus, the president appoints all major party leadership positions and effectively controls the composition of the CSC.

The party leadership, in turn, exercises strong control over nominations and appointments, beginning with the lists of endorsed candidates for both legislative and subnational elections. Lists are prepared by a nomination committee whose members are appointed by the party chairman, though the means of actually compiling the lists have changed over time (Lin 1987).[7] With the rise of independent opposition candidates after 1980, the provincial KMT branch began to recommend the lists based in part on informal opinion inquiries and in part on somewhat

---

[6] The president (again, in his capacity of chairman of the party) nominates one list for these elected posts. The second list is composed by delegates of the party Congress, typically in contending factions, though they, like the president, must accommodate the balance of forces within the party leadership as a whole. Following a rule adopted in the Thirteenth Congress in 1988, delegates cast a bloc vote for the two lists, with the number of candidates nominated on each list exactly equal to the number of open seats; in effect, election was under a closed-list procedure. Only with the Fourteenth Congress in 1993 were Central Committee members granted greater leeway in voting for individual candidates.

[7] Given that Taiwan's is an SNTV system, these lists are of course not closed, and are best thought of as party endorsements. For the supplementary elections of 1969, 1972, and 1975, the provincial KMT branch solicited opinions from party members, assessed the findings, and submitted them to party headquarters which would then draw a list for the party chair to ratify.

more systematic straw polls of party cadres (Huang 1996). In 1989, prior to the first legislative election following the formation of recognized opposition parties, the KMT held a closed primary (Robinson and Baum 1993).[8]

Had primaries become the principal means of nomination, the party leadership's control over legislators would have been greatly compromised, although the party could still have limited or preselected candidates for the primary. However, neither the party leadership nor all KMT legislators saw the primary system as desirable, and after 1992 its weight in candidate selection was reduced.[9] The party leadership returned to giving preference to those who performed well on internal evaluations, including such factors as whether incumbents had been cooperative with the party whip in the Legislative Yuan.

In addition to the lists compiled for district elections, there are thirty at-large seats allotted to political parties in proportion to their share of the total vote; six additional seats are reserved for Chinese living overseas. These closed-list PR seats further enhance party discipline by providing an additional way for the party leadership to reward the faithful and compensate those who do not receive nominations for district seats.

The president's powers extend de facto to the appointment of the cabinet. In premier-presidential systems, the premier chooses the cabinet in consultation with party leaders in the legislature, to whom they are ultimately accountable. In Taiwan, it is the president who appoints the premier, and the Central Standing Committee – not the party's legislative leadership – ultimately approves cabinet changes.[10] As a result, the president effectively exercises appointment power down to the rank of deputy ministers.

A final source of presidential power is the control that is exercised as

---

[8] Elections were also held for provincial assembly, city councillors, country magistrates, and mayors.

[9] Turnout rates in primaries were very low and candidates from some districts (such as urban constituencies with a high concentration of civil and military service, intellectuals, and mainlanders) were better able to mobilize their supporters than candidates in others (such as those from rural constituencies or urban constituencies with a high concentration of businesspeople, self-employed, and workers). Thus the primary did not really identify the most electable candidates, and in fact disproportionately represented the "nonmainstream" faction; we return to this below.

[10] Taiwan's system does permit a somewhat different form of "cohabitation" than the French system; it is possible that the president could be forced for larger political reasons to appoint a premier who is not from the president's faction; this happened when Hau, of the nonmainstream faction, was premier from March 1991 to February 1993; we return to the issue of factionalism below.

party chairman over appointments to managerial positions in KMT-owned enterprises (KOEs). In total, KOE assets would place it equal to the sixth largest conglomerate in Taiwan; the KMT is undoubtedly one of the richest political parties on earth (Liáng 1995). As in the Japanese system of *amakudari,* control over these positions is used like a bond; the leadership can reward legislators for faithful service or provide "parking spaces" for those who lose election or reelection bids until they can reenter the electoral game.

THE ELECTORAL SYSTEM AND PARTIES

Although the powers of the president are significant, his or her behavior is ultimately a function of the wider political and electoral setting in which he or she operates and of the separation of purpose between himself or herself and legislators. We distinguish between three factors that are germane in this regard: the increase in political competition and the entry of new forces into the political system; the design of the institutions through which electoral competition occurred, namely the SNTV system; and, the declining cohesion of the ruling party and the intensification of intraparty factionalism. As we will see, these three factors are closely related and have mutually reinforcing effects.

Increasing Political Competition

To gauge the effect of increased party competition, it is important to understand the role of elections under the authoritarian status quo ante. Provincial, county, city, and township elections have been a regular feature of Taiwan's politics since 1950, but opposition parties were banned and efforts to create them repressed. At the national level, the KMT held guaranteed majorities in the National Assembly and Legislative Yuan; these majorities were partially manufactured by the seating of legislators who were elected in 1947 under the pretense of representing mainland districts. These senior legislators began to die in the 1960s, necessitating a series of "supplemental" elections to fill vacant seats (in 1969, 1972, 1975, 1980, 1983, 1986, and 1989). The final removal of the aging legislators was a matter of some delicacy for the party,[11] but

---

[11] A voluntary plan for their retirement proved unsuccessful in 1988, and in 1990 – undoubtedly with the nod of the party leadership – the Council of Grand Justices decided that the "senior parliamentarians" should be terminated.

the decision to retire them in 1990 set the stage for the first fully competitive elections for the Legislative Yuan.[12]

The ban on opposition parties and the tight central control over nominations combined to eliminate electoral surprises. However, the KMT did cultivate an electoral base in the state sector – particularly the military, civil service, and public school teachers – and in the rural areas, where the land reform of the early 1950s had been popular. The "iron votes" of the military proved particularly useful in solving the vote division problem under SNTV; we return to this problem in more detail below. In the countryside, the KMT forged alliances with the leaders of local factions and clientele networks and played a coordinating role. The party fostered agreements among local factions that prevented them from engaging in "excessive" competition; if necessary, the party also exercised discipline over defectors (Lin 1987; Rigger 1993; Chen 1995; Dickson 1996). Because of the control exercised by local party and factional leaders, the KMT could not only count on votes from rural households, they could also count on these votes being targeted to specific candidates, again helping to solve the vote division problem.

After 1977, the electoral system became more competitive, although KMT candidates faced no officially recognized political opposition until the supplemental elections of 1989. In the provincial and local elections of 1977, individual dissidents joined with several prominent KMT liberals to form a loosely organized opposition camp, subsequently known as the *dangwai* (literally translated as "outside the party"). In June 1986, Chiang Ching-kuo signaled his willingness to initiate political reform and begin indirect negotiations with the opposition.[13] When these negotiations broke down, a group of opposition leaders announced the formation of the Democratic Progressive Party (DPP). The government chose not to suppress the new illegal entity, lifted the ban on political associations, and the DPP was retroactively legalized.

The DPP proved surprisingly effective in overcoming its own internal divisions while the KMT became increasingly split. Electoral data in Table 6.4 show an unmistakable erosion of voter support for the KMT after 1986. Following setbacks in the December 1992 Legislative Yuan

---

[12] The first fully competitive elections for the Legislative Yuan occurred in 1992.

[13] Chiang called for the creation of a blue-ribbon committee to review political reform. Virtually all issues were placed on the table: a restructuring of the National Assembly; local autonomy; martial law; civic organizations; social reform; and further reforms of the party itself.

Table 6.4. *National-level Election Results: 1986–1996*

		KMT Share	
Date	Offices Contested	Popular Vote	Seats
1986	National assembly, supplemental	68.3	81.0
	Legislative yuan, supplemental	69.9	80.8
1989	Legislative yuan, supplemental	60.1	71.3
1991	National assembly	71.2	78.1
1992	Legislative yuan	53.0	59.6
1995	Legislative yuan	46.1	51.8
1996	President	54.0	

Source: Central Electoral Commission.

elections, the party showed its continued dominance in the local elections held in December of 1993. But the legislative elections of 1995 provided a rude shock – were it not for electoral rules that transformed KMT's vote plurality into a legislative majority, the KMT would have lost control of the legislature in the mid-1990s.

Taiwan's Electoral Laws: SNTV in a Presidential System

The incentives associated with the country's single nontransferable vote system were critical in fostering new parties. As we have seen (Cox and McCubbins, ch. 2), SNTV is a candidate-centered system par excellence. Many legislators are elected from a single district, but each voter can cast only one vote; moreover, the votes a candidate obtains cannot be transferred to other candidates of the same party. Under an SNTV system, any political party that has the potential to win more than two seats from a district faces a vote-division problem; in any particular district, parties may run too many or too few candidates and may fail to equalize the votes among their nominees efficiently.[14]

This issue, however, is less significant for our purposes than the politician's "product differentiation" problem. Given intraparty competition, politicians must devise a strategy to distinguish themselves from other candidates of their own party who seek election in the same district.

---

[14] There has been a substantial debate over whether large versus small parties, or ruling versus opposition parties are more prone to such errors (see Cox and Rosenbluth 1993; Cox and Niou 1994; Cox 1995).

This intraparty competition gives rise to a particularly egregious separation of purpose. Numerous studies have demonstrated how parties use pork, particularly public construction projects, to assist individual candidates in cementing personal support bases and securing campaign contributions (Curtis 1988, 67, 70, 184; Inoguchi 1990; Ramseyer and Rosenbluth 1993; Fukui and Fukai 1996, 180–84; Woodall 1996).

There are two further features of Taiwan's constitution and electoral laws that are likely to exacerbate the incentives for legislators to pursue pork. First, unlike Japan, Taiwan is a presidential system (Cox and Rosenbluth 1993; McCubbins and Noble 1995; Shugart and Haggard, ch. 3). In a parliamentary system such as Japan, the party leadership holds an important and credible threat over backbenchers; if their demands threaten the reputation of the government as a whole, the party risks losing elections. In a presidential system, however, the president holds no such threat because of the separate election of the two branches; indeed, it is the president who must accommodate himself to the interests of the legislature.

A second factor that is likely to intensify the struggle for pork are differences in district magnitude (Shugart and Haggard, ch. 3). Japan has medium-sized electoral districts; each district is represented by three to five assembly members. By contrast, in Taiwan the size of the electoral districts varies widely. Taipei County has sixteen seats and two other major urban districts have nine seats while, at the other extreme, there are five districts with two seats and five districts with only a single seat. On average, the districts are larger than in Japan; two-thirds of Taiwanese legislators are elected in districts with a magnitude of five or higher. The larger the district, the more volatile the electoral game, the greater the risk of party nomination errors (Cox and Niou 1994), and the lower the incumbency advantage. Incumbents in Taiwan have very low reelection rates by Japanese and American standards (Sheng 1996). Most importantly, the higher the district magnitude, the more intense the intraparty competition.

There is one characteristic of Taiwan's electoral system that might have mitigated rent-seeking by legislators during the period under review. A strong ideological or ethnic cleavage may serve to discipline voters; both the DPP and New Party have had at least some success in convincing their constituents to accept their parties' instructions to split their votes among candidates, even in the absence of access to pork (C. Y. Lin 1995; J. W. Lin 1995). On the other hand, these cleavages may also serve to exacerbate competition. For example, these cleavages generated rifts between radical and moderate Taiwanese nationalist factions within the DPP.

Factionalism

As we have seen (Cox and McCubbins, ch. 2; Shugart and Haggard, ch. 3), the internal factionalization of parties is an important determinant of the cohesiveness and decisiveness of policy. The larger the number of factions that must be accommodated, the larger the division of purpose, the more veto gates, the larger the coalition required to enact legislation, and the more expansive the resulting logrolls.

Prior to the creation of the New Party in 1993, the main factional conflict in the party was between the Lee Teng-hui's "mainstream" faction and the "nonmainstream" faction of mainlanders that represented the old guard in the party; the latter stood to lose substantially from Lee's effort to transform the party into an electoral machine. In late 1993, portions of the nonmainstream faction broke away to form the New Party, creating a three-party system. After the departure of the New Party, the KMT again saw an increase in factionalism. This factionalism, however, was less ideological in nature; it was associated with the incentives induced by the SNTV system itself (Shubert 1992; Hood 1996).

In the wake of his election to the presidency in 1991, Lee accommodated the growing divisions within his own ranks through a masterful, but ultimately problematic, compromise; he chose as his premier a prominent general, Hau Pei-tsun, from the nonmainstream faction. This choice averted a potential threat from *the* key political force that any democratizing leader had to appease – the military.[15] However, as a result, Taiwan underwent a period when two major, but opposing, factions within the party were represented not only within the cabinet but also in two key posts.

Given that Lee had a Ph.D. in economics while Hau was a former general with little expertise in economic affairs, "cohabitation" appeared to provide for a natural division of policy labor; Lee would manage the economy, including the budget, while Hau would attend to issues of

---

[15] Hau was extremely influential not only within the party (the CSC) but also within the military; as Chief of Staff, most generals in key command or administrative positions had been advanced by Hau. To assume the premiership, Hau had to retire from the military, permitting Lee to restructure the military leadership, promote Hau's rivals, and expand his own links to military factions.

defense and law and order. However, the premier's formal control over the budget process provided an opportunity for the nonmainstream faction to extend its influence into economic issues, an area in which it had previously been poorly represented. Moreover, while Lee had the support of the new KMT legislators from the mainstream faction, the rise of the opposition and the threat of outright factional defection – which ultimately came to pass – meant that he needed to appease nonmainstream legislators as well.[16]

Summary

Democratization and electoral reform wrought a profound transformation in Taiwan's political institutions and, correspondingly, in the incentives facing the president and legislators. At the beginning of the transition, the system was characterized by a high unity of purpose. Partisan competition and electoral reform frayed that unity, as legislators were compelled to respond to the opposition. However, the system was also characterized by two further features that made party unity difficult, namely, the SNTV system and the emergence of serious intraparty factionalism.

ELECTORAL REFORM AND FISCAL OUTCOMES

To understand how the increasing division of purpose operated on fiscal policy, we must first identify the interests represented by the new parties. We then examine the effects of factionalism and the influence of SNTV on legislative incentives with respect to fiscal policy.

The Changing Issue Space in Taiwan's Politics

In its early phases, the opposition was concerned primarily with forcing the pace of political liberalization. Once that had been achieved, the opposition turned its attention to identity and ethnic politics. As numerous studies have noted, the rise of the DPP can be interpreted as a reassertion of Taiwanese nationalism. The creation of the New Party, in

---

[16] An important issue in this regard was the management of the "tenured" legislators elected in the late-1940s and in "supplemental" elections to represent mainland districts, who had been resisting the public call for their retirement and the growing number of opposition legislators on the other; we return to this issue below.

turn, represented the mainlander reaction (Cheng and Hsu 1996a). However, the opposition's emphasis on identity politics proved to be ephemeral. Since the late 1970s, and particularly following the electoral reforms, the KMT had made a strong effort to incorporate talented Taiwanese into the party. Given that both the party and government bureaucracy were increasingly indigenized and the president himself was Taiwanese, it became increasingly difficult for the DPP to characterize the KMT as a mainlander party. The extreme nationalist stance of the radical wing of the DPP, which called for Taiwan's independence, also tended to alienate middle-class and business voters. But a more moderate nationalist stance carried little electoral punch; despite the official pronouncements of the KMT that it remained committed to reunification with the mainland, President Lee's diplomacy repeatedly showed his willingness to assert Taiwan's de facto independence.

The New Party faced a somewhat similar set of problems in playing the ethnic card. Commitment to reunification with the mainland generated support among the mainlander community and galvanized the party faithful, but it held forth little promise of expanding the New Party's electoral base to the Taiwanese majority.

New empirical work on issue cleavages and public opinion in Taiwan finds increasing evidence of the salience of economic cleavages as well as new issues such as the environment. As Yun-han Chu (1994, 90) finds in his analysis of the 1992 election, "the social welfare issue is a separate conflict dimension that transcends the prevailing national identity-based conflict dimensions."[17] These new cleavages affected budgetary politics by increasing the salience of welfare spending and by generating electoral bidding among contending parties.[18]

In 1987, the KMT coupled its pledge of political reform with the commitment to create a "welfare state" by the end of the century. The government inaugurated a heavily subsidized health insurance program for farmers in 1989, a program for low-income households in 1990, and

[17] The sources of these new cleavages are multiple; they include the disruptive effects of trade liberalization on small business and agriculture, a slowing of the growth of rural incomes and a widening of the urban – rural income differential, intense pressure on wages from an appreciating exchange rate and the "hollowing out" of the economy, and the deterioration in income distribution associated with the bubble economy of 1986–1990 and the emergence of a Taiwanese *nouveau riche*.

[18] Certain social welfare measures predated the transition period, including limited insurance, health, and social relief programs. But these programs were all initiated from above and tended to benefit the KMT's core base of support, including the military, civil servants, and teachers (Cheng and Schive 1996, 18).

a separate health program for the handicapped in 1991. In the 1991 National Assembly elections, the DPP fared poorly by campaigning on a Taiwanese independence platform. Prior to the 1992 Legislative Yuan elections, the party turned its attention to public policy and introduced its own "welfare state" platform. The DPP promised an extensive array of entitlement programs, including universal health insurance, subsidized housing, government-guaranteed retirement income for the elderly, and pensions for old age farmers (Cheng 1995).

However, it was really with the formation of the New Party and the fundamental realignment of the party system in the summer of 1993 that the KMT entered a bidding war with the opposition on social welfare issues. In 1993, the DPP took up the issue of reducing health premiums for workers; the structure of premiums had previously favored the KMT's political base in the state sector. In its 1994 electoral campaign, the DPP called for universal pensions for senior citizens, to which the KMT responded by drafting a policy guideline for social welfare and by promising to adopt a national health program. In 1995, an election year, the national health plan was implemented – five years ahead of schedule. The government also attempted to appeal to its base by adopting old age farmer pensions and expanding civil service pensions as well as experimenting with a more general means-tested pension program. For its campaign in the December 1995 legislative election, the DPP again reiterated its proposal for the reduction of insurance premiums for workers. The New Party joined the bandwagon with a white paper on welfare that advocated the renovation of military residential compounds and a number of new welfare programs, including unemployment pension and national retirement pension plans.

The Fiscal Effects of Factionalism

In addition to intense partisan conflict, we have noted that the KMT also had to deal with growing factionalism within its own ranks. One mechanism for maintaining party unity, as well as solving the demands for pork associated with SNTV more generally, was the Six-Year National Development Plan (SYNDP). Launched in 1991, the SYNDP was a massive public works program. Although it included some 700 items, the big ticket items in the plan were a series of major public infrastructure, transportation, and communication projects that blanketed the entire country. Most notably, the program incorporated four major initiatives: a coastal expressway on the western side of the island; a second inland freeway in the north; a north–south high-speed railway; and new mass transit systems for both Taipei and Kaoshiung, the country's second largest city and, not coincidentally, a bastion of DPP support.

As with all such infrastructure initiatives, this one was not without substantive justification.[19] However, the motivations for the plan were also clearly political. The SYNDP was cobbled together relatively quickly by premier Hau's cabinet, with particular assistance from the Minister of Transportation, Dr. Jian You-shing, who was one of the cabinet ministers handpicked by President Lee. Both factions saw potential gains. By initiating a massive economic plan (and mimicking Chiang Ching-kuo's "ten major projects" of the early 1970s), Hau was able to make a political statement in a policy area that the president had dominated while forging new ties between the nonmainstream faction and Taiwanese business elites. However, given the divisible nature of this type of public works spending, the mainstream faction benefited from the SYNDP as well, permitting it to cement yet closer ties with the local factions that were increasingly the building blocks of the "new" legislative party (Cheng and Hsu 1996b).

The initial version of the plan was massive, including 775 projects and estimated spending of NT$8,200 billion (or US$303 billion), roughly eight times the size of the central government annual budget in the early 1990s. Much of the spending was to acquire land, which in itself provided tremendous opportunities for landholders, including small farmers. But the proposed engineering and construction expenditure was substantial as well (Li 1993, 21).

Traditionally, much public works spending was channeled to Veterans Engineering Services (VES). The largest construction company in Taiwan, VES was owned by the Commission on Veterans Affairs and provided opportunities for retired military personnel; it thus represents a perfect example of the way in which government spending was used to maintain core bases of support within the state sector. But SYNDP was extensive enough to accommodate private construction firms as well, thus fitting the political agenda of the mainstream faction in nurturing ties with both large and small Taiwanese entrepreneurs.

[19] The Council on Economic Planning and Development (CEPD) rightly argued that the country's infrastructure was overtaxed, and it had been close to two decades since President Chiang Ching-kuo had launched a similar set of major infrastructure initiatives. An effort to repeat that plan in the late 1970s and early 1980s was interrupted by the second oil shock.

Smaller projects and ancillary spending for the SYNDP passed through the regular budget, but the big items – the highways, mass transit systems, and rail link – were packaged into three special budgets, each for a two-year period (Phase 1, FY 1992–1993; Phase 2, FY 1994–1995; and Phase 3, FY 1996–1997); these special budgets typically ranged between 5% and 10% of the total central government budget.[20] A big political advantage of using the special budget mechanism was that it reduced the frequency that the government's proposal would have to amass legislative support; in effect, two years of spending would get authorized at once.

The first phase of the special budget authorized spending NT$153 billion (one third in the first year, two thirds in the second); this amount was later increased to NT$173.28 billion due to cost overruns. However, only 48% of the budget was spent, as many specific projects were either not started or were severely behind schedule. Roughly 87% of Phase 1 was financed by government borrowing and bonds. The second phase had a new, additional budget of NT$170 billion, again one third was to be spent in the first year and two thirds were to be spent in the second year; it was 100% debt-financed. The utilization of the budget in Phase 2 was even lower than for Phase 1, leading the government to adjust these two combined special budgets downward by NT$100 billion in January 1995. Phase 3 for 1996 and 1997 fiscal years has a new, additional budget of NT$170 billion, again, one third is allocated for the first year, two thirds is allocated for the second year; it too is 100% debt-financed (Republic of China Executive Yuan 1991, 1993, 1995).

There is ample evidence that the budget proposals were inflated, leading to shortfalls in overall spending relative to the original plan; at the same time, however, individual projects experienced severe cost overruns in implementation (Ministry of Audit, n.d.). For example, the Chiang Kai-Shek International Airport expansion project was budgeted for NT$5.7 billion, but the successful bid came in at NT$2.7 billion, showing an overestimate of costs at 52%. On the other hand, Taipei's mass transit system was budgeted for NT$261.6 billion but cost NT$444.5 billion (70% overrun); nuclear power plant #2 was budgeted for NT$22 billion but cost 39.16 billion (178% overrun), and the second north Taiwan freeway project, budgeted for NT$51.8 billion, cost NT$118.75

[20] Aside from the three special budgets associated with the SYNDP, the Executive Yuan also initiated a fourth special budget for the acquisition of F-16 fighter jets in FY 1996.

billion (204% overrun) (*Commercial Times* 1996). As we will see, these cost overruns were related to the rise of money politics that we associate with SNTV.

After the Legislature Yuan elections of December 1992, Premier Hau was ousted, reestablishing a greater unity of purpose within the government. The SYNDP was quickly consolidated by his successor, Premier Lien Chan, a faithful follower of President Lee during the previous factional struggles. Spending on infrastructure proposals declined in the early 1990s (Table 6.3). In 1995, the budget was consolidated into 12 major items, and the total cost reduced from NT$8,200 billion to NT$2,900 billion (*United Daily News* 1995). As the concern with budget deficits and corruption in government spending mounted, fueled in part by the excesses of the SYNDP, Premier Lien redefined the government's primary budgetary task as one of retrenchment. In the spring of 1996, the government finally announced that rebalancing the budget by the next century would be a policy goal.

Despite the rhetoric of budget cutting, legislators of both factions and all parties proved reluctant to wield the knife on the government's budget proposals (*Independent Evening News* 1995). Legislative cuts tended to be minimal and the "cuts" were imposed only in the context of phenomenal growth in the proposed budgets. The budget for the most controversial project, the high-speed railway, provides an example of how the budget-cutting exercise is itself highly disingenuous. When first presented to the Legislative Yuan for review in the spring of 1994, legislators vetoed the entire item. However, the reason for this legislative veto was not on the basis of the project per se, but that the Executive Yuan did not allow sufficient private participation in the project; legislators were thus able to express concerns about the project while signaling that they were ultimately receptive to its passage. The following year – an election year – the Executive Yuan revised the plan and trimmed the budget and legislators passed it with cross-party support, with the DPP party whip explicitly allowing his party's legislators to vote their preferences (*China Times* 1995; *United Daily News* 1995).

Another example comes from the budgetary fight for the 1997 fiscal year. Shih Tai-sheng, a KMT legislator, openly opposed the agreement reached in interparty negotiations over public works spending, arguing that the legislature never took its responsibility to cut public construction spending seriously (*China Times* 1996). In the midst of public criticism of cost overruns and collusive bidding, the president made a remark that the budgetary figures for public construction projects were indeed inflated, and the premier responded that the Executive Yuan would voluntarily trim them. Hence, in the 1997 FY budget review, a consensus emerged that the central government's public construction budget should be trimmed by 15%. However, legislators proved reluctant to go along with an interparty agreement for a 10% reduction of the central government's subsidies to *local* construction, subsidies that are particularly useful to individual legislators; the committee reviewing this budgetary item ultimately recommended a 4% reduction (*China Times* 1996).

Money Politics in Taiwan

As the foregoing analysis of the SYNDP demonstrates, there is ample prima facie evidence of the importance of pork-barrel spending in Taiwan's politics. However, it is also important to emphasize a second element of the SNTV story – the role of money politics in the running of political campaigns. We expect that campaigns characterized by intense intraparty rivalry, heightened by high-magnitude districts, would be expensive, thus providing strong incentives to cultivate ties with business. Prior to the transition to democratic rule, the KMT's control over the budget, well-funded political projects (such as youth corp activities), and their own enterprises aided it in collecting funds for its electoral campaign and in staffing the huge party bureaucracy. The KMT could and did easily subsidize the candidates it nominated. Democratization forced a separation of the party from the state. The party had to wean itself from state coffers while economic liberalization reduced the opportunity for KMT-owned enterprises to enjoy monopoly profits.

However, just as the capacity of the party to subsidize political campaigns was declining, the economy was creating a new middle and entrepreneurial class that stood ready to make investments as the political market opened up. Young leaders from the nonmainstream faction[21] began to enlist business support and even encouraged businesspeople to run for legislative office on the KMT ticket. After being removed from key party positions, several nonmainstream elites began to mobilize support from the business community in the late 1980s, triggering a parallel effort by the mainstream faction to court ties with both big business and regional business leaders (Su 1992, 48). Recruiting Taiwanese business elites into party ranks was one factor in helping the mainstream faction to alter the political balance within the party (Cheng and Hsu 1996b).

[21] Notably John Kuan, then head of the KMT's Department of Organization.

The new role of business had two effects on economic policy, one programmatic, one more directly related to the demands of SNTV politics. On the one hand, the KMT sought to position the party on the center right by identifying more openly with the private sector at both the national and subnational levels. Business sought to free itself from burdensome regulations, and particularly from restraints on the range of its investment activities, while also maintaining the advantages that flowed from the stability and competence of KMT rule. As Chu (1994) concludes, the KMT and the private sector "both see the need for the involvement of an active state in the process of industrial upgrading, both put economic growth before environmental considerations, both favor a slow growth in social welfare spending, and both support a state-orchestrated exclusion of organized labor from the economic policy-making." A detailed analysis of public opinion at the time of the 1992 legislative elections shows substantial majorities of respondents scoring the KMT as more pro-growth and pro-development than the opposition (Hsieh and Niou 1996).

However, the courting of business also found reflection in the quest for pork, particularly with respect to land-use policy. As in Japan, the central government controls the bulk of government fiscal resources in Taiwan; however, local governments in Taiwan have more discretionary power in allocating subsidies coming from the central government as well as more autonomy in urban planning than their counterparts in Japan. The central government has passed ordinances and plans for urban development for the whole island, and the provincial government of Taiwan has broad planning powers, but county governments retain substantial discretion over implementation, particularly in the critical issue of zoning. Given the scarcity of land, the country's rapid growth, and the explosion of land prices, the discretion built into the zoning process constitutes a major source of rent-seeking. Zoning takes many years to complete and even upon completion revisions are still possible. Party leaders, legislators, local politicians, and business at all levels have become increasingly intertwined in what Fukui and Fukai (1996, 280) have called *electoral keiretsu* – policy and political circles that generate pork and rents that are in turn offered as political donations.

One of the more interesting developments is the direct entry of businesspeople into politics. A report by the Taipei Society (1992, 1–3, 1–9ff) shows that there were more businesspeople-turned-candidates for the December 1992 legislative election than in any previous election. Most of the businesspeople running for office were nominated by the

KMT and aligned with the mainstream faction. The rise of business-people-politicians shows more clearly than anything else how the formal powers of the president and party hierarchy are in fact heavily conditioned by electoral calculations. Given the cost of running electoral campaigns, the KMT must often choose between nominating well-qualified candidates without independent financial bases and allowing self-nominating businesspeople, particularly those with strong support from local factions, to run under the KMT label. This choice is not an easy one. Such candidates are not only self-financed, but their affiliation with particular local factions alleviates to some extent the problem of vote division for the party; the KMT in effect buys a seat. Moreover, if the party rejects the candidate as unsuitable, the candidate might run for one of the opposition parties or help to finance another opposition candidate. However, the nomination of businesspeople-candidates leaves the party open to charges of corruption, while the very costs of campaigning guarantee that legislators will want to make a return on their investment through the policy and budget process. This tendency of money politics to compound itself is one reason why increasing calls are being heard for fundamental reforms of the electoral system.[22]

Summary

Our review of fiscal politics shows strongly the influence of increasing separation of purpose within the political system. The rise of new parties produced a renewed interest in welfare spending and programmatic bidding among the parties. At the same time, the combination of intraparty factionalism and SNTV provided strong incentives for pork-barrel expenditures and the cultivation of ties with local business. These difficulties were only partly reversed by the reduction of intraparty factionalism after 1992; not until the late 1990s did corruption and fiscal laxity become salient electoral issues in their own right, producing new efforts at fiscal consolidation.

AN EMERGENT SEPARATION OF POWERS: THE PRESIDENT, THE LEGISLATURE, AND THE MAKING OF FISCAL POLICY

As in a number of other presidential systems, the formal power to draft, compile, and propose the budget in Taiwan lies in the Executive Yuan

---

[22] Similar reform movements occurred earlier in Japan.

(Article 57). A more distinctive feature of budgeting in Taiwan is found in Article 70 of the Constitution: "The Legislative Yuan shall not make proposals for an increase in the expenditures in the budgetary bill presented by the Executive Yuan." Under a controversial ruling by the Court of Grand Justice (Interpretation #281), Article 70 was interpreted to imply that the Legislative Yuan also could not reallocate funds across spending categories. As Baldez and Carey (Chapter 4) show, such a rule increases the agenda-setting power of the president. If the Legislative Yuan enacts a new program, the government is required to budget for it. But, since legislators do not initiate the budget and cannot increase the level of spending proposed by the executive, the executive can stymie legislative initiative by simply funding programs at a minimal level.

This constraint would appear to inoculate the budgetary process from interbranch bargaining and from the tendency of the SNTV system to generate pork-barrel expenditures. The null hypothesis on the role of the electoral and party system is that the concentration of powers trumps the emerging division of purpose and that the president should be able to limit particularism. Yet the existence of formal executive powers does not tell us how those powers will be deployed; in addition to the president's interest in his or her own reelection, he or she also must accommodate backbenchers and maintain the ruling party's narrowing majority within the legislature.

We show, first, that KMT and opposition legislators have exploited several means for influencing budget outcomes that had been dormant prior to the transition, including various mechanisms for signaling, the strategic use of budget cuts, and threats of delay and stalemate. We also show how the executive is constrained by the reversionary point (Cox and McCubbins, ch. 2) if no budget is passed. Second, we show that the structure and process of budgeting changed in predictable ways following the transition to more democratic rule, and we trace the emergent division of powers in fiscal policy making. The role of the National Security Council in the budget process was eliminated and KMT legislators designed new institutions to voice their policy preferences, including significant changes in the legislature's committee structure. Third, we show that these changes are manifest not only in the budgetary process but also in the organization of the party within the legislature. Electoral reform has included efforts by ruling party legislators to expand their voice within their party while simultaneously solving some of the collective action problems that necessarily arise as a result of greater organizational decentralization. Finally, we show that through his role as party chair, the president was able to limit the devolution of power to the legislature in important ways.

Drafting the Budget Bill

As in many presidential and parliamentary systems, the initial drafting of the budget is an executive exercise. The Executive Yuan is required to finalize the policy guidelines for the following fiscal year by the end of October.[23] In doing so, the Executive Yuan draws on reference materials from three core ministries (Finance, Foreign Affairs, and Defense) as well as a number of executive agencies, several of which serve as monitors on the programs submitted by other ministries and agencies.[24]

The party hierarchy inserts its views into the policy process in July, when a draft of the policy guidelines and accompanying documents are sent to the Central Standing Committee (CSC) for discussion and approval. As we have seen, the CSC only indirectly represents the ruling party in the legislature. Since 1988, KMT legislators have routinely requested to meet with government and party leaders before or during the budget compilation process. In 1988 and again in 1993, the premier (Yu Kuo-hwa and Hau Pei-tsun, respectively) promised to hold such meetings; even though a meeting was held with KMT legislators after the budget bill was submitted in late February, the premier's promise was never honored (*United Daily News* 1987; *Taiwan Daily* 1992).

The draft guidelines come back to the cabinet in August. After the cabinet incorporates the CSC's views, the guidelines are ready to be decreed by the president and turned over to the major administrative units of the government for the drafting of specific policy plans and budget estimates. In drafting estimates for continuing programs, line

---

[23] The policy guidelines include an overview of the state of the nation, the government's broad policy objectives, as well as more specific initiatives.

[24] The Council on Research and Evaluation (CRE), the Council on Economic Planning and Development (CEPD), and the National Science Foundation (NSF) are the three gatekeepers; by contrast, the role of the Director-General of Budget, Accounting, and Statistics (DGBAS) is the largely administrative one of preparing the technical guidelines for budgeting. All of the agencies involved in formulating the guidelines are directly under the Executive Yuan except for the Department of Auditing, which is part of the Control Yuan, and the Central Bank, which is nominally independent though its chairman is appointed by the president.

ministries typically use the previous year as a reference point. All new projects must be preapproved by the cabinet; to create new spending categories or programs, line ministries must first get relevant laws or regulations amended, a process that necessarily passes through the executive and the ruling party.[25]

The government then faces the task of how to aggregate and reconcile ministerial demands; this task is delegated to a small Planning and Budget Review Group (PBRG) within the Executive Yuan, convened by the vice premier (Yang 1991, 133–34).[26] The PBRG is essentially an agent for the premier in managing the budget-making process within the executive branch. Prior to the transition to democratic rule, the PBRG was vested with the task of controlling the overall level of the government budget and minimizing deficits. The PBRG did not set firm upper limits on the budget for a given ministry; rather, the budgeting process was an informal bargaining game between the PBRG, the line ministries, and their subunits.[27] Since the PBRG had the power to ask a ministry or agency to redraft its budget, ministers would typically exercise fiscal restraint; in effect, ministers knew their own weight in the eyes of the premier, and they knew that the PBRG was aware of the importance the premier attached to each ministry. An important exception was that the defense budget was beyond the reach of the PBRG, hammered out by the Ministry of Defense and the premier directly.

[25] If new projects exceed some specified thresholds, they must also be submitted to one of three gate-keeping bodies for analysis. As noted above, the gatekeeper agencies are the CRE, CEPD, and NSF. The threshold for economic development projects is NT$500 million; for science and technology projects, the thresholds are NT$10 million for annual appropriations and NT$30 million over the life of the project. Programs singled out by the Executive Yuan or regarded by the line ministries as critical are also sent to the CEPD, CRE, and NSF for preview irrespective of their size.

[26] There are several interesting differences between the PBRG and the cabinet, or the Executive Yuan Council as it is formally known. The cabinet is a formal organization stipulated in the Constitution (Article 58), presided over by the premier, and including the vice premier, ministers, chairmen of commissions, and ministers without portfolio. The cabinet makes all final decisions on statutory or budgetary bills before sending them to the Legislative Yuan. The PBRG is not a statutory entity. The group is dominated by "control" ministries; it excludes all line ministers and heads of agencies except for the Minister of Finance and includes ministers without portfolio, the director of DGBAS, the secretary-general of the Executive Yuan, and the governor of the Central Bank.

[27] For those ministries with revenue-generating units under their jurisdiction (for example, the Ministry of Economic Affairs oversees over a dozen state-owned enterprises), revenue estimates are sent to the Ministry of Finance.

The role of the PBRG as an agent of the premier, and ultimately as an agent of the president, was revealed starkly in the early 1990s when the executive itself took policy initiatives that sharply increased spending. After 1995, however, increasing budget deficits became a salient political issue, and the PBRG became more assertive by setting budget limits for each line ministry (Su 1994, 230).

The Director-General of Budget, Accounting, and Statistics (DGBAS) reviews the budgets from various organizations, in conjunction with the revenue budget produced by MOF, and reports to PBRG on the way the budget will be balanced – if it is to be balanced – before turning it to the premier for approval. With the seal of the premier, DGBAS integrates the ministry budgets into a budget bill, which is then submitted to the cabinet for approval before being forwarded to the Legislative Yuan for deliberation. This is usually done in the second half of February.

Prior to the lifting of the Temporary Provisions and the transition to democracy, the president had a second opportunity to assert his preferences; once cleared of the cabinet, the budget bill was routed through the National Security Council. An artifact of martial law, the NSC was directly accountable to the president. With the abolition of the Temporary Provisions in 1991, the status of the NSC was called into question by the opposition. In 1993, the President secured legislative support for its continuance, though its role was circumscribed to considering only foreign policy and defense issues. Once sanctioned by the NSC, the budget bill typically sailed smoothly through the legislative branch. Facing no electoral competition, and heavily dependent on the executive, legislators had little incentive to challenge the government's budget.

Deliberation within the Legislative Yuan

With the opening of the political system after 1986, however, long-ritualized procedures took on new political significance. After clearing the procedure committee and being scheduled for the plenum,[28] the premier, accompanied by the head of DGBAS and the Minister of Finance, presented the government's budget bill. The plenum then votes on whether the budget bill should be returned to the Executive Yuan (for redrafting and resubmission) or be reviewed by the Legislative Yuan;

[28] In theory, the procedure committee can block or accelerate the process, though to date the KMT has maintained a thin majority in the committee and this has not become a choke point.

this stage constitutes the first reading of the bill. Because the KMT has had a legislative majority, there has been no controversy at this stage of the process.

The budget bill then goes to the Committee of All Committees (CAC), a committee of the whole legislature.[29] Representatives of the government elaborate the technical aspects of the budget before the CAC; the CAC then sets the agenda and schedules the committee review process. A formal vote is required for the CAC to forward the bill to the budget review committees. The CAC can, however, vote to return the bill to the Executive Yuan for redrafting and resubmission. Again, because of the KMT's legislative majority, the budget has never been returned to the government at this stage, although the opposition has proposed it. In the spring of 1987, the opposition argued that the government's budget did not meet the constitutional requirement that 15% of spending be devoted to education, science, and culture. The plenum rejected this motion, but the premier publicly promised to correct this error within three years (*Taiwan Daily* 1988.[30]

Since 1991, there has been substantial change in the process of committee review of the budget; most importantly, legislative oversight has increased significantly. Prior to the reforms of that year, the CAC determined how the budget bill would be divided for the purpose of committee review. Four to six ad hoc committees were set up to review the budget bill, chaired by members of the budget committee.[31] The reform decentralized the review process; the budget bill is now reviewed by ten committees that correspond roughly with the twelve standing.[32] The

---

[29] The CAC has a lower quorum and is chaired not by the speaker, as in plenum, but by the chairs of the budget review committees on a rotating basis.

[30] The premier actually corrected the problem in only two years.

[31] The Budget Review Groups were: I. Budget Committee, Interior Affairs Committee; II. Budget Committee, Education Committee, Border Minorities Committee, Overseas Chinese Committee, Judiciary Committee, and Legal-Regulatory Committee; III. Budget Committee, Economic Committee, Finance Committee, and Transportation-Communication Committee; IV. Budget Committee, Foreign Affairs Committee, and Defense Committee.

[32] Following the budget reforms, the number of standing committees was reduced to ten. The Judiciary and Legal committees and the Mongolian and Tibetan Committee and the Internal Committee are combined for the purpose of budget review. The ten committees are: Budget Committee; Interior Affairs Committee (subsumed the now defunct Border Minorities Committee); Education Committee, Judiciary Committee, Legal-Regulatory Committee; Economic Committee; Finance Committee; Transportation-Communication Committee; Foreign Affairs Committee (subsumes now defunct Overseas Chinese Committee), and the Defense Committee.

budget review committees are now chaired by the chairmen (or "convenors") of the relevant standing committees rather than members of the budget committee; large committees (which can have a maximum of eighteen members) have three convenors whereas smaller ones have one or two. The convenors of each committee are not chosen by seniority; instead, they are elected by committee members. All legislators seek to chair a committee in the first session of every year, especially in the first and third year of the three-year electoral cycle.

With respect to committee assignments, each legislator can join only one committee, but committee membership can change every legislative session. In principle, each legislator is free to sign up for any committee he or she chooses. In fact, self-nomination produces oversubscription for desirable committees; not surprisingly, the finance, economic, transportation, and communication committees are the most popular. Given that demand for chairmanships and desirable committee assignments outstrips their supply, some coordination is required. The party caucus in the legislature has assumed this role and has devised a solution: Party members simply rotate among committees and chairmanships. This solution is facilitated by the fact that there are six sessions in each three-year term and that both chairs and memberships can change with each session. Before the December 1995 legislative elections, the ruling party's majority in the plenum was comfortable enough for it to control virtually all committees, though even then it could at most control two out of three convenors on the larger committees. After those elections, the KMT's legislative majority fell to the narrowest of margins – only three seats – and the party failed to orchestrate successfully the staffing of less desirable committees; in the second (fall) session of 1996, the KMT lost its majority in four committees. We predict that as the party caucus becomes better organized, this is unlikely to happen again; we discuss this process in more detail below.

The loss of these committee chairs sheds light on the ramifications of divided government. First, opposition convenors could simply refuse to set the agenda for consideration of the budget bill; in the spring of 1996, several convenors deliberately shelved the government's bill to consider other matters. Second, opposition convenors could allow their copartisans to filibuster by launching extensive criticisms of particular budget items. Neither of these powers proved fatal to the government's budget; once in the chair again, a ruling party convenor could rule favorably on a motion for cloture or steer the committee back to the budget bill. But, the budget bill is unlike other bills; if it does not pass, the legislature has the option of passing its own temporary provisions. Thus, Taiwan's presidential system is no different than other presidential systems; it is only the continuing capability of the KMT to garner legislative majorities that averts the possibility of deadlock that is associated with divided government.

Each budget review committee initially invites ministers and heads of agencies to provide reports and face interpellation. At this stage, all legislators can attend and participate, and many do, rushing from committee to committee to make statements on electorally-salient issues. As a result, the level of interpellation has skyrocketed (Lee 1993, 115). Some indication of the effects of electoral reform on legislative scrutiny of government can be gathered from an analysis of *zhixun*, formal inquiries for information to which the executive must, according to the Constitution (Article 71), respond. During the eighty-first session of the First Legislative Yuan (1988), legislators made a total of 1956 such inquiries, already a dramatic increase from those submitted prior to 1986. During the third session of the Second Legislative Yuan (1994), 4,875 were submitted (Johnson 1995, 4–5).

When the specific budget lines are reviewed, only members of the budget review committee and the main budget committee can participate. Members of the budget committee are allowed to vote in each review committee; for that reason the ruling party has jealously guarded its control of the budget committee. The KMT's share of seats in the Legislative Yuan dropped to just over 50% in 1996, but the KMT holds 60% of the seats in the budget committee. This majority permits the party to deploy a mobile vote troop that can be dispatched to the budget review committees.

If an item remains intact through the review process, it is passed. If an item is controversial, then the committee debates and votes on amendments; interparty negotiations arranged by party whips are increasingly frequent at this stage.

The reasons for the reform of the committee structure are straightforward. Prior to the transition, the budget committee was monopolized by the aging legislators who were elected in 1947 and 1948; they exercised tight control over the process and exchanged support for the government's budget bills for various personal perks and sinecures for themselves, relatives, and factional followers. With the supplemental elections, and in anticipation of the replacement of the entire legislature in the 1992 elections, the newer KMT legislators had an interest in gaining access to the budget process. One way to dilute the power of the aging legislators and provide opportunities for newcomers was to expand the number of review committees and decentralize the budget review process.

The constraints of Article 70, however, appear to make legislators' interests in gaining greater access to the budget-review process somewhat puzzling. The budget-review committees do not have the option of increasing spending on favored projects; they can only deliberate on whether an item should be cut and, if so, by how much. Before the democratic transition, budget cuts were rare; opposition legislators and a handful of senior KMT legislators occasionally attached "notes" or "side-resolutions" to signal the Executive Yuan of their interests, but these notes and side-resolutions were not legally binding. In theory, legislators could retaliate in the following year by cutting the budget, but given the party's control over the legislature, this was highly unlikely (Yang 1991, 164; Lee 1993, 210).

Following electoral reform, especially after the KMT's legislative majority was drastically reduced after the formation of the New Party in 1993, party discipline has weakened and the government's budget is usually cut at the committee review stage. To understand why legislators do this requires an analysis of the executive–legislative game. The power of the legislature to cut the budget induces the executive to make larger budget requests than it might otherwise; the Executive Yuan builds enough spending into the budget to satisfy a majority of legislators and guarantee that it is veto proof, *even when some cuts are made*. This pattern was particularly visible between 1989 and 1992 when the executive itself was introducing budgets with large spending increases and budget deficits. Since executive and legislative preferences over spending do not necessarily coincide, budget cutting, or threats of budget cutting, can be used at the margin to secure or safeguard projects of legislative interest. Legislators make cuts to show those policy areas in which legislative interests are greatest (those receiving the smallest cuts) or where legislative and executive preferences over the composition of spending diverge (those receiving the largest cuts). The scale of overall legislative cuts remains small and has always taken the form of across the board percentage point cuts for very broad spending categories. These cuts demonstrate to voters legislative involvement in the oversight process while avoiding actions that would be politically costly.

When the individual budget review committees have voted, the budget committee aggregates its resolutions and sends the bill to the CAC. If there are still unresolved issues, the budget committee will summarize the controversy and hand it over to the CAC. At this stage, the party leadership is able to reverse committee decisions by restoring cuts (Hsu 1994, 54); this has on occasion triggered opposition boycotts and further interparty negotiation (*United Daily News* 1990; *China Times* 1992; *China Times* 1993; *Taiwan Daily* 1994). The bill is then read by the plenum; this is known as the second reading. Interparty negotiations spill over into the plenum, where the opposition presents various drafts of temporary provisions; in effect, these drafts represent their counter-budget were the proposed budget not to pass. The bill is read by the plenum for the third and final time for cosmetic changes; if passed, a statutory budget is born.

Endgame: Executive-Legislative Relations

After the budget bill has been passed, the Executive Yuan has two options: accept it or veto it in whole or in part within ten days and return it to the Legislative Yuan for reconsideration (Constitution, Article 57, Section 3). Although this power appears to reflect a line item veto, the premier does not have the power to promulgate the remainder of the budget. The veto power is also conditional upon the consent of the president. Given that the president appoints the premier in the first place, this provision effectively grants the president the veto (Article 57, Section 3). To override the premier's request for reconsideration requires a two-thirds vote in the Legislative Yuan. Only if overridden is the premier forced to accept the budget or resign.

The veto power has never been used. The Executive Yuan has always struck a bargain with the Legislative Yuan over the budget before the deadline. The absence of the veto may be due to the executive's anticipation of legislators' interests in initially drafting the budget. Additionally, the constitution does not require the Legislative Yuan to act in a specified period of time on the premier's request for reconsideration. In theory, the Legislative Yuan can postpone the premier's request for reconsideration indefinitely. Consequently, even with the two-thirds majority provisions governing override, wielding the veto raises the spectre of deadlock.

Second, the legislature influences the reversionary point, though there is still ambiguity on this point. Article 49 of the Budget Law states that "if a part of the budgetary bill fails to pass the Legislative Yuan, leaving no statutory budget by the stipulated date [May 31], the Legislative Yuan shall decide by resolution temporary provisions and notify the

Executive Yuan. Temporary provisions include both an implementation guideline in the absence of a statutory budget and a procedural guideline for completing the budget review process."

If the legislature really had the power to draft a temporary budget of its choosing, *Articles 57 and 70 would have no significance whatsoever.* The legislature would completely control the reversionary point and could thus dictate the budget directly. However, no such temporary provisions have been enacted, in part because the executive is anxious to avoid them and in part because the meaning of Article 49 of the Budget Law remains constitutionally ambiguous. On the one hand, Article 70 is in the Constitution while the measures on temporary provisions are only in the Budget Law. If the legislature were to seek to exploit the Budget Law to increase or reallocate spending, they would clearly leave themselves open to challenge by the Council of Grand Justices, which has established its powers of judicial review. Second, there is legal precedent for a restrictive interpretation of the meaning of the temporary provisions in the provincial budget law (Local Autonomy Law [1994], Article 23), which holds that if there is no budget by the deadline the temporary provisions will simply maintain the previous year's spending levels; during the budget debate of 1996, the government itself suggested that the Local Autonomy Law should serve as a guide if there was deadlock in the budget review at the national level.

Yet even such a restricted outcome, not to mention political deadlock or the prospect of wider legislative prerogative in drafting the temporary provisions, is a constraint on the executive. In 1996, the principal opposition party, the Democratic Progressive Party, presented a draft temporary resolution to signal its preferred outcome to the statutory budget; its contents are revealing.[33] The DPP's temporary provisions allowed all

[33] The draft resolution stipulated that the government could implement those budgetary items that had been approved (i.e., those that all parties have agreed on), but also proposed freezes on government outlays in a number of categories that would have been a major annoyance for the government: personnel expenses for extra-regular employees; maintenance expenses; travel expenses; materials and supplies (primarily materials for government special projects and medical supplies); new equipment and investment; subsidies and transfers (e.g., bloc grants for local governments and domestic and international obligation); projects contracted out; relief and promotion (scholarship and government awards, but not social reliefs); special expenses of chief administrators of various government units; the reserve fund. The draft temporary provision also stipulates that for consolidated operational expenses, designated operational expenses and management expenses, the budget for current fiscal year or estimates for next fiscal year will apply, whichever is the lower. In sum, the opposition would not shut down the government

ongoing programs to continue at previously funded levels, but they stripped the budget of new spending initiatives advanced by the ruling party, including public construction and a new welfare bill.

The Organization of the Party in the Legislature

The changes in legislative organization that we have just outlined were mirrored in changes in the organization of the ruling party itself. Prior to the transition to democratic rule, the KMT maintained a "branch office" in the Legislative Yuan that basically served to dictate to, and monitor, legislators. Outside the Legislative Yuan, the Central Standing Committee maintained a Central Policy Affairs Council (CPAC) under its direct authority to coordinate party interests with respect to the other branches of government and to mediate interbranch conflicts. The CSC, however, was itself largely under the authority of the president in his capacity of head of the party. The head of CPAC was not a legislator and, in effect, he served as little more than a liaison officer for the KMT leadership.

In the second half of the 1980s, the party organization in the Legislative Yuan was restructured to give legislators a greater voice; this reorganization was the result of the KMT's increasing difficulty in maintaining its majority. In 1992, following the electoral reform, the KMT legislative party branch was reorganized into a KMT party caucus, initially headed by a secretary selected by the party leadership (i.e., the president) but later elected by KMT legislators (Chen 1994, chs. 4, 6). As we have seen from the discussion of committee chairmanships and assignments, the caucus has played a key role in resolving certain collective action problems that have been associated with the increasing decentralization of the budget process.

Under CPAC, three important new bodies were created: a Party-Government Coordination Committee (PGCC); an Inter-Party Coordination Committee (IPCC); and a Policy Research Committee (PRC). The PRC provides legislators with at least some analytic tools to evaluate policy proposals whereas the IPCC serves to manage negotiations with other parties. The most important of these new bodies is the PGCC.

or interrupt existing services, but would tie the hands of the government with respect to initiating new investment projects or policy initiatives, including in the welfare area.

Though the head of the PGCC is selected by the KMT party leadership, the party has consistently chosen a senior legislator. Under the PGCC are ten party committees corresponding with the ten standing committees of the Legislative Yuan, each headed by a commissioner elected by the KMT members of each legislative committee. A high ranking KMT legislator has revealed that the PGCC regularly surveys KMT legislators with respect to the policy programs that most affect their constituencies and that they would most like to see included in the budget. Such representation is currently indirect, as it is ultimately the executive, not the legislators, who pick and choose the programs to include in the budget bill. However, through the PGCC, the CPAC, and the shadow budget committees, the Central Standing Committee now has considerable intelligence on the interests of legislators.

Failed Reforms: Mirror of the Future?

In the early 1990s, there were proposals from legislators for at least five further institutional changes in the budget process. Proposals for a seniority system, a congressional budget office, and the creation of an appropriation committee garnered at least some support from legislators of all three parties (Peng 1993). Proposals for the creation of a more "interactive" budgeting process within the KMT and for the creation of special discretionary funds for legislators were of primary interest to the KMT. The opposition parties raised particular objections to the proposal for special funds. Yet, despite the fact that some of these changes could be achieved through ordinary legislation (including the seniority system, the creation of an appropriation committee, and the creation of the Congressional Budget Office), none of the reform proposals passed. Our interviews suggest that their failure had to do with staunch executive opposition as well as with the ability of the president to sway KMT legislators. Those legislators defying the party leadership risked being penalized both with respect to renomination and future career advancement. Without ruling party support, opposition legislators were unable to garner sufficient support to pass the reforms. Nonetheless, an analysis of these failed reforms is highly revealing of legislative interests.

Perhaps the most important challenge to executive dominance was the effort on behalf of KMT legislators after 1992 to involve themselves more directly and actively in the policy-making process. Legislators advanced a complicated plan under which all bills, including the budget bill, would pass through the CPAC for study and referral to the PGCC.[34] Both the executive and the party hierarchy strongly resisted this proposal and it was not adopted. Despite the informal and indirect channels through which legislative preferences are made known to the Executive Yuan during the drafting process, there is still no mechanism through which legislators can *directly* influence the drafting of the budget to guarantee inclusion of favored projects.

Other intraparty reform proposals have also met stiff executive and party resistance. One proposal made in 1992 suggested that CPAC be hived off from the CSC and placed directly under the authority of the party leader, in effect giving the party in the legislature coequal status with the traditional party hierarchy (Chen 1994, ch. 4). This idea was not endorsed by party elders, many of whom were nonmainstream faction members. Given that the CSC remains under presidential control, however, it was clearly not only the opposition faction that disliked the idea; it was the president himself. The CPAC continues to fall under the CSC, though it is now headed by a senior KMT legislator.

The absence of a seniority system creates important inefficiencies, not only for the legislature as a whole but also for the ruling party. A seniority system would not only allow legislators to gain specific policy expertise but it would also allow them to work in issue areas of particular concern to their constituents. The current competition for desirable committee assignments provides opportunities for the opposition. The continuous reshuffling of committee assignments means few legislators accumulate either expertise or the capacity to make credible commitments to interest groups, constituencies, or line ministries about what they can do in the budget-review process. The KMT party leadership and the party whip, however, have been reluctant to see the establishment of a seniority system.

The Executive Yuan and the party hierarchy have also resisted the formation of a congressional budget office capable of collecting statisti-

---

[34] If disputes arose (that is, if CPAC or PGCC did not endorse the bill), then the KMT's legislative caucus would vote on it. If the KMT party caucus – attended by at least one half of the KMT legislators – voted against it by a simple majority, then the decision would go to CPAC and then to the Central Standing Committee (CSC) of the KMT for ratification. If the CSC disagreed with the decision of the party caucus (by simple majority), then the caucus would still enjoy an ultimate override with a two-third majority vote (with a quorum of two-thirds of all KMT legislators) (Chen 1994, ch. 4).

cal data and conducting independent economic analysis. Backed by a CBO, the Legislative Yuan could come up with a credible alternative to the government's budget, which could be used either as a weapon in the budget process or as a means of usurping greater budgetary authority from the executive over time. Instead of a CBO, the Legislative Yuan was allowed to set up a Legislative Consultation Center (LCC) in January 1989, in anticipation of the last of the supplemental elections; however, it has only half a dozen staff working on budget issues (Republic of China 1992–1995; Peng 1993; Huang 1996).

A third proposal centers on the capacity of the legislature to control and monitor the way funds are actually spent. While the Legislative Yuan authorizes government spending, the Executive Yuan (and more specifically DGBAS) actually appropriates government money. The Legislative Yuan cannot halt appropriations; it cannot even audit them. By the time the auditor-general of the Department of Auditing (which is part of the Control Yuan) completes the report on the actual expenditure during the previous year, the budget proposal for the next fiscal year has already been completed by the Executive Yuan; moreover, these timetables are stipulated in the Constitution. If the Legislative Yuan were to appropriate, it would need investigative power, power that now resides in the Control Yuan. These ideas have been resisted by both the Executive Yuan and the Control Yuan.

A final and particularly revealing reform proposal emanating from KMT legislators has been the request for a spending category called "local public construction expenditure." This idea originated in the provincial assembly. Although the first effective opposition party was not formed until 1986, a loosely organized opposition known as the *dangwai* appeared in the mid-1970s, concentrating its efforts on contesting provincial assembly elections. Facing pressure from the new political opposition, the KMT allowed its provincial legislators to "recommend" local construction projects for inclusion in the provincial budget (*United Daily News* 1987; *China Times* 1988). Initially, this was done only for KMT members and only during election years, but it quickly became an annual practice. When the opposition learned of it, they demanded and, ultimately, were granted a share of this slush fund. The KMT caved in primarily to silence the opposition and to prevent them from boycotting the provincial review process. To date, however, national legislators have been unsuccessful in securing such access to pork for themselves.

CONCLUSION

We have analyzed how electoral reform and the gradual introduction of democratic politics affected the policy-making process as well as specific fiscal outcomes. The gradual nature of Taiwan's transition from 1986 to 1996, the continuing powers of the president, and the still incomplete control legislators and politicians have exercised over political institutions might lead one to conclude that little real change occurred. We have demonstrated, however, that the increasing division of purpose, manifest in the rise of competitive political parties, in the SNTV system, and in intraparty factionalism have all influenced the president's role in fiscal policy making. Over time, the president has become increasingly attentive to legislative interests. Most importantly, the president and the ruling party have had to cultivate ties with new constituencies (business, the middle class, and environmentalists), largely via private-regarding policy – that is, by providing more targeted and particularistic pork-barrel expenditures. We have also traced how political change affected the structure and process of fiscal policy making by strengthening the legislature and thus expanding the separation of powers.

In 1997, the government initiated a process of constitutional revision, intended precisely to reduce the interbranch conflicts we have outlined. However, the process of negotiation with the opposition ended up limiting its achievements in this regard, and may even increase interbranch conflict in the future. On the one hand, the new constitution appeared to introduce parliamentary features. One third of legislators can move a vote of no confidence and, after a three-day grace period, a simple majority of legislators can remove the premier.[35] The Legislative Yuan is now allowed to initiate impeachment proceedings against the president, although the final decision on impeachment remains in the hand of the National Assembly. Moreover, the Legislative Yuan now only needs an absolute (rather than two-thirds) majority in the legislature to override the cabinet veto power regarding any bill or legislative resolution. This means that the executive branch needs to have at least half, rather than one third, of legislators to exercise a veto, and can be sidelined altogether in the case of divided government.

On the other hand, the powers of the president were also enhanced in certain ways that serve to offset these apparent parliamentary elements.

---

[35] The constitution stipulates that the Legislative Yuan can exercise this power only once vis-à-vis the same premier in a year.

Upon the passage of a vote of no confidence, the premier can suggest that the president dissolve the Legislative Yuan, sending all legislators home to face reelection; this reduces the separation of powers and thus the incentive for interbranch cooperation. The president also gained the power to appoint and dismiss the premier without the consent of the Legislative Yuan. The fact that the Legislative Yuan can offer no confidence motions means that the partisan composition of the legislature is a crucial variable in understanding the political dynamics of the system. The president can choose a premier if his party has the majority in the Legislative Yuan; otherwise, his appointee can be ousted by a vote of nonconfidence. But this apparent legislative power will depend very much on the cohesion and discipline of opposition parties; lack of majority support is not the same thing as being opposed by a cohesive majority. Moreover, the ability of the president to dismiss the Prime Minister suggests that the system is not one in which the cabinet is solely responsible to the legislature, but rather a "president-parliamentary" hybrid that is, in the end, more presidential than parliamentary.

It is also interesting to note that the constitutional revision did not change Taiwan's electoral laws. Despite the backlash against money politics and corruption, the incentives associated with that system remain in place until consensus can be reached to revise it.

We thus expect that many of the features of the system that we have outlined here will continue to operate, as will the pressures for more complete separation of powers that we have noted. If and when the KMT's electoral margin narrows, or divided government emerges, we can expect interbranch cooperation to be more difficult. We can also expect the legislature to push for reforms such as the formation of a CBO, the adoption of a seniority system and stricter controls over committee convenorships and assignments. These changes, in turn, will require further reforms of the legislative party itself, reforms that will undoubtedly foster the formation of a more active and powerful legislative party organization. Once this occurs, the challenge to the old hierarchy of the ruling party will be profound, its raison d'être will be called into question, and the transition from a party-dominant system to a fully democratic one will be complete. Taiwan is now very far down that road, but with all the policy challenges that systems of divided powers and purpose pose.

PART III

Regulatory Policy Cases

7

Political Institutions and Economic Development

The Case of Electric Utility Regulation in Argentina and Chile

WILLIAM B. HELLER and MATHEW D. MCCUBBINS

INTRODUCTION

Economic development and long-term capital investment go hand in hand. Public utilities, such as power and communications, are particularly important in the relationship between development and investment: Not only do utilities require major capital inputs, but they are fundamental building blocks for economic development. Studying utilities, therefore, can provide key insights into economic development.

Utility regulation has a profound effect on utility investment, productivity, and costs. But, utility regulation is also redistributive, providing either the utility with monopolistic rents or consumers with prices less than the marginal cost of delivering the service. Political interference in production and pricing of utility services tends to be economically inefficient, as economic criteria often are low on the list of considerations for political decisions. Politically motivated redistributive efforts often drive away sources of long-term capital investment and hence seriously impede economic development.

The problem is not simply that political considerations in policy making lead to bad policies. They do sometimes, but even politically motivated policy can be attractive to investors. Moreover, investment is motivated not by economic efficiency but by profit, and even wildly inefficient policies can attract investment – albeit, wildly inefficient investment. The problem is that the conflict inherent in policy making makes it difficult to know whether, when, or how policy will change. Since any investment decision depends on predictions of the stability (and favorability) of regulatory policy (and the likely range of policy change), it is necessary to be able to look at the give and take of political conflict.

Judgments about the likelihood of regulatory policy change are based upon two *political factors*: regulatory predictability (i.e., resoluteness) and regime stability. Regulatory predictability implies that the regulatory process, in which prices and levels of service are set, is not arbitrary. If the condition of regulatory predictability holds, then investors can forecast their returns over time and hence can calculate the value of their investment. Further, labor, suppliers, and consumers of the utility's services must believe that the payments, contracts, and prices will be kept within the parameters promised by the regulation or they will strive to disrupt or change the regulatory process. If the regulatory "war of all against all" breaks out, then predicting consequent changes in regulatory decisions will be extremely difficult. Regime stability refers to the way the government regulates the industry. The questions here are at a higher level; for example, will the utility, labor, or consumers have property rights or representation in the regulatory process? If either of these two political factors seem problematic, then there is little basis for judging regulatory promises and, hence, private investment and social cooperation toward reforms will be discouraged.

Following Cox and McCubbins (Chapter 2), we will argue that three characteristics of the regulatory process are important determinants of regulatory predictability: assignment of agenda control over regulatory policy changes, the definition of the reversionary regulatory policy (i.e., the policy that obtains in the absence of policy change), and the number of veto gates (i.e., places in the process where it is possible to reject policy changes) in the regulatory process. First, if a veto player with a stake in the reversion has agenda control, then an investor can take comfort in the expectation of an *ex ante* veto. Second, the more extreme[1] the reversionary policy, all else constant, the more likely is policy change; conversely, if the reversion constitutes some veto player's ideal policy, then policy change under normal circumstances is highly unlikely. With respect to the third characteristic, the more players there are who control veto gates, the more likely it is that the current policy will be resolute. This observation hinges on an important premise: Policy cannot legally be changed unless there exists some alternative policy that all veto players prefer to the reversionary policy.

Regulatory predictability does not, of course, exist alone. Even when the regulatory process is stable and predictable, the potential for changes

---

[1] We define "extreme" here as a point sufficiently far from all the veto players' ideal points.

in government or its goals might make it difficult to predict future returns on investment. Unpredictability arises because such changes could in turn generate unpredictable changes in the regulatory regime itself. In order to understand investment and regulatory decisions, therefore, it is necessary to examine regulatory structures on the one hand, and the possibility that the regulatory structures will themselves be overturned or ignored, on the other.

To that end, in this chapter we look both at regulations and regulatory processes and at the politics and processes of government formation and policy making. We proceed as follows. In the next section, we examine the role of institutions in fostering regulatory predictability. Here we argue that incentives within the regulatory structure for private investment mean little unless they are nested in a political context that makes them durable. Our argument hinges on the role of political institutions in protecting a specific policy. In the third section, we briefly consider the difference between stability that results from a convergence of preferences and that which results from the construction of veto gates. We then look in the fourth section at electricity regulation in its political and institutional context, in Argentina and Chile. While we find efficient and apparently similar regulatory frameworks in both countries, they came about through very different political circumstances and regulatory mechanisms (for a detailed description of policies to promote competition in both countries, see Hogan 1996). The final section concludes.

INSTITUTIONAL DETERMINANTS OF REGULATORY PREDICTABILITY: VETO GATES, REVERSIONARY POLICY, AND AGENDA CONTROL

A necessary condition for policy *change* is that policy makers prefer some policy other than the status quo. There are a number of reasons why changing policies might become attractive. A new government might come to power, reflecting new (or hitherto ignored) demands and priorities; better information might become available to policy makers (via generational replacement or new advisory teams, for example) that supports more efficient alternative policies; policy makers might want to adjust policy in response to extragovernmental pressures, as from interest groups or rival political parties; or technology may develop to render old regulatory structures irrelevant or even harmful. Each of these possibilities carries the danger that policy change will reduce the return to investors with sunk costs in the affected industries.

There are three features of the process that investors can consider in order to predict the consequences of their actions and thus to make reasoned investments. First, investors can identify who holds veto power over policy change. In the United States, for example, utilities hold an *ex ante* veto in that they control the proposal power to change rates. Public utilities commissions can veto proposed changes. If any veto player has a stake in current policy, then the status quo will endure, thereby protecting the expected return on investments. A second key variable, therefore, is the policy that obtains, if no new policy is enacted, the reversionary outcome. Often, the reversionary outcome is the status quo; but, this need not be the case, as illustrated by policies that are subject to sunset provisions. Under such policies, the reversionary outcome is not the status quo, but rather the eventual cessation of existing policy. Federal spending in the United States for the Department of Education, for example, reverts to zero dollars in the absence of new appropriations for it in the annual budget. With regard to regulatory policy, a reversionary outcome could include a sunset provision that calls for deregulation via termination of the relevant regulatory agency. In the United States, the reversionary outcome is the existing rate structure and service schedule. Finally, an investor would be wise to consider the agenda setters, who dictate whether and what proposed changes will be considered. In the United States, as noted above, proposal power belongs to the utilities. In Chile, it is the regulatory agency that proposes changes to the existing policy. We will discuss the dynamics of each of these elements of the policy-making process in turn.

A common approach to instituting a commitment is to increase the number of veto players with authority to block policy changes. A political process that increases the number of veto players, while making no other changes, will be more biased toward maintaining reversionary policy.[2] Hence, government commitment to stable policy or process is easier in presidential, bicameral-legislative (where the chambers have equal powers), and federal constitutional systems, as well as multiparty systems where no single party controls a majority of legislative seats, for in each case we see a multiplicity of veto players.

---

[2] Stable policies or processes, however, do not necessarily encourage investment. Current policy may be difficult to change but may be also averse to investment. Therefore, the investors must evaluate the degree to which the reversionary policy suits their goals for rate of return.

The combination of agenda control, veto power, and reversionary outcome affects the stability of regulatory policy. Thus, the level of private investment in utilities is, at least partially, a function of these three institutional features. To see how this might work, let us first consider a simple agenda structure where agenda control is granted to the regulator and the utility lacks the ability to veto changes in the reversionary policy. Under this scenario, the regulator would pick its ideal policy. When the utility's ideal point is closer to the regulator's ideal point than to the reversion, then the utility is made better off; otherwise, the utility is made worse off.

Next, consider a slight variation of this agenda, where the utility is granted a veto over changes to the reversion policy. Under this regulatory process, the utility has a chance to protect its interests. For example, if the utility's ideal point is in fact closer to the reversion than it is to the regulator's ideal point, then the utility will veto proposals to change policy to the regulator's ideal point. Given these preferences and an agenda that allows the utility to veto policy change, the regulator would only offer the utility a proposal that is closer to both the regulator's ideal point *and* the utility's ideal point than it is to the reversion. The regulator does this in anticipation of the utility's veto power. *Thus, by changing the regulatory process, in granting the utility a veto, the regulatory policy can move closer to the utility's ideal policy.*

Now consider the agenda structure where the utility again has a veto and the reversionary policy lies between the ideal point of the utility and the ideal point of the regulator. In this circumstance, there is no proposal that makes both the regulator and the utility better off than the reversion. The equilibrium outcome, then, is the reversion.

Finally, consider the agenda structure where the utility initiates changes to the regulatory policy, and the regulator has a veto, as is often the case in the United States. In this case, the utility's best strategy is to select a policy that both the regulator and the utility prefer to the reversion. This scenario directly parallels the case when the utility has a veto and the regulator proposes a new policy – the only difference is that the two players switch roles.

The notion of vetoing a policy proposal implies that there is some other policy – the reversionary policy – is preferred. The existence of veto players and a reversionary policy, then, leads us to make the following predictions:

- When the reversion lies between veto players or when it is itself the most preferred policy of at least one veto player, the reversion will obtain.
- When the reversion is relatively more extreme, by contrast – that is, as it becomes more likely that all veto players (and, of course, whoever has proposal power) will agree on some alternative to it – the outcome will be something other than the reversion.

In order to analyze regulatory policy, we must look not only at regulatory incentives but also at the authority and preferences of regulators, the ease of changing regulatory processes, and reversionary policy. Further, especially in light of the past experience of many low- and middle-income countries, we should consider what happens when key players are denied a veto. Formal vetoes mean little when they are unbalanced – that is, controlled by one or more players with identical preferences. Where veto gates are few or unbalanced *and* exclude important actors such as the military, we must consider also the specter and consequences of dissatisfaction, not only with regulatory outcomes and process, but also with the entire political structure. It is to this analysis that we now turn.

THE DETERMINANTS OF REGIME STABILITY

As explained in Chapter 2, the determinants of regime stability are unity of purpose and separation of powers. If policy makers agree on the structure of regulatory decision making, then the process for deciding regulatory policy will be stable. Such unity of purpose among policy makers could arise if division would allow those who could topple the government to come to power, or if there is a unity of purpose among those to whom the government is accountable. As long as this unity of purpose holds, we expect that the regulatory process will be stable.

Suppose, however, that policy makers are divided on the issue of regulatory structure. If competing factions all prefer some alternative to the status quo, but disagree over which of the alternatives should be chosen, unity of purpose disappears. Then, for the existing regulatory structure to be stable, the competing factions must be able to check each other's proposed changes. That is, in a divided society, a system of separation of powers must exist, so that competing factions hold a veto over proposed changes in the existing regulatory institutions (Cox and McKelvey 1984; Tsebelis 1995). Otherwise, chaos is a likely result.

Separation of powers stacks the deck in favor of preserving the reversion, hence allowing for regulatory stability.

UTILITY REGULATION IN ARGENTINA AND CHILE

In the next two sections, we turn our attention to the specifics of agenda control, veto authority, and political risk and regime stability in Argentina and Chile. These two countries, with their similar political systems but different regulatory rules and outcomes, present a stark contrast.[3] One of the key regulatory differences between the two countries is where agenda power lies: In Chile, the regulators mostly control the agenda; in Argentina, by contrast, the regulators' agenda power is quite limited. Argentine regulators may exercise agenda power only at specified intervals and, in fact, they share agenda authority with producers, distributors, and even users. ENRE, the national electricity regulatory body in Argentina, can propose new policies unilaterally, for example, only when issuing or renewing licenses. It must respond, however, to proposals for change (e.g., to alter price-setting formulas or tariff structures) emanating from consumers as well as generators and distributors. While the government's (specifically, the Secretaría de Energía's) 20%-share in CAMMESA (Compañía Administradora del Mercado Mayorista Eléctrico Sociedad Anónima – the corporation that administers the wholesale electricity market) gives it special veto powers over decisions taken by CAMMESA's board, it has no more authority to make proposals in that area than the generators, transmission companies, and distributors with whom it shares ownership.

This difference in the regulators' agenda power can be a subtle but important factor in investor calculations of expected returns. To anticipate the discussion below, in Chile, political risk is minimal. The Constitution makes it very difficult for politicians who want to change the regulatory regime to succeed and, moreover, the general success of liberalizing policies means that those who want to roll them back are in a decided minority. The regulatory regime itself is quite formal (i.e., specific about what can be changed, how much, and under what circum-

---

[3] The contrast stems from the mirroring principle (McCubbins et al. 1989, 444). Argentina's regulatory regime, open to participation (and to conflict) on all sides, reflects Argentine politics as that country works to shake off its turbulent political past. And Chile's regulatory regime, insulated from politics and largely free from the need to respond to conflict, reflects Pinochet's position and power at the time *el legislador* set it into law.

stances), so that while regulators have a great deal of authority to propose policy change, they are very limited in the proposals that they can make. Under these conditions, investors have little to fear from rogue regulators and so should be untroubled by the CNE's agenda authority.

In Argentina, political risk has decreased, but it is still not clear whether the present favorable investment climate is well-entrenched or merely dependent on the whims of President Menem and his economic team (hence the international as well as domestic concern over Menem's sacking of Economy Minister Cavallo). Under these circumstances, investors have held on to substantial agenda control, which can serve as added protection against the policy whims of elected officials.

Electricity Regulation and Regulatory Outcomes in Argentina

In this section we examine the privatization and concomitant regulation of Argentine electricity. To this end, we first sketch the extent to which the electricity sector is privatized. We next look at rate-setting rules and processes. The structure of rate setting defines veto gates, reversionary outcomes, and agenda control in utility regulation. We then situate these rules within the larger political context of electoral, legislative, and constitutional processes. By identifying agenda setters, veto players, and reversionary policy, we can formulate and test hypotheses against available data on rates and rate structures.

Privatization and Regulatory Predictability. Privatization and hence regulation of electric utilities in Argentina is a new phenomenon.[4] The current system, designed for private enterprise, is unique in that it divorces utility earnings from their capital-investment costs. Of further interest, while provisions for rate of return on capital have been abandoned, the regulatory scheme essentially provides for rate of return on variable costs such as labor, administration and organization, fuel, and so forth, reflecting the importance of labor to the governing coalition. This regulatory scheme appears to be consistent with a "mirroring" principle (McCubbins et al. 1989); that is, those who create the policy seek to ensure that it operates in a way consistent with *their* interests, even after they have left or been removed from power.

The government and the workers of SEGBA (Servicios Eléctricos del Gran Buenos Aires) reached an agreement on selling SEGBA (with some

---

[4] The process began in 1989, but the first sales took place in 1992.

shares going to workers) in September 1989 (González Fraga 1991, 95). By 1994, the government had sold majority stakes to three distribution firms, serving a total of 3,954,333 customers; six transmission companies, accounting for a total of 14, 971 kilometers of lines; and 21 generating plants, ranging in capacity from 47 to 1400 megawatts, for a total capacity of 10,203 megawatts. The government held 39% of shares for itself, distributed 10% to workers, and sold the rest on the stock market.[5] It sold between 51% and 60% of generating plant shares on the stock market, keeping between 30% and 47% for itself and distributing the balance to workers in the affected plants (ENRE 1994a, 20, 25, Table 2). Purchasers involved in the original sale included Chilean companies as well as companies from France and Spain (Hannon 1993, 96; Rausch 1993, 185). Privatization of so many state holdings in just two years suggests that investors find the Argentine regulatory formula attractive.

The Regulation of Generation, Transmission, and Distribution

Electricity generation, transmission, and distribution are regulated under Law 24065 and Decree 1398/92. As in most countries, there are different regulatory procedures for each of these three aspects of electricity provision.

Electricity generation is essentially unregulated, with no need for (prospective) generators to obtain permission prior to building or adding to generating facilities. When it comes to *selling* electricity, generators operate in two markets: In one, they can contract to sell their output among themselves and directly to distributors and large consumers, at any price that both parties can agree to (Law 24065, Article 5).[6] In the second, they supply energy at the "spot" price[7] on the basis of the marginal cost of meeting immediate demand (ENRE 1994a, 39–40).[8] Generators "also are remunerated for their available capacity," through a fixed, per-megawatt sum that is added into the spot price (ENRE 1994a, 40).

---

[5] One transmission firm, Transcomahue, was bought by the provincial-government firms EPEN and ERSE.

[6] Note that the rules governing implementation of the electricity law prohibit owners of generating facilities from holding licenses to distribute electricity (Decree 1398/92, Article 9).

[7] The spot price is calculated hourly by the Compañía Administradora del Mercado Mayorista Eléctrico Sociedad Anónima (CAMMESA).

[8] In periods of high demand, therefore, the "spot" price will be much greater than the production cost of the most efficient producers.

Electricity transmission and distribution are classified as public services. Transmission companies may not buy and sell electricity. Like distributors, they are considered natural geographical monopolies and are obliged to supply access to transmission lines as long as they have capacity to spare, for which they charge a fixed transport fee (see footnote 10). Distribution companies (but not transmission companies) can buy their energy either directly from a generator for a contracted price, or they can buy electricity in the "producers' market"[9] at a three-month "stabilized" spot price intended to approximate what would prevail in a free market (ENRE 1994a, 46).[10]

The national electricity regulating body (Ente Nacional Regulador de la Electricidad, or ENRE) regulates transmission and distribution companies and, for the most part, both are covered by the same regulatory provisions.[11] The transmission and distribution companies control the agenda, insofar as they can propose changes to rates, but they also must obtain permits from ENRE in order to build, operate, or extend their facilities (Law 24065, Article 11). The process through which such permits are granted is replete with public hearings and public notice and comment (much like that provided for in the U.S. Administrative Procedure Act; see also Resolución ENRE No. 39/94). They must also obtain ENRE approval for mergers, buyouts, or service cutbacks; such approval, like approval of operating licenses, requires a well-defined process of public notice, hearing, and comment. The reversionary policy when ENRE rejects a request is the status quo policy (i.e., ENRE holds an *ex ante* veto over regulatory change); should ENRE fail to act, neither

---

[9] A producer's market is a "spot" market where the price is calculated by a company dedicated only to that task (e.g., in Argentina, CAMMESA).

[10] This price combines long-term estimates of the output of the most economical production technology (over the long term) available (i.e., hydroelectric), weekly estimates of the probability of breakdowns and the concomitant costs of ensuring sufficient capacity to maintain uninterrupted supply, and daily calculation – given input availability (for example, hydroelectric generation grows more expensive during dry spells) – of the most efficient type of generator. Decisions as to the standard for an efficient generator, as well as estimates of future demand and probability of breakdowns, are made by the regulatory body, leaving quite a bit of leeway for the "spot" price to differ from what would be the free-market price.

[11] Unless otherwise specified, we shall refer generically to distribution companies to cover both aspects of supply. We focus mainly on distribution, not because regulation of transmission companies is transparent or uninteresting – it is neither – but because transmission-specific regulations are in a different category from distribution. In any case, the fixed transmission prices are factored into retail prices straightforwardly.

rejecting nor accepting a request, then policy reverts to the utility's proposal.

Pricing Under the New Regime

While the wholesale electricity market is largely unregulated, with prices subject basically to the pressures of supply and demand, the retail market is not. Distributors operate regional monopolies under five-year licenses from ENRE and, therefore, do not face market competition. The licenses stipulate a tariff structure, which then serves as the basis for all price adjustments.

The reversionary pricing policy, then, is the initial tariffs agreed to at the beginning of the licensing period, adjusted according to a number of criteria set forth in the electricity law. As circumstances and technologies are not constant, distributors may request adjustments to the initial structure, thereby controlling the agenda over price changes. Such requests must be approved by ENRE, which holds veto authority over them. Rate-change requests are subject to challenge on several fronts (Law 24065, Article 45; Resolución ENRE No. 39/94); ENRE may call hearings on rate adjustments, for example, if it believes that a company's rates are "unjust, unreasonable, unjustifiably discriminatory, or preferential" (Law 24065, Article 48; and see Resolución ENRE No. 39/94). *In the event of ENRE inaction (i.e., no ruling within 120 days), the licensee may institute its requested changes as if they had been approved.*[12] Thus, the distribution companies control, to some extent, the reversionary policy. Together with their control over the agenda, the regulatory process should seem quite attractive to investors, as it is predictable and controllable. If the initial tariffs in the contract are favorable, then investors should be quite happy to commit their resources.

The distribution companies' control over the reversionary policy indicates that the government designed the regulatory structure to ensure that private investors would continue to garner a satisfactory rate of

---

[12] This gives the licensee only partial control over the reversion because, should ENRE later reject the requested change, the licensee must return to the old rate structure and reimburse customers for any difference in payments (Law 24065, Article 47). How this plays out, however, is unclear. Therefore, industry's role in agenda setting remains a potent tool for investors to help ensure the preservation of profitable regulatory structures.

return beyond the tenure of the enacting coalition. Again, this is consistent with the "mirroring" principle as discussed previously.

In many countries, including such disparate cases as Japan, the United States, and Mexico, utility prices are regulated so that residential users are charged a lower rate than many other types of users. Prices fit this description in Argentina when its electric utilities were state-owned enterprises. Moreover, prior to privatization, prices were often unpredictable (Covarrubios and Maia 1994a), particularly for commercial users. As a general rule, industry tends to pay less for electricity than other consumers, due both to its relatively elastic demand for energy (Kahn and Gilbert 1994, 13) and to the fact that energy for industry tends to be cheaper to deliver because it comes in larger quantities and at higher tension. If prices reflect cost of delivery, then the ratio of residential to industry prices should always be greater than one. As can be seen in Table 7.1, before privatization in 1989–1990, the ratio of residential to industrial prices was in fact above unity. Table 7.1 also shows that, prior to privatization, low-demand residential users were charged far less than high-demand residents, commercial users, and small industry.

In the leadup to privatization, however, prices were adjusted. While commercial users were still charged more than any other class of consumers, by 1991, low- and high-demand residential users were facing roughly equal prices and small and large industry both saw significant price drops. These changes more than doubled SEGBA's total average tariff from spring 1990 to spring 1992 (Covarrubios and Maia 1994b, A-40, Table 2). This doubling in the total average tariff, given the increase in electricity consumption overall (see Table 7.2), implies that the utility's revenues increased greatly and that utilities were increasing capacity to fulfill previously unmet demand.[13] The increase in prices for residential consumers is a nontrivial change with respect to revenue for the utilities, since residential consumption is both inelastic and accounts for nearly 50% of overall electricity sales (see Table 7.3). We also see evidence of increasing profitability for Argentine electric utilities. For example, consider EDENOR, the electricity distribution company for the northern region of Argentina. EDENOR's balance sheet reported net

---

[13] As of 1991, average revenue for electricity (total sales divided by total sales in Gwh) was only 79% of average financial cost, defined as total operating cost, plus payments on debt interest and principal, minus depreciation, divided by total sales in Gwh (Campos and Esfahani 1994, Table 2b).

Table 7.1. *Preprivatization Rate Ratios by Consumption Category (SEGBA)*

Ratio of Prices Between	1987	1988	1991
Residential low/Large industry	1.48	2.47	2.10
Small industry/Large industry	2.45	2.98	1.58
Residential high/Large industry	2.38	2.41	2.07
Commercial/Large industry	2.38	2.93	2.63

All figures rounded to nearest 100th of a cent.
Source: Heidarian and Wu 1994, 20.

Table 7.2. *Total Electric Energy Consumption in Argentina*

Year	Consumption (billion kilowatt hours)
1990	46
1991	49
1992	53
1993	58
1994	61

Source: Energy Information Administration, Office of Energy Markets.

Table 7.3. *SEGBA Electricity Sales (MWh)*

Year	Residential	Commercial	Industrial
1990	5187890	1425959	4226193
1991	5554000	2134881	4074052

Sources: Secretaria de Energia, Subsecretaria de Energia Electrica, Direccion Nacional de Prospectiva.

losses in 1992 and 1993 but they have begun to turn it around with net gains in both 1994 and 1995 (see Table 7.4).[14] This increase in profitability is attractive to investors, particularly if they are convinced that the

[14] The losses in the first couple of years after privatization can be attributed to the enormous inefficiency of the state-run companies, which the private owners inherited.

Table 7.4. *Postprivatization*
Annual Profits, Argentina
(EDENOR)

Year	Net Income (thousands of pesos)
1992	−52,304
1993	−65,814
1994	1,386
1995	46,530

Source: Data supplied by ENRE.

existing regulatory structure is sustainable. In fact, the utility's agenda-setting role with respect to policy change offers the investor confidence in regulatory sustainability, and thus gives rise to regulatory predictability.

The regulatory regime that was created for privatized electric utilities privileges status-quo tariffs. Private utilities, under this new structure, retain monopoly proposal power for changes in regulatory policy. Rational utilities, therefore, will make proposals for policy change only when it will guarantee higher rates of return than the status quo. The regulatory process, replete with hearings and open challenges, essentially gives companies a veto over new policy and thus makes regulatory policy predictable. Hence, by adjusting prices before privatization in order to make SEGBA profitable and by credibly committing to a regulatory structure that stacks the deck in favor of the status quo, the government guaranteed the preservation of tariffs that were favorable to investment. The new pricing structure was credible as long as the regulations underpinning it were seen as stable. This is the topic to which we next turn.

Regime Stability. The new regime in Argentina is attractive to investors because utilities control the agenda over proposed tariff changes and because the reversionary price structure was set up to be profitable. But why would investors believe that the regulatory regime is credible? After all, Argentine politics in the twentieth century have been typified by intense, often violent, class and urban-rural conflict. The provinces' strong voice in politics magnified this conflict. Further, political leaders usually have faced both an interventionist military and an opposition that sought radical economic redistribution.

Political control was particularly desirable because the state owned key sectors of the Argentine economy. State ownership of public utilities was one of the few things that radical party politicians and Peronists agreed on. Whatever the basis for this agreement – economic philosophy, nationalism, political experience, ideology – it effectively opened the coffers of state-owned enterprises to the party in power. As a result, politicians in power have sought two things above all else: to eliminate the opposition and to extract as much as they could from the economy before they themselves were removed from office.

For most of the twentieth century, Argentina's governments have been unified, either under Peronist, Radical/Conservative, or military control. During their tenure in office, each had opportunities to unilaterally impose its own policies. But, the separation of powers system in Argentina allows for the division of purpose within the society to yield divided government. Indeed, in the 1980s, President Alfonsín faced a divided legislature. Divided government, in this instance, seemed destined to follow the same pattern of policy stalemate and political upheaval as in the past, but it did not. The violence of the past caused the parties to compromise in this case: Alfonsín structured a compromise between the moderate factions within both his own Peronist Party and the Radicals who held the legislature. It was under these conditions that privatization was possible (Hill and Abdala 1996).

The 1988 elections brought unified government back in under the Peronist *Partido Justicialista* (PJ) but the newly elected Peronist president, Menem, and other moderate Peronists proved willing to work with moderates in the Radical/Conservative Party even against the wishes of their more extreme copartisans. With the military on the sidelines and the public sector in shambles, control of government was both less tenuous and less profitable than in the past. Thus, while there are still some risks of investing in Argentina relative to investments in other developing countries, the new political environment and new regulatory regime reduced the risks in the near term, making investment more attractive and privatization feasible.

Indeed, the new political climate is reflected in the setting of electricity tariffs. Table 7.5 provides a representative glance at electricity rates for different user categories from the moment of privatization to April 1994.[15] This table shows that the price adjustments made before priva-

---

[15] The table shows the tariff structure for EDENOR S.A., one of the three regional-monopoly distribution companies that were created from SEGBA's distribution network. The other two, which have similar tariff structures, are EDESUR S.A.,

Table 7.5. *Postprivatization Electricity Tariffs, Argentina (EDENOR[a])*

Users	Class[b]	Initial Tariff	April 1993	November 1993 April 1994
Small	T1-R1	0.061	0.061	0.066
	T1-R2	0.056	0.055	0.051
	T1-G1	0.108	0.108	0.104
	T1-G2	0.083	0.083	0.078
	T1-G3	0.063	0.062	0.057
Medium	T2	0.067	0.067	0.062
Large[c]	T3-BT	0.048	0.047	0.042
	T3-MT	0.046	0.045	0.040
	T3-AT	0.043	0.043	0.038

[a] Excluding charges for public lighting, etc.
[b] User classes are defined as follows: *Low demand:* T1-R1, residential < 300 kWh; T1-R2, residential > 300 kWh; T1-G1, general < 1600 kWh; T1-G2, general > 1600 kWh and < 4000 kWh; T1-G3, general > 4000 kWh (all bimonthly). *Medium demand:* T2; *High demand:* T3-BT, low tension, T3-MT, medium tension; T3-AT, high tension.
[c] Rates are shown for mid-demand hours. Peak- and low-demand rates are comparable, and all are equal within categories by April 1994 (Ministerio de Economia y Obras y Servicios Publicos 1992, Subanexo #).
Source: ENRE 1994a, 53. The initial tariff rate is for Sept/Oct 1992.

tization appear to have continued after privatization: Industry's electricity prices have dropped while residential prices have remained fairly steady, if not increased. By and large, however, prices have been fairly stable, far more stable than in previous years.

The compromise policies of the early 1990s were followed by some important political reforms. Prior to 1994, senators were elected from two-member districts by plurality rule in provincial legislatures. It was thus unlikely for a province to have split party representation in the Senate. The rules governing senatorial elections were amended in 1994, and senators now are directly elected in three-member districts under a rule that gives two seats to the party winning the most votes, with the second-place party taking the third seat. Thus, where the old electoral rules reinforced the "winner-take-all" pathology attributed to presidential systems (Linz 1990), the 1994 constitutional amendments undercut this tendency. Further, the amended Constitution not only reduces provincial governments' power, but also the stakes of interprovincial con-

and EDELAP S.A. More recent ENRE data, supplied by Hanna Robles, confirm that this trend has continued into early 1996.

flict, by prohibiting unfunded mandates and stipulating revenue sharing among provinces (Article 75.2). By institutionalizing compromise (cf. Lijphart 1984) and ensuring that the majority cannot deny vital resources to the minority, these reforms made reversionary policy a more acceptable alternative and hence increased the importance of each branch of government's veto authority. In Madisonian terms, the reforms made it feasible for ambition to counter ambition and, thus, gave life to constitutional checks. This makes all policy change, and particularly change that runs roughshod over all opposition, much more difficult.

What do these recent changes mean in terms of investment and prices? We argue that willingness to invest is a function of reversionary policy plus the interaction of regulations, regulatory processes, and political stability. In Argentina, there are three distinct periods of interest with respect to investment and regulatory prices – pre-1992, 1992–1994, and post-1994 – corresponding to bouts of privatization and of constitutional revision. With respect to pricing, we should observe that utility pricing prior to 1992 should follow a political logic, not an economic one. While we do not pretend to analyze policy makers' incentives we do expect prices to be erratic during this period, with unpredictable changes as political circumstances change, and for the tariff structure to favor the constituents to whom the politicians are electorally accountable. Table 7.6 presents average tariff levels for residential, commercial, and industrial users of electricity for April and October, 1988–1991. These data show considerable price instability. The data presented in Table 7.1 also support the latter contention, showing that the ratio of prices favored certain user groups over others.

We would also have expected prices to then stabilize in 1992 for two reasons. First, the government sought to create an initial tariff to encourage investment upon the initiation of privatization. Second, the utilities under the new regulatory structure retained monopoly proposal power for changes from the initial tariff. Indeed, as Table 7.6 indicates, prices stabilized in 1992 for all three user categories. Table 7.5 shows evidence that tariffs were stable between 1993 and 1994.

Investment should be lower where price risk and political uncertainty are high (i.e., an adequate return is uncertain), all else being constant. Thus, we should observe that private investment should have increased from 1992 to the present. Figure 7.1 shows that installed capacity has increased for at least the years for which we have data (installed capacity is a reasonable proxy for investment in generating equipment). Further-

Table 7.6. *Argentine Tariff Structure: 1988–1992 (US$/kWh)*

		Residential Tariff	Commercial Tariff	Industrial Tariff
Pre-1992				
	Apr-88	6.28	8.05	3.06
	Oct-88	8.93	14.12	5.68
	Apr-89	2.30	3.70	1.43
	Oct-89	3.83	10.17	5.58
	Apr-90	4.93	14.02	7.14
	Oct-90	11.16	17.88	8.70
	Apr-91	9.59	10.80	6.42
	Oct-91	9.49	10.68	6.35
1992				
	Jan-Feb	8.52	15.32	9.04
	Mar-Dec	9.71	16.94	9.94

Source: OLADE.

more, utilities will shy away from major investments if they fear that they won't be allowed to recoup their costs, much less earn a profit. This implies, for example, that in a situation of political uncertainty, distributors will invest relatively more heavily in variable inputs for maintaining the existing grid instead of investing capital to upgrade or extend it. This is a testable proposition, although we do not have the data to check it. If we did, we would expect to observe a clear increase in capital investment by distribution companies in the wake of the 1994 constitutional revisions and their confirmation by the public with the peaceful reelection of President Menem. Generators, as we have shown in Figure 7.1, also increased their investments as their future became more secure.[16]

Finally, the higher are utility prices, the more attractive it is for large users to opt out of the system and instead generate their own power. When an uncertain market keeps prices high enough that self-generation is an attractive alternative, self-generation should be fairly common. We note in this regard that, in the absence of the political stabilization we identify with constitutional amendments and Menem's reelection, self-

[16] The situation for transport companies is murkier, as they remain heavily regulated and are permitted to invest only on request from electricity generators or buyers (we thank Hanna Robles of ENRE for this clarifying observation).

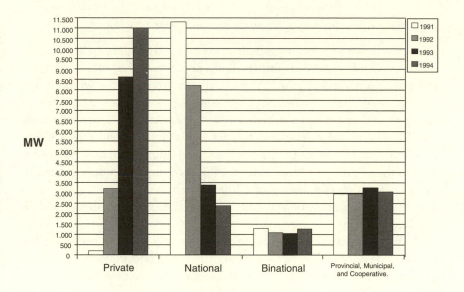

Ownership Type

Figure 7.1.   Installed Capacity by Type of Ownership, Argentina
Source: http://www.mecon.ar/energia/energ_anuario/zip/tapa.htm which contains "IN-FORME DEL SECTOR ELECTRICO" of the SUBSECRETARIA DE ENERGIA, Dirección Nacional de Prospectiva, MINISTERIO DE ECONOMIA Y OBRAS Y SERVICIOS PUB-LICOS SECRETARIA DE ENERGIA, TRANSPORTE Y COMUNICACIONES, Republic of Argentina.

generated electricity in Argentina was projected to rise from some 3400 GWh in 1991 to 5480 in the year 2000 (Covarrubios and Maia 1994b, A-42, Figure 7). In the more certain political climate that prevails today, increased capital investment should improve economies of scale and hence prices, and future estimates of self-generation should decline. Indeed, it has, as the development of new self-generation capacity has recently dropped to near zero, while cogeneration has increased to take advantage of the more favorable pricing structure.[17] Moreover, during the period from 1991 through 1994, the number of self-generators dropped from 1839 to 1601.[18]

---

[17] As noted in a personal communication with Felix Helou, legal advisor on economic regulation at ENRE. Also, see http://www.mecon.ar/energia/energ_anuario/zip/tapa. htm which contains Dirección Nacional de Prospectiva, Republic of Argentina.

[18] See http://www.mecon.ar/energia/energ_anuario; /zip/tapa.htm.

Electricity Regulation and Regulatory Outcomes in Chile

Throughout most of the twentieth century in Argentina, frequent military coups and suspended constitutional processes led to increased political uncertainty and economic risks. Only recently has the winner-take-all quality of Argentine politics been seemingly overtaken by a spirit of compromise. In Chile, Pinochet's 1973 military coup overturned an admirable history of democratic politics. This led to a host of societal problems, including both civil unrest and human rights violations. Rather than inject an added measure of uncertainty to economic decision making, however, the legacy of Chile's nearly two decades of dictatorship is a high degree of stability in both the political regime and in regulatory policy.

Prior to privatization, Argentina set up a profitable reversion for electric utility regulation and then set up a regulatory system that was predictable and, indeed, favorable to utilities. As discussed above, political and institutional changes served to reinforce this structure. Similarly, Pinochet set up a profitable reversion and predictable utility regulation process. This structure in Chile favored utility profit motives.[19] Evidence of favorable conditions for investment is revealed in Table 7.7, as we observe a change in prices that we can trace to early in Pinochet's regime. Table 7.7 shows an increase in the average annual tariff, for both residential and large industry consumers, when comparing an early five-year period of Pinochet's regime with the last five-year period of his tenure,

Table 7.7. *Average Electrical Energy Prices in Chile (US$ cent/kWh)*

	Residential Tariff[a]	Large Industry[a,b]
5 Year Period		
1975–1979	4.20	2.63
1984–1988	8.91	4.15

[a] Series until 1980 may not be comparable with post 1980.
[b] Load Factor = 0.548, high voltage.
Source: Prices until 1980 from OLADE, various issues, from 1981 on, Philippi 1991.

[19] It is interesting to note that Pinochet, while raising tariffs to encourage private investment, continued to favor the agriculture sector with moderate, consistent prices. This is not surprising, since the agriculture sector is a key supporter of his regime.

after his new regulatory structure was given a chance to settle in. Also note that, as expected, Chile's largest electric power supply company, ENDESA, has been quite profitable over the same period (see Table 7.8).[20] Moreover, constitutional change, making changes in the regulatory regime sustainable in the short run, allowed for more stable policies than we might otherwise predict. We now turn to examine the underpinnings of this stability in the context of Chilean electricity regulation.

As in Argentina, the electricity sector in Chile is regulated by a single body – the National Energy Commission (CNE). Guidelines for electricity regulation are spelled out in fine detail in Ministry of Mines Decree 1, 1982 (as amended by Law 18.922, 1990). Also as in Argentina, certain classes of service are unregulated. In general, prices may be freely contracted for large users (over 2000 kW), short-term service (less than twelve months), and users with special service requirements (DFL 1, Article 90).

While the law regulating electricity generation and distribution explicitly leaves certain classes of service unregulated, it nonetheless links regulated and nonregulated prices. Decree 1, 1982, stipulates that the prices set by the CNE "may not differ by more than 10 percent from contracted prices" in the nonregulated market (Law 24065, Article 101). This clause ties the two classes of prices – regulated and unregulated –

Table 7.8. *Chile: Average Electricity Prices (US$ cent/kWh) and ENDESA Profits: 1982–1990*

Year	Residential Tariff	Small Industry Tariff	Large Industry Tariff	ENDESA profits (US $millions)
1982	8.80	7.55	5.52	
1983	7.45	6.45	1.78	101
1984	6.18	5.31	3.84	33
1985	6.40	5.56	3.78	−65
1986	6.48	5.62	3.81	50
1987	7.06	6.19	4.29	62
1988	8.23	7.60	4.78	179
1989	9.24	8.62	5.45	106
1990	8.77	8.18	5.17	104

Source: Spiller and Martorell 1994, 43, 47, Tables B:IX, and B: XIII.

[20] The dip into unprofitability in 1985 coincides with bad economic times in general.

together and carries with it the potential to set up a rather interesting incentive structure for utility investment strategies.

In its rate-setting role, the CNE – again, like its Argentine counterpart – is supposed to take into account the real costs of producing, transmitting, and distributing electricity. To this end, it sets maximum allowable rates that are supposed to reflect the long-run marginal costs of operations (Silva 1991, 25; Spiller and Martorell 1994, 36). The result is intended to approximate prices and profits under a competitive market, not the rate-of-return regulation used prior to 1980 (Spiller and Martorell 1994, 30).

Tariff Regulation. Chilean rate-setting procedures make rate setting predictable. Where ENRE in Argentina must respond to all complaints and, often, hold public hearings, less is required of the CNE. In some cases, as when generating companies register complaints about what they see as unfair regulated rates, CNE is under no obligation to take any action at all (so long as regulated rates are within 10% of unregulated rates – DFL 1, 1982, Article 101). In those cases where a response is required, the manner and degree of the response are spelled out in the law. This makes rate setting transparent and, along with the fact that costs are calculated on the basis of long-term investments (DFL 1, 1982, Article 105), gives companies an incentive to invest in efficient and durable physical plants.

Prices at the distribution end of the electricity pipeline are set on the basis of wholesale, or "node" prices plus value added in distribution. Node prices for electricity are set twice yearly to "reflect an average of the marginal costs of supply incurred in generation and transmission" (DFL 1, 1982, Article 97).[21] To the extent that capital costs are factored into this calculation, they are aggregated and averaged across all generating and transmitting companies. Company-specific capital costs are not included in the calculation of distribution value added. They are determined, along with administrative and operating costs, on the basis of a "model company" whose characteristics CNE defines (DFL 1, 1982, Article 106). By creating and referencing a "model company," in the regulation, the authors of the legislation sought to sustain their market reforms through administrative structure and process (cf. McCubbins et

---

[21] Node prices "are computed using indexing formulae that depend on fuel costs, equipment costs, dam levels, exchange rate, and so on" (Spiller and Martorell 1994, 37).

al. 1989). In short, distributors (except, perhaps, CHILECTRA as discussed below) have little direct control over prices. While they are assured of recouping their cost of buying electricity on the wholesale market, they have no such assurance with respect to returns on their capital investments. For that, they need to invest as efficiently as possible, in order to keep their own costs in line with those of the CNE's "model" company.[22]

In defining the tariff-influencing characteristics of a "model" company, and hence the costs that utilities may recoup through tariffs, the CNE divides companies into three classes. "Low density" (of which there are 7) companies, with fewer than 20,000 customers; "medium density" (17) companies, with between 20,000 and 1 million customers; and "high density" (1 – CHILECTRA, a publicly owned, integrated company) companies that serve more than 1 million users (Spiller and Martorell 1994, 32). "Model" costs are set separately for each class of company, and how closely they approximate costs for companies in a competitive market depends on how accurate the CNE's calculations are, which depends crucially on how competitive the market actually is. As the best source of information on company costs is the companies themselves, estimated costs for medium-density companies should be fairly accurate, costs for low-density companies should be somewhat less accurate, and costs for the single high-density company ought to be overestimated.

As noted above, regulated wholesale prices are set to reflect generating companies' long-run marginal costs. The twist to this scheme is that CNE-determined node prices "cannot diverge by more than 10% from prices [for equivalent tension and power levels] not subject to price regulation" (DFL 1, 1982, Article 101). The intent here is to ensure that nodal prices do not diverge too much from market prices. If generators can use regulated prices as a focal point for collusion, however, this creates an interesting incentive problem with regard to whether to sell their output in the unregulated or the regulated market: The problem is, the existence of the regulated market could take the competitive pressure out of the unregulated market. As in any free market, the fewer compa-

[22] The CNE-defined "model" company represents a "typical," efficient firm. Existing distribution and transmission companies can challenge the CNE's estimates, however (DFL 1, 1982, Article 107). When challenged, the CNE may accede to the utilities' estimates of costs; if not, then the characteristics of a "model" company are calculated as a weighted average of CNE and industry figures. This rule gives electric utilities as a group a fair amount of indirect authority to set their own rates.

nies that compete in the unregulated market, all else being constant, the higher will be the unregulated price and, therefore, the regulated price as well. A company that does not enter into the unregulated market is not, however, denied the ability to sell its product. On the contrary, it can then sell its output on the regulated market *at guaranteed prices*. Hence, collusive, cartellike behavior would be rewarded through higher prices on the regulated market.

There is in fact no fixed reversionary tariff in Chile, although the reversion is predictable and depends on market forces or, absent a competitive market, on well-defined formulas for approximating one. The reversion is essentially whatever the market will bear, and firms that allocate investment inefficiently will see their profits drop as a result. To the extent that the regulatory formulas are well-designed, then, electricity pricing should contribute to more efficient economic development in general.

Results of Chilean Electricity Regulation Reform. On the one hand, then, investment capital should have gravitated toward Chile's electric utilities. Further, as such investment would have been channeled into efficient generation and transmission facilities, Chile should have seen an impressive increase in installed capacity over the same period. On the other hand, to the degree that generators operate in uncompetitive markets (due to market structure or to collusion), and to the degree that CHILECTRA acts as a monopolist in the single largest market in Chile, electricity prices should have held steady or at least dropped far less than might be expected given the increase in installed capacity. As a result, electricity generation should be highly profitable in spite of the CNE's continuing efforts to set tariff rates equal to long-term marginal costs and, therefore, bring profits down to minimal levels.

What we observe in Chile meets our expectations. As can be seen in Table 7.9, the amount of electricity generated in Chile has risen steadily, with prices changing little throughout the 1980s, as seen in Table 7.8. Further, electricity self-generation has continued to rise since privatization (see Spiller and Martorell 1994, 41, Tables B:VI, B:VII). This suggests that prices still are high enough to make it worthwhile for relatively inefficient producers to continue generating electricity rather than buying it off the grid.

Chile's electricity regulatory system has sparked new investment. The question is, what are the chances that this particular regulated system will last?

Throughout Pinochet's regime (1973–1989), Chile's government fo-

Table 7.9. *Electricity
Generation, Chile
(thousands of kWh)*

Year	Total
1989	17,727,469
1990	18,321,400
1991	19,807,554
1992	22,167,280
1993ᵖ	23,331,924

Source: Instituto Nacional de
Estadisticas 1994, Table 234–
01, 169.

cused on economic liberalization and political stability. By the time
Pinochet left power, the electricity sector was just one of many segments
of the economy that had been privatized and opened up to market
forces. In essence, the free market became the reversionary policy. We
next argue that this reversion is well-protected by the Constitution that
Pinochet introduced in 1980.

Regime Stability. Chile's Constitution privileges the status quo. Chile
has a separation of powers system with a bicameral legislature, like Argentina, with each chamber possessing a veto over policy. Rules that skew
representation in favor of conservative, rural areas, and a two-member
district system that gives a strong boost to the second-strongest party in
a district virtually guarantee that supporters of the policies put in place
under Pinochet always have the ability to veto changes to them. Not only
is it difficult for a single party to win more than 50% of lower-house
seats (see Caviedes 1991; Godoy Arcaya 1994), but a constitutional
provision (Article 45) for appointed (8-year terms) and lifetime senators
has thus far denied a Senate majority to Pinochet's old antagonists.[23]
    As a result, it would be very difficult for a government that sought to

---

[23] Pinochet's government appointed its own supporters to the Senate positions. In the
1989 elections that preceded Pinochet's withdrawal from the forefront of politics,
the opposition Concertación won about 58% of the elected seats in both the House
of Deputies and the Senate. It was able to occupy only 47% of Senate seats,
however, because of the designated senators. In 1993, Concertación parties jointly
won about 55% of elected Senate seats, but only 46% of total Senate seats. The
Concertación's share of the popular vote in 1989 and 1993 was 52.1 and 55.5%,
respectively (Auth 1994, 347).

reverse policies enacted under Pinochet's rule to do so. Unless *Concerta-ción* lists and candidates begin to win by overwhelming majorities throughout the country, their opposition is likely always to hold a powerful check. And even if the *Concertación* were to sweep aside its opponents, it remains in effect a coalition of parties with distinct policy goals (see especially, Drake 1993, 4; Auth 1994, 347). As it stands now, the present governing coalition – onetime opponents of Pinochet and, it was presumed, all he stood for – stands in support of economic liberalism and the economic model promoted by Pinochet's regime (Godoy Arcaya 1994, 305).

Drastic changes in regulatory policy or goals, therefore, are unlikely in Chile. Those who might oppose current policies cannot expect to control all the various segments of the policy-making process, so they cannot expect to change policy. Moreover, if 1993 electoral outcomes are any indication, voters approve of the liberalizing bent of the current government. Perhaps more to the point, Pinochet and the military returned to the barracks, but they still pose a tacit threat to all who might consider significantly changing the status quo. This situation will remain unchanged until 1997, when the balance of power in the Senate may shift as a result of the appointment of eight new members by the president.

CONCLUSION

Chile's success in privatizing the electricity sector (and other utilities, such as telecommunications) has been seen as a victory for institutional engineering. Chile's privatized electricity sector seems to have developed steadily and healthily over time, while Argentina's development looks much more erratic. Now that Argentina has privatized electric utilities, the question arises as to whether its development will begin to parallel that of Chile. Spiller and Martorell (1994) argue that it will not, because Chile has had the time to develop calmly, with "strong political support for maintaining the financial viability of the companies," an opportunity denied Argentina. Further, electricity regulation in Chile is decentralized, while in Argentina it remains centralized in the federal government (Spiller and Martorell 1994, 49).

There is undoubtedly much truth to this view. The level of regulatory risk, after all, is tightly linked to the decisiveness of policy making – the ease with which regulatory procedures allow regulators to force utilities to reallocate the incidence of charges, for example. We have argued here, however, that investment strategies look to a much more basic source of risk: regime instability. While this has been only a distant concern in Chile, it has been an urgent concern in Argentina. But, the future may bring changes. We contend that constitutional reform has transformed Argentine politics to some extent, providing a foundation for profitable enterprise comparable to that built up over many years in Chile. By contrast, changes in the makeup of the Chilean Senate could constitute a shift in its policy preferences, as we expect the new appointees to be either part of the president's party or at least members of a party other than the Conservatives. In Argentina, now that the constitutional incentives lead to compromise and not confrontation (and the military threat is but a pale caricature of what it once was; see, e.g., Sims 1996), investors and firms can look forward to a more favorable future.

The task for any government that wishes to privatize its utilities is to establish a regulatory structure that is both favorable to private investment and sustainable without sacrificing service. Private entities must be satisfied that the political risk of investing in regulated utilities is counterbalanced by a sufficiently tempting expected rate of return. If, however, the rate of return is not exorbitantly high, then cautious investors must be convinced that a more conservative rate of return is politically sustainable. Our theory of privatization and political risk establishes that regulatory predictability and regime stability are two conditions that encourage private investment in public utilities. When a government and its regulatory structure meet these conditions, private investors can reasonably conclude that the commitment to the process is credible. Evidence from Argentina and Chile, as presented here, indicates that these conditions are, in fact, critical to the economic growth of key sectors within developing nations.

8

Power Politics

Elections and Electricity Regulation in Taiwan

STEPHAN HAGGARD and GREGORY W. NOBLE[1]

The drive for economic reform in developing countries is usually associated with trade liberalization, price reform, deregulation, and the sale of state-owned enterprises. Some of the most important reforms, however, center on economic activities that are typically regulated even in the market economies of advanced industrial states. These reforms focus primarily on the supply of water and power, finance, transportation, and telecommunications. The key policy objectives in regulating these markets are to stimulate an adequate level of investment to meet demand, to avoid the exercise of market power by natural monopolists, and to set prices in a way that encourages efficiency in the production and consumption of the regulated goods and services.

Electric power is a particularly important case because it is central to virtually all economic activity. The regulation of electric power is vulnerable to a number of political problems, particularly when utilities are state-owned (Joskow and Schmalensee 1985; Levy and Spiller 1994; Spiller and Viana Martorell 1994; Guasch and Spiller 1995; Heller and McCubbins, ch. 7). First, capital-intensive utilities such as electricity generate enormous cash flows; as a result, political authorities may be tempted to tap this stream of revenue and divert it to political supporters rather than use it for investment purposes. Even if the government does not behave in this fashion, the political system may generate a second problem – inefficiencies in the structuring of prices. Politicians do not

[1] We would like to thank Nick Cullather, Will Heller, Phil Keefer, Mathew McCubbins, Matthew Shugart, and Chris Woodruff for comments on earlier drafts. T. J. Cheng and Roger Noll were particularly helpful. Tonia Pizer and David Johnson provided research assistance. We are also thankful to Val de Beausset and Chi Schive of the Council for Economic Planning and Development and to numerous officials from the Ministry of Economic Affairs and Taipower for their cooperation.

necessarily have incentives to encourage efficient marginal cost pricing; electoral or interest group pressures can lead them to distort prices to favor suppliers or particular classes of users (Stigler 1971; Peltzman 1976).[2] Finally, as governments seek to privatize industries, they face the problem of assuring private investors while simultaneously guaranteeing competitive behavior. Because investments in the utilities sector are large, lumpy, and immobile, they are vulnerable both to expropriation and to ex post changes in the pricing structure. If governments are incapable of making credible commitments to protect property rights or to ensure stable regulation, private (and even public) investors will underinvest.

Taiwan offers an intriguing case for comparative analysis of electricity regulation because, unlike many other developing countries, it has largely avoided these problems. The country has enjoyed a relatively stable regulatory environment, without egregious distortions in pricing; additionally, it has encouraged sustained investment in electricity generation and transmission.

One popular explanation for this outcome is the existence of a "developmental state," with a strong and insulated bureaucracy at its core (Johnson 1982; Wade 1990). This argument has some surface plausibility: The state-owned Taiwan Power Company (Taipower) was long led by a stable cadre of technocrats, most of whom were trained by the company itself. Taipower took the initiative in most investment and pricing decisions, usually with little apparent political oversight from the Legislative Yuan (Taiwan's Congress) or even the Minister of Economic Affairs.

Closer scrutiny reveals that Taipower was *never* autonomous from the top political leadership. Actions taken at different points in the company's history reveal that Taipower's rate of return, its pricing and investment decisions, top leadership, and even basic legal status were all subject to change by the top officials in the Economics Ministry, most of whom were not (as in Japan) career civil servants but rather presidential appointees. Despite Taipower's considerable day-to-day operating independence, it was always subject to oversight by the executive and the ruling party; this was even more true after the transition to democratic rule in the mid-1980s. Moreover, the developmental state model assumes

---

[2] Regarding production, prices may be distorted as a result of regulations that lead to the excessive use of labor. Regarding consumption, governments frequently extend favorable rates to particular classes of users, a practice that not only affects the efficiency of energy use but also distorts the broader allocation of resources.

a relatively constant political structure that bears little resemblance to Taiwan even during its authoritarian period; the model is especially ill-suited to understand the transition to democratic rule.

In this chapter, we show how institutional arrangements, the separation of power and purpose, and the constituencies to which the KMT appealed affected the nature, coherence, and credibility of regulatory policy. We build our analysis around a comparative statics analysis of three periods. The first half of the chapter contrasts the early authoritarian period (1949–c.1960) with the latter more "consolidated" authoritarian phase (1960–1986); the second half of the chapter addresses the democratic period (1986–present). During the first two periods we focus primarily on investment and pricing decisions. During the democratic period, we extend our analysis to cover four policy areas: (1) the level and structure of prices; (2) the management of outages; (3) the politics of plant siting; and (4) the emergence of a privatization program. Our analysis of the authoritarian period shows that considering separation of purpose is useful not only for understanding domestic developments but also for identifying international actors who may place checks on executive discretion. Finally, we show how electoral reform results in a new, and welcome, separation of powers and purpose.

In the early authoritarian period, the KMT effectively eliminated all political challengers and established a regime characterized by a powerful executive and the monopoly of a single party. Such a system should be highly decisive (Shugart and Haggard, ch. 3), but the party was *internally* factionalized, allowing a limited division of powers to emerge with respect to the making of energy policy. Accommodating these factional and legislative pressures contributed to substantial biases in energy pricing. Government policy favored state-owned industry at the expense of both commerce and residential users.[3]

These arrangements might very well have persisted, yielding the types of distortions that are only too frequent in developing countries. However, a full mapping of the political arrangements governing electricity regulation must take into account the role of the United States. Initially, the United States tolerated the KMT's preferences; in effect, there was a unity of purpose between the two countries driven by U.S. strategic interests. The government initially had few incentives to raise prices or to force Taipower to generate the revenues needed for investment be-

---

[3] In the early authoritarian period, the military, party functionaries, and the civil service were the core KMT constituencies.

cause the United States was providing substantial financial support; it was fully rational for the government to tap Taipower's revenues and to extend subsidies to its clients.

However, the United States maintained agenda control through its aid policy, and when its preferences changed so did the political game. The KMT retained a veto over U.S. proposals, but only at the high cost of reverting to a lower level of assistance. Driven by balance of payments concerns and an interest in limiting financial commitments to its clients, the United States began to reevaluate its overall aid policy in the late 1950s and early 1960s. In Taiwan, the U.S. aid mission began to press for a number of reforms that would reduce aid dependence and make the country more self-sufficient. In the important energy sector, these included a decrease in implicit subsidies, price increases, and a push to generate investment resources internally. The United States also sought changes in the regulatory structure to guarantee that its preferences would be secure. Legislative involvement in the policy process was reduced, eliminating a division of powers through which rent-seeking forces within the party had exercised some influence. Policy shifted to a rate-of-return method of regulation that committed the government to the profitability of Taipower.

Given its political dominance and the absence of effective electoral or institutional checks, the party could have ignored its own commitments, particularly as U.S. aid declined. However, the end of U.S. aid had additional effects. It encouraged economic reforms that strengthened private property rights, made the country more dependent on foreign investment and multilateral assistance, and set the country on the path of export-led growth. As in Chile, increasing dependence on foreign and domestic exporters and foreign lenders placed strong constraints on domestic decision making, particularly when placed in the context of Taiwan's geopolitical isolation; external and externally *oriented* actors continued to exercise a check on government policy. The government continued to pay off its core constituency, but the unity of powers and purpose within the government and the long time horizon of the government permitted a coherent and credible industrial strategy focused on building new plants to supply power to a rapidly growing domestic and foreign private sector.

As the KMT liberalized the political system, it faced new electoral, legislative, and interest group pressures in designing energy policy. Electoral reform meant an increasing separation of both powers and purpose, as the legislature reasserted its prerogatives and legislators faced electoral incentives quite different from those of the president. The full effects of these new political conditions were partly delayed by the prolonged nature of the transition, important continuities in the constitutional powers of the president, and the fact that the KMT maintained its legislative majority. However, ample evidence suggests that the changing constitutional conditions made the executive more sensitive to the legislature and made legislators more sensitive to interest group pressure. We show how the new politics affected the rate structure (tilting rates toward new business constituents), the capacity of Taipower to invest (slowing it by allowing local resistance), and the regulatory institutions themselves (opening them to greater legislative and interest group involvement).

THE AUTHORITARIAN PERIOD: POLITICAL INSTITUTIONS, CONSTITUENCIES, AND EXTERNAL CHECKS

The central feature of Taiwan's politics in the postwar period has been the dominance of the Kuomintang (Nationalist Party or KMT) that relocated to Taiwan following its defeat by the Communists on the mainland in 1949. Initially organized along Leninist lines, the party had been plagued by extreme factionalism on the mainland (T-s. Ch'ien 1950). Chiang Kai-shek exploited the civil war to declare Martial Law in 1948, banning the formation of competing political parties. Following the move to Taiwan, Chiang consolidated his authority within the party, drawing particularly on his control over the military and intelligence apparatus.[4] He quickly invoked external threats and a tenuous international diplomatic position to promulgate "Temporary Provisions," under which the constitution was effectively revised and authority concentrated in the president. The combination of strong presidential powers and the ban on national-level electoral competition and opposition parties[5] allowed the KMT to monopolize the country's complicated five-branch governmental structure. In sum, there was broad unity of both powers and purpose, although some internal factionalism remained.

Despite its fundamentally authoritarian character, the KMT was not

---

[4] Most of the regional warlords and factional leaders chose not to follow the KMT to Taiwan, leaving Chiang Kai-shek and his followers from the Whampoa (Huangpu) military academy in clear control; Chiang took advantage of this dominance to carry out a major internal reform of the party in 1950.

[5] In order to increase both local and Western support, the party did allow elections for subnational office, but this competition was tightly controlled.

oblivious to the need to develop a wider base of support among the majority of indigenous Taiwanese. A wide-ranging land reform built a tacit base of rural support, and economic reforms launched in the 1950s signaled a rapprochement with the local manufacturing sector (see Jacoby 1966; Gold 1986; Haggard 1990, ch. 4; Wade 1990; Haggard and Pang 1994; Cullather 1996). The early reforms strongly favored priority industrial users in Taipei and Kaohsiung over commercial enterprises or households (Jacoby 1966, 177–8).

However, it is important to emphasize that there were no *institutional* incentives for the president or legislators to be responsive to either rural or private sector constituents. Not only was political competition at the national level effectively banned, but the KMT elite was overwhelmingly mainlander and had few personal or clientele ties with the local private sector or landed elite; nor did the party depend on either for political or financial support. Through party-sponsored and other controlled organizations, the KMT penetrated the educational system, unions, farmers' associations, and civil society more generally. Though the private sector grew rapidly, business concentration was actively discouraged (Cheng 1993); the government tightly controlled business organizations, and the private sector had few formal channels for representation within the ruling party or the bureaucracy (Chu 1994, but see also Kuo 1995, chs. 4–6).

The core domestic constituency of the KMT government was the government apparatus itself. Within the government, important conflicts of interests existed. On the one hand, an important technocratic cadre argued early for economic reforms (Haggard and Pang 1994). Initially, these forces were significantly outnumbered by the military, police, civil servants, teachers, and other functionaries that accompanied the government when it moved to Taipei in the late 1940s. The KMT used this numerical advantage and quickly established direct control over the commanding heights of the economy (Cheng 1993). The large state-owned enterprise sector and government ownership of the financial system provided an additional channel for state patronage, particularly to the military.

We would expect energy pricing policy to show favoritism toward these core constituencies. We find that energy policy did indeed favor these interests. Preferential rates for certain classes of users are outlined in Table 8.1. These preferential rates can be divided into two categories. One type are subsidies aimed at the provision of public goods, such as railways, water supply, street lights, and schools. The other type of

Table 8.1. *Taipower Preferential Rates*

Consumer	Discount	Basis of Policy
Military use	30%	MOEA Order. Methods of water and electricity conservation and fee payment for military units is under the Ministry of Defense.
Military dependents	Under 800 units per month: 50%; 801–1000 units per month: 30%	Regulations for preferential treatment for military personnel and families.
Agriculture	Reduction of flat rate according to rate of use	Regulations concerning agricultural development and scope and standards of agricultural energy use
Railways	5%	Article 65 of Power Utility Law, but not less than cost of provision.
Water supply	30%	Article 65.
Street lights	50%	Article 65; not less than half of normal lighting cost.
Schools	Flexible prices parallel to noncommercial rates	

Source: Taiwan Power Company.

preferences includes those for important political clienteles, particularly agriculture and military dependents.

Were we to confine ourselves to the domestic level, the political system appears to constitute a recipe for policy disaster: a relatively coherent institutional structure, albeit with some important policy divisions, at the service of an inefficient state-centered clientele. However, domestic politics in Taiwan cannot be properly understood without also considering international influences. Throughout the 1950s, the KMT regime relied heavily upon American military might, diplomatic support, and economic assistance. U.S. aid supplied a large share of the government budget, and American advisors played a crucial policy role in the postwar economy, including in the transition to export-led growth (Haggard and Pang 1994). This influence extended to the area of electric power. Taipower was the dominant recipient of U.S. project aid in the period 1951–1964, receiving nearly 70% of total U.S. capital assistance to infrastructure. Aid provided the majority of Taipower's investment budget in every year until 1963, when aid began to phase out and the company was forced to rely on internally generated funds for capital spending (Jacoby 1966, 177).[6] The aid allocation process subjected Taipower, and the government more generally, to agenda control that would have been lacking under other circumstances. Formally, the KMT held final veto power; it could have walked away from U.S. aid, but only at high cost. An outline of the policy-making process shows the significance of the United States in changing the policy status quo and setting the stage for a more coherent energy strategy.

THE AUTHORITARIAN PERIOD: THE REGULATORY STRUCTURE AND THE EVOLUTION OF POLICY

Until 1988, when the government promulgated regulations allowing for private cogeneration, the generation, transmission, and marketing of electric power in Taiwan was in the hands of Taiwan Power Company (Taipower), a state-owned corporation with its ownership split between the Central Government (66.7%), the Taiwan Provincial Government (27.3%), and several other agencies.[7] Taipower has an independent board of directors and a budget separate from that of the Economics Ministry; these organizational features gave Taipower a greater degree of statutory independence than public utilities in other developing countries.

Despite these signs of independence, the hierarchical structure of government guaranteed that Taipower fell under direct central government control. The Chiangs personally appointed the presidents of Taipower. The KMT leadership also appointed the chairmen, who tended to come from the bureaucracy, and either directly or indirectly appointed the board members who represented the actual stockholders.[8] The premier

---

[6] AID financed six large hydroelectric and three large thermoelectric power plants during the peak aid years.

[7] Other government agencies hold 5%, with minuscule shares held by the Taipei Municipal Government and private shareholders.

[8] The most important stockholder was the government itself.

controlled all appointments to the succession of interministerial coordinating bodies within the Ministry of Economic Affairs – the ministry that oversaw power policy.[9] The premier, in turn, served at the pleasure of the Chiangs.

Until recent organizational changes, Taipower sent its requests for rate adjustments to the National Corporations Commission of the Ministry of Economic Affairs, which then sent them to the Minister's office and up to the Executive Yuan if the rate change involved an overall rate increase. A similar process governed the approval of investments, though the executive was typically involved more extensively in investment decisions. During the aid period, the U.S. aid mission had a veto over projects.[10] Beginning in the 1960s when aid declined, Taipower could submit requests for projects under certain thresholds (currently NT$ 1 billion). For projects above the threshold, Taipower has had to obtain the express approval of the National Corporations Commission, which reviews the proposals with special attention to the reserve margins for electricity, rate of return, siting, and infrastructural requirements.[11] For larger and more complex projects, the National Corporations Commission does not have the capacity to rule on Taipower plans alone; for these projects, its role shifts to coordinating decision making between the Ministry of Economic Affairs and other relevant agencies. A common device – typical of other aspects of economic policy making in Taiwan (Noble 1999b, chs. 2, 4) – has been to form ad hoc committees of scholars and other experts to review proposals, which are then passed up to the Council on Economic Planning and Development and are ultimately given to the Executive Yuan for final approval.

In sum, the decision-making structure in the authoritarian period was generally hierarchical. Nonetheless, the president and his cabinet delegated substantial authority over rate-setting to Taipower, guaranteed its rate of return, and generally encouraged a long-term, developmentalist

[9] The interministerial coordinating bodies of the Ministry of Economic Affairs are The Public Utilities Rate Deliberation Committee (1960–1966), the Energy Policy Deliberation Small Group (1968–1979), and the Energy Commission.

[10] Though it controlled the approval process and modified projects, it supported almost all of those proposed by Taipower between 1951 and 1963.

[11] "Requests" for Taipower to revise or delay its plans are not uncommon and on occasion the National Corporations Commission does reject proposals. In 1982, for example, it recommended to the Minister of Economic Affairs that the Number 4 nuclear plant be delayed because it would create surplus capacity.

approach to utility pricing and investment. These outcomes can be traced to U.S. influence in the decision-making process.

The energy situation in Taiwan in the immediate postwar period was chaotic. The island had been bombed extensively and the main hydroelectric unit had sustained damage and neglect. Moreover, the interests of the American advisors and their technocratic allies within the government conflicted with those of core KMT constituents. The Americans wanted utility pricing not only to reflect costs of delivery but also to generate the internal savings required to meet investment needs. Limiting implicit subsidies was seen as key to reducing Taipower's voracious appetite for funds from both the United States and from the central government's budget. These policy changes were not limited to rate adjustments but rather required a fundamental reevaluation of Taipower's assets and a modification of the depreciation schedule (*Industry of Free China 2, 4*, October 1954, 50).

The political leadership, by contrast, saw the provision of cheap power as a political tool, providing benefits to the state-owned enterprise sector that dominated industrial output, particular clienteles, and to the nascent private manufacturing sector. In the early period of reconstruction, the United States tolerated KMT preferences. From 1949 through 1954, increases in power rates significantly lagged behind changes in the general price index. If June 15, 1949 (when the New Taiwan dollar was adopted following a stabilization) is taken as the baseline (100), the general price index reached 630 in May 1954. Industrial power rates, however, increased to only 225, and average lighting rates increased to only 450 (*Industry of Free China 2, 4*, October 1954, 49).

Beginning in 1953, conflicts between the government and the U.S. aid mission intensified (Tung 1996). From 1953 through 1958, rate increases had to be formally authorized by the Legislative Yuan; this process established a division of powers, and provided a political channel for forces, both inside and outside the government, that opposed the rate hikes. Of the five authorized rate adjustments between 1953 and 1960, all were below those proposed by Taipower (Taipower 1994, 42). In 1954, rate hikes and power cuts were particularly contentious. Party members, state-owned enterprises, and the private sector all expressed concerns about the effect of rate hikes on the overall price level, a subject on which the government was particularly sensitive given its history with hyperinflation on the mainland. Editorials from the time show substantial private sector resistance to shifting the burden of price increases and outages onto private firms, given that state-owned enterprises were the heaviest users and were rightly suspected of securing special deals. Demands for outright budget subsidies were raised by all users (*Industry of Free China 2, 4,* October 1954, 29–36, 46–54).

Despite these new political channels for the airing of domestic interests, the U.S. aid mission stepped up its efforts to influence the course of policy (Tung 1996). The first coherent pricing formula was set up in 1953 under U.S. pressure. The second price rise in 1955 was again due to the Mutual Security Mission, and a third price increase following a subsequent depreciation came following a threat to withhold aid. In 1958, the aid mission again called for price increases in response to new congressional legislation requiring that aid recipients seek greater self-reliance. The government responded by establishing a target rate of return for the company, which had a corresponding effect on prices and generated a new rate formula in 1960; again, the threat of aid termination was crucial (Jacoby 1966, 135; Tung 1996, 22–24).

The battle over prices was directly related to the American effort to increase investment by Taipower and to reduce its dependence on aid funds. Under American pressure, the government agreed to reinvest the income taxes and defense taxes payable by the company, along with the interest and bonuses of the public-owned shares of the company for a full fifteen years. Before this reinvestment act was passed, all aid funds were temporarily frozen by the United States. American involvement extended to oversight of the investment plans themselves. All proposals from Taipower had to be prepared using the evaluation methods prescribed by the Federal Power Commission and other U.S. agencies; the proposals were further reviewed by the private American consulting firm, J. G. White, which checked on costs, the purchase of equipment, and the supervision of construction (Jacoby 1966, 195–96; personal communication, Val de Beausset [J. G. White], May 10, 1996).

The United States was not content to secure discrete rate changes; it also sought to change the institutional structure and process through which rates were set; it hoped to guarantee Taipower's income and to diminish the voice of those clamoring for lower rates. We have already noted how establishing a target rate of return forced price increases in 1960. In the drafting of the aid budget for 1961, the United States made the establishment of a Utility Rate Commission a condition for a large loan for a power generating project. The Commission was to have full authority to decide utility rates free of control from the Legislative Yuan ("U.S. Aid and the Power Rate" 1960).

A wholesale revision of the legislation governing the power sector quickly followed. The initial drafting of this legislation was done by Taipower, and a draft was sent to the Ministry of Economic Affairs in 1961 for consultations among various government ministries and agencies; U.S. aid officials routinely participated in such meetings. The basic legislation – still in force in early 2000 – confirmed that the company would be guaranteed a minimum rate of return of 6% (Chung-hua Institution of Economics 1993). In 1968, at the urging of the World Bank (Taipower 1988, 14), Taipower's stipulated rate of a return was raised to a "target range" of 9.5 to 12% (Hsu 1995, 4; Tung 1996, 24). The principle that energy pricing reflect real costs and that China Petroleum and Taipower generate sufficient rate of return to support long-term development was reaffirmed in statute in the 1973 "Energy Policy for the Taiwan Area" (Liang 1986).

The gradual reduction of U.S. aid raises the puzzle of why the KMT did not revert to its old ways. The answer has to do with a reconfiguration of the KMT's constituency in addition to the other political advantages of a profitable Taipower. The surge of private demand for power associated with the successful export-led growth strategy and increasing shortages provided the incentives for the government to grant Taipower autonomy in setting the overall tariff level and in generating adequate investment resources.[12] Moreover, the resources generated by Taipower's new-found profitability could also be used for other political ends. The structure of government guaranteed that this new strategy could be pursued coherently and credibly.

In the 1950s and early 1960s, most investment was in hydroelectric power. In the early 1960s, the government aggressively turned its attention to the development of thermal power, which only surpassed hydroelectric power as a source of electricity in 1962. Though total installed capacity grew at more than 10% a year in the 1960s, it was still not sufficient to meet demand. In 1968, a new set of "Principles of Energy Development in the Taiwan Area" placed priority on the development

---

[12] Generous allowances for "construction-work-in-progress" (CWIP) provided one means of achieving this objective. Rate of return regulation specifies a given rate of return on capital investments. The sum of the capital investment on which profit is made is called the rate base; rules governing the rate base are therefore critical for determining actual returns. In Taiwan, the rate of return is revenue after taxes divided by the rate base. The rate base includes the present value of investments plus net operating capital minus net unrepaid debt on completed work. See Cohen, McCubbins, and Rosenbluth (1995, 191).

of electric power and stipulated that new nuclear and coal-fired plants would be assigned to peak load generation.

The coherence of government meant that it was well-positioned to allow rates to respond quickly to changes in energy prices, even when large and painful adjustments were required. The government passed on virtually the entire cost of the two oil shocks directly to consumers; Taipower adjusted global rates upward 80% on January 27, 1974 and undertook three large rate adjustments of 30%, 18%, and 29% over the course of 1979–80. Even with these increases, the average annual change in the real cost of electricity outstripped the annual average increase in prices over the 1970s by 2.1 percentage points. As a result, Taipower substantially increased its debt burden. Nonetheless, the utility managed to increase prices at a rate higher than that of overall inflation (Kim and Smith 1989, 189, 193), a substantial accomplishment when compared to declining real revenues in the face of inflation among most major Latin American utilities (Spiller and Viana Martorell 1994), not to mention the difficulties of adjusting energy prices in the United States!

DEMOCRATIZATION IN TAIWAN: CONSTITUTIONAL DESIGN, ELECTORAL REFORM, AND POLITICAL COMPETITION

Beginning in the late 1970s, Taiwan's authoritarian political order began to undergo a transformation, but political liberalization was very gradual and tightly controlled from the top. It is useful to distinguish between several distinct phases of the transition. During an initial phase (1977–1986), the government tolerated opposition but did not allow any changes in political institutions. Martial law remained in place and powers remained unified, but preferences within the party began to diverge. During a second transitional phase (1986–1991), the ruling party lifted martial law and permitted an opposition party to form, but the institutional legacies of the authoritarian period remained in place, including the Temporary Provisions and a legislature that was not elected under fully competitive conditions. After a series of constitutional reforms in 1991–1992, the government became more fully democratic, and a greater separation of both powers and purpose emerged (see Cheng and Haggard, ch. 6).

The greatest element of continuity during the transition was the ruling party's control of a powerful presidency. Lee Teng-hui assumed the presidency in 1988 on the death of Chiang Ching-kuo; in 1990 Lee

Teng-hui was elected by the National Assembly, which was still dominated by aging legislators elected to represent mainland districts after
1949. Not until 1991 did he give up his martial law powers. The controversial issue of the direct election of the president was not resolved until
mid-1994. Presidential elections held in 1996, under the threat of Chinese military maneuvers, produced an impressive victory for the incumbent. However, conflict over the nomination split the KMT in 1999 and
caused it to lose the presidential election in 2000.

Although the constitutional powers of the president appear limited
and resemble those found in premier-presidential systems, Taiwan's system was in fact presidential.[13] Despite factional challenges, the president
served as chairman of the ruling party, which gave him influence over
legislators through the nomination process (Cheng and Haggard, ch. 6).
However, after 1986, and to some extent earlier, the president and ruling
party were forced to operate in a political setting characterized by steadily increasing political competition. Provincial, county, city, and township elections had been a regular feature of Taiwan's politics since the
early 1950s, but these contests were closely controlled by the KMT.[14]
The major institutional break occurred in 1986, when President Chiang
Ching-kuo effectively allowed an opposition party, the Democratic Progressive Party (DPP), to form. In 1991, the Supreme Judicial Court
ordered the complete renewal of the Legislative Yuan and the National
Assembly. The resulting elections, held in 1991 and 1992, yielded comfortable majorities for the ruling party. However, in 1993 internal factionalism within the KMT split the party; a dissident faction of mainlanders opposed to Lee's political reforms and foreign policy broke away
to form the New Party. In 1995, the KMT maintained its legislative
majority by only the slimmest of margins – three seats – and secured
only a plurality of the popular vote.

In sum, although the KMT retained the presidency and its legislative
majorities until 2000, electoral constraints began to weigh on public
policy from the early 1990s. The DPP actively contested elections, drawing on its major advantage of claiming to represent the interests of
indigenous Taiwanese. After 1993, the KMT was further squeezed by

---

[13] See Cheng and Haggard, this volume, ch. 6.
[14] Not until the provincial and local elections of 1977 did individual dissidents for
the first time challenge the government by forming a loosely organized opposition
camp. To the embarrassment of the ruling party, the new movement succeeded in
winning 35% of the seats in the provincial legislature, establishing itself as an
important presence on the political scene.

the emergence of the New Party. The New Party sought both to represent the interests of the conservative elements of the mainlander community and to expose money politics and corruption within the government. With restraints lifted on the formation of interest groups, all parties had to compete for the support of a variety of new associations; of particular importance for energy and power policy was the rise of a vocal environmental movement (Hsiao 1992).

One key to the KMT's continued electoral success was its ability to play the challenging political game associated with the country's electoral laws, the single nontransferable vote (SNTV) system (Winckler 1984; Nathan 1993, 432; Cox and Niou 1994; Cox 1997). Under this system, parties must be able to allocate or spread votes so that they are not wasted on the leading candidates. Despite some decline in the capacity to discipline its own ranks, the KMT had greater organizational capability to do this than its rivals.[15] On the other hand, the SNTV system itself placed important constraints on public policy making (Cox and McCubbins, ch. 2; Shugart and Haggard, ch. 3). By forcing candidates from the same party to compete against one another in the same district, an SNTV system generates strong incentives to cultivate a personal vote and to differentiate oneself from copartisans.

Candidate-centered electoral systems require substantial financial resources to run campaigns and to provide constituent services. We would thus expect legislators of all parties to court business support. This was particularly true, however, of the KMT (Shiao 1996). To remain a viable electoral force, the KMT needed both direct funding and financially viable Taiwanese candidates. To secure these objectives, the party's identification with and links to the private sector became more open at both the national and subnational levels, with corresponding charges of corruption and "money politics" from the opposition; indeed, these changes played a central role in defeating the party in the 2000 presidential elections.

---

[15] The ability for the KMT to control its own internal factions and nominations may be eroding. In late 1993, portions of the nonmainstream faction broke away to form the New Party, an undeniable loss to the KMT. The party has also seen increasing factionalism of a less ideological sort. Legislative races have attracted a larger number of candidates than the party can expect to accommodate while pursuing the rational electoral strategy under SNTV of limiting nominations and seeking to divide the vote among candidates within a district as evenly as possible (Nathan 1993; Cox and Niou 1994). This internal fracturing constitutes one of the most substantial challenges to the KMT.

The KMT's attentiveness to business concerns was heightened by the changing economic environment that coincided with Taiwan's democratization. After two decades of rapid growth in labor-intensive exports, and another decade and a half in which Taiwan successfully upgraded its industrial structure, Taiwan's private investment and economic growth rates began to slip in the late 1980s. Between the revaluation of the New Taiwan dollar after the Plaza accord, and the emergence of new investment opportunities following economic reform in Southeast Asia and China, foreign and domestic investors increasingly looked away from Taiwan. In response, the government developed bold new plans to establish Taiwan as an "Asia Pacific Regional Operations Center" for global corporations. However, inducing major multinationals to establish regional headquarters in Taiwan would be impossible if the government could not guarantee the provision of a stable supply of electricity.

In sum, during the consolidated authoritarian period, the KMT was characterized by a high degree of institutional centralization and an unusual autonomy from both electoral and interest group pressures; both powers and purpose were unified. The transition to democracy meant greater electoral and interest group constraints and greater pressures for particularism. These pressures were only partly counterbalanced by a strong party organization, automatic majorities in the legislature (until 1992), and a strong presidency.

We would thus expect to see the rate structure and the provision of services become more attentive to key legislative constituents, and we would expect greater difficulty in politically sensitive decisions, such as price increases or plant siting. We would also expect the regulatory process increasingly to reflect the institutional as well as political interests of legislators.

POLICY IN THE DEMOCRATIC PERIOD

Since the executive remained relatively powerful vis-à-vis the legislature, which the KMT continued to dominate, we would not necessarily expect radical changes in policy as a result of the transition to democratic rule. However, both the increase in electoral competition and the pecularities of the SNTV system combined to have an influence on policy. By far the most important consequence of democratization was a sudden wave of opposition to the siting of new electricity facilities, including transmission lines, power stations, and, most notably, the planned Number Four nuclear power plant. We show that this opposition resulted not simply from new programmatic concerns associated with political liberalization (the need to respond to new pressures for environmental legislation) but also from the influence of particularistic concerns on the part of legislators. The slowing of new investment – a sharp change from the authoritarian period – forced Taipower to manage an increase in power outages in addition to convincing the government to permit new private power producers and, eventually, to privatize Taipower itself.

Second, we find substantial evidence in energy and electricity policy of the KMT's effort to reconfigure its political base so as to become more directly responsive to private sector interests. Old KMT constituencies lost their clout, and biases against important new constituencies fell away. Both the design of the privatization program and the management of outages show business' new political influence on policy. Finally, we show that the changes in constitutional arrangements were reflected in the structure and process of electricity policy making and oversight. The regulatory structure for approval of rate changes became considerably more open and transparent and, even though the executive branch managed to retain influence through continuing control over appointments, the general direction of institutional change allows us to make predictions about how policy making will evolve in the future.

Power Rates

Taipower does not generally publicize its costs in providing service; we can thus make no judgment from published rates about the extent to which prices reflect marginal costs. We do have cost and price data from one study for 1978, 1980, and 1981, however, and these can serve as a baseline for saying something about the general direction of relative price movements (Kim 1989); the data are reported in Table 8.2. The ratio of revenue to the cost of supply across all classes of users during these years

Table 8.2. *Cost of Service by Class of Customer: 1978–1981*

	(Average revenue/supply cost)			
	Residential	Commercial	Industrial	Total
1978	0.74	1.71	1.05	1.02
1980	0.73	1.64	0.95	0.94
1981	0.81	1.79	1.00	1.03

Source: Kim 1989, Table 6.3, 193.

was 1.02. The ratio for residential users was 0.74; the industry average was 1.05, close to the overall average; and the average revenues from commercial users were 1.71 times the cost of supplying them. Though not definitive, these data suggest that policy tilted in favor of industrial and particularly residential use in the 1960s and 1970s at the expense of commerce.

The second oil shock produced a number of innovations in pricing designed to promote conservation and increase the efficiency of energy use. The government replaced the decreasing block rate schedule for industrial energy charges with a flat rate applicable to all energy consumption. Time-of-use pricing was introduced for industrial customers contracting more than 100 kw in an effort to shift demand to off-peak hours.[16] During the 1980s, the differential between peak and off-peak rates gradually widened. In 1989, seasonal pricing was introduced.

Tables 8.3 through 8.5 outline in some detail the evolution of the rate structure throughout the 1980s. These tables thus permit a comparison with the 1981 baseline in Table 8.2 and capture the series of post-oil shock price adjustments that gradually lowered prices in line with decreasing energy costs. All of the adjustments of the 1980s and 1990s involve overall price decreases, though there are increases in some usage categories.

For comparative purposes, the first significant feature of the rate structure is that rates are set by broad classes of users and by the technology of delivery (low, high, and extra-high tension) rather than by narrow end uses; this stands in contrast to a number of developing countries where rates are set by a variety of quite particularistic end uses. There are three broad classes of use: (1) "lighting," which covers residential and small commercial use and is billed on a metered basis; (2) "combined lighting and power" for non-industrial institutional users, including large commercial users, which is billed on the basis of both a demand charge (NT$ per kW per month) and an energy charge (NT$ per kWh); and (3) "power" for industrial use,[17] which combines demand and energy charges with a more complex rate structure including peak-load and seasonal pricing.

In analyzing changes in rates, it is useful to distinguish adjustments in

---

[16] For technical analyses, see Sheen, Chen, and Yang 1994; Sheen, Chen, and Wang 1995.

[17] This category may include office buildings if they are linked on the same site as the factory.

Table 8.3. *Changes in Rate Schedule I: Metered Rates (NT$ / kWh)*

	Date of Rate Change								
	10/1/80	2/15/81	3/17/83	7/25/84	12/1/86	3/1/87	1/1/88	2/1/89	6/1/91
I. Noncommercial									
1-100 kWh	2.30	2.50	2.40	2.40	2.20	2.15	2.10	2.20[c] 2.00	2.20
101-300 kWh	2.90	3.20	3.10	3.10	2.85	2.00	2.50	2.70[c] 2.30	2.70[c] 2.30
over 301 kWh	3.80	4.20	4.10	4.10	3.78	3.68	2.90	3.30[c] 2.60	3.30[c] 2.60
II. Commercial									
100-300 kWh	5.60	6.00	5.90	5.90	5.23	5.23	2.90	3.30[c] 2.60	3.30[c] 2.60
over 301 kWh	6.30	6.80	6.70	5.90	5.23	5.23	2.90	3.30[c] 2.60	3.30[c] 2.60
Memo-authorized rate adjustment, percent	28.67	7.79	−3.25	−1.61[a] −1.87[b]	−2.10	−4.75[a] −3.32[b]	−15.14[a] −5.07[b]		−1.32

[a] Lighting
[b] Power
[c] Summer season rates

Sources: Ministry of Economic Affairs, Energy Commission, *Taiwan Energy Statistics 1990, 241.* Ministry of Economic Affairs, Energy Commission, *Taiwan Energy Statistics 1994, 257.*

Table 8.4. *Changes in Rate Structure II: Combined Lighting and Power (Demand Charge, NT$ per kW per month; Energy Charge, NT$ per kWh)*

Date	10/1/80		2/15/81		3/17/83		7/25/84		12/1/86		1/1/88		2/1/89		6/1/92	
	Non-commercial	Commercial	Non-commercial	Commercial	Non-commercial	Commercial	Non-commercial	Commercial	Non-commercial	Commercial	Non-commercial	Commercial	Non-commercial	Commercial	Non-commercial	Commercial
I. Demand charge																
Low tension By installed capacity	138.00	156.00	141.00	165.00	141.00	165.00	141.00	165.00	134.00	157.00	134.00	134.00	134.00	134.00	134.00	134.00
By contracted maximum demand	192.00	216.00	198.00	228.00	148.00	228.00	198.00	228.00	188.00	217.00	188.00	188.00	188.00	188.00	168.00	168.00
High tension By Contracted maximum demand	177.00	201.00	180.00	210.00	180.00	210.00	180.00	210.00	171.00	200.00	171.00	171.00	171.00	171.00		
II. Energy charge																
first 60 hours	1.50	3.00	1.65	3.25	1.65	3.25	1.65	3.25	1.57	3.09	1.40	1.60	1.44[a] / 1.37	1.65[a] / 1.56	1.44[a] / 1.37	1.65[a] / 1.56
61–120 hours	1.70	3.30	1.90	3.60	1.90	3.60	1.90	3.60	1.80	3.09	1.60	1.40	1.65[a] / 1.56	1.65[a] / 1.56	1.65[a] / 1.56	1.65[a] / 1.56
over 120 hours	2.00	3.70	2.25	4.05	2.15	3.85	2.15	3.85	2.04	3.09	1.60	1.40	1.65[a] / 1.56	1.65[a] / 1.56	1.65[a] / 1.56	1.56

[a] Summer rates

Sources: Ministry of Economic Affairs, Energy Commission, *Taiwan Energy Statistics 1990*, 242; Ministry of Economic Affairs, Energy Commission, *Taiwan Energy Statistics 1994*, 258.

Table 8.5. *Changes in Rate Schedule III: Power Rates (Demand Charge, NT$ per kW per month; Energy Charge, NT$ per kWh)*

Date	10/1/80	2/15/81	3/17/83	7/25/84	12/1/86	1/1/88	2/1/89	5/26/90	6/1/91	6/1/92
I. Low tension										
demand charge[a]	186.00	195.00	195.00	195.00	185.00	185.00	185.00	185.00	185.00	165.00
Energy charge										
first 1000 kWh	1.76	1.90	1.82	1.82	1.73	1.60	1.65[b]	1.65[b]	1.65[b]	1.65[b]
1001–10,000 kWh	1.76	1.90	1.82	1.82	1.73	1.60	1.56[c]	1.56[c]	1.56[c]	1.56[c]
over 10,000 kWh	1.76	1.90	1.82	1.82	1.73	1.60	1.48[d]	2.03[d]	2.03[d]	2.09[d]
							0.98[e]	0.91[e]	0.84[e]	0.8[e]
II. High tension										
regular service rates										
Demand charge[a]	180.00	186.00	186.00	186.00	177.00	177.00	177.00	171.00	177.00	213.00
Energy charge	1.68	1.83	1.75	1.75	1.66	1.51	1.56[f]	1.56[f]	1.56[f]	
							1.48[g]	1.48[g]	1.48[g]	
Time of use rates										
Demand charge[a]										
On peak	180.00	186.00	186.00	186.00	177.00	177.00	177.00	177.00	177.00	213.00
Off peak	36.00	37.20	37.20	37.20	35.40	35.40	35.40	35.40	35.40	42.60
Energy charge										
On peak	1.92	2.12	2.12	2.12	2.01	1.82	1.82	1.88	1.88	1.89
						2.91	2.64	2.64	2.78	2.78	2.95
Off peak	1.33	1.43	1.27	1.12	1.06	0.96	0.96	0.88	0.81	0.77
					0.97	0.86	0.86	0.79	0.72	0.70
Semi-peak				—	1.94	1.76	1.76	1.79	1.79	1.78

III. Extra-high tension
regular service rates

Demand charge[a]	174.00	180.00	180.00	180.00	171.00	171.00	171.00	171.00	171.00	207.00
Energy charge	1.63	1.77	1.69	1.69	1.60	1.45		1.50	1.50	—
							1.42	1.42	1.42	
Time of use rates										
Demand charge[a]										
On peak	174.00	180.00	180.00	180.00	171.00	171.00	171.00	171.00	171.00	207.00
Off peak	34.80	36.00	36.00	36.00	34.20	34.20	34.20	34.20	34.20	41.40
Energy charge										
On peak	1.89	2.04	2.04	2.04	1.99	1.80	1.80	1.86	1.86	1.88
					2.85	2.60	2.60	2.76	2.76	2.93
Off peak	1.30	1.80	1.29	1.09	1.03	0.93	0.93	0.67	0.80	0.76
					0.95	0.85	0.85	0.78	0.71	0.69
Semi-peak	—	—	—	—	1.90	1.73	1.73	1.78	1.78	1.77

[a] Demand charge by contracted maximum demand
[b] Summer/not time of use
[c] Nonsummer/not time of use
[d] Peak
[e] Off-peak
[f] Summer/not time of use
[g] Non-summer

Sources: Ministry of Economic Affairs, Energy Commission, *Taiwan Energy Statistics 1990, 273;* Ministry of Economic Affairs, Energy Commission, *Taiwan Energy Statistics 1994, 258.*

the overall level of prices from alterations in their structure. The general trend in average rates has been down, though there were increases in some categories. For example, power rates to industrial users show a steady decline from 1983 to 1988, and though they appear to recover some of that decline in 1992, this is an artifact of the introduction of seasonal rates.

Because there are economies of scale involved in electricity supply, the cost per unit of energy delivered is lower at higher quantities and tension levels; this has to be taken into account when interpreting the data in Tables 8.3 through 8.5. However, when placed against the revenue-to-cost ratios available for 1978–1981, it appears that the move toward the unification of commercial and noncommercial rates has in fact reduced an important bias in the system. Taipower data on the average price paid by broad classes of customers show that commercial prices fell from more than double the noncommercial rates before 1985, to 30% higher than in 1989, to a 24% difference in 1994. Most of this change was achieved by decreasing progressivity for commercial users.

Though the data do not permit an equally firm judgment on this score, there also appears to be a reduction of the bias in favor of large users, which included a number of state-owned enterprises concentrated in energy-intensive sectors. Also noteworthy is the fact that Taipower began to reduce the preferential rates outlined in Table 8.1 as well; subsidies to the military, villages of military dependents, and agriculture were eliminated with the last replaced by a budget allocation. This action, taken by the Fair Trade Commission, itself a product of the democratic era, was based on the grounds that such subsidies were unfair to other consumers.

What accounts for these changes in the level and structure of rates? The official justification for the rate cuts of the 1980s focused on purely economic factors, and we certainly do not deny their significance. Declining oil prices, an appreciating exchange rate that further lowered the local currency cost of imported energy, and the increasing efficiency of Taipower's operations all had an effect on costs (Taipower 1994, 44). However, there is also evidence that the reduction of rates reflected an assertion of government oversight driven by new political concerns. It is highly unlikely that Taipower would independently petition the government for rate *decreases*, particularly given its ability to shift "excess" profits to its own workers in the form of employee bonuses. Through most of the late 1980s, Taipower stayed within its target range for rate of return despite the price cuts. Nonetheless, the government continued to cut rates, including a large rate cut in 1988 that favored residential and particularly commercial consumers. In the 1990s, the rate of return fell sharply, reaching a low of 5.78% in 1993 before rebounding somewhat in 1994. Thus the opening of the political system corresponded with an abandonment of the long-standing practice of rigorously maintaining Taipower's mandated rate of return. We also have direct evidence of political efforts, albeit not successful, to influence rates. For example, in December 1996, legislators led by the DPP passed a resolution calling on Taipower not to raise prices through the rest of the year.

Changes in the rate structure can also be given a political interpretation. Due to the opening of electoral politics, we would expect the KMT to widen its basis of support. The abandonment of preferences for specific social groups such as military dependents fits that expectation perfectly, as does the effort to favor both consumers and certain types of business users. Seeking to position itself at the center-right of the political spectrum, it was advantageous to the KMT to decrease the bias against nonindustrial private sector firms, a class that consists largely of small Taiwanese commercial enterprises. The introduction of flat rates for industrial users marked an official turn away from the promotion of heavy industry that had been initiated at the beginning of the 1970s in response to the oil crisis. However, it also marked a reduction in government support for energy-intensive state-owned enterprises and larger firms in favor of the smaller enterprises that continue to be the backbone of the Taiwanese manufacturing sector.

The Politics of Investment: The Problem of Siting

The economic rationale for the government's decision to allow prices and profitability to fall becomes even more puzzling when considered in the context of Taiwan's long-term power needs (Li 1995). In the last decade, conservation measures have pushed the growth of energy consumption under that for overall economic growth; the energy demand elasticity for 1984–1994 was 0.84. Power consumption, however, has outstripped economic growth; the elasticity of power consumption is about 1.1. Commercial use has seen the fastest growth, a fact that is not surprising given the rapid growth of services and the easing of earlier biases against the sector.

For the first four decades of KMT rule, Taipower's strategy for managing supply bottlenecks was to build new generating plants as quickly as possible; the regulatory structure and pricing policy encouraged reinvestment. As Table 8.6 shows, this expansion came to a screeching halt

Table 8.6. *Taipower Installed Capacity and Reserve Margins*

Year	Installed Capacity (Kw)	Annual Increase (%)	System Peak Load (Kw)	Gross Reserve Margins (%)
1945	275,255	—	119,023	56.7%
1949	275,655	0.1%	148,649	46.1%
1952	331,545	8.7%	231,675	30.1%
1953	363,108	9.5%	270,760	25.4%
1954	393,914	7.9%	316,512	19.6%
1955	493,414	25.9%	336,113	31.9%
1956	520,414	5.5%	385,483	25.9%
1957	541,231	4.0%	442,958	18.2%
1958	582,141	7.6%	506,514	13.0%
1959	632,751	8.7%	561,911	11.2%
1960	709,191	12.1%	635,234	10.4%
1961	923,420	30.2%	719,210	22.1%
1962	923,420	0%	769,655	16.6%
1963	1,039,920	12.6%	856,784	17.6%
1964	1,129,990	8.7%	985,599	12.8%
1965	1,186,196	5.0%	1,066,225	10.1%
1966	1,475,196	24.4%	1,242,531	15.8%
1967	1,579,621	7.1%	1,417,100	10.3%
1968	1,940,261	22.8%	1,615,800	16.7%
1969	2,245,261	15.7%	1,848,300	17.7%
1970	2,720,261	21.2%	2,131,400	21.6%
1971	2,774,261	2.0%	2,399,300	13.5%
1972	3,519,261	26.9%	2,733,500	22.3%
1973	4,124,261	17.2%	3,133,700	24.0%
1974	4,358,061	5.7%	3,451,600	20.8%
1975	5,300,394	21.6%	3,765,200	29.0%
1976	5,883,642	11.0%	4,301,700	26.9%
1977	7,019,642	19.3%	4,817,800	31.4%
1978	7,682,705	9.4%	5,629,700	26.7%
1979	8,182,705	6.5%	6,069,800	25.8%
1980	9,055,705	10.7%	6,702,700	26.0%
1981	10,158,650	12.2%	6,796,700	33.1%
1982	11,868,614	16.8%	6,918,000	41.7%
1983	12,412,594	4.6%	7,807,500	37.1%
1984	12,959,494	4.4%	8,517,400	34.3%
1985	15,969,794	23.2%	8,716,300	45.4%
1986	16,594,494	3.9%	9,900,300	40.3%
1987	16,588,824	0%	11,113,400	33.0%
1988	16,588,934	0%	12,330,600	25.7%
1989	16,593,554	0%	13,421,700	19.1%

Year	Installed Capacity (Kw)	Annual Increase (%)	System Peak Load (Kw)	Gross Reserve Margins (%)
1990	16,882,874	1.7%	14,510,500	14.1%
1991	18,382,874	8.9%	15,320,700	16.7%
1992	19,246,805	4.7%	16,703,900	13.2%
1993	19,354,725	0.6%	17,666,200	8.7%
1994	20,983,225	8.4%	18,610,200	11.3%
1995	21,897,970	4.4%	19,932,900	9.0%
1996	23,762,670	8.5%	21,761,500	8.4%
1997	25,735,412	8.3%	22,237,000	13.6%

Sources: Taiwan Dianli Gongsi, *Tongji Nianbao* (Taipower, *Statistical Yearbook*) 1975, 197; Council for Economic Planning and Development, *Taiwan Statistical Data Book* 1998, 106, and *TSDB 1982* 94. Gross Reserve Margin = (installed capacity minus peak load)/installed capacity.

in 1986–1987. The result was a decline in the reserve margin to under 10% in the mid 1990s. Typically, the utility prefers to maintain a reserve margin of 20–30% to handle the possibility of equipment failures and natural disasters, and the company even resorted to scheduled outages during peak hours.

The reason for the slowdown in investment and the sluggish growth of installed capacity is tied to two interrelated features of the changed political environment. Much weight has been placed on the rise of a vocal environmental movement that opposed a number of large Taipower investments (Hsiao 1992). These environmental forces would have been impotent, however, had they not been accompanied by an increase in electoral and legislative competition.

The history of Taipower's ill-fated Number 4 nuclear reactor demonstrates the interaction of central and local level politics in this process. After being shelved for purely economic reasons in 1982, the idea for a fourth nuclear reactor complex was resubmitted to the Executive Yuan for approval in 1984. Despite the fact that the government had completed the acquisition of the land in 1983, opposition both inside and outside the KMT stopped proceedings on the initiative. In April 1985, 55 KMT legislators and 6 independents issued separate written group interpellations requesting the Executive Yuan to stop work on the power plant; interestingly, it was the KMT legislators – facing increasing electoral competition – who focused on safety and disposal of nuclear waste while the opposition targeted cost overruns in Taipower's budget (*Lianhe Bao*, April 9, 1985).

Upon its formation in 1986, the DPP quickly took the lead in questioning the safety of nuclear plants, exploiting a series of safety incidents at existing facilities (Yang 1994). Opposition peaked again in February 1988 when reports of leaked radioactive material focused attention on mismanagement at Taipower's facilities. The press and legislators of both parties called for investigations and improved discipline and security at the plants, and the government once again postponed the project; as Taipower put it euphemistically, "the government decided that the enhancement of public communication should be carried out prior to the construction" (*Annual Report 1991*, 25).

The construction of the first two units was again approved by the Executive Yuan in 1991, and by the Executive and newly elected Legislative Yuan in 1992. Obtaining approval was not easy. The business community strongly supported the plant, and President Lee staked the prestige of the KMT on the issue, defining the Number 4 plant as a "test case" of KMT rule. Yet, the vote was still close. More than 40% of legislators, *including many KMT members*, declined to support the plant (Liang 1995; Yang 1994).

However, this time the launching of the government's effort to secure support for the plant and other projects was accompanied by the formal initiation of a "Taipower Power Development Donation Fund." In 1988, the government had attempted to woo local support for its activities by offering subsidies of approximately 9% to residents of areas adjacent to nuclear power plants. The formation of the Donation Fund marked a recognition of the importance of local politics and vastly expanded Taipower's political foray into the distribution of pork. In 1992, Taipower contributed more than NT$1 billion to more than 200 local governments, farmers' associations, fisherman's associations, and schools in the vicinity of existing nuclear facilities. In 1994, Taipower's contributions had increased to NT$1.4 billion and their activities had greatly expanded. Taipower's district offices and power stations threw themselves into "public-interest" activities, "including education and culture activities, environmental sanitation, medical aid, comforts to low-income families and the handicapped, religious celebrations, folk festivals, recreation activities and sports" (*Annual Report 1994*, 17).

Particular effort was focused on influencing the outcome of a local referendum by residents of Kungliao, where the fourth nuclear reactor complex was to be sited; Taipower pledged to pay the town $11 million annually plus a one-time subsidy of $64 million during construction, or an average of about $700 per person. Nonetheless, the referendum, later ruled illegal by the government, overwhelmingly rejected the Taipower offer (*Far Eastern Economic Review*, June 30, 1994, 22). Despite its continuing majority, the party's ability to command had obviously weakened; achieving its objectives has required precisely the pork-barrel politics that one would expect from a candidate-centered electoral system that encourages a high degree of particularism.

In July 1994, the budget for the Number 4 plant passed the legislature by a narrow majority. Yet this did not prove to be the end of the issue. In early 1996, the opposition took advantage of the temporary absence of several KMT representatives to pass a new measure to stop the plant. The KMT called upon a rarely used constitutional device designed to reduce instability; the rule allows the executive to resubmit bills that have already been passed; but, unless the legislature can sustain a two-thirds majority, the original vote holds. Following substantial opposition efforts to keep the legislation bottled-up in committee, the party did succeed in forcing a vote on the override and ultimately on the bill itself. However, the Executive Branch won only after making some concessions, causing defections from its own ranks, and sparking substantial demonstrations that led to the worst clashes between police and citizens since the early 1980s (*Zhongguo Shibao* October 19, 1996).[18] Moreover, the DPP, which boycotted the final vote, has continued to threaten that it would use legislative oversight of Taipower's budget to stop operation of the plant and that if the KMT slipped below half of the sitting legislators, they would pass comprehensive antinuclear legislation (*Zhongguo Shibao*, October 9 and 10, 1996). KMT majorities sustained in the 1998 legislative elections have allowed it to proceed with the plant, but the politics surrounding the process have changed definitively (*Gongshang Shibao*, March 18, 1999).

Service Provision: Managing Outages

As we have seen, curtailments are not new in Taiwan. Problems of reconstruction made them a feature of the economic landscape in the 1950s, and the extraordinary pace of Taiwan's growth put strain on the

---

[18] One key concession was ruling out the possibility of a planned Number 5 plant (*Gongshang Shibao*, October 18, 1996).

system in the 1960s despite the rapid growth of installed capacity. When curtailments were necessary, the company consistently focused them on a few, large-scale, low-value added industries dominated by state-owned enterprises, such as steel, cement, and petrochemicals (see, for example, *Far Eastern Economic Review*, June 13, 1963). Taipower justified this approach as imposing the lowest economic costs; it also benefited Taipower by minimizing transactions costs and the number of customers inconvenienced by outages. The affected industries complained but to little avail.

Beginning in the late 1980s, the problem of outages and how the government was going to manage them again became politically salient. As we have seen, the debate surrounding the siting of new plants made the old engineering strategy of increasing capacity infeasible. Moreover, the government now faced more politically threatening protests from customers. For example, the steel industry, a bright spot in the general weakening of industrial investment in the late 1980s, threatened to reduce its investment plans unless supply could be guaranteed (Xu 1992, 1994). Similar to its response to the oil crisis, Taipower again turned to an aggressive strategy of incentive-based demand management (Xu 1992, 1994; Energy Commission 1995). The company sweetened its program of voluntary curtailment, in which consuming industries agreed to accept occasional curtailments during periods of peak demand in return for lower rates.

However, the voluntary curtailment schemes also proved inadequate and, as enforced outages of up to 20% of demand became more common, business became more vociferous in its demands for supply guarantees. Curtailment procedures, initially determined solely by Taipower, became an issue for the Minister of Economic Affairs and ultimately for the cabinet as a whole. The government switched to a procedure where curtailments were not concentrated on existing users but on new larger users of all types. If capacity were still not adequate, whole geographic districts would be subjected to outages, reportedly on the belief of some top officials that if the public experienced the consequences of inadequate capacity, public support for environmental and NIMBY demands would wilt and support for building new capacity would emerge. Taipower executives objected to this approach as both economically and politically dangerous, but they were overruled. All of northern Taiwan became subject to occasional widespread outages or brownouts.

However, the strategy of targeting new users and the mass public also proved vulnerable to protest, particularly from important business users.

When brief curtailments resulted in large losses for Taiwan's spectacularly successful semiconductor industry, the industry appealed to legislators and the government was forced to relent and institute a special exemption for capacity expansion by existing firms (*Gongshang Shibao*, June 23, 1995; *Electronic Engineering News*, August 7, 1995). When Taipower's president Zhang Simin was sacked in 1994, many observers attributed his ouster to the failure to stem the tide of brownouts, despite the fact that his hands were largely tied by larger political dynamics.

The analysis of curtailments contains in microcosm many of the important shifts in Taiwan's overall energy policy – from a nearly exclusive emphasis on overcoming supply constraints by building new plants, to an increasing reliance on incentives by significantly restructuring the rate system, to an evolving set of curtailment schemes that explicitly took into account the social and political consequences of alternative means of allocating shortages.

Politics and the Structure of Regulatory Institutions

The final effect of democratization that we analyze focuses on the institutions through which policy is made and overseen. More open politics has been accompanied by changes in the regulatory process, changes designed to accommodate new political actors and the Legislative Yuan itself.

One interesting piece of evidence in this regard concerns the pattern of appointments and the political ambitions of those holding regulatory positions. Until the mid-1980s, Taipower had a strong reputation for engineering competence, skill in dealing with the international financial community, and lack of corruption in procurement. It was better in engineering than management or accounting and failed to consider scenic and environmental issues in plant siting, but it nonetheless enjoyed a generally positive public image.

Beginning in 1984, however, as Taipower came under closer opposition and legislative scrutiny for cost overruns and safety issues, regulators began to preempt criticism by taking a more critical stance toward the company. An important example of this phenomenon was the critical stance taken by a new Secretary General of the MOEA's National Corporations Commission, Wang Yuyun, appointed in July 1985. Wang was a Taiwanese businessman, a novel choice for the post that reflected the long-run KMT electoral strategy of integrating more Taiwanese into the party. Wang almost immediately announced cuts in the budget of SOEs, including a substantial cut in Taipower's capital budget. He called for changes in the rate structure and publicly criticized Taipower for inefficiency. He also forced out the long-time president of Taipower, Chen Lan'gao (Sun 1985a; Sun 1985b). Such actions would have been unnecessary and unheard of during the authoritarian period.

Broader political changes were also reflected in the creation of new consultative and oversight bodies, even though their precise role is formally advisory. To date, the executive has maintained control over appointments to these new oversight bodies, and their composition has closely mirrored the core constituencies of the new KMT. A number of these bodies have been grouped within the Ministry of Economic Affairs under the Industrial Development Consultative Committee (IDCC) and have served the primary purpose of increasing contact between business and government.

The IDCC's Energy Committee provides a forum for consultation on the broad outlines of energy policy. The committee has thirty-seven members. Ten of these members are drawn from the bureaucracy: seven from various parts of the Ministry of Economic Affairs, one from the Economic Planning Agency, one from the Atomic Energy Agency, and one from the Council on Economic Planning and Development. Thirteen are "experts and scholars," and the remaining fourteen represent industry and commerce, including one representing the peak business associations, five industry associations – including the most energy intensive ones such as paper, petrochemicals, and steel – as well as the major state-owned enterprises: Taipower, China Petroleum, and China Steel. The striking feature of this committee is the strong representation of the government, its appointees, and major energy users; absent are journalists, union representatives, and other ministries that may represent competing clienteles such as consumers or environmental groups.

In the electricity area, Taipower submits proposals for rate changes to the MOEA, which are then passed through the Energy Commission to the Oil and Electricity Prices Consultation Committee (OEPCC) for review; the insertion of this oversight body constitutes a change from the past. OEPCC makes its recommendations to MOEA, which has the authority to approve changes unless they involve a change in the entire pricing structure, in which case they are passed up to the Executive Yuan. The OEPCC is also an advisory commission, and it consists primarily of scholars and experts. The committee does, however, include three members of the Legislative Yuan, a departure from the past. Moreover, the scholars and experts are themselves subject to appointment by the executive. To date, the role of these committees has been only advisory, but we predict that developments in these institutions will parallel those in the legislature, with increasing involvement and voice for legislators in the oversight process.

CONCLUSION

At first glance, the broad outlines of Taiwan's regulatory system seem to contradict a number of the orienting hypotheses developed in this volume. A highly authoritarian government facing few constitutional checks ultimately created a stable regulatory system that encouraged a high level of investment until the 1980s. In recent years, despite the complete transformation of the political system, the regulatory structure has remained relatively stable. The executive continues to set the broad outlines of policy, and the legislature appears to have exerted little influence over pricing.

On closer inspection, however, the case of Taiwan confirms and extends our comparative institutional approach. While Taipower appeared to enjoy a high degree of operating autonomy, it was always subject to oversight by the top political leadership. During the 1950s, when the ruling party was still prone to factionalism and the Legislative Yuan had some influence over policy, subsidies were extended to favored political groups. In effect, U.S. aid allowed the KMT to pursue pricing policies that were inimical to generating the long-term *domestic* investment required to meet rapidly rising demand.

However, the United States was not content to finance the KMT unconditionally, and it gradually moved to exercise its agenda control. Once in place, Taipower's growth-oriented strategy proved self-sustaining. The efficient provision of power fueled the rapid expansion of private investment, both domestic and foreign. Continuity in the political structure – with a tight unity of both powers and purpose – prevented legislators or private interests from capturing energy policy. The strong position of the president and the ruling party up until 2000 allowed the government to take a long-term perspective on economic growth and to reap the gains from sustained investment in infrastructure such as electric power.

As we would expect, democratization has changed the politics of energy policy in Taiwan, despite the continuity in KMT rule. An environmental movement has arisen, competing parties have seized on environmentalism and opposition to nuclear power as electoral issues, and some backbench KMT politicians have joined them in preventing new electricity investments, in part because the SNTV electoral system puts a premium on individual credit-claiming. Democratization, particularly the KMT's quest for business support, affected the rate structure by providing incentives for the government to equalize energy charges across different classes of business users. The most important effect of democratization, however, has been the increasing difficulty in making new investments, particularly in generating facilities such as the Number 4 nuclear power plant. This, in turn, had a number of further consequences. The dangerous drop in reserve margins stemming from inadequate investment pushed the government to rationalize the rate structure and to increase the efficiency with which electricity is used.

More recently, political limits on investment have even forced the government to open up the electricity market to independent power providers through the Independent Power Producers (IPP) program and to make plans ultimately to dismantle and privatize Taipower (Hsu 1995). Politics has entered into the privatization process in ways that are predictable given the demands of an SNTV system; liberalization and deregulation provide an opportunity for the KMT to cement ties with important private business interests who can provide support for the party, even if the bidding for entry is conducted in a relatively fair and transparent fashion. All of the seven entrants in the first round of IPP bidding were backed not only by big business groups but also by specific legislators, in the case of Hualong by the head of the group, Wong Daming, who was for a time a "golden bull" legislator – an entrepreneur-turned-politician capable of funding his own campaigns. Such political backing appears to have played little role in the actual awarding of contracts, but it is likely to be extremely important in the second phase of the program, which involves the rezoning and acquisition of land. Private firms are likely to be well-positioned to overcome local opposition to new electricity facilities because of their greater freedom to dispense largesse, enter into local business alliances, and hire gangsters to pressure local protesters.

A final consequence of democratization is institutional. Political liberalization has led to the creation of more open oversight mechanisms that provide opportunities for legislators and interest groups to participate in rate-setting. If and when Taipower needs to raise rates, these groups may well turn into a source of opposition. Similar developments have already bedeviled attempts to rationalize telephone rates (*Zhong-guo Shibao* September 9, 1996; *Gongshang Shibao*, September 19, 1996).

The Taiwan case has several implications for a political theory of regulation. First, external constraints can serve as an important check on executive discretion, *but only if external actors wield credible threats to exercise their agenda control or veto*. Second, the rationalization of the rate structure in Taiwan provides additional support for the proposition that even in economies that have been relatively well-managed under authoritarianism, democratization may enhance efficiency. The transition to democracy reduced the influence of cronies and constituents in the state sector, empowered private-sector beneficiaries of reform, and enshrined procedures that are increasingly transparent. Electoral reform, however, does not always lead to greater efficiency, particularly in systems with candidate-centered electoral rules. Political openness in Taiwan has also slowed much-needed investment.

Our analysis of the Taiwan case also has a number of policy implications. First, the evidence reviewed here provides further argument in favor of an export-led growth strategy. By increasing the political weight of externally oriented actors who are sensitive to input prices, Taiwan's externally oriented strategy no doubt contributed to sustaining Taipower's growth-oriented investment strategy. Second, while privatization and the introduction of competition through "independent power provider" schemes can be helpful in increasing flexibility and efficiency, they are not a substitute for institutional reforms that strengthen and streamline the structures of regulatory oversight. Electricity generation may be relatively amenable to expanded competition, but distribution to the user is likely to remain a natural monopoly and even bulk transmission is unlikely to support a genuinely competitive market with a large number of providers. Regulating a large number of IPP firms and contracts is likely to prove even more difficult than overseeing one state-owned enterprise or a handful of geographically distinct investor-owned utilities with local monopolies, particularly given the incentives generated by a SNTV electoral system. To date, these problems have been partly overcome by a strong president; however, the increase in electoral competition has revealed that the president's power is ultimately contingent on retaining legislative majorities. Inadequate regulation of the IPPs or newly privatized electricity companies could easily lead to instability and scandals that would undermine both the willingness of private companies to invest in the utility sector and the willingness of the public to countenance further privatization.

Thus far, Taiwan has enjoyed a relatively effective and efficient electric power sector in both the authoritarian and democratic periods. Maintaining that effectiveness will depend at least as much on improving regulatory structures as on privatization. Ultimately, the outcome will be affected by an increasingly competitive political system and by the capacity of the ruling party to organize itself to avoid the excesses of candidate-centered politics; we address this theme in more detail in our analysis of budgetary politics (Cheng and Haggard, ch. 6).

9

Privatization in Transition Economies

Politics as Usual?

PHILIP KEEFER and MARY SHIRLEY

Despite recent scholarly attention to liberalizing economies, there remain important unanswered questions about why countries choose the reform policies or paths that they do. This article examines the reform of state-owned enterprises (SOEs) in Poland, a premier-presidential country that was able to overcome both a separation of power and separation of purpose and achieve successful reform. We compare the reform process in Poland to that of its neighbor Czechoslovakia,[1] who adopted a parliamentary system rather than a premier-presidential system like Poland's. Since both countries emerged from Soviet control at similar times and with similar histories, and since both embarked on similar attempts to privatize, Poland and the Czech Republic present us with a natural experiment in the effects of institutional variation.

We argue that three institutional factors explain the different approaches to reform initially taken by the two countries. First, we observe that there was greater institutional separation of power in Poland, as it is a premier-presidential system while Czechoslovakia is parliamentary. Second, Poland's electoral system promoted fragmentation in governing coalitions. This enabled more interests – especially rural interests – to veto reform proposals. Because these rural interests tended to be opposed to privatization and the restructuring of SOEs, legislative politics in Poland was characterized by a separation of purpose on these issues. Combined with the separation of powers, this created a tendency toward gridlock in attempts to achieve SOE reform. Third,

---

[1] The policy changes that we analyze overlap the period during which Czechoslovakia became two independent countries, the Czech Republic and Slovakia. We have endeavored throughout to refer to Czechoslovakia for policy changes prior to the breakup and to the Czech Republic in the period following.

SOE insiders in Poland enjoyed greater control under that country's preexisting legal regime than did insiders in Czechoslovakia. Thus, both the differences between the two countries' electoral institutions and their property rights gave opponents of reform greater leverage in Poland.

The combination of these institutions led to a situation where both powers and purpose were separated in Poland. In Chapter 2, Cox and McCubbins hypothesize that – all else being equal – greater separations of power and purpose have two effects: First, they make changing policy more difficult, causing policy to be more resolute; and second, they engender more private- rather than public-regarding policies. As our comparisons of the Polish and Czech cases make clear, however, these hypotheses proved valid. To accomplish their reforms, Poland was required to rely on particularistic politics. Their reforms provided asymmetric benefits to the groups who were enfranchised in either the legal or political system. Rural interests received their agricultural subsidies, and SOE insiders received a larger share of the rents from the Polish government's privatization efforts. Poland was also slower to begin reforms than was Czechoslovakia.

This chapter begins with a comparison of the reform outcomes in Poland and Czechoslovakia (and the present Czech Republic). We then turn to a more detailed examination of separation of power and purpose in the two countries, and show how this separation was a greater obstacle to reform in Poland. The last sections of the chapter demonstrate that both the possibilities for making concessions across policy dimensions, and the reversionary outcomes confronting key veto players, can permit reform to progress despite institutional limitations.

THE REFORM OF STATE-OWNED ENTERPRISES IN CZECHOSLOVAKIA AND POLAND

There are essentially two strategies for reforming SOEs: They can be privatized, or the budget constraints under which they operate can be hardened. Czechoslovakia and Poland pursued different combinations of these strategies. The Czech Republic proceeded to privatize SOEs rather quickly, while Poland chose to tighten budget constraints. These key choices are described in this section.

Different Reforms with Similar Outcomes

Following the transition, Poland and Czechoslovakia quickly privatized small state-owned SOEs, mostly in the retail sector. Czechoslovakia directly sold these SOEs to the highest bidder. In Poland, a May 1990 law first transferred ownership of small trade establishments to local governments, municipalities, or communes (Hashi 1995, 12; *EIU Country Report: Poland* 1990, 10). Czechoslovakia (and subsequently the Czech Republic) also moved quickly to privatize large enterprises, through auctions and voucher methods, while Poland proceeded more slowly, granting considerable authority to SOE insiders to hold up a privatization with which they disagreed. Tables 9.1a and 9.1b demonstrate that by June 1994, 90% of state-owned SOEs in the Czech Republic had been privatized, compared to only 46% in Poland. Most of the Czechoslovak SOEs were sold to outside owners (raising some US$ 4 billion in

Table 9.1a. *Percentage of State Owned Enterprises Sold by 1994*

	Czech Republic	Poland
Outside owner	32	3
Management/employee Buyout	0	14
Vouchers	22	6
Resources	9	0
Other	23	23
Subtotal	90	46
Still in states' hands	10	34
TOTAL	100	100

Table 9.1b. *Foreign Exchange, in Millions of US $*

Poland (1988–1995)	Czech Republic (1993–1995) Plus Czechoslovakia (1988–1992)	Czech Republic (1993–1995)
$2,294	$4,203	$2,294
$1,297	$4,010	$2,128

foreign exchange), while in Poland privatization was through management/employee buyouts or through leases or liquidations.

Although it lagged in privatization, by comparison to the Czech Republic, Poland was stricter about exposing SOEs to hard budget constraints. Both countries eliminated direct budget transfers to SOEs, and in both there was a build up of arrears and bad loans to the banking system.[2] However, in the Czech Republic, some 6,000 SOEs received debt relief when their loans were taken over by a "consolidation bank" created in 1991, while the National Property Fund has used the proceeds from privatization to provide debt relief and loan guarantees.[3] Compared to Czechoslovakia, bankruptcy proceedings and company liquidations were much more common in Poland. From 1990 to October 1995 Poland had liquidated 1,343 large SOEs in poor financial condition (CEEPN 1996, p. 386). By contrast, in Czechoslovakia the bankruptcy law that passed Parliament in 1991 was put into effect only in April 1993, and cumbersome procedures and overloaded courts have kept most filings from making it to court. By the end of 1995, only 833 bankruptcies had been declared, overwhelmingly by small, new private SOEs.[4]

Although they pursued different reform strategies, the two countries received nearly identical scores on several measures of progress in transition, as reported by the European Bank for Reconstruction and Development and indicated in Table 9.2. The policies of the two countries should have created greater incentives for SOEs to improve productivity

[2] Gray and Holle (1996) report that bad loans amounted to 20% of the stock of bank debt in Poland in 1992. In the Czech Republic, bad debts were about 19% of outstanding bank loans to enterprises by the end of 1992 (International Monetary Fund 1995).

[3] National Property Fund transfers to enterprises amounted to CZK 2 billion in 1993 and 2.6 billion in 1994 (International Monetary Fund 1995). Moreover, although credit to enterprises has fallen in both countries, it has fallen faster in real terms in Poland. In 1992, credit to SOEs fell by 20% in Poland, compared to an inflation rate of 46% while in the Czech Republic it fell by 11% that year, while inflation was also 11%. In 1993, credit declined by 6% in Poland, when inflation was 37% in the Czech Republic the numbers were 14% and 21%, respectively (World Bank 1994; International Monetary Fund 1995).

[4] A study by Jiri Koda of the Ministry of Economy of 480 cases filed in 1995 found that 29.2% were self-employed entrepreneurs and 51% were small, privately held companies (U.S. Department of State 1996, cable from the American Embassy in Prague). This suggests that of only 20% of all bankruptcies, about 17 in all, were former SOEs.

and they should potentially have increased the share of the private sector in GDP. Notwithstanding the slower pace of privatization in Poland, the shares of the private sector in GDP and employment were similar in the two countries by 1994 (Table 9.3), and labor productivity recovered faster in Poland (Table 9.4). It might even be argued that more painful, and politically unpopular, adjustments were made in Poland; Poland has experienced consistently higher levels of unemployment than the Czech

Table 9.2. *Progress in Transition*

	Czech Republic	Poland	Difference
Private share of GDP, mid-1995	70%	60%	10%
Large scale of privatization	4	3	1
Small scale privatization	4	4	—
Enterprise restructuring	3	3	—
Price liberalization	3	3	—
Trade and foreign exchange	4	4	—
Competition policy	3	3	—
Banking reform	3	3	—
Securities markets and nonbank financial institutions	3	3	—
Legal reform	4	4	—

Source: European Bank for Reconstruction and Development Transition Report 1995 (London: EBRD, 1995), page 11–12. See EBRD notes for details on classification system.

Table 9.3. *Private Sector Share of the Economy and Employment*

	% of GDP		% Employment	
	Poland	Czech Republic	Poland	Czech Republic
1989	28	11	47	16
1990	31	12	49	20
1991	42	17	50	30
1992	47	28	54	40
1993	52	45	57	60
1994	52	56	59	65

Source: World Bank 1996b.

Table 9.4. *Labor Productivity*

	Index of Industrial Labor Productivity	
	Poland	Czech Republic
1990	100	100
1991	96	82
1992	109	82
1993	125	81
1994	141	85

Sources: Czech statistical yearbook 1994; Polish statistical yearbook 1995; 1993; Indicators of the Economic and Social Development of the Czech Republic, 1995.

Table 9.5. *Unemployment*

	(% of Labor Force)	
	Czech Republic	Poland
1990	0.3	3.5
1991	2.8	9.2
1992	3.0	12.9
1993	3.0	14.9
1994	3.3	16.5
1995	3.2	15.2
Jan. 1996	3.0	15.4

Source: World Bank 1996b.

Republic (Table 9.5), which adds greater credence to the argument that Poland was more aggressive in hardening budget constraints to restructure SOEs during this period.[5]

---

[5] It is sometimes argued that unemployment in the Czech Republic might be low because laid off workers are rapidly absorbed by the dynamic new service sector (where many of the new private businesses are found in transitional economies), masking the extent of adjustment in the industrial sector. However, it is at least as likely that the absorption by the service sector in Poland biases its adjustment down relative to the adjustment in the Czech Republic. Services have grown faster in Poland – 21.8% from 1988 to 1994, compared to 11% for the Czech Republic – and started out as a larger share of the economy to begin with – 43% of GDP in 1991 versus 36% in Czechoslovakia (World Bank 1996a; Gelb and Singh, 1994).

Existing Explanations for SOE Reform Choices in Transition Economies

Why did Poland's rate of privatization lag that of the Czech Republic? One common explanation is that the Poles were in general less supportive of free markets than were the Czechs. However, Times Mirror surveys in May 1991 showed more than 80% of respondents in both Czechoslovakia and Poland generally approving of movement to a free market economy (Times Mirror Center for the People and the Press, 1992).

The literature has suggested several alternative answers. The first, advanced by Frydman and Rapaczynski (1993), Boycko, Shleifer, and Vishny (1994), Johnson and Kowalska (1994), Milor (1994), and others, emphasizes the relative strength of insiders (workers and managers). The consensus among these scholars is that insiders were strong in Poland thanks to the Solidarity movement. Solidarity was at the vanguard of political reform, and the pressure it put on the communist government even in the early 1980s led to worker councils receiving the right to hire and fire managers and to veto management decisions. In Czechoslovakia, where the communist government chose to repress rather than to co-opt organized worker dissent, unions were quiescent both inside SOEs and in the transition to democracy.

The events of the 1980s explain why Solidarity was important in the early part of the transition, and why SOEs insiders had significant authority inside SOEs in Poland. It does not explain, however, why SOE insiders maintained their influence after the fall of the communist regime. Indeed, there are several reasons to think that insiders should have become more powerful in Czechoslovakia and weaker in Poland after the transition to democracy. First, there were more SOE insiders in Czechoslovakia; Czech industrial employment was 46% of total employment, compared to only 29% in Poland. With the advent of democracy and elections, the larger number of Czech insiders should have increased their influence relative to insiders in Poland. Moreover, the Solidarity movement members who were instrumental in the Polish transition constituted much less than a majority of voters in Poland, and were outnumbered 2 to 1 by the members of the official trade union (OPZZ), which Lewis (1994) reports had 4.5 million members in 1990. Second, once the fight against communism in Poland had been won, other issues came to the fore which divided the Solidarity movement. Third, strike activity, which was important in Solidarity's influence over the communist government, seemed to lose some of its effectiveness in the postcommunist era. Strikes were seldom employed, offering corroborative evidence that Solidarity's strength had declined.[6]

A second theory suggests that the privatization decision turns on its employment consequences. Assuming that privatization leads to greater unemployment, governments, sensitive to the demands of employees in SOEs, are reluctant to privatize the greater is initial unemployment (Rodrik [1995], and Aghion and Blanchard [1994] present sophisticated versions of this somewhat crudely summarized argument). One can find support for this position in the observation that Poland began with a higher rate of unemployment than Czechoslovakia, and was also more reluctant to privatize. However, Poland undertook other measures after the initial period – such as more effective enforcement of bankruptcy law and harder budget constraints – that workers in state-owned enterprises might also have been expected to oppose, given this logic. In addition, Polish SOE reform efforts, including continual expansion of the set of SOEs to be privatized, have continued throughout the 1990s, even as unemployment in the country consistently exceeded Czech unemployment levels by a large margin.

OUR EXPLANATION

To better understand the reform choices made in Poland and Czechoslovakia, we turn to a closer analysis of three issues: (1) the degree of the separation of power existing in the two countries, (2) the extent to which separation of power in Poland was matched by a separation of purpose, leading to indecisiveness vis-à-vis reform, and (3) the role of other factors – particularly the possibility of tradeoffs across policy dimensions and the existence of different reversionary outcomes for various veto players – in narrowing the separation of purpose in Poland.

It is important to note that the differences we find between Poland and the Czech Republic can be traced to varying levels of separation of purpose among veto players other than the president and the legislature,

---

[6] From January to September 1990, the nadir of the Polish recession, there were only 131 strikes involving 31,200 workers, in a country with almost 40 million people (*EIU Poland* 1990:4, 7). The Suchocka government did face more serious strike activity, but even when nearly the entire Silesian mining industry struck in 1993 for several weeks, following motor industry strikes earlier in that year, the government made no significant concessions (*EIU Poland* 1993:1, 7). Under communism, worker strikes had a political character that broadened support for them in society at large. This almost certainly changed in the postcommunist era.

as may typically be the case. The extent of executive–legislative separation of purpose in the two countries was quite similar. In both countries, legislation is initiated by the cabinet and submitted to the parliament for approval. In Poland, the president exhibited unity of purpose with reformers on the issue of SOE reform. Walesa was generally favorable to economic reform. In 1990, he asked the government to enact more than two dozen liberalization measures by decree, given the Sejm's failure to approve them (Banks 1991). In Czechoslovakia, the coalition government favored reform.

The key ministries concerned with SOE reform in the two countries were Finance and Industry. The Finance Ministry initiated privatization proposals, making the Minister of Finance the key agenda setter. The Industry Ministry was the "founding" ministry of most nonagricultural SOEs; it was endowed with certain rights to oversee, initiate, and even veto reform efforts as they affected individual firms. Moreover, in the period under consideration, strong free-market reformers headed the finance ministries in both countries.[7]

The Pace of Privatization: Electoral Laws, Veto Power, and Separation of Purpose

In privatizing, the influence of different groups depended entirely on a group's ability to exert pressure on other veto players involved in negotiating SOE reform. The difference in groups' influence can be traced to the institutions governing Poland's and Czechoslovakia's transitions to postcommunist government. Poland's electoral institutions allowed small parties to have greater influence on legislative outcomes than in Czechoslovakia. In particular, the small parties representing rural interests and firm insiders (i.e., firm workers and managers) had considerably more legislative influence in Poland because of the prevailing electoral rules. Because their support was essential to the governing coalition, rural

---

[7] The finance ministries in both countries were headed by strong free-market reformers in the period under consideration. In Czechoslovakia, one of the most ardent free-market reformers of any transition country, Vaclav Klaus, became Finance Minister. Similarly, in Poland, after the Solidarity landslide in June 1989, the Finance Minister (Leszek Balcerowicz) and the Minister of Industry (Tadeusz Syryczyk) were widely regarded as strongly committed to free markets. One important exception to the embrace of free markets in Poland was in the agriculture portfolio, where a member of the communist-allied Peasants' Party was named Minister of Agriculture and deputy prime minister (*EIU Country Report Poland* 1989:4, 6).

interests and firm insiders in Poland exercised greater influence over veto players and agenda setters.[8] Progress on SOE reform therefore required mollifying these two interests. These groups would have had significantly less influence, and both the pace and modes of privatization would have more closely resembled privatization outcomes in Czechoslovakia, if Polish political and electoral institutions had more closely mimicked those of Czechoslovakia. However, because these actors controlled veto gates in the decision-making process in Poland but not in Czechoslovakia, it was more difficult to negotiate SOE reforms in Poland.

Electoral Laws

When Czechoslovakia and Poland adopted their posttransition electoral arrangements, they both chose proportional representation and allowed very large district magnitudes (the maximum number of candidates and, hence, parties that could take office in the district) for the main legislative chamber. Poland had thirty-seven constituencies, with five to seventeen members in each; Czechoslovakia had eight constituencies, averaging approximately nineteen seats per constituency. The combination of large district magnitudes and proportional representation promotes multiple parties. However, relative to Poland electoral rules in Czechoslovakia created greater disincentives to defect from positions taken by party leaders, and fewer incentives for smaller parties to form.[9]

Party discipline was weaker in Poland because rules gave ample scope for individual preference voting (i.e., voters could select particular candidates rather than cast their ballots for a party list established by party leaders). Preference votes in Poland determined the first candidates who would hold seats, and list ordering determined candidate selection only if, after preference votes were exhausted, there remained extra seats to which a party was entitled in a constituency.[10] These rules reduced a member of parliament's incentives to vote with the party, undermining

---

[8] We provide evidence in the next section that rural interests were, at best, ambivalent toward privatization. Also, for details of the Polish and Czechoslovak transitions, see Linz and Stepan (1996).

[9] For Polish electoral rules, see Millard (1992), 840. For Czechoslovak rules, the source is the electoral law downloaded from the Internet.

[10] That is, if preference votes were concentrated on three candidates in a twelve-seat district, but the party received sufficient votes to take six seats, the first three seats were filled by the candidates who received the preference votes, while the other three seats were filled according to their ranking on the party list.

party discipline. Czechoslovakia did have a weak form of individual preference voting, but a candidate had to obtain more than 10% of the vote cast for his party in order to displace a candidate higher up on the party list. Party leaders therefore had greater leverage over party members in Czechoslovakia than in Poland.

Voting threshold limits are the fraction of the total vote that a party must capture in order to be entitled to any parliamentary seats at all. Where these are lower, smaller parties are encouraged to run. For the 1991 elections, Poland had a minimum national vote threshold of 5% only for 69 seats awarded at the national level. The remaining 391 seats in the Sejm had no threshold requirement. Any party could take one of these seats, no matter what its percentage of the national vote, as long as it had sufficient votes concentrated in one constituency to qualify for office (Lijphart Elections Archive). In contrast, Czechoslovakia had a 5% vote threshold for single parties in either the Czech or Slovak areas of the country. This threshold rose for coalitions: 2 parties had to achieve a 7% threshold, 3 parties a 9% threshold, and 4 or more parties, 11%. These thresholds discouraged the defection of unhappy factions from larger parties into coalitions. Polish rules therefore encouraged electoral fragmentation, while Czechoslovakian rules discouraged fragmentation.[11]

Unity of Purpose in the Czech Republic

The ultimate impact of threshold rules is evident in Table 9.6a-c, a comparison of 1991 parliamentary elections in Poland and 1990 and 1992 elections in Czechoslovakia. In Czechoslovakia 7 parties surpassed the 5% threshold and won seats in 1990, and 6 in 1992. Civic Forum received over 50% of the vote in the Czech portion of the country in the early election; its successor alliance, the Civic Democratic Party-Christian Democratic Party (ODS-KDS), gained nearly 50% of seats in the Czech fraction of the House of the People in 1992. The level of fragmentation in Czechoslovakia prior to the dissolution of the country

---

[11] The evidence does not allow us to distinguish between the possibility that Czechoslovaks had a more convergent set of opinions, lending themselves to larger parties, and the hypothesis that electoral incentives were responsible for the more concentrated outcomes in the Czechoslovak case. However, given that regional, religious, and ethnic divisions were likely to have been at least as deep in Czechoslovakia as in Poland, it seems implausible that preference differences entirely explain differences in fragmentation.

Table 9.6a. *1991 Polish Parliamentary Election Results (the Sejm)*

Party	% of Vote	Seats Won
Democratic Union (UD)	12.31	62
Alliance of the Democratic Left (SLD)	11.98	60
Catholic Election Action (WAK) (the leading party in this coalition is ZChN)	8.73	49
Centre Democratic Accord (Centrum)	8.71	44
Peasant Party-Programmatic Alliance (PSL)	8.67	48
Confederation for Independent Poland (KPN)	7.5	46
Liberal Democratic Congress (KLD)	7.48	37
Peasant Accord (PL-Rural Solidarity)	5.46	28
Solidarity (Labor Solidarity)	5.05	27
Others (20 parties)	N/A	59

Table 9.6b. *1990 Czech Parliamentary Elections (Federal Assembly)*

Party	Percent of Czech Vote	Percent of Slovak Vote	Percent of Assembly Seats
Civic Forum	51.6	—	170 (Civic Forum plus PAV)
Public Against Violence (PAV)	—	34.9	
Communist Party	13.6	13.6	47
Christian Democrat coalition	8.7	13.6	40
Slovakian, Moravian, Hungarian ethnic parties (3)	8.5	19.7	43
Social Democrat, Farmers, Greens	11.2	6.9	0

Note: The assembly was bicameral, with a total of 300 seats; Civic Forum and Public Against Violence had an absolute majority in both.

Source: Poland: Millard 1992; Banks 1990; *EIU Country Report: Czechoslovakia.*

indicates that there were two key veto players. One was the party of Vaclav Klaus, Civic Forum in the 1990 elections and the Civic Democratic Party in 1992. The other was the Public against Violence party (PAV); together, these two parties had a parliamentary majority.

Table 9.6c. *June 1992 Czech Parliamentary Elections (House of the People)*

Party	Percent of Vote	Percent of Seats (out of 99)
Civic Democratic Party-Christian Democratic Party (ODS-KDS)	29.7	38
Left Block (Communist Party of Bohemia and Moravia and the Democratic Left of the CSFR, or LB)	14.1	17.5
Social Democrats	6.5	8
Liberal Social Union (LSU, Alliance of Czechoslovak Socialist Party, Agrarian Party, Green Party)	6.5	8
Christian and Democratic Union-Czechoslovak Peoples' Party	6.3	7.5
Republican Party	6	7
Civic Democratic Alliance (ODA)	5.9	7
Movement for Self-managing Democracy	5.9	7
Others	19.1	—

Note: The Federal Assembly had two chambers, each with a Czech and Slovak component. The Slovak Republic was created soon after the election. Reported are the results for the Czech parliament that emerged from the elections and the dissolution.

Source: EIU Country Report: Czechoslovakia 1992:3, 8.

The key parties in the Czech Republic – the Civic Forum and the Public Against Violence – enjoyed a unity of purpose on the major issues of the day, and in particular SOE reform. It is widely observed that Civic Forum in the 1990 elections and the Civic Democratic Party in 1992, the parties of Vaclav Klaus, were strong proponents of reform. Dissidents had little leverage, as the results of the 1992 elections proved. The PAV was also in favor of economic reform, and of privatization specifically; moreover, it was unlikely to leave the government even if its most preferred privatization policy were not passed.

The proprivatization policy preferences of the Klaus parties are widely recognized. The strongest evidence that the PAV supported some privatization is that, following the dissolution of Czechoslovakia, the Slovakian government that was led by the successor party of PAV did not halt privatization.[12] All observers clearly view the PAV and Civic Forum as linked with respect to reform efforts, much closer to each others' than to other parties' reform preferences (see, e.g., EIU Czechoslovakia 1990, 2 and 1990, 3, describing PAV as the Slovak counterpart of Civic Forum).

At the same time, the costs to PAV of leaving the government over disagreements regarding privatization were high, further cementing unity of purpose. At the time that privatization decisions were made, the most significant intracoalition issue had to do with the possible dissolution of Czechoslovakia into two nations. Most observers conclude that Klaus' preference (or at least the preference of his party) was for dissolution of the country (in part to divest himself of a voting population that was less in tune with his policy preferences than the Czechs). The preferences of PAV (known as the Movement for a Democratic Slovakia at the time of dissolution debates) was for a level of autonomy greater than the existing extremely federalized arrangements, but less than full independence. It was arguably more important to PAV to exercise leverage over this process and remain in government even if its preferred privatization outcome were not achieved.[13]

Separation of Purpose in Poland

In Poland, many more parties won seats and none had a large share of total seats. Low party discipline and fragmented government coalitions suggest that there were many more effective veto players in Poland than in Czechoslovakia. Were veto players more likely to exercise their authority in Poland? There are two reasons to suspect that they would. First, the costs of a veto (bringing down a government) were not high in Poland relative to Czechoslovakia. Those parties even moderately opposed to SOE reform could credibly threaten to leave the government in

---

[12] It did abandon the mass privatization process preferred by the Civic Democratic Union, but replaced it with an auction system over which it exercised tighter control.

[13] In the endgame leading up to dissolution, Klaus pursued a goal of complete dissolution; the PAV attempted to obtain a less drastic resolution, confederation, but ultimately and quickly acceded to a complete split (*EIU Country Report Czechoslovakia* 1992:4, 8). However, since the PAV wanted to control postdissolution Slovakia (and ended up doing precisely that), even if it had anticipated this result it was still in its interest to influence the dissolution process.

order to block it. "Defectors" from a government coalition frequently found relatively close allies in the opposition, and in any case had significant possibilities of joining any new coalition that emerged. At various times there were labor parties both inside the government coalition (Labor Solidarity) and outside it. Similarly, there were agricultural interests in both the governing coalition and in the opposition under both the Olszewski and Suchocka governments. In Czechoslovakia, on the other hand, to defect from the governing coalition meant uniting either with nationalists or communists. Because of electoral rules, a faction that left the Civic Forum and joined the opposition could potentially lose its representation in Parliament unless the faction aligned itself with one of these parties, neither of which were viable political options. Evidence of this shows up in the 1992 election. The Civic Democratic Alliance and the Civic Movement split off from Civic Forum prior to the election, but the latter earned no seats in the election, and the former surpassed the 5% threshold with only 0.9% of the vote to spare.[14]

Considerable evidence affirms the existence and strength of multiple veto players in Poland. Most conspicuously, governments in Poland were extremely unstable. The Olszewski government lasted from December 1991 until June 1992; the Suchocka government from July 1992 until September 1993. Labor Solidarity, with only twenty-seven seats in the Polish Sejm, helped form the Suchocka coalition; it was also the party that presented the motion of no confidence that eventually brought down the government. Parties with a rural base were also strong in all governments, reflecting the prominence of agricultural issues in a country in which agriculture provided 25% of total employment, compared to only 12% in Czechoslovakia (World Bank 1996a).

Two small parties that were crucial to government formation in Poland represented SOE insiders (Labor Solidarity), who opposed privatization, and rural interests (Rural Solidarity or Peasant Accord), who may have favored privatization in principle, but were opposed to privatization in agriculture and agroprocessing.[15] The opposition of rural

---

[14] At the same time, it should be emphasized that the range of disagreement inside the Civic Forum could have been substantially less than that inside Solidarity, simply because of a greater convergence of preferences. Nevertheless, the institutional setup increased the political gains from exacerbating rather than closing differences in Poland.

[15] Millard (1992) derives party preferences from policy stances taken during the 1991 parliamentary elections (to the extent that they could be gleaned from the campaign). Among those that were members of the government coalition, the Liberal

parties in Poland to SOE reform arose from fear that reform of agro-industrial SOEs would harm their interests. As late as 1994, there was evidence of strong political resistance to adjustment in agroindustry (World Bank 1994, 11). Indeed, only 2 of the parties that won seats in the 1991 elections, the KLD and UD (with fewer than 25% of the seats in the Sejm), were unambiguously in favor of privatization, so that any winning coalition had to include less fervent supporters. No parties in the Czechoslovakian governing coalitions opposed privatization, although they disagreed on approaches. Even if they had, the costs of exercising vetoes were higher in Czechoslovakia, so that Vaclav Klaus was better able than his Polish counterpart to push his favored reform strategy.[16]

This analysis provides an explanation for the influence of SOE insiders in Polish privatization policy. They exerted influence over parties such as Labor Solidarity, which in turn were able to exercise veto power over privatization policies not because of their strong support among the general public (Labor attracted little over 5% of total votes), but because of an electoral system that gave it exceptional leverage over its coalition partners. If the electoral laws of Czechoslovakia had been transplanted to Poland, it is likely that the influence of SOE insiders, and rural interests, would have been considerably less.[17]

Not only was there conflict among coalition partners, there was also considerable conflict within parties. Fractures within Solidarity and shift-

---

Democratic Congress (KLD) and Solidarity Peasants (PL) were the most laissez-faire (although PL excluded agriculture from this free-market emphasis); the Democratic Union of Mazowiecki advocated moderate interventionism (although the precise nature of the interventions were not defined); while Labor Solidarity was interventionist and opposed to rapid privatization. The Liberals and the Democratic Union supported proreform Balcerowicz, who was strongly resented by the others. The Centrum (Walesa's party during the presidential elections) and the Christian National Union (ZChN), the leading force in WAK, were more populist, as was the KPN (not a former Solidarity party); the ZChN favored privatization, but only if former communists were excluded from benefiting. The Centrum favored privatization, but also intervention to save state enterprises from collapse; it was against inflation, but also against tight money.

[16] Three of the remaining parties were primarily concerned with nationalistic or ethnic issues (Silesian and Moravian, Slovakian, and Hungarian, respectively), not with economic issues. The final party was the revived Communist Party. There were no overtly labor-oriented parties, except for possibly the Communist Party, nor were there farmer parties.

[17] We provide evidence in the next section that rural interests were, at best, ambivalent toward privatization. Also, for details of the Polish and Czechoslovak transitions, see Linz and Stepan (1996).

ing party allegiances were apparent throughout the 1989–1990 period. Several times, Rural Solidarity staged independent protests against the government. In the roundtable discussions with the communist government that constituted the basis for the transition, Solidarity insisted on the formal recognition of Rural Solidarity (*EIU Poland* 1989:2, 6). In the local elections held on May 27, 1990, Solidarity (which was not technically a party) supported an ad hoc array of Citizens' or Civic Committees that won 41% of the places; 52.5% went to independent candidates and smaller parties, and 6.5% to the Polish Peasants' Party. Early in 1990, the Center Alliance and the Democratic-Social Movement emerged from Solidarity (Banks 1990; 1991). Obviously, by the 1991 elections, the pace of party creation had accelerated considerably.

Given the role of different narrow interests as veto players in Polish politics, we would expect that SOE reform in Poland, unlike Czechoslovakia, would have depended on the possibility of making policy trade-offs that would serve to mollify these interests and to unify separate purposes, particularly those of rural and labor interests. The following sections provide evidence that this occurred. The process was facilitated by reversionary outcomes that made these interests more willing to compromise. Rural interests, facing a rapidly declining agricultural sector, were increasingly willing to sacrifice their SOE reform preferences for the restoration of some agricultural subsidies. SOE insiders, confronted with potentially catastrophic macroeconomic conditions, were more willing than otherwise to accept hard budget constraints, effectively reducing subsidies to SOEs. At the same time, because their control of SOEs in the absence of reform was stronger than the control exercised by their counterparts in Czechoslovakia, SOE insiders in Poland were able to obtain privatization legislation that was more favorable to their interests.

Manufacturing Unity of Purpose in Poland

The foregoing arguments suggest that political fragmentation provided more and different veto gates in Poland that slowed SOE reform there relative to Czechoslovakia. However, while privatization did proceed more slowly in Poland than in Czechoslovakia, SOE reform more broadly did not. The similarity of policy outcomes can be traced to two factors: (1) the set of salient policies that were under discussion in the two countries; and, (2) the reversion outcomes on salient policy issues. While neither the set of salient issues nor the reversion outcomes were the same in the two countries, these two factors interacted in such a way that the Polish government was able to overcome the considerable separation of purpose that existed among its key political actors whereas the Czech government was able to maintain its initial unity of purpose among its key actors. The effect of these differences was to allow the Polish agenda setter to make tradeoffs across policy dimensions that advanced SOE reform. The following section focuses on the policy tradeoffs that persuaded agricultural interests not to oppose SOE reform in Poland. The final section of the chapter discusses the policy proposals that defused the opposition of firm insiders.

The passage of the 1990 privatization law demonstrates two different ways in which support from rural interests was shored up. First, concessions to rural interests were made in the privatization law itself. The 1990 privatization law passed nearly unanimously, with 328 votes in favor and only 2 against. However, it was highly contentious and went through 17 drafts before reaching Parliament on July 13. After the legislation was submitted to the Sejm, different members attempted to make 30 amendments. Most disagreement surrounded the form that privatization would take, which is discussed in subsequent sections on SOE insiders. However, rural interests were also at stake, since of the 30 amendments, the only one that passed granted agricultural workers the right to buy shares at preferential rates in SOEs with which they had long-standing trading relationships (*EIU Poland* 1990:3, 9).[18]

At the same time, concessions were made to rural interests on a second policy dimension at approximately the same time that privatization legislation was under Sejm consideration, suggesting that these two policy dimensions were linked. Actions favorable to agriculture were taken beginning in June 1990, the same month that privatization legislation was approved by the Sejm. At that time, agricultural tariffs began to rise again and, by mid-1993, agriculture became the second most protected sector after automobiles. In addition, the Agency for Agricultural Markets (ARR) was created to stabilize farm products markets and to protect farm incomes. Minimum prices were also introduced for wheat, rye, and milk (World Bank 1994, 98–99).

---

[18] This raises the question of why the government did not include such a provision in the bill submitted to the Sejm. One likely explanation is that this bill was the product of the Industry and Finance Ministries, offering the Agriculture Ministry less opportunity to intervene.

The willingness of agricultural interests to accept privatization in return for policy concessions on agriculture was likely to have been increasing throughout the period. By 1990 the economic position of agriculture had deteriorated considerably because of price and trade liberalization. In September 1989, the government reduced import tariffs on all agricultural and agroindustrial products (World Bank 1994, 98). The average farmer's income fell 40% more than the average wage in nonagricultural sectors between 1985 and 1990. The situation had not bottomed out, however, since the terms of trade for agricultural products continued to deteriorate, by more than 60% in 1990–1991 (World Bank 1994, 96).

It is worth emphasizing that these tradeoffs would not have been feasible in some political environments. For example, if the rural situation in Poland had been good, rural interests would have been more difficult to persuade on privatization. Another way to underline the possibly ephemeral nature of these tradeoffs is to observe that in Czechoslovakia, should the Public Against Violence have actually opposed privatization, instead of merely preferring a different modality of reform, it would have been difficult to have constructed a tradeoff to secure their support. The principal policy dimension that concerned veto players in Czechoslovakia, apart from economic liberalization and privatization, was ethnic and nationalistic issues. Czechoslovakia had no significant agricultural parties, but did have active political movements concerned with national or minority issues: the protection or enhancement of political rights in Moravia and Silesia, Slovakia and for Czechoslovaks of Hungarian descent, a minority that is concentrated in Slovakia. For both the leaders of the Civic Forum and the Public Against Violence, the dissolution of the country into the Czech Republic and Slovakia was the most significant intracoalition issue.

However, the Civic Forum wanted the most dramatic reforms on both dimensions: fast and massive privatization, and dissolution of the country. The PAV was less insistent on dissolution and more content with the existing autonomy arrangements. If, in addition, the PAV had opposed privatization, there was no trade that Vaclav Klaus could have offered in order to have achieved the remarkable privatization policies that in fact emerged in the country. The reversionary outcomes on both dimensions would have been more satisfactory to PAV than any combination of significant reform proposals that Klaus could have proposed, so PAV would have vetoed any such proposals.

Gaining the Agreement of SOE Insiders

The previous section explained how tradeoffs between SOE reform and agricultural policies persuaded rural interests in Poland to go along with SOE reforms. It does not tell us why another key veto player (firm insiders) did not prevent reform. Our hypothesis is that differences in reversion outcomes for another salient policy, stabilization, explain the persistence of SOE reform in Poland despite the veto power exercised by firm insiders. If Poland had instead faced the more benign macroeconomic outlook of Czechoslovakia, reform would have slowed.

Fiscal stabilization and SOE reform are linked in a straightforward manner. The fiscal and monetary adjustments that a country has to make to combat inflation can have the additional effect of tightening SOE budget constraints, since governments trying to reduce the fiscal deficit to slow inflation are likely to reduce SOE subsidies. The greater the fiscal adjustment, therefore, the greater also is the likely reduction in these subsidies. Harder budget constraints would have led to greater observed productivity improvements, independent of ownership changes.

Poland confronted raging inflation in 1990, verging on hyperinflation – the inflation rate in January 1990 was nearly 80%, and 589% for the entire year, compared to 6% in Czechoslovakia that year. Even in 1991, when Czechoslovakian inflation surged to its highest level (57%; World Bank 1996), it never approached Polish highs (Vanous 1992, 1993, 1995, 1996). Without reform on the macroeconomic front, therefore, Poland confronted a significantly worse reversion scenario than did Czechoslovakia.

SOE insiders in Poland certainly preferred softer budget constraints for SOEs than did the Finance Minister. But they also preferred stabilization to continued hyperinflation. Consequently, although insiders would naturally have preferred that the burden of fiscal adjustment be borne by other segments of society, there were clearly important compromise policies across the two dimensions that the Finance Minister could propose and that SOE insiders would not veto. In particular, because of the severity of the macro crisis, the Finance Minister could construct veto-proof budget proposals that demanded greater belt-tightening from SOEs than would otherwise have been the case. If SOE insiders had confronted the Czechoslovakian reversion point for stabilization, the Finance Minister would have been more limited in his ability to propose policies that would achieve SOE reform.

This argument explains the association of fiscal adjustment and the increase in labor productivity in Poland, and predicts that these two outcomes would have been accompanied by a reduction in subsidies to SOEs. Data on government finances suggests that Poland implemented a fierce fiscal adjustment in 1990, when the government budget deficit went from 6% of GDP to a significant surplus. Although the deficits returned to the levels of 1989 in 1991 and 1992, the following years saw a significant and sustained fall that lasted through the end of the period (Table 9.7).[19] Moreover, there was a significant and sustained decline in direct government subsidies as a percentage of GDP throughout the period.[20] According to Kharas (1991), most of these subsidies went to mining, while manufacturing subsidies averaged only 8.5% of the previous year's level. While there is no breakdown available on the destination of these subsidies, the decline was likely to have been felt most by industrial interests, since mid-1990 saw the restoration of nonindustrial subsidies and protective measures for the agricultural sector.

Of course, insiders might have been able to avoid restructuring if they could use soft credits from the financial system to make up for the shortfall in subsidies. This does not seem to have happened, however. Domestic credit to SOEs remained constant, at approximately 18% of GDP, from 1990 to 1991 (using GDP from World Bank 1996, and credit to SOEs from World Bank 1994, Table 3.3). Industrial output (largely

Table 9.7. *Polish Budget Deficits: 1989–1995*

Year	Deficit (−) or Surplus (+) (% of GDP)	Subsidies (% of GDP)
1989	−6.03	10.56
1990	3.72	7.7−
1991	−6.67	5.12
1992	−6.66	3.27
1993	−2.43	3.87
1994	−2.19	4.08
1995 (prel.)	−2.62	1.76

Source: World Bank 1996.

[19] The return to high budget deficits in 1991 was largely due to a decline in revenues amounting to 3% of GDP, an increase in wage expenditures of approximately 2% of GDP, and an increase in transfers from 17.9% to 20.3% of GDP (World Bank 1994).

[20] Kharas (1991) reports an even larger 70% drop in subsidies in 1990, almost twice as large as in Table 9.7.

SOEs) declined from 1990 through 1992 by more than 14% a year; it increased by .3% in 1993 and 2% in 1994 and 1995. Moreover, the evidence shows that most bad loans that confronted the banking system in 1994–1995 were made in 1990 and 1991, suggesting that soft credits did not fully compensate for the decline in fiscal subsidies.[21]

COMPARING POLICY APPROACHES IN POLAND AND CZECHOSLOVAKIA

The first sections of this chapter have addressed two questions that have received little attention in prior research: Why did SOE insiders exercise significant influence in Poland? and Why did veto players opposed to privatization and hard budget constraints end up accepting them? The third puzzle, which we address in this section, is why the approaches of privatization chosen by the two countries differed, and in particular, why SOE insiders embraced mass privatization in the Czech Republic but resisted it in Poland. Here again, the key to the puzzle seems to lie with the distinct reversionary outcomes in the two countries. Those outcomes were more favorable to SOE insiders in Poland, and forced policy makers to propose privatization policies that granted SOE insiders greater control over the privatization process. Reversionary outcomes were less favorable to SOE insiders in Czechoslovakia, who in any case enjoyed weaker veto power, allowing policy makers to devise privatization processes that gave insiders less control than they enjoyed in Poland.

Prior to the 1990 privatization law Polish insiders could continue to control their SOEs through the employee councils under the 1981 Law on State Enterprises that the communist government passed in response to pressure from Solidarity.[22] Alternatively, they could liquidate their SOE under the 1981 law. The law allows the founding organ of the state enterprise (such as the Ministry of Industry) to liquidate the SOE (sell off its assets) if the Minister of Finance does not object to the liquidation within two weeks and if any one of the following conditions prevails: (1) the SOE does not pay a "dividend" (an asset tax on the capital contributed by the state); (2) the SOE's activities are no longer possible

---

[21] Gray and Holle (1996, 7) find in their survey of Polish SOEs that two thirds of the bad loans to SOEs originated in 1990 and 1991, before the adoption of banking reforms.

[22] Following the declaration of martial law in December 1981, employee councils saw their legal rights to SOE governance restricted in fact, if not in law, but the legal basis for extensive council control was not modified (Szomburg 1993, 78).

for legal reasons; or (3) more than one-half of the enterprise's assets are composed of other business entities or have been leased to other persons. Frydman et al. (1993, 169) report that liquidation under the 1981 Law on State Enterprises does not require the approval of the employee council, but is a viable mode of privatization only for enterprises that do not pay a particular debt to the state. These enterprises have generally been in serious financial difficulties.

For insiders in successful enterprises, this legal framework was highly satisfactory. Their SOEs were in no danger of being subjected to involuntary liquidation under the Law on State Enterprises, since they were always in a position to pay their "dividend" to the state. This meant that, at their discretion, they could continue to govern the SOE and receive whatever stream of benefits this offered them. Moreover, as the rash of "spontaneous privatizations" confirmed, the Law on State Enterprises also provided legal justification for SOE insiders to formally take possession of the SOE, by arranging a private placement of SOE assets through a friendly ministry (Frydman et al. 1993, 183). The only important reform in the SOE legal framework that these insiders would have valued would have been more convenient legal instruments for allowing them to formally take over the SOEs that they controlled.

Less successful SOEs, or those that thought they might be less successful, confronted more serious risks of forced liquidation under the Law on State Enterprises. Insiders in these SOEs would have preferred to see the repeal of these articles of the Law on State Enterprises. This was unlikely, however, since more successful SOEs and the proprivatization elements in the government would have opposed repeal. As a second choice, they would have preferred a new privatization law that gave them greater control over privatization proceedings than they had over liquidation. Such a law would have been acceptable to successful SOEs as well.

If we compare the privatization laws that were approved in Poland with those approved in Czechoslovakia, it becomes clear that the former, but not the latter, offered SOE insiders advantages over their reversionary outcomes. The Polish Law on Privatization of 1990 left less successful enterprises no worse off than they were before, since it continued to permit involuntary liquidations. However, the law improved the situation of SOE insiders in successful SOEs, because it gave them formal veto power over any efforts to privatize the SOE ensuring that, if they chose to accept privatization, they would be able to extract the maximum rents out of the transaction. Of course, the law that was ultimately passed in 1990 also included the provision in the law that workers could buy up to 20% of shares at half price; more substantial subsidies were demanded, but rejected by the Sejm (in part because of compromises designed to attract the support of rural interests).[23]

The mass privatization program pursued in the Czech Republic would not, however, have been superior to the reversion points confronting the insiders in Poland. Like the program in the Czech Republic, the mass privatization proposals considered in Poland reduced the control of SOE management and employee councils, vesting it in privatization funds. As a result, insiders resisted these. Of course, a mass privatization law ultimately passed in Poland, the 1993 Law on National Investment Funds and their Privatization. However, it further entrenched the veto power of SOE insiders over implementation, and was therefore unobjectionable to them. Under the 1993 law, the designation of SOEs for privatization was to be decided by the Council of Ministers upon receipt of a motion by the appropriate minister (from the SOE's founding ministry). This motion could be submitted only if neither the director nor the workers council had forwarded an objection with reasons within forty-five days of notification. The workers council could formulate an objection only with the support of the general meeting of workers. So for purposes of this law, the general assembly of workers, the directors of SOEs, the founding ministry, *or* the entire council of ministers could veto any privatization. This left SOE insiders no worse off than they had been previously, and so they did not object to it.

Maintaining Unity of Purpose in the Czech Republic

Why did SOE insiders in Czechoslovakia acquiesce to mass privatization? Earlier sections of this chapter point to the weaker veto power of insiders there.[24] However, even if they had enjoyed strong veto power, insiders confronted worse reversion outcomes in Czechoslovakia and would therefore have been willing to accept a privatization law that offered less control than SOE insiders enjoyed in Poland.

Under the communist regime, employee councils had legal rights to

---

[23] The total value of this privilege cannot be greater than the average annual earnings of workers over the previous twelve months, multiplied by the number of workers in the SOE.

[24] Insiders in Poland had both legislative influence, because of the electoral structure, and influence through the Ministry of Industry. Czech insiders enjoyed institutional influence only through the Ministry of Industry.

SOE governance only since 1987, when Czechoslovakia (under pressure from the Soviet Union) passed a new law on state enterprises that allowed the election of self-managed bodies and directors within the SOEs. In practice, however, existing communist party cells in the SOEs monitored the election of employee councils, controlled the nominations for enterprise mangers, and often allowed only one candidate. In June 1989, a few months before the Velvet Revolution, even these insider powers were reduced when a law on state planning was passed reinforcing the control of the state over the economy (Milor 1994, 17). Consequently, at the time of the political transition, SOE insiders did not have the right to veto efforts to liquidate or sell state SOEs (confirmation of this requires identifying the communist-era legislation governing this issue).

Managers of Czechoslovakian state-owned enterprises did have some de facto discretion to direct the use of SOE assets. They were able to set up private companies to either purchase output from their SOEs or to sell inputs to them on favorable terms, or to lease or transfer capital assets from the SOEs. However, these latter options were illegal (Mladek 1993, 137). Moreover, unlike the Polish case, the pretransition government retained the right to accept or reject the management choices of the workers' council, and continued to appoint managers directly (Frydman et al. 1993, 52). Since the government had the authority to replace managers, and to sell SOE assets (following the specific procedures set out in the laws governing state enterprises), insiders would, therefore, have preferred privatization proposals that gave them less control than Polish insiders successfully obtained.

The mass privatization program that was approved offered managers the possibility of low levels of monitoring from diffuse ownership, reducing their risks of job loss. In addition, the voucher scheme that was ultimately adopted also allowed SOE managers to propose privatization projects, which, as Milor notes, generally prevailed over proposals from other sources.[25] In Poland, though, managers had greater formal veto

---

[25] Interviews conducted by Milor (1994) revealed that 90% of the recommendations from the founding ministries (typically Industry) to the Privatization Ministry were approved; in case of disagreements, a special committee headed by the Prime Minister made the final decision. Management proposals succeeded, first, because they enjoyed information advantages over other "bidders." Second, as Milor (1994, 41) argues, is that managers constituted a well-organized group with a powerful and centralized Industry Association, with strong ties to officials in various ministries (founding ministries of their enterprises and others). Founding ministries tended to look favorably on their proposals in making recommendations to the Ministry of Privatization. Given the strong desire for speedy transfer of ownership,

power over privatization proposals, since even SOE level worker committees could block privatization attempts.

By identifying the distinct reversion points in the two countries, we can begin to explain the apparent contradiction in the attitudes of firm insiders toward mass privatization in Poland and Czechoslovakia. In Poland, insiders rejected the limitations on their authority that mass privatization might represent, while in Czechoslovakia managers preferred mass privatization precisely because they were hoping to take advantage of the dispersion of ownership that mass privatization provided. In the Polish case, since managers already had control of SOEs, this advantage was not an attraction of mass privatization.[26] In the Czechoslovakian context, manager control was already weak, and mass privatization represented the possibility of improvement – particularly compared to alternatives that involved concentrated outside ownership. This discussion suggests that the key actors in the Czechoslovakian case confronted fewer obstacles in privatizing than the key actors in the Polish case. In Poland, it was more difficult for firm insiders to be persuaded to support mass privatization efforts. Ultimately, however, the Polish government succeeded in promoting privatization and the two countries enjoyed similar economic progress.

POLICY IMPLICATIONS AND CONCLUSION

In this chapter, we compare the privatization efforts undertaken in Czechoslovakia (and the present Czech Republic) and Poland, discussing both the pace of privatization and the outcome of privatization in these two countries. Because of their similar histories and similar attempts to privatize their state-owned enterprises, many relevant factors may be

and the information advantages of the SOEs, these recommendations would have been difficult to overturn. According to Milor and others, the decisions selecting the winning privatization proposals were not based on any published criteria. It is not surprising, then, that although SOE managers were initially against mass privatization, after interviews with managers Milor (1994, 42) concludes that they came to see it as advantageous.

[26] Milor (1994, 24) argues that it was exactly because of the possibility that existing managers would be entrenched by a program of mass privatization that there was opposition to this plan in Poland. Since the status quo entrenched managers even more firmly than mass privatization would have, and the Czechoslovakian leaders – who also would have resisted entrenching firm management – nevertheless proceeded with mass privatization, this does not seem to be a complete explanation of the failure of mass privatization in Poland and its success in Czechoslovakia.

held constant, allowing us to focus clearly on the institutional differences between the two countries. We find key differences in the pace of privatization in the two countries, as well as in the distributive content of the final outcomes. As Cox and McCubbins would have predicted in Chapter 2, we trace Poland's slower privatization process to a greater separation of purpose, a separation of purpose that was inflamed by electoral rules that gave small parties pivotal policy-making power. The key actors in Czechoslovakia, on the other hand, enjoyed an initial unity of purpose that they were able to maintain throughout the transition process. Despite proceeding more slowly, Poland was able to achieve results quite similar to the outcome of privatization in the Czech Republic, because they could make critical policy concessions to entice key veto players to agree to privatization strategies. Ultimately, we argue it was the ability to construct these tradeoffs that allowed Poland to achieve results that in the end, resembled those obtained in the Czech Republic.

As predicted for this type of case by Cox and McCubbins in Chapter 2, however, the resulting policy in Poland had more particularistic ingredients than in Czechoslovakia. That is, although both countries finally achieved similar levels of privatization, some important distributional consequences did arise from the institutional differences. First, because farming interests were enfranchised in the political process, they were able to get agricultural subsidies in exchange for their votes for privatization. Second, because SOE insiders were enfranchised in the *legal* process, they were able to protect their own interests by trading their support for privatization for rents. Thus, these two constituencies in Poland were able to consume a disproportional share of the newly created surplus due to electoral and legal institutions. It remains to be seen whether these initial differences in who won and lost will have long-term repercussions on inequality of the distribution of income in the two countries.

We conclude that separation of purpose is a critical dimension within presidential systems and that we cannot understand policy outcomes without probing into both the natures of the separation of power and the separation of purpose, as well as the reversionary outcomes. Poland and the Czech Republic, though similar in many respects, had different institutional structures and confronted very different levels of interest conflict. The Polish government was characterized by more parties with more disparate interests than the Czech government. This heightened separation of purpose in Poland and generated significant problems in implementing privatization policies. Had the degree of separation of purpose not been explicitly studied in these case studies, we believe we would have missed the critical dynamics affecting privatization in Poland and Czechoslovakia. In short, we emphasize that both separation of power and separation of purpose must be explored if we are to provide accurate and compelling explanations for specific policy outcomes.

It is often claimed that policy recommendations must be tailored to individual country characteristics. The particular characteristics that are important, however, are usually determined in an ad hoc manner by leaders (or lenders) acting strategically. This paper uses a systematic framework for assessing whether reforms fall within the set of policy actions that are politically feasible – that can overcome the opposition of those groups that exercise veto power in the policy-making process in a country. While the merits of fast versus slow reform, and SOE-by-SOE versus mass privatization are undoubtedly important to understand, in many countries, the menu of feasible options is a short one that does not provide the luxury of these choices.

10

Conclusion

Policy Making in Presidential Systems

STEPHAN HAGGARD, MATHEW D. MCCUBBINS, and
MATTHEW SOBERG SHUGART

For some time, comparative politics has witnessed a strange debate about whether institutions "mattered" for political and policy outcomes.[1] For a discipline in which the analysis of institutions is arguably its central comparative advantage, this must have seemed to an outsider like a particularly strange bout of self-doubt. The debate was, in the end, useful because it forced those who focus on institutions to confront the null hypothesis that structural and social factors are the primary determinants of policy. In so doing, it has pushed institutionalists to come to address the interactions between institutions and social interests, and to put greater emphasis on empirical demonstrations of institutions' effects.

Initially, these empirical demonstrations focused on major constitutional arrangements, such as the difference between authoritarianism and democracy, or between parliamentary and presidential rule. We believe there is still merit in plowing these fields; but these distinctions are too broad for many purposes and thus have sometimes yielded only ambiguous results. What is required is more nuanced analysis that looks to variations within these large categories and to interactions among different institutions.

The "new institutionalism" does precisely that. Thus we are seeing an efflorescence of important comparative findings on the effects of particular institutions on policy, including federalism (Weingast 1995), bicameralism (Tsebelis and Money 1997), decree powers (Carey and Shugart 1998), cabinet formation (Laver and Shepsle 1996), and legislative committee systems (Shepsle 1989).

In this book, we have taken a similar line of attack. After Cox and McCubbins's general theoretical overview of the logic of institutionalist

---

[1] For a survey, see Cox and McCubbins, this volume, or Milner 1998.

analysis, Shugart and Haggard advanced some hypotheses concerning the functioning of presidential systems. One motivating factor behind this line of inquiry is the large and growing literature on the advantages of parliamentarism and the failings of presidential rule (particularly in Latin America, and more recently in the former socialist states). These claims of the relative merits of the two systems struck us as dubious.[2] More importantly, we believed that much hinged on the nature of presidential rule itself, which probably exhibits an even wider range of variation than parliamentarism, which is similarly diverse.

A second theoretical motivation grew out of the literature on economic reform (Haggard and Webb 1993). One finding of the Cox and McCubbins chapter is that decisive policy and resolute policy appear to demand somewhat contradictory institutional capabilities (Haggard and Kaufman 1992, 1995). The initiation of reform requires decisiveness, and in turn, a certain concentration of decision-making authority; but resolute policy requires that the status quo not be easily overturned, which requires less concentrated decision making.

Further, the contributors to the volume shared the sense that many institutional analyses have operated in a vacuum, isolating particular institutional elements (such as legislative committees), without locating them within a context of other institutional actors with whom they interact. For example, critics of presidentialism worried about the effects of divided government. But the deleterious effects of divided government may be partially offset if the president has proactive and reactive powers. We have tried to avoid this problem by looking at the different elements of presidentialism as constitutive of a policy-making *system;* the various powers of the president interact not only with his legislative interlocutors but with the political parties in which both executive and legislative action is embedded.

What we found, in a series of policy case studies, was that institutional structure, in particular the design of separation of powers and separation of purpose, have implications for the shape of public policy. The effective number of veto players, which is determined largely by constitutional divisions of power and by electoral systems, shapes how a state makes the decisiveness – resoluteness tradeoff. More veto players, whether in the form of different branches of government, more parties in a coalition, or disunited parties, mean that decisions entail higher

---

[2] We have detailed this criticism elsewhere; see Shugart and Mainwaring 1997, or Haggard and Kaufman 1995.

transaction costs, and so are more difficult to make. For the same reason, however, more veto players make policy more resolute, thereby guarding against the possibility of ever-changing, unpredictable policies. Similarly, more veto players mean that policy will be more private-regarding, as each demands a particularistic payoff in exchange for supporting any deal.

We also found that a certain unity of purpose is important to coherent policy making in presidential systems. In our sample of cases, the late Alfonsín years present ample evidence of the potential disabilities of a presidential system in which there is a polarized party system. In those years, not only were the two biggest parties far apart ideologically, with neither in the majority, but there were a few small parties, each based in a single province, that blackmailed the president, exchanging fiscal handouts for short-term coalitional support. Thus, the Argentine case in the latter years of Alfonsín's presidency demonstrates clearly the pitfalls of separation of purpose in presidential systems.

In Chapters 2 and 3, we argued that the likelihood of a separation of purpose increases with the presence of a number of features of the electoral process, including: nonconcurrence of presidential and congressional elections; incongruence of the congressional majority's constituency with that of the president, such as with malapportionment of even one house; staggering of elections, such that there is not full renewal of legislative seats at each election; and candidate-centered electoral formulas, which tend to reduce the salience of national issues in congressional races. This last element of the institutional picture is especially important: Many of the disabilities attributed to presidentialism are in fact due to peculiarities of the party system, and in turn how parties are shaped by electoral rules.

In Taiwan's SNTV system, for example, parties must develop strategies to divide the vote relatively evenly among their own candidates in any given district, or risk electing fewer than the maximum number of candidates that could be elected, given their share of the vote. The chapters on Taiwan by Cheng and Haggard and Haggard and Noble provide a number of examples of increases in the ruling party's interest in catering to particularistic constituencies as its majorities became less secure after 1992.

The cases further affirmed the importance of the nature of presidential power. Presidential regimes take a wide array of forms, and presidents' powers vary widely. While most have at least weak *reactive* power in the form of a veto, many also have important *proactive* powers, most notably decree power. The effects of reactive powers, for example, appear in Chile. Baldez and Carey note that recent Chilean tax policy has been very stable in part because the reversion point (a law enacted in 1990 and extended in 1993) is more progressive than Congress has subsequently been able to enact.

The effect of proactive powers also appeared in the cases. Restrictions on legislative amendments are also found to have potentially important effects in Chile and Taiwan, particularly where they limit Congress's authority to increase the amount of spending from the amount in the budget submitted by the president. Even where such powers exist, outcomes are shaped by the reversion point in case of failure to agree. In Argentina, Chile, and Taiwan, only the president may initiate the budget and Congress cannot increase spending, but different reversionary points in each case affect how much leverage the president enjoys. In Chile, the reversion point is current policy in most policy areas (including, as noted, taxation), but is the president's proposal in the case of spending. This contrasts with Taiwan, where the legislature may pass a temporary resolution, though the Constitution prohibits the legislature from increasing spending over levels proposed by the executive.

The use and abuse of decree powers is often touted as a potentially problematic component of presidential rule. The authority to issue new laws by decree exists in Argentina, and has proven important in some reforms, including the regulatory ones that Heller and McCubbins discuss. But the ultimate origin of these decree powers is frequently misunderstood; they may be less important than is thought, and may even have perverse effects. For example, the president in Taiwan is usually considered quite powerful, but does not have decree powers. As we have argued throughout, unity of purpose may prove more important than a particular power. In Argentina, authority delegated from Congress (rather than the president's constitutional decree powers) proved to be the most important factor in most of Menem's reforms. However, Heller and McCubbins note that such decree power may have negative effects on investor perceptions in a variety of regulatory areas, precisely because it implies the ability for the president to overturn existing policy, thereby increasing uncertainty.

These positive observations can be turned into policy prescriptions. Presidential systems of certain sorts are prone to particularism; as we noted, this tendency toward particularism is greatest where presidentialism coexists with electoral systems that tend to weaken parties or malapportion legislatures. Strengthening reactive powers of the presidency has been a common means of coping with such systems, but a more promising one lies in reform of the electoral process and legislative apportionment itself. While it might seem strange to suggest that countries undertake constitutional reform in order to achieve greater economic efficiency, Shugart and Haggard point out that a number of countries have done just that.

What we have termed the paradox of presidentialism – legislators elected from provincial constituencies and/or via candidate-centered electoral rules tend to be even more particularistic under presidentialism – is one of the prime sources of pressures to engage in distributive fiscal policy and the provision of pork. Thus, if legislative constituencies could be brought somewhat more into line with the presidential constituency through balancing local interests with national party interests and limiting malapportionment, the pressures for such policy problems would be diminished. It might be argued that such systems are unlikely to reform themselves. However, recent electoral reforms that combine single-member districts with national PR lists in some presidential systems, such as Bolivia and Taiwan, necessarily create a national-oriented check upon regional interests in the legislature. Moreover, economic reforms that empower urban middle-class constituencies and the recent reelection of reform-minded presidents (Cardoso and Menem) suggest that the political will for reducing the gap between the incentives of legislators and of presidents may be emerging.

While confirming some of our expectations about the role of party systems, the cases also opened up some extensions of our work where further reflection and research is required. Jones' chapter on Argentina demonstrates that some of the advantages that we attribute to strong parties can also turn into pathologies if the power of party leaders is not checked internally by democratic mechanisms. The Mexican system is, of course, not fully democratic, but nonetheless shows at the extreme how parties can be creatures of their leadership rather than constituents. In other presidential systems, such as Venezuela, we see strong, hierarchical parties colluding with their counterparts rather than competing vigorously to reflect the public-policy demands of constituents. The collusion of such inwardly oriented parties is largely responsible for extensive corruption.

Clearly, more work is needed both on the internal organization of parties, and on how different party systems and also individual parties might affect interest group organization and lobbying. Parties operating under electoral rules that mandate intraparty competition may have a greater propensity to generate demands for pork-barrel expenditure than would legislators responding only to their localized constituencies (see also Carey and Shugart 1995). Centralized parties and closed-list electoral rules partly solve this problem, but shift the locus of interest group activity to the center, opening avenues for "big" corruption and "partyarchy" (Coppedge 1994; Shugart 1998) where other checks do not exist.

Another extension of our work is in the mediating effects that federalism may have on presidential rule. Argentina, for example, exhibits a number of institutional features, such as closed lists, that imply strong parties. But party nominations in Argentina's parties are primarily controlled by party leaders in the provinces. As a result, Argentine presidents, even under unified government, face a party rank and file determined to increase transfers of revenues to provincial party leaders; Jones shows that this was an important component of Alfonsín's fiscal problems, and even extended into the Menem era (see also Willis et al. 1998).

In the case of Poland, we saw that separation of power between the president and the legislature was not an important factor in shaping reform of state-owned enterprises (SOEs), but that an important separation of powers and purpose occurred nonetheless. In this case, the president, who wields fairly weak reactive powers, was not centrally involved in battles over privatization. Rather, a separation of purpose that stemmed largely from the electoral system led to a fragmented party system, and in turn to a kind of de facto SOE-federalism in which firm managers wielded considerable influence over proposed policy changes. This effective veto allowed them to demand payoffs in exchange for their support of reform, ensuring that reforms would take a particularistic, private-regarding form. Keefer and Shirley show that in neighboring Czechoslovakia, where there were fewer veto players (and unity of purpose among them), the government acted more decisively, and Czech reforms took a public-regarding form.

In sum, we have presented a theory of institutional effects on policy. The cases presented regarding budgetary and regulatory policy in Argentina, Chile, Poland, and Taiwan provided substantial support for that. Although there is more work to be done, we believe this volume demonstrates that institutional analysis is sufficiently advanced to generate both predictions and recommendations for institutional design.

References

Ackerman, Bruce A. and William T. Hassler. 1981. *Clean Coal/Dirty Air: Or How the Clean Air Act Became a Multibillion Dollar Bail-out for High Sulfur Coal Producers and What Should Be Done About It.* New Haven: Yale University Press.

Aghion, Philippe and Olivier Blanchard. 1994. "On the Speed of Transition in Central Europe," in Stanley Fischer and Julio Rotemberg, eds., *NBER Macroeconomics Annual 1994,* 283–320. Cambridge, Mass.: The MIT Press.

Aguero, Felipe. 1992. "The Military and the Limits to Democratization in South America." in Scott Mainwaring, Guillermo O'Donnell, and J. Samuel Valenzuela, eds., *Issues in Democratic Consolidation: The New South American Democracies in Comparative Perspective.* Notre Dame, Ind.: University of Notre Dame Press.

Aguero, Felipe. 1994. "The Military in the Constitutions of the Southern Cone Countries, Brazil and Spain," *El Papel de los Partidos Politicos en el Retorno a la Democracia en el Cono Sur,* 153–198. Washington, D.C.: Wilson Center.

Alesina, Alberto and Geoffrey Carliner. 1991. *Politics and Economics in the Eighties.* Chicago: University of Chicago Press.

Alesina, Alberto and Howard Rosenthal. 1995. *Partisan Politics, Divided Government, and the Economy.* Cambridge: Cambridge University Press.

Alesina, Alberto and Guido Tabellini. 1990. "A Positive Theory of Fiscal Deficits and Government Debt." *Review of Economic Studies* 57: 403–414.

Alt, James E. and Robert C. Lowry. 1994. "Divided Government, Fiscal Institutions, and Budget Deficits-Evidence from the States." *American Political Science Review* 88: 811–828.

American Political Science Association, Committee on Political Parties. 1950. *Toward a More Responsible Two-Party System.* New York: Rinehart.

Ames, Barry. 1995a. "Electoral Rules, Constituency Pressures, and Pork Barrel: Bases of Voting in the Brazilian Congress." *The Journal of Politics* 57, 2: 324–343.

Ames, Barry. 1995b. "Electoral Strategy under Open-List Proportional Representation." *American Journal of Political Science* 39, 2: 406–433.

Aramouni, Alberto and Ariel Colombo. 1992. *Críticas al Liberal-Menemismo.* Buenos Aires: Fundación Proyectos para el Cambio.

Archer, Ronald P. and Mathew Soberg Shugart. 1997. "Presidential Power and its Limits in Colombia," in Scott Mainwaring and Matthew Soberg Shugart, eds., *Presidentialism and Democracy in Latin America*, 110–159. New York: Cambridge University Press.

Arellano, José Pablo. 1996. Interview. Santiago, Chile.

Arnold, R. Douglas. 1990. *The Logic of Congressional Action*. New Haven: Yale University Press.

Atlas, Cary M., Thomas W. Gilligan, Robert J. Hendershott, and Mark A. Zupan. 1995. "Slicing the Federal Government Net Spending Pie: Who Wins, Who Loses, and Why." *American Economic Review* 85: 624–629.

Auth, José. 1994. "Elecciones presidenciales y parlamentarias de 1993." *Estudios Públicos* (fall): 339–361.

Banks, Arthur S., ed. 1990. *Political Handbook of the World 1990*. Binghamton, N.Y.: CSA Publications, State University of New York.

Banks, Arthur S., ed. 1991. *Political Handbook of the World 1991*. Binghamton, N.Y.: CSA Publications, State University of New York.

Bartos, O. J. 1995. "Modeling Distributive and Interactive Negotiations." *Annals of the Academy of Political and Social Science* 542: 48–60.

Bauer, Raymond A., Ithiel de Sola Pool, and Lewis Anthony Dexter. 1963. *American Business and Public Policy: The Politics of Foreign Trade*. New York: Atherton Press.

Bawn, Kathleen. 1993. "The Logic of Institutional Preferences: German Electoral Law as a Social Choice Outcome." *American Journal of Political Science* 37: 965–989.

Becker, Gary S. 1985. "Public Policies, Pressure Groups, and Dead Weight Costs." *Journal of Public Economics* 28: 329–347.

Bensel, Richard F. and E. Sanders. 1979. "The Effect of Electoral Rules on Voting Behavior: The Electoral College and Shift Voting." *Public Choice* 34: 69–85.

Beyme, Klaus von. 1985. *Political Parties in Western Democracies*. New York: St. Martin's Press.

Birnbaum, Jeffrey H. and Alan S. Murray. 1987. *Showdown at Gucci Gulch: Lawmakers, Lobbyists, and the Unlikely Triumph of Tax Reform*. New York: Random House.

Black, Jerome. 1978. "The Multicandidate Calculus of Voting: Applications to Canadian Federal Elections." *American Journal of Political Science* 22: 609–638.

Black, Jerome. 1980. "The Probability-choice Perspective in Voter Decision Making Models." *Public Choice* 35: 565–574.

Blais, Andre and Robert K. Carty. 1987. "The Impact of Electoral Formulae on the Creation of Majority Governments." *Electoral Studies* 6: 99–110.

Blais, Andre, Rachel Desrosiers and Francois Renaut, 1974. "L'effet en Amont de la Carte Electorale." *Canadian Journal of Political Science* 7: 648–672.

Boeninger, Edgardo. 1996. Interview, January, Santiago, Chile.

Boycko, Maxim, Andrei Shleifer, and Robert W. Vishny. 1994. "Voucher Privatization." *Journal of Financial Economics* 35: 249–266.

Boylan, Delia M. 1998. "Pre-emptive Strike: Central Bank Reform in Chile's

Transition from Authoritarian Rule." *Comparative Politics* 30, 4: 443–462.

Brady, David and Mark A. Morgan. 1987. "Reforming the Structure of the House Appropriations Process: The Effects of the 1885 and 1919–1920 Reforms on Money Decisions," in Mathew D. McCubbins and Terry Sullivan, eds., *Congress: Structure and Policy*, 207–234. New York: Cambridge University Press.

Bresser Pereira, Luiz Carlos, José María Maravall, and Adam Przeworski. 1993. *Economic Reforms in New Democracies*. New York: Cambridge University Press.

Brocato, Alejandro. 1996. Multiple interviews, May–June, Buenos Aires, Argentina.

Brody, Richard A. and Benjamin I. Page. 1973. "Indifference, Alienation, and Rational Decisions." *Public Choice* 15: 1–17.

Buchanan, James M., Robert D. Tollison, and Gordon Tullock, ed. 1980. *Toward a Theory of the Rent-Seeking Society*. College Station: Texas A&M University.

Buchanan, James M. and Gordon Tullock. 1962. *The Calculus of Consent: Logical Foundations of Constitutional Democracy*. Ann Arbor: University of Michigan.

Burnham, Walter Dean. 1982. *The Current Crisis in American Politics*. Oxford: Oxford University Press.

Cain, Bruce E. 1978. "Strategic Voting in Britain." *American Journal of Political Science* 22: 639–655.

Cain, Bruce E., John Ferejohn, and Morris P. Fiorina. 1987. *The Personal Vote: Constituency Service and Electoral Independence*. Cambridge: Cambridge University Press.

Calder, Kent. 1988. *Crisis and Compensation: Public Policy and Political Stability in Japan, 1949–1986*. Princeton: Princeton University Press.

Callieri, Claudio. 1996. Multiple interviews, May–June, Buenos Aires, Argentina.

Campbell, Donald T. 1975. " 'Degrees of Freedom and the Case Study." *Comparative Political Studies* 8: 178–193.

Campos, Jose Edgardo and Hadi Salehi Esfahani. 1994. "The Political Foundations of Public Enterprise Reform in Developing Countries." Unpublished typescript, The World Bank, Washington, DC.

Carey, John M. 1994. "Los efectos del ciclo electoral sobre el sistema de partidos y el respaldo parlamentario al ejecutivo." *Estudios Públicos* 55: 305–314.

Carey, John M. 1996. *Term Limits and Legislative Representation*. New York: Cambridge University Press.

Carey, John M. 1997. "Strong Parties for a Limited Office: Presidentialism and Political Parties in Costa Rica," in Scott Mainwaring and Matthew Soberg Shugart, eds., *Presidentialism and Democracy in Latin America*, 199–224. New York: Cambridge University Press.

Carey, John M. 1998. "Electoral Reform and the Chilean Legislative Party System." Unpublished manuscript.

Carey, John M. Octávio Amorim Neto, and Matthew Soberg Shugart. 1997.

"Appendix: Outlines of Constitutional Powers in Latin America," in Scott Manwaring and Matthew Soberg Shugart, eds., *Presidentialism and Democracy in Latin America*, 440–460. New York: Cambridge University Press.

Carey, John M. and Matthew Soberg Shugart. 1995. "Incentives to Cultivate a Personal Vote: A Rank Ordering of Electoral Formulas." *Electoral Studies* 14: 417–439.

Carey, John M. and Matthew Soberg Shugart, ed. 1998a. *Executive Decree Authority: Calling Out the Tanks or Just Filling Out the Forms?* New York: Cambridge University Press.

Carey, John M. and Matthew Soberg Shugart. 1998b. "Calling Out the Tanks or Just Filling Out the Forms?" in John M. Carey and Matthew Soberg Shugart, eds., *Executive Decree Authority: Calling Out the Tanks or Just Filling Out the Forms?*, 1–29. New York: Cambridge University Press.

Casper, Gretchen. 1995. *Fragile Democracies: The Legacies of Authoritarian Rule*. Pittsburgh: University of Pittsburgh Press.

Caviedes, Cesar. 1991. *Elections in Chile: The Road toward Redemocratization*. Boulder, Colo.: Lynne Rienner Publishers, Inc.

Central and Eastern European Privatization Network. 1996. "Privatization in Central and Eastern Europe 1995." in Andreja Böhm, ed., *Annual Conference Series, No. 6. Ljubljana:* CEEPN.

Central Electoral Commission. Various years. *Reports on Elections*.

Chen, Ming-tong. 1995. *Pai hsi cheng chih yu Taiwan cheng chih pien chien* (Factionalism and Taiwan's Political Change). Taipei: Yeh-dan Publishing.

Chen, Shong-san. 1994. *Kuo-hui chih-tu jie-tu* (Understanding the Congressional System in Taiwan). Taipei: Yeh-dan Publishing.

Cheng, Tun-jen. 1993. "Guarding the Commanding Heights: The State as Banker in Taiwan," in Stephan Haggard, Chung H. Lee and Sylvia Maxfield, eds., *The Politics of Finance in Developing Countries*, 55–92. Ithaca: Cornell University Press.

Cheng, Tun-jen. 1995. "Democratic Transition and Economic Policymaking in Korea and Taiwan." Paper presented at the American Political Science Association convention, Chicago.

Cheng, Tun-jen and Stephan Haggard, ed. 1992. *Political Change in Taiwan*. Boulder, Colo.: Lynne Rienner Publishers, Inc.

Cheng, Tun-jen and Yung-ming Hsu. 1996. "Issue Structure, the DPP's Factionalism, and Party Realignment," in Hung-mao Tien, ed., *Taiwan's Electoral Politics and Democratic Transition*, 137–173. Armonk, N.Y.: M. E. Sharpe.

Cheng, Tun-jen and Yung-ming Hsu. Forthcoming. "Interest Groups, Entrepreneurship, and Party Politics," in Hung-mao Tien, ed., *Political Development in Hong Kong and Taiwan*. Hong Kong: Oxford University Press.

Cheng, Tun-jen and Chi Schive. 1996. "What Has Democratization Done to Taiwan's Economy?" Paper presented at conference on Taiwan: A Decade of Democratization: Record, Prospects, and Implications, George Washington University, Washington, D.C.

Ch'ien, Tuan-sheng. 1950. *The Government and Politics of China*. Cambridge: Harvard University Press.

China Times. May 30, 1992, 4. Taipei.

References

China Times. May 29, 1993, 4. Taipei.

China Times. January 3, 1988, 2. Taipei.

China Times. February 9, 1995, 7. Taipei.

China Times. May 31, 1996. Taipei.

China Times. June 1, 1996. Taipei.

Chou, Yu-kou. 1994. *Lee Teng-hui, 1993.* Taipei: Wu Publishers.

Chu, Yun-han. 1994. "The Realignment of Business-Government Relations and Regime Transition in Taiwan," in Andrew MacIntyre, ed., *Business and Government in Industrializing Asia*, 113–141. Ithaca: Cornell University Press.

Chung-hua Institution of Economics. 1993. "Wuguo Dianyefa Xiuzheng Caoan Zhi Yanju (A Study of Preliminary Modifications of the Electricity Act in Taiwan)." Taipei: Energy Commission, Ministry of Economic Affairs, June.

Cohen, Linda, Mathew McCubbins, and Frances M. Rosenbluth. 1995. "The Politics of Nuclear Power in Japan and the United States," in Peter F. Cowhey and Mathew McCubbins, eds., *Structure and Policy in Japan and the United States*, 177–202. New York: Cambridge University Press. *Commercial Times.* June 12, 1996. Taipei.

Commercial Times. June 12, 1996. Taipei.

Constable, Pamela and Arturo Valenzuela. 1989–1990. "Chile's Return to Democracy." *Foreign Affairs* 68, 5 (Winter): 169–187.

Constable, Pamela and Arturo Valenzuela. 1991. *A Nation of Enemies.* New York: W. W. Norton & Company, Inc.

Cooper, Joseph, David W. Brady, and Patricia A. Hurley. 1977. "The Electoral Basis of Party Voting: Patterns and Trends in the U.S. House of Representatives," in Louis Maisel Louis and Joseph Cooper, eds., *The Impact of the Electoral Process*, 133–165. Beverly Hills: Sage Publications, Inc.

Cornell, Nina, Roger G. Noll, and Barry R. Weingast. 1976. "Safety Regulation," in C. Schultze and H. Owen, eds., *Setting National Priorities*, 457–504. Washington, D.C.: Brookings Institution.

Costa, Rossana. 1996. Interview. Santiago, Chile.

Council on Economic Planning and Development. 1993. "Cheng-fu tsai-wu tuai kuo-nai tsong-ti ching-chi fa-tsang chih ying-hsiang (Government Debt and Its Effect on the Economy)." Unpublished paper.

Council on Economic Planning and Development. 1996. "*Sheu-hui fu-li chih-chu tuai tsong-ti ching-chi fa-tsang chih ying-hsiang* (Social Welfare Expenditures and Their Effects on Economic Development)." Unpublished paper.

Covarrubios, Alvaro J. and Suzanne B. Maia. 1994a. " 'Reforms and Private Participation in the Power Sector of Selected Latin American and Caribbean and Industrialized Countries," v. 1, *Discussion of Issues.* World Bank, Latin America and the Caribbean Technical Department, Regional Studies Program, *Draft report #33.* March.

Covarrubios, Alvaro J., and Suzanne B. Maia. 1994b. " 'Reforms and Private Participation in the Power Sector of Selected Latin American and Caribbean and Industrialized Countries," v. 2, *Appendices.* World Bank, Latin America and the Caribbean Technical Department, Regional Studies Program, *Draft report #33.* March.

Cowhey, Peter F. and Mathew D. McCubbins, ed. 1995. *Structure and Policy in*

Japan and the United States. Cambridge, New York: Cambridge University Press.

Cox, Gary W. 1984. "Strategic Electoral Choice in Multi-Member Districts: Approval Voting in Practice?" *American Journal of Political Science* 28: 722–738.

Cox, Gary W. 1987a. "Electoral Equilibrium under Alternative Voting Institutions." *American Journal of Political Science* 31: 82–108.

Cox, Gary W. 1987b. *The Efficient Secret: The Cabinet and the Development of Political Parties in Victorian England*. Cambridge: Cambridge University Press.

Cox, Gary W. 1994. "Strategic Voting Equilibria under The Single Nontransferable Vote." *American Political Science Review* 88: 608–621.

Cox, Gary W. 1995. "Is the Single Non-Transferrable Vote Superproportional? Evidence from Japan and Taiwan," Unpublished manuscript, University of California, San Diego.

Cox, Gary W. 1997. *Making Votes Count: Strategic Coordination in the World's Electoral Systems*. New York: Cambridge University Press.

Cox, Gary W. and Octavio Amorim-Neto. 1997. "Electoral Institutions, Cleavage Structures, and the Number of Parties." *American Journal Of Political Science* 41:149–174.

Cox, Gary W. and Samuel Kernell, ed. 1991. *The Politics of Divided Government*. Boulder, Colo.: Westview Press.

Cox, Gary W. and Mathew D. McCubbins. 1991. "Divided Control of Fiscal Policy," in Gary W. Cox and Samuel Kernell, eds. *The Politics of Divided Government*, 155–175. Boulder, Westview Press.

Cox, Gary W. and Mathew D. McCubbins. 1993. *Legislative Leviathan: Party Government in the House*. Berkeley: University of California Press.

Cox, Gary W. and Richard D. McKelvey. 1984. "A Ham Sandwich Theorem for General Measures." *Social Choice and Welfare* 1:75–83.

Cox, Gary W. and Emerson Niou. 1994. "Seat Bonuses Under the Single-Non Transferrable Vote System: Evidence from Japan and Taiwan." *Comparative Politics* 26: 221–36.

Cox, Gary W. and Frances Rosenbluth. 1993. "The Electoral Fortunes of Legislative Factions in Japan." *American Political Science Review* 87: 577–589.

Cox, Gary W. and Matthew Soberg Shugart. 1995. "The Absence of Vote Pooling: Nomination and Vote Allocation Errors in Colombia." *Electoral Studies* 14, 4 (December): 441–460.

Cox, Gary W. and Matthew Soberg Shugart. 1996. "Strategic Voting under Proportional Representation." *Journal of Law, Economics, & Organization* 12: 299–324.

Crisp, Brian F. and Juan C. Rey. 2000. "The Sources of Electoral Reform in Venezuela," in Matthew Soberg Shugart and Martin P. Wattenberg, eds., *Mixed-Member Electoral Systems: The Best of Both Worlds?* Oxford: Oxford University Press.

Cuckierman, Alex. 1992. *Central Bank Strategy, Credibility and Independence: Theory and Evidence*. Cambridge, Mass: The MIT Press.

Cullather, Nick. 1996. " 'Fuel for the Good Dragon: The United States and

References

Industrial Policy in Taiwan, 1950–1965." *Diplomatic History* 20, 1 (Winter): 1–25.

Curtis, Gerald. 1988. *The Japanese Way of Politics*. New York: Columbia University Press.

Czech Republic. 1994. *Statisticka rocenka Ceske Republiky – Statistical Yearbook of the Czeck Republic*. Prague: Czech Statistical Office.

Czech Republic. 1995. *Indicators of the Economic and Social Development of the Czech Republic*. Prague: Aggregate Information Branch.

Dahl, Robert A. 1956. *A Preface to Democratic Theory*. Chicago: University of Chicago Press.

Dahl, Robert A. 1967. *Pluralist Democracy in the United States: Conflict and Consent*. Chicago: Rand McNally.

Della Sala, Vincent. 1993. "The Permanent Committees of the Italian Chamber of Deputies: Parliament at Work?" *Legislative Studies Quarterly* 18: 157–83.

Dickson, Bruce J. 1996. "Kuomintang before Democratization: Organizational Change and the Role of Elections," in Hung-mao Tien, ed., *Taiwan's Electoral Politics and Democratic Transition*, 42–78. Armonk, N.Y.: M. E. Sharpe.

Dirección de Información Parlamentaria. 1996. Reference files of the Dirección de Información Parlamentaria, Congreso de la Nación, Buenos Aires, Argentina.

D'Onofrio, Francesco. 1979. "Committees in the Italian Parliament," in John D. Lees and Malcolm Shaw, eds., *Committees in Legislatures*. Durham, N.C.: Duke University Press.

Drake, Paul. 1993. "Obstacles to Policy Changes in Chile," Unpublished manuscript. University of California, San Diego.

Dromi, Roberto and Eduardo Menem. 1994. *La Constitución Reformada: Comentada, Interpretada y Concordada*. Buenos Aires: Ediciones Ciudad Argentina.

Durrieu, Marcela. 1996. Multiple interviews, May–June, Buenos Aires, Argentina.

Duverger, Maurice. 1954. *Political Parties: Their Organization and Activity in the Modern State*, trans. Barbara and Robert North. New York: John Wiley & Sons.

Duverger, Maurice. 1980. "A New Political System Model: Semipresidential Government." *European Journal of Political Research* 8: 165–187.

Earle, John S., Roman Frydman, and Andrzej Rapaczynski. 1993. *Privatization in the Transition to a Market Economy: Studies of Preconditions and Policies in Eastern Europe*. New York: St. Martin's Press.

Eaton, Kent. 1997. "The Politics of Tax Reform: Economic Policy Making in Developing Presidential Democracies." Ph.D. diss., Yale University.

Economist Intelligence Unit. Various issues. *Country Report: Argentina*. London: Economist Publications.

Economist Intelligence Unit. Various issues. *Country Report: Czechoslovakia*. London: Economist Publications.

Economist Intelligence Unit. Various issues. *Country Report: Czech Republic and Slovakia*. London: Economist Publications.

Economist Intelligence Unit. Various issues. *Country Report: Poland*. London: Economist Publications.

El Mercurio. 1993. "Resultos Electorales." *Electronic Engineering News*. C2–C5.

Energy Commission, Ministry of Economic Affairs, Republic of China. 1995. "Dianyuan Buzu Shiqi JianshaoYongdian Banfa (Method for Controlling Electricity Use in Times of Insufficient Electricity Supply)," Unpublished manuscript.

Ente Nacional Regulador de la Electricidad. 1994. *Informe Anual 1993/1994*, Vol. 1. Buenos Aires: ENRE.

Feliu, Olga. 1994. "Informe sobre el proyecto de ley de presupuestos del año 1995." Unpublished manuscript. Santiago.

Feliu, Olga. 1996. Personal communication. Santiago, Chile.

Fenno, Richard. 1978. *Home Style: House Members in Their Districts*. Boston: Little, Brown.

Feo, Alberto. 1996. Interview, May 16, Buenos Aires, Argentina.

Ferejohn, John. 1974. *Pork Barrel Politics: Rivers and Harbors Legislation, 1947–1968*. Stanford, Calif.: Stanford University Press.

Fiorina, Morris P. 1977. *Congress: Keystone of the Washington Establishment*. New Haven: Yale University Press.

Fiorina, Morris P. 1980. "The Decline of Collective Responsibility in American Politics." *Daedalus, Journal of the American Academy of Arts and Sciences*, 109, 3.

Fiorina, Morris P. 1981. *Retrospective Voting in American National Elections*. New Haven: Yale University Press.

Fiorina, Morris P. 1992. *Divided Government*. New York: Macmillan.

Fiorina, Morris P. and Roger Noll. 1979. "Majority Rule Models and Legislative Elections." *Journal of Politics* 41: 1081–1104.

Fisher, S. L. 1974. "A Test of Anthony Downs' Wasted Vote Thesis: West German Evidence." Unpublished paper prepared for the Public Choice Society, New Haven, Conn.

Ford, Henry Jones. 1898. *The Rise and Growth of American Politics*. New York: Macmillan.

Freeman, John Lieper. 1955. *The Political Process: Executive Bureau-Legislative Committee Relations* New York: Random House.

Frydman, Roman and Andrzej Rapaczynski. 1993. *Privatization in Eastern Europe: Is the State Withering Away?* New York: Central European University Press.

Frydman, Roman, Andrzej Rapaczynski, and John S. Earle. 1993. *The Privatization Process in Central Europe*. Central European University Privatization Project.

Fukui, Haruhiro and Shigeru Fukai. 1996. "Pork Barrel Politics, Networks, and Local Economic Development in Contemporary Japan." *Asian Survey*. 36, 3 (March): 268–286.

Garman, Christopher, Stephan Haggard, and Eliza Willis. 1996. "Decentralization in Latin America." Paper presented at the annual meeting of the American Political Science Association, San Francisco, California.

References

Geddes, Barbara. 1994. *Politician's Dilemma: Building State Capacity in Latin America*. Berkeley: University of California Press.

Gibson, Edward L. 1996. *Class and Conservative Parties: Argentina in Comparative Perspective*. Baltimore: Johns Hopkins University Press.

Gibson, Edward L. and Ernesto Calvo. 1997. "Electoral Coaliticus and Market Reforms: Evidence from Argentina." Paper presented at the Fundación Gobierno y Sociedad and Centro de Estudios para el Desarrollo Institucional (CEDI) Conference Democracia, Reformas Económicas, y Diseño Institucional, Buenos Aires, Argentina.

Godoy, Oscar. 1996. Interview, January, Catholic University, Santiago, Chile.

Godoy Arcaya, Oscar. 1994. "Las elecciones de 1993." *Estudios Públicos* (fall) : 301–337.

Gómez de la Fuente, Pedro and Carolina Pérez Colman. 1995. *Glosario Electoral Argentino*. Buenos Aires: Centro Editor Argentino.

González Fraga, Javier, A. 1991. "Argentine Privatization in Retrospect," in William Glade, ed., *Privatization of Public Enterprises in Latin America*, 75–98. San Francisco: International Center for Economic Growth, Institute of the Americas, and Center for US-Mexican Studies.

Gopher://fenir.psp.cz:70/oo/parleng/volzak (Online source for Czech electoral law of 1995).

Gray, Cheryl and Arnold Holle. 1996. "Bank-led Restructuring in Poland (II): Bankruptcy and its Alternatives." *Policy Research Working Papers #1651* Policy Research Department, The World Bank.

Grofman, Bernard and Arend Lijphart, ed. 1986. *Electoral Laws and Their Political Consequences*. New York: Agathon Press.

Grupo Sophia. 1997. *Informe Sobre el Presupuesto Nacional 1997*. Buenos Aires: Grupo Sophia.

Guasch, J. Luis and Pablo Spiller. 1995. "Regulation and Private Sector Development in Latin America." Unpublished manuscript.

Guasch, J. Luis and Pablo Spiller. 1996. *Managing the Regulatory Process: Concepts, Issues and the Latin America and Caribbean Story Book*. Unpublished manuscript.

Gunther, Richard. 1989. "Electoral Laws, Party Systems, and Elites-The Case of Spain." *American Political Science Review* 83: 835–858.

Haggard, Stephan. 1990. *Pathways from the Periphery: The Politics of Growth in the Newly Industrializing Countries*. Ithaca, N.Y.: Cornell University Press.

Haggard, Stephan and Robert Kaufman, ed. 1992. *The Politics of Economic Adjustment* Princeton: Princeton University Press.

Haggard, Stephan and Robert R. Kaufman. 1995. *The Political Economy of Democratic Transitions*. Princeton: Princeton University Press.

Haggard, Stephan and Chien-kuo Pang. 1994. "The Transition to Export-led Growth in Taiwan," in Joel Aberbach, David Dollar, and Ken Sokoloff, eds., *The Role of the State in Taiwan's Development*. Armonk, N.Y.: M. E. Sharpe.

Haggard, Stephan and Steven B. Webb, ed. 1993. *Voting for Reform: Democracy, Political Liberalization, and Economic Adjustment*. New York: Oxford University Press.

Hannon, Paul. 1993. *Argentina: A New Era*. London: Euromoney Publications.

Harris, Fred R. 1993. *Deadlock or Decision: The U.S. Senate and the Rise of National Politics.* New York: Oxford University Press.

Hashi, Iraj. 1995. "Employee-Ownership and Enterprise Behaviour: Evidence from Poland's Privatisation by Liquidation." Unpublished manuscript, Centre for European Research in Economics, Staffordshire University.

Hau, Yu-mei. 1981. *Chung-kuo kuo-min-tang ti-ming chih-tu chih yen-chiu* (A Study of the KMT's Nomination System). Taipei: Cheng-chung.

Heidarian, Jamshid and Gary Wu. 1994. *Power Sector Statistics for Developing Countries (1987–1991).* Washington, D.C.: World Bank.

Heller, William B. 1995. *Legislative Institutions, Parliamentary Process, and Cabinet Coalitions: Structure and Policy in Postwar Italy and Western Europe.* Ph.D. diss. University of California at San Diego.

Heller, William B. 1997. "Bicameralism and Budget Deficits: The Effect of Parliamentary Structure on Government Spending." *Legislative Studies Quarterly* 22: 485–516.

Hill, Alice and Manuel Angel Abdala. 1996. "Argentina: The Sequencing of Privatization and Regulation" in Brian Levy and Pablo T. Spiller, eds., *Regulations, Institutions, and Commitment: Comparative Studies of Telecommunications.* 202–249. Cambridge: Cambridge University Press.

Hood, Steven J. 1996. "Political Change in Taiwan: the Rise of Kuomintang Factions." *Asian Survey* 36, 5: 468–482.

Hsiao, Hsin-huang Michael. 1992. "The Rise of Social Movements and Civil Protests," in Tun-jen Cheng and Stephan Haggard, eds., *Political Change in Taiwan,* 57–72. Boulder, Colo.: Lynne Rienner Publishers, Inc.

Hsieh, J. F. S and Emerson Niou. 1996. "Issue Voting in the Republic of China on Taiwan's 1992 Legislative Yuan Election." *International Political Science Review* 17, 1: 13–27.

Hsu, Chien-ying. 1994. *"Tang-chien hsien-cheng chang yu-kuan li-fa-yuan wen-ti hsu-tang: cheng-shih wei-yuan hui chi chuan-hsien wen-ti* (Further Study of the Constitutional Power of the Legislative Yuan: The Jurisdiction of Standing Committees)." *Li-fa-yuan hsin-wen* (Legislative News) 44–58.

Hsu, George Jau-Yuan. 1995. "The Restructuring of the Electric Power Industry in Taiwan," Unpublished manuscript, Center for Energy and Environmental Studies, Chung-Hua Institution for Economic Research, Taipei, Taiwan.

Huang, Den-wei. 1996. *"Chiu mei-kuo kuo-hui yu-suan-ju chih chih-tu lun wuo-kuo shih-fou hsu sheuh-li kuo-hui yu-suan-ju* (On the need for a Congressional Budget Office in Taiwan: Learning from American Experience)," *Li-fa-yuan hsin-wen* (Legislative News) 58–69.

Huang, Jau-yuan. 1995. "Constitutional Change in Democratic Taiwan." Ph.D. diss., Boston, Harvard Law School.

Huang, Teh-fu. 1996. "Elections and the Evolution of the Kuomintang" in Hung-mao Tien, ed., *Taiwan's Electoral Politics and Democratic Transition: Riding the Third Wave,* 105–136. New York: M. E. Sharpe.

Huber, John D. 1992. "Restrictive Legislative Procedures in France and the United States." *American Political Science Review* 86: 675–687.

Huber, John D. 1998. "How Does Cabinet Instability Affect Political Performance? Portfolio Volatility and Health Care Cost Containment in Parliamentary Democracies." *American Political Science Review* 92: 577–591.

Independent Evening News. April 26, 1995, 3. Taipei.

Industry of Free China. Various dates, see individual citations.

Inoguchi, Takashi. 1990. "The Political Economy of Conservative Resurgence under Recession: Public Policies and Political Support in Japan, 1977–83," in T. J. Pempel, *Uncommon Democracies* 189–225. Ithaca: Cornell University Press.

International Financial Statistics. 1990, 1992, 1996, 1997. Washington D.C.: International Monetary Fund Statistics Department.

International Monetary Fund. September 1995. "Czech Republic: Selected Background Studies." *IMF Country Staff Report* No. 95/85.

Jacobson, Gary C. 1990. *The Electoral Origins of Divided Government: Competition in U.S. House Elections, 1946–1988.* Boulder, Colo.: Westview Press.

Jacoby, Neil. 1966. *U.S. Aid to Taiwan: A Study in Foreign Aid and Self-Help, and Development.* New York: Praeger.

Jefe de Gabinete de Ministros. 1996. Decisión Administrativa N° 1. Buenos Aires, Argentina.

Johnson, Chalmers A. 1982. *MITI and the Japanese Miracle: The Growth of Industrial Policy, 1925–1975.* Stanford, Calif.: Stanford University Press.

Johnson, David C. 1995. "The Effect of Democratization on the Legislative Yuan's Role in the Budget Formulation Process," Unpublished manuscript, University of California, San Diego.

Johnson, Simon and Marzena Kowalska. 1994. "Poland: The Political Economy of Shock Therapy," in Stephan Haggard and Steven B. Webb, eds., *Voting for Reform: Democracy, Political Liberalization, and Economic Adjustment.* New York: Oxford University Press.

Johnston, Robert J. and Charles J. Pattie. 1991. "Tactical Voting in Great Britain in 1983 and 1987 – An Alternative Approach." *British Journal of Political Science* 21: 95–108.

Jones, Mark P. 1994. "Electoral Laws and the Survival of Presidential Democracies." Ph.D. diss., University of Michigan.

Jones, Mark P. 1995. *Electoral Laws and the Survival of Presidential Democracies.* Notre Dame, Ind.: University of Notre Dame Press.

Jones, Mark P. 1997. "Evaluating Argentina's Presidential Democracy: 1983–1995," in Scott Mainwaring and Matthew Soberg Shugart, eds., *Presidentialism and Democracy in Latin America,* 259–299. New York: Cambridge University Press.

Jones, Mark P., Pablo Sanguinetti and Mariano Tommasi. 1998. "Politics, Institutions, and Public Sector Spending in the Argentine Provinces," in James M. Poterba and Jürgen von Hagen, eds., *Budget Institutions and Fiscal Outcomes,* 135–150. Chicago: NBER-University of Chicago Press.

Joskow, Paul L. and Richard Schmalensee. 1983. *Markets for Power: An Analysis of Electric Utility Deregulation.* Cambridge, Mass.: The MIT Press.

Kahn, Edward and Richard Gilbert. 1994. "International Comparisons of Electricity Regulation." Paper presented at the 17th Annual International Conferences of the International Association of Energy Economists, Stavanger, Norway.

Katz, Jonathan and Brian Sala. 1996. "Careerism, Committee Assignments, and the Electoral Connection." *American Political Science Review* 90: 21–33.

Katz, Richard S. 1980. *A Theory of Parties and Electoral Systems*. Baltimore, Md.: Johns Hopkins University Press.

Katz, Richard. 1986. "Intraparty Preference Voting," in Bernard Grofman and Arend Lijphart, eds., *Electoral Laws and their Political Consequences*, 85–103. New York: Agathon.

Katzenstein, Peter J. 1985. *Small States in World Markets: Industrial Policy in Europe*. Ithaca, N.Y.: Cornell University Press.

Kharas, Homi. 1991. "Restructuring Socialist Industry: Poland's 1990 Experience." Mimeo, The World Bank.

Kiewiet, D. Roderick and Mathew D. McCubbins. 1988. "Presidential Influence on Congressional Appropriations Decisions." *American Journal of Political Science* 65:131–143.

Kiewiet, D. Roderick and Mathew McCubbins. 1991. *The Logic of Delegation: Congressional Parties in the Appropriations Process*. Chicago: University of Chicago Press.

Kim, Yoon Hyung. 1989. "Financial Management and Corporate Organization," in Yoon Hyung Kim and Kirk R. Smith, eds., *Electricity in Economic Development: the Experience of Northeast Asia*, 187–224. New York: Greenwood Press.

Kim, Yoon Hyung and Kirk R. Smith, ed. 1989. *Electricity in Economic Development: the Experience of Northeast Asia*. New York: Greenwood Press.

Krueger, Anne O. 1974. "The Political Economy of the Rent Seeking Society" in James M. Buchanan, Robert D. Tollison, and Gordon Tullock, eds., *Toward a Theory of the Rent-Seeking Society*, 51–70. College Station, Tx: Texas A&M University.

Kuo, Cheng-Tian. 1995. *Global Competitiveness and Industrial Growth in Taiwan and the Philippines*. Pittsburgh: University of Pittsburgh Press.

Laakso, Markku. 1987. "Thresholds for Proportional Representation: Reanalyzed and Extended" in Manfred J. Holler, ed., *The Logic of Multiparty Systems*, 383–390. Dordrecht: Kluwer Academic Publishers.

La Época. 1995. "Josefina Bilbao Se Sumó a Lamentos por Posible Reducción Presupuestaria." 28: 21.

Lancaster, Thomas D. 1986. "Electoral Structures and Pork Barrel Politics." *International Political Science Review* 7, 1 (January): 67–81.

Latin American Weekly Report. 1984–1988. London: Latin American Newsletters.

Laver, Michael and Norman Schofield. 1990. *Multiparty Government: The Politics of Coalition in Europe*. Oxford: Oxford University Press.

Laver, Michael and Kenneth A. Shepsle. 1990a. "Coalitions and Cabinet Government." *American Political Science Review* 84: 873–890.

Laver, Michael and Kenneth A. Shepsle. 1996. *Making and Breaking Governments: Cabinets and Legislatures in Parliamentary Democracies*. New York: Cambridge University Press.

Lee, Chih-yang. 1993. *"Li-fa-yuan yi-chueh kuo-chia chong-yu-suang-an kuo-cheng chi yen-chiu'* (Legislative Processes of the National Budget)." Unpublished Masters's thesis in public policy, National Chung-hsing University.

Lehmbruch, Gerhard, and Philippe C. Schmitter. 1982. *Patterns of Corporatist Policy-making*. London: Sage.

Lemieux, Peter. 1977. *The Liberal Party and British Political Change: 1955–1974*. Ph.D. diss., Massachusetts Institute of Technology.

Leng, Shao-chuan and Cheng-yi Lin, 1993. "Political Change on Taiwan: Transition to Democracy?" *The China Quarterly* 136, December: 808.

Levy, Brian and Pablo Spiller. 1994. "Regulation, Institutions, and Commitment in Telecommunications: A Comparative Analysis of Five Country Studies" in Michael Brcho and Boris Pleskovic, eds., *Proceedings of the World Bank Annual Conference on Development Economics 1993 Supplement to the World Bank Economic Review and the World Bank Research Observer*. Washington D.C.: The World Bank.

Levy, Brian and Pablo Spiller, ed. 1996. *Regulations, Institutions, and Commitment: Comparative Studies of Telecommunications*. New York: Cambridge University Press.

Lewis, Paul G. 1994. "Political Institutionalisation and Party Development in Post-communist Poland." *Europe-Asia Studies* 46, 5: 779–799.

Ley de Administración Financiera. 1992. Ley de Administración Financiera y de los Sistemas de Control del Sector Público Nacional (Ley N°. 24.156).

Ley de Presupuesto. 1995. Ley de Presupuesto General de Gastos y Cálculo de Recursos de la Administración Nacional (Ley N°. 24.447).

Li, Laura. 1993. "Contractual Relationships: Economic and Foreign Relations in the Six Year Plan," *Sinorama* February: 20–28.

Li, Shuo-jung. 1995. "Government Plans and Policies on Private Sector Investment in Taiwan's Power Sector," Unpublished manuscript, Energy Commission, Ministry of Economic Affairs, Taiwan, Republic of China.

Liang, Chi-Yuan. 1986. "Energy Supply and the Viability of the Economy of Taiwan, The Republic of China," in Ronald C. Keith, *Energy, Security, and Economic Development in East Asia*, 109–137. London: Croom Helm.

Liang, Rongqu. 1995. "Taiwan Heneng Kaifa de Guoji Guan (An International Perspective on the Development of Nuclear Power in Taiwan,)" *Jinri Jingji* 330, 2.95: 49–53.

Liang, Yung-huan. 1995. *"Yi-er-yi chia tang-tsi shih-yeh tsong-lung* (An Overview of 121 KMT Enterprises,)" *Tsai-hsuen* April: 102–110.

Lijphart, Arend. 1971. "Comparative Politics and the Comparative Method." *American Political Science Review* 65: 682–698.

Lijphart, Arend. 1977. *Democracies in Plural Societies: A Comparative Exploration*. New Haven: Yale University Press.

Lijphart, Arend. 1984. *Democracies: Pattern of Majoritarian and Consensus Government in Twenty-one Countries*. New Haven: Yale University Press.

Lijphart, Arend. 1991. "Constitutional Choices for New Democracies." *Journal of Democracy* 2: 72–84.

Lijphart, Arend. 1992. *Parliamentary versus Presidential Government*. Oxford: Oxford University Press.

Lijphart, Arend. 1994. *Electoral Systems and Party Systems: A Study of Twenty-Seven Democracies, 1945–1990*. New York: Oxford University Press.

Lijphart, Arend and Robert W. Gibberd. 1977. "Thresholds and Payoffs in List Systems of Proportional Representation." *European Journal of Political Research* 5: 219–230.

Lijphart Elections Archive. *Poland: Formulaic Matrix*. Website, University of California, San Diego (http://dodgson.ucsd.edu/lij/plndmat.html).

Lin, Chau-yi. 1995. "The Electoral System and Institutionalization of Factionalism in Taiwan," Paper presented at the First Annual Taiwan Studies Conference in North America, New Haven, Yale University.

Lin, Chi-lang. 1987. *Chung-kuo kuo-min-tang fu-hsuen cheng-cheu chih yen-chiu* (A Case Study of the KMT's Electoral Campaign Policy). Taipei: Cheng-chung.

Lin, Jih-wen. 1995. "Social Cleavages and Political Competition under the Single Non-transferable Vote System," Paper presented at the first annual Taiwan Studies Conference in North America, Yale University.

Linz, Juan J. 1990. "The Perils of Presidentialism." *Journal of Democracy* 1: 51–69.

Linz, Juan J. 1994. "Presidential or Parliamentary Democracy: Does It Make a Difference?" in Juan Linz and Arturo Valenzuela, eds., *The Failure of Presidential Democracy, Vol. I Comparative Perspectives*, 3–90. Baltimore: Johns Hopkins University Press.

Linz, Juan J. and Alfred Stepan. 1996. *Problems of Democratic Transition and Consolidation*. Baltimore: The Johns Hopkins University Press.

Linz, Juan J. and Arturo Valenzuela, ed. 1994. *The Failure of Presidential Democracy*. Baltimore: Johns Hopkins University Press.

López Murphy, Ricardo. 1996. Interview, Buenos Aires, Argentina.

Loveman, Brian. 1993. *The Constitution of Tyranny: Regimes of Exception in Spanish America*. Pittsburgh: University of Pittsburgh Press.

Loveman, Brian. 1998. "When You Wish upon the Stars: Why the Generals (and Admirals) say Yes to Latin American 'Transitions' to Civilian Government," in Paul W. Drake and Mathew D. McCubbins, eds., *The Origins of Liberty: Political and Economic Liberalization in the Modern World*, 115–145. Princeton: Princeton University Press.

Lowi, Theodore. 1979. *The End of Liberalism: The Second Republic of the United States*. New York: W. W. Norton.

Lundberg, Eric. 1979. "Fiscal and Monetary Policies," in Walter Galenson, ed., *Economic Growth and Structural Change in Taiwan*, 263–307. Ithaca: Cornell University Press.

Lupia, Arthur and Mathew D. McCubbins. 1994. "Learning from Oversight: Fire Alarms and Police Patrols Reconstructed." *Journal of Law, Economics, and Organization* 10: 96–125.

Lupia, Arthur and Mathew D. McCubbins. 1998. *The Democratic Dilemma: Can Citizens Learn What They Need to Know?* New York: Cambridge University Press.

Macey, Jonathan R. 1992. "Separated Powers and Positive Political Theory –

References

The Tug of War Over Administrative Agencies." *Georgetown Law Review* 80: 671–703.

Madison, James, Alexander Hamilton, and John Jay. 1961. *Federalist Papers.* New York: Penguin.

Mainwaring, Scott. 1991. "Politicians, Parties, and Electoral Systems: Brazil in Comparative Perspective." *Comparative Politics* October: 21–43.

Mainwaring, Scott. 1997. "Multipartism, Robust Federalism, and Presidentialism in Brazil," in Scott Mainwaring and Matthew Soberg Shugart, eds., *Presidentialism and Democracy in Latin America*, 55–109. New York: Cambridge University Press.

Mainwaring, Scott and Matthew Soberg Shugart, ed. 1997a. *Presidentialism and Democracy in Latin America* New York: Cambridge University Press.

Mainwaring, Scott and Matthew Soberg Shugart. 1997b. "Conclusion: Presidentialism and the Party System," in Scott Mainwaring and Matthew Soberg Shugart, eds., *Presidentialism and Democracy in Latin America*, 394–439. New York: Cambridge University Press.

Mainwaring, Scott and Matthew Soberg Shugart. 1997c. "Juan Linz, Presidentialism, and Democracy: A Critical Appraisal." *Comparative Politics* 29: 449.

Maxfield, Sylvia. 1997. *Gatekeepers of Growth: The International Political Economy of Central Banking in Developing Countries.* Princeton: Princeton University Press.

Mayhew, David. 1974. *The Electoral Connection.* New Haven: Yale University Press.

McConnell, Grant. 1966. *Private Power and American Democracy.* New York: Knopf.

McCubbins, Mathew D. 1985. "The Legislative Design of Regulatory Structure." *American Political Science Review* 29: 721–748.

McCubbins, Mathew D. 1991a. "Government on Lay-Away: Federal Spending and Deficits under Divided Party Control," in Gary W. Cox and Samuel Kernell, eds., *The Politics of Divided Government*, 113–153. Boulder, Colo.: Westview Press.

McCubbins, Mathew D. 1991b. "Party Governance and U.S. Budgets: Divided Government and Fiscal Stalemate," In Alberto Alesina and Geoffrey Carliner, eds., *Politics and Economics in the Eighties*, 83–122. Chicago: University of Chicago Press.

McCubbins, Mathew D. and Gregory W. Noble. 1995. "Perceptions and Realities of Japanese Budgeting," in Peter H. Cowhey and Mathew D. McCubbins, eds., *Structure and Policy in Japan and the United States*, 81–118. New York: Cambridge University Press.

McCubbins, Mathew D., Roger G. Noll, and Barry R. Weingast. 1987. "Administrative Procedures as an Instrument of Political Control." *Journal of Law, Economics, and Organization* 3: 243–277.

McCubbins, Mathew D., Roger G. Noll, and Barry R. Weingast. 1989. "Structure and Process, Politics and Policy: Administrative Arrangements and the Political Control of Agencies." *Virginia Law Review* 75: 431–482.

McCubbins, Mathew D. and Talbot Page. 1987. "A Theory of Congressional

Delegation" in Mathew D. McCubbins and Terry Sullivan, eds., *Congress: Structure and Policy*, 409–425. Cambridge: Cambridge University Press.

McCubbins, Mathew D. and Frances Rosenbluth. 1995. "Party Provision for Personal Politics: Dividing the Vote in Japan" in Peter Cowhey and Mathew D. McCubbins, eds., *Structure and Policy in Japan and the United States*, 35–55. Cambridge: Cambridge University Press.

McCubbins, Mathew D. and Thomas Schwartz. 1984. "Congressional Oversight Overlooked: Police Patrols versus Fire Alarms." *American Journal of Political Science* 28: 165–179.

McNollgast. 1992. "Positive Canons – The Role of Legislative Bargains in Statutory Interpretation." *Georgetown Law Journal* 80: 705–742.

Merbilha, Oscar. 1996. Interview, Bueuos Aires, Argentina.

Milgrom, Paul R., Douglass C. North, and Barry R. Weingast. 1990. "The Role of Institutions in the Revival of Trade: The Law Merchant, Private Judges, and the Champagne Fairs." *Economics and Politics* 2:1–23.

Millard, Frances. 1992. "The Polish Parliamentary Elections of October 1991." *Soviet Studies* 44, 5: 837–855.

Milner, Helen V. 1998. "International Political Economy: Beyond Hegemonic Stability." *Foreign Policy* 110:112–123.

Milor, Vedat. 1994. "Political Economy of Public Enterprise Reform and Privatization in the Czech Republic and Poland." Finance and Private Sector Development Division, Private Policy Research Department, Washington D.C.: The World Bank.

Mladek, Jan. 1993. "The Different Paths of Privatization: Czechoslovakia, 1990–?" in John S. Earle, Roman Frydman, and Andrezej Rapaczynski, *Privatization in the Transition to a Market Economy: Studies of Preconditions and Policies in Eastern Europe*, 463. New York: St. Martin's Press.

Moe, Terry M. 1990a. "Political Institutions: the Neglected Side of the Story," *Journal of Law, Economics and Organization* 6 (Special Issue): 213–253.

Moe, Terry M. 1990b. "The Politics of Structural Choice: Toward a Theory of Public Bureaucracy," in Oliver E. Williamson ed., *Organization Theory: From Chester Barnard to the Present and Beyond*, 116–153. New York: Oxford University Press.

Moe, Terry M. and Michael Caldwell 1994. "The Institutional Foundations of Democratic Government: A Comparison of Presidential and Parliamentary Systems," *Journal of Institutional and Theoretical Economics* 150, 1: 171–195.

Molinelli, N. Guillermo. 1991. *Presidentes y Congresos en Argentina: Mitos y Realidades*. Buenos Aires: Grupo Editor Latinoamericano.

Molinelli, N. Guillermo. 1996a. "Sobre Nuestra Democracia." *Revista Jurídica del Centro de Estudiantes de la Universidad de Buenos Aires* 8(November): 4–13.

Molinelli, N. Guillermo. 1996b. Multiple interviews, May–June, Universidad de Buenos Aires.

Moody, Peter R. Jr. 1992. *Political Change on Taiwan: A Study in Ruling Party Adaptability*. New York: Praeger.

References

Mustapic, Ana María. 1996. Interview, May 22, Universidad Torcuato Di Tella, Buenos Aires, Argentina.

Mustapic, Ana Maria and Natalia Ferreti. 1995. "El Veto Presidencial Bajo los Gobiernos de Alfonsín y Menem." Buenos Aires: Universidad Torcuato de Tella.

Myerson, Roger. 1994. "Incentives to Cultivate Favored Minorities Under Alternative Electoral Systems." *American Political Science Review* 87: 856–869.

Myerson, Roger and Robert Weber. 1993. "A Theory of Voting Equilibria." *American Political Science Review* 87: 102–114.

Nathan, Andrew J. 1993. "The Legislative Yuan Elections in Taiwan." *Asian Survey* 33, 4 (April): 424–438.

Nino, Carlos Santiago. 1996. "Hyperpresidentialism and Constitutional Reform in Argentina," in Arend Lijphart and Carlos H. Waisman, eds., *Institutional Design in New Democracies: Eastern Europe and Latin America*, 161–174. Boulder, Colo.: Westview Press.

Noble, Gregory. 1999a. "Opportunity Lost: Partisan Incentives and the 1997 Constitutional Revisions in Taiwan," *The China Journal* 41 (January): 89–114.

Noble, Gregory. 1999b. *Regimes and Industrial Policy: The Politics of Collective Action in Japan and Taiwan*. Ithaca, N.Y.: Cornell University Press.

Nohlen, Dieter, ed. 1993. *Enciclopedia Electoral Latinoamericano y del Caribe*. San Jose, Costa Rica: Instituto Interamericano de Derechos Humanos.

Noll, Roger G. 1987. "The Political Foundations of Regulatory Policies," in Mathew McCubbins and Terry Sullivan, eds., *Congress: Structure and Policy*, 462–492. New York: Cambridge University Press.

Noll, Roger G. 1989. "Economic Perspectives on the Politics of Regulation," in Richard Schmalensee and Robert D. Willig, eds. *Handbook of Industrial Organization*, Volume II, 1253–1287. Amsterdam, New York: North-Holland.

North, Douglass C. 1981. *Structure and Change in Economic History*. New York: N.W. Norton.

North, Douglass C. 1990. *Institutions, Institutional Change, and Economic Performance*. New York: Cambridge University Press.

North, Douglass C. and Barry R. Weingast. 1989. "Constitutions and Commitment: The Evolution of Institutions Governing Public Choice in Seventeenth-Century England." *The Journal of Economic History* 49: 803–832.

O'Donnell, Guillermo. 1994. "Delegative Democracy." *Journal of Democracy* 5,1: 55–69.

O'Donnell, Guillermo. 1996. "Illusions About Consolidation." *Journal of Democracy* 7, 2: 34–51.

O'Donnell, Guillermo and Phillippe C. Schmitter. 1986. *Transitions from Authoritarian Rule: Tentative Conclusions About Uncertain Democracies*. Baltimore: Johns Hopkins University Press.

Oficina Nacional de Presupuesto. 1996. Circular N° 2/96: Incorporación del Presupuesto Preliminar al Proceso de Formulación de Presupuesto para el Ejercicio 1997.

References

Olson, Mancur. 1965. *The Logic of Collective Action: Public Goods and the Theory of Groups.* Cambridge: Harvard University Press.

Olson, Mancur. 1982. *The Rise and Decline of Nations: Economic Growth, Stagflation, and Social Rigidities.* New Haven: Yale University Press.

Ordeshook, Peter C. and Olga Shvetsova. 1994. "Ethnic Heterogeneity, District Magnitude, and The Number of Parties." *American Journal of Political Science* 38: 100–123.

Orpis, Jaime. 1996. Interview, January. Santiago, Chile.

Página/12. 1994–1997. Various issues. Buenos Aires, Argentina.

Palfrey, Thomas. 1989. "A Mathematical Proof of Duverger's Law," In Peter C. Ordeshook, ed., *Models of Strategic Choice in Politics*, 69–93. Ann Arbor: University of Michigan Press.

Palma, Andrés. 1996. Interview, January. Santiago, Chile.

Pasquino, Gianfranco. 1986. "Party Government in Italy: Achievements and Prosperity," in Richard. S. Katz ed., *The American and European Experiences of Party Government.* Berlin: DeGruyter.

Peltzman, Sam. 1976. "Toward a More General Theory of Regulation." *The Journal of Law and Economics* 19, 2 (August): 211–240.

Peng, Nu-ning. 1993. "*Chiang-hua li-fa-yuan yu-suan sheng-yi gong-neng chi yen-chiu* (A Study of Legislative Budgetary Review)." Masters thesis in public policy, National Chung-hsing University.

Peng, Pai-hsien. 1993. *Juay-chiu hsiau-lu cheng-fu* (In Pursuit of Government Efficiency). Taipei: New Society Foundation.

Pesce, Miguel. 1996. Interview, May 17, Buenos Aires, Argentina.

Pion-Berlin, David. 1997. *Through Corridors of Power: Institutions and Civil-Military Relations in Argentina.* University Park: Pennsylvania State University Press.

Poder Ejecutivo Nacional. 1994. Decreto 2329/94, Veto Parcial de Ley N° 24.447 de Presupuesto de la Administración Nacional para el Ejercicio de 1995.

Poder Ejecutivo Nacional. 1995. Decreto 1040/95, Veto Parcial de Ley N° 24.624 de Presupuesto de la Administración Nacional para el Ejercicio de 1996.

Porto, Alberto. 1990. *Federalismo Fiscal: El Caso Argentino.* Buenos Aires: Editorial Tesis.

Porto, Alberto and Pablo Sanguinetti. 1996. "Political Determinants of Regional Redistribution in a Federation: Evidence from Argentina." Unpublished manuscript, Instituto Torcuato Di Tella, Buenos Aires, Argentina.

Posner, Richard A. 1975. "The Social Cost of Monopoly and Regulation." *Journal of Political Economy* 83: 807–827.

Powell, G. Bingham. 1982. *Contemporary Democracies: Participation, Stability, and Violence.* Cambridge: Harvard University Press.

Power, Timothy J. 1998. "The Pen is Mightier than the Congress: Presidential Decree Power in Brazil," in John M. Carey and Matthew Soberg Shugart, eds., *Executive Decree Authority: Calling Out the Tanks or Just Filling Out the Forms?*, 197–230. New York: Cambridge University Press.

Przeworski, Adam. 1991. *Democracy and the Market: Political and Economic*

Reforms in Eastern Europe and Latin America. New York: Cambridge University Press.

Przeworski, Adam and Henry Teune. 1970. *The Logic of Comparative Social Inquiry*. New York: Wiley-Interscience.

Putnam, Robert D. 1993. *Making Democracy Work: Civic Traditions in Modern Italy*. Princeton: Princeton University Press.

Rae, Douglas W. 1971. *The Political Consequences of Electoral Laws*, 2d ed. New Haven: Yale University Press.

Ramseyer, J. Mark and Frances M. Rosenbluth. 1993. *Japan's Political Marketplace*. Cambridge: Harvard University Press.

Rausch, Alejandro E. 1993. "Privatization in Argentina," in V. V. Ramanadham, ed., *Constraints and Impacts of Privatization*. London and New York: Routledge.

Reed, Steven R. 1994. "Democracy and the Personal Vote: A Cautionary Tale from Japan." *Electoral Studies* 13: 17–28.

Republic of China, Council on Economic Development and Planning. Various years. *Taiwan Statistical Data Book*.

Republic of China, Executive Yuan. "*Chung-yang cheng-fu tsong yu-suan-an* (Central Government Budget Bills)." Various issues, Taipei.

Republic of China, Executive Yuan. 1991. "*Chung-yang cheng-fu hsing-chien chong-ta-chiau-tung chien-shih chi-hua ti-yi-chi kong-cheng te-bei yu-suan-an* (Special Budget on Major Transportation Projects Undertaken by Central Government, Phase One, Fiscal Years 1992 and 1993)." Taipei.

Republic of China, Executive Yuan. 1993. "*Chung-yang cheng-fu hsing-chien chong-ta-chiau-tung chien-shih chi-hua ti-er-chi kong-cheng te-bei yu-suan-an* (Special Budget on Major Transportation Projects Undertaken by the Central Government, Phase Two, Fiscal Years 1994 and 1995)." Taipei.

Republic of China, Executive Yuan. 1995. "*Chung-yang cheng-fu hsing-chien chong-ta-chiau-tung chien-shih chi-hua ti-san-chi kong-cheng te-bei yu-suan-an* (Special Budget on Major Transportation Projects Undertaken by Central Government, Phase Three, Fiscal Years 1996 and 1997)." Taipei.

Republic of China, Shung-chih-pu (Ministry of Auditing). N.D.a. "*Chung-yang cheng-fu hsing-chien chong-ta-chiau-tung chien-shih chi-hua ti-yi-chi kong-cheng te-bei chueh-suan-sheng-heu bao-kau* (The Auditing Report on Special Budget for Major Transportation Projects Undertaken by Central Government, Phase One, Fiscal Years 1992 and 1993)." Taipei.

Republic of China, Shung-chih-pu (Ministry of Auditing). N.D.b. "*Chung-yang cheng-fu hsing-chien chong-ta-chiau-tung chien-shih chi-hua ti-er-chi kong-cheng te-bei chueh-suan-sheng-heu bao-kau* (The Auditing Report on Special Budget for Major Transportation Projects Undertaken by Central Government, Phase Two, Fiscal Years 1994 and 1995)." Taipei.

Republic of Poland. 1993. *Rocznik Statystyczny 1993*. Warsaw: Glowny Urzad Statystyczny.

Republic of Poland. 1995. *Rocznik Statystyczny 1995*. Warsaw: Glowny Urzad Statystyczny.

Reuters News Service. 1996. "Chilean Senators Reject Constitutional Reforms." April 11.

Rigger, Shelley. 1993. "Electoral Strategies and Political Institutions in the Republic of China on Taiwan," Fairbank Center Working Papers, No. 1, Taiwan Studies Workshop, Harvard University.

Riker, William. 1982. *Liberalism against Populism: A Confrontation between the Theory of Democracy and the Theory of Social Choice*. San Francisco Calif.: W. H. Freeman.

Ripley, Randall B. and Grace A. Franklin. 1976. *Congress, the Bureaucracy and Public Policy*. Homewood Ill.: Dorsey Press.

Robinson, James and Julian Baum. 1993. "Party Primaries in Taiwan: Footnote or Text in Democratization?" *Asian Affairs* Summer: 88–99.

Rodríguez, Héctor C. 1996. Interview, May 10, Buenos Aires, Argentina.

Rodríguez, Héctor C. and Rubén Ventulle. 1995. "El Control Público Moderno." *Boletín Informative del Secretariado Permanente de Tribunales de Cuentas 21,* January–April: 3–13 and May–August 5–15.

Rodrik, Dani. 1995. "The Dynamics of Political Support for Reform in Economies in Transition." *Journal of the Japanese and International Economies* 9: 403–425.

Rogowski, Ronald. 1989. *Commerce and Coalitions: How Trade Affects Domestic Political Alignments*. Princeton: Princeton University Press.

Root, Hilton L. 1994. *The Fountain of Privilege: Political Foundations of Economic Markets in Old Regime France and England*. Berkeley: University of California Press.

Rosales, Willian. 1996. "Measuring Party System Changes in Democratic Transitions: Chile and Uruguay." Rochester, NY: McNair Undergraduate Research Project.

Rose, Richard. 1983. "Elections and Electoral Systems: Choices and Alternatives." in Vernon Bogdanor and David Butler, eds., *Democracy and Elections*. Cambridge: Cambridge University Press.

Rosenbluth, Frances. 1989. *Financial Politics in Contemporary Japan*. Ithaca, N.Y.: Cornell University Press.

Sabsay, Daniel A. and José M. Onaindia. 1994. *La Constitución de los Argentinos: Análisis de Su Texto Luego de la Reforma de 1994*. Buenos Aires: Errepar. University of California.

Sala, Brian. 1998. "In Search of the Administrative President: Presidential 'Decree' Powers and Policy Implementation in the United States," in John M. Carey and Matthew Soberg Shugart, eds., *Executive Decree Authority: Calling Out the Tanks or Just Filling Out the Forms?*, 254–273. New York: Cambridge University Press.

Sanguinetti, Pablo and Mariano Tommasi. 1997. "Los Determinantes Económicos e Institucionales de los Déficits en los Presupuestos Provinciales: Argentina 1983–1996." Unpublished manuscript, Banco Interamericano de Desarrollo.

Sartori, Giovanni. 1968. "Political Development and Political Engineering," in John D. Montgomery and Albert O. Hirschman, eds., *Public Policy*, 261–298. Cambridge: Cambridge University Press.

Sartori, Giovanni. 1994. "Neither Presidentialism nor Parliamentarism," in Juan J. Linz and Arturo Valenzuela, eds., *The Failure of Presidential Democracy*

Volume 1: Comparative Perspectives, 106–118. Baltimore: Johns Hopkins University Press.

Sawers, Larry. 1996. *The Other Argentina: The Interior and National Development.* Boulder, Colo.: Westview Press.

Schattschneider, Elmer E. 1960. *The Semisovereign People: A Realist's View of Democracy in America.* New York: Holt, Rinehart, and Winston.

Schattschneider, Elmer E. 1963. *Politics, Pressures, and the Tariff: A Study of Free Private Enterprise in Pressure Politics, as Shown in the 1929–30 Revision of the Tariff.* Hamden, Conn.: Archon Books.

Schick, Allen. 1980. *Congress and Money.* Washington D.C.: The Urban Institute.

Schubert, Gunter. 1992. "Constitutional Politics in the Republic of China: The Rise of the Legislative Yuan." *Issues and Studies* 28: 21–37.

Scully, Timothy. 1995. "Reconstituting Party Politics in Chile," in Scott Mainwaring and Timothy R. Scully, eds., *Building Democratic Institutions: Party Systems in Latin America*, 100–137. Stanford, Calif.: Stanford University Press.

Senado de Chile. 1995. *Diario de sesiones del Senado. Legislatura 332, Extraordinaria, Sesión 17, en miércoles 22 de noviembre de 1995 (Anexo de documentos).* Valparaíso, Chile.

Shapiro, Martin. 1986. "APA: Past, Present, and Future." *Virginia Law Review* 72: 447–492.

Sheen, J-N, C-S Chen, and J-K Yang. 1994. "Time-of-Use Pricing for Load Management Programs in Taiwan Power Company." *IEEE Transactions on Power Systems* 9, 1 (February): 388–395.

Sheen, J-N, C-S Chen, and J-K Yang. 1995. "Response of Large Industrial Customers to Electricity Pricing by Voluntary Time-of-use in Taiwan." *IEEE Proceedings: Generation, Transmission, Distribution* 142, 2 (March): 157–166.

Sheng, Shing-Yuan. 1996. "Electoral Competition and Legislative Participation," Unpublished diss., University in Michigan.

Shepsle, Kenneth A. 1979. "Institutional Arrangements and Equilibrium in Multidimensional Voting Models." *American Journal of Political Science* 23: 27–59.

Shepsle, Kenneth A. 1989. "The Changing Textbook Congress," in John Chubb and Paul Peterson, eds., *Can the Government Govern?*, 238–266. Washington, D.C.: The Brookings Institution.

Shepsle, Kenneth A. and Barry R. Weingast. 1987. "The Institutional Foundations of Committee Power." *American Political Science Review* 81: 85–104.

Shiao, Chyuan-Jeng. 1996. "Elections and the Changing State-Business Relationship," in Hung-Mao tien ed., *Taiwan's Electoral Politics and Democratic Transition: Riding the Third Wave*, 213–225. Armonk N.Y.: M.E. Sharpe.

Shirk, Susan L. 1993. *The Political Logic of Economic Reform in China.* Berkeley and Los Angeles: University of California Press.

Shugart, Matthew Soberg. 1985. "The Two Effects of District Magnitude: Venezuela as a Crucial Experiment." *European Journal of Political Research* 13: 353–364.

References

Shugart, Matthew Soberg. 1992. "Leaders, Rank and File, and Constituents: Electorlal Reform in Colombia and Venezuela." *Electoral Studies* 11, 1: 21–45.

Shugart, Matthew Soberg. 1995. "The Electoral Cycle and Institutional Sources of Divided Presidential Government." *American Political Science Review* 89, 2 (June): 327–343.

Shugart, Matthew Soberg. 1998. "The Inverse Relationship Between Party Strength and Executive Strength: A Theory of Politicians' Constitutional Choices." *British Journal of Political Science* 28: 1–29.

Shugart, Matthew Soberg and John Carey. 1992. *Presidents and Assemblies: Constitutional Design and Electoral Dynamics*. Cambridge: Cambridge University Press.

Shugart, Matthew Soberg and Scott Mainwaring. 1997. "Presidentialism and Democracy in Latin America: Rethinking the Terms of the Debate," in Scott Mainwaring and Matthew Soberg Shugart, eds., *Presidentialism and Democracy in Latin America*, 12–54. New York: Cambridge University Press.

Silva, Ernesto. 1991. "El Nuevo Niño Prodigio de la Bolsa." *Revista de la Facultad de Ciencias Economicas y Administrativas de la Universidad Católica* 5: 23–28.

Sistema de Información Financiera, Oficina Nacional de Presupuesto (SIDIF) Staff. 1996. Communications, May–June, Buenos Aires, Argentina.

Sims, Calvin. 1996. "Argentine Military for Rent; Turns Swords into Tin Cups," *The New York Times* (January 29) A1.

Spafford, D. 1972. "Electoral Systems and Voters' Behavior: Comment and a Further Test." *Comparative Politics* 5: 129–134.

Spiller, Pablo T. and Luis Viana Martorell. 1994. "How Should It Be Done? Electricity Regulation in Argentina, Brazil, Uruguay and Chile." Typescript, University of California, Berkeley.

Stallings, Barbara. 1992. "International Influence on Economic Policy: Debt, Stabilization, and Structural Reform," in Stephan Haggard and Robert R. Kaufman, eds., *The Politics of Economic Adjustment* 41–88. Princeton: Princeton University Press.

Stepan, Alfred and Cindy Skach. 1993. "Constitutional Frameworks and Democratic Consolidation: Parliamentarism and Presidentialism." *World Politics* 46: 1–22.

Stewart, Charles, III. 1989. *Budget Reform Politics: The Design of the Appropriations Process in the House of Representatives, 1865–1921*. New York: Cambridge University Press.

Stewart, Charles, III. 1991. "Lessons from the Post-Civil War Era" in Gary W. Cox and Samuel Kernell, eds., *The Politics of Divided Government*, 203–238. Boulder, Colo.: Westview Press.

Stigler, George. 1971. "The Theory of Economic Regulation." *Bell Journal of Economic and Management Science* 2: 3–21.

Stone, Alec. 1992. *The Birth of Judicial Politics in France: The Constitutional Council in Comparative Perspective*. New York: Oxford University Press.

Strom, Kaare. 1990a. "A Behavioral Theory of Competitive Political Parties." *American Journal of Political Science* 38: 303–335.

Strom, Kaare. 1990b. *Minority Government and Majority Rule*. Cambridge: Cambridge University Press.

Strom, Kaare, Ian Budge, and Michael J. Laver. 1994. "Constraints on Cabinet Formation in Parliamentary Democracies." *American Journal of Political Science* 38: 303–335.

Su, Tsai-tsu. 1994. "*Cheng-fu yu-suan chueh-tse mo-shih chi tang-tau* (Models of Government Budgetary Decision-making)." *National Chung-shan University Forum* June: 239–243.

Sun, Manpin. 1985a. "*Wang Yuyun Chizha Guoyinghui* (Wang Yuyun Lords it Over the National Corporations Commission)." *Tianxia* October: 26–35.

Sun, Manpin. 1985b. "*Chen Langao shi Taidian de Gongchen huo Zuiren* (Is Chen Langao Taipower's Meritorious Official or its Criminal?)." *Tianxia*, July: 62–70.

Surballe, Rossana. 1996. Multiple interviews, May–June, Buenos Aires, Argentina.

Szomburg, Jan. 1993. "The Decision-making Structure of Polish Privatization," in John S. Earle, Roman Frydman, and Andrezej Rapaczynski, *Privatization in the Transition to a Market Economy: Studies of Preconditions and Policies in Eastern Europe*. New York: St. Martin's Press.

Taagepera, Rein and Matthew S. Shugart. 1989. *Seats and Votes: The Effects and Determinants of Electoral Systems*. New Haven: Yale University Press.

Taiwan Daily. April 11, 1988, 2. Taipei.

Taiwan Daily. March 19, 1992. Taipei.

Taiwan Daily. May 26, 1994, 2. Taipei.

Taiwan Power Company. 1988. "Taiwan Dianli Jianshi (xia) (A Short History of Electric Power in Taiwan, Part II)," *Taidian Yuekan* 310.

Taiwan Power Company. 1994. *Taiwan Power Company Financial Information*. Taipei: Taiwan Power Company.

Taiwan Power Company. *Annual Reports*.

Taylor, Philip. 1960. *Government and Politics in Uruguay*. New Orleans, La.: Tulane University Press.

Thies, Michael F. 1994. *Majority Party Decision Making and Policy Change: The Liberal Democratic Party and Japanese Fiscal Policy*. Ph.D. diss. University of California at San Diego,

Tien, Hung-mao. 1989. *The Great Transition: Political and Social Change in the Republic of China*. Stanford, Calif.: Hoover Institution Press.

Tien, Hung-mao, ed. 1996. *Taiwan's Electoral Politics and Democratic Transition: Riding the Third Wave*. Armonk N.Y.: M. E. Sharpe.

Truman, David B. 1951. *The Governmental Process: Political Interests and Public Opinion*. New York: Alfred Knopf.

Tsebelis, George. 1995. "Decision Making in Political Decisions: Veto Players in Presidentialism, Parliamentarism, Multicameralism, and Multipartism." *British Journal of Political Science* 25: 289–325.

Tsebelis, George and Jeanette Money. 1997. *Bicameralism*. Cambridge: Cambridge University Press.

Tung, An-chi. 1996. "Growth with Debt: U.S. Aid and Taiwan's Electricity

Enterprise." Academica Sinica Institute of Economics Discussion Paper #9624, Taipei, Taiwan.

United Daily News. December 7, 1987, 2. Taipei.

United Daily News. December 10, 1987. Taipei.

United Daily News. April 25, 1990, 2. Taipei.

United Daily News. February 9, 1995, 4. Taipei.

United Daily News. March 11, 1995, 4. Taipei.

"U.S. Aid and the Power Rate." November 1960. *Far Eastern Economic Review* 225.

Valdes, Juan Gabriel. 1995. *Pinochet's Economists: The Chicago School in Chile.* New York: Cambridge University Press.

Valenzuela, Arturo. 1978. *The Breakdown of Democratic Regimes: Chile.* Baltimore: Johns Hopkins University Press.

Valenzuela, Arturo. 1993. "Latin America: Presidentialism in Crisis." *Journal of Democracy* 4, 4 (October): 3–16.

Vallejos, Cristina. 1996. Multiple interviews with Vallejos, May–June, Buenos Aires, Argentina.

Vanous, Jan, ed. *Czech Republic Monthly Economic Monitor.* Various Issues.

Vanous, Jan, ed. *Polish Monthly Economic Monitor.* (May 27, 1992; March 22, 1993; January 16, 1995; December 15, 1995; March 18, 1996).

Wade, Robert. 1990. *Governing the Market: Economic Theory and the Role of Government in East Asian Industrialization.* Princeton: Princeton University Press.

Weingast, Barry R. 1979. "A Rational Choice Perspective on Congressional Norms." *American Journal of Political Science* 23: 245–262.

Weingast, Barry R. 1995. "The Economic Role of Political Institutions: Market-Preserving Federalism and Economic Development." *Journal of Law Economics & Organization* 11:1–31.

Weingast, Barry and William Marshall. 1988. "The Industrial Organization of Congress." *Journal of Political Economy* 96: 132–63.

Weingast, Barry R., Kenneth A. Shepsle, and Christopher Johnsen. 1981. "The Political Economy of Benefits and Costs: A Neoclassical Approach to Distributive Politics." *Journal of Political Economy* 89: 642–664.

Weldon, Jeffrey. 1997. "The Logic of *Presidencialismo* in Mexico," in Scott Mainwaring and Matthew Soberg Shugart, eds. *Presidentialism and Democracy in Latin America.* New York: Cambridge University Press.

Weyland, Kurt. 1997. " 'Growth with Equity' in Chile's New Democracy." *Latin American Research Review* 32, 1: 37–68.

Williamson, Oliver. 1975. *Markets and Hierarchies: Analysis and Antitrust Implications.* New York: The Free Press.

Willis, Eliza, Stephan Haggard, and Christopher Garman. 1999. "The Politics of Decentralization in Latin America" *Latin American Research Review* 34, 1: Winter 7–56.

Wilson, Rick. 1987. "An Empirical Test of Preferences for Political Pork Barrel: District Level Appropriations for River and Harbor Legislation." *American Journal of Political Science* 30: 729–753.

Winckler, Edwin. 1984. "Institutionalization and Participation on Taiwan: from

Hard to Soft Authoritarianism." *The China Quarterly* 99 (September): 481–499.

World Bank. 1994. *Poland: Growth with Equity: Policies for the 1990s*. Report No. 13039-POL. Washington, D.C.

World Bank. 1995. *Bureaucrats in Business: The Economics and Politics of Government Ownership*. New York: Oxford University Press for the World Bank.

World Bank 1996a. *World Development Report*. New York: Oxford University Press.

World Bank 1996b. *Multiquery Database. A Tool for Cross-Country Comparisons*. Washington, D.C.

Woodall, Brian. 1996. *Constructing Japan: Pork Barrel Politics*. Berkeley: University of California Press.

Wu, Weng-hong. 1995. "*Chiang-hua cheng-fu chi-chu kuei-mo yu chieh-kou chieh-tse chi tao* (On Strengthening the Budgetary Decision-making Process)," National Policy Dynamic Analysis, May 2–4.

Wynia, Gary W. 1995. "Argentina's New Democracy: Presidential Power and Legislative Limits," in David Close, ed., *Legislatures and the New Democracies in Latin America*, 71–87. Boulder, Colo.: Lynne Rienner Publishers, Inc.

Xu, Zhiyi. 1992. "*Lun Taiwan Diqu Dianli Duanque Wenti ji Yin ying Duice* (The Problem of Electricity Curtailments and Countermeasures in the Taiwan Region)." *Taiwan Yinhang Jikan* (Bank of Taiwan Quarterly): 43, 3: 66–81.

Xu, Zhiyi. 1994. "*Tan Dianli Duanque Wenti yu Duice* (On Electricity Shortages and Countermeasures)." Paper presented at the Annual Conference of the Association of Energy Economics, Taiwan, Republic of China.

Yang, Chih-heng. 1991. "*Yu-suang cheng-chi hsueh de kou-chu* (Politics of the Budget)." Institute for National Policy Research: Taipei.

Yang, Mali. 1994. "Taidian Guanbuliao Hedian? (Is Taipower Incapable of Managing Nuclear Power?)." *Tianxia* 8.94: 87–94.

Zagorski, Paul W. 1992. *Democracy versus National Security: Civil-Military Relations in Latin America*. Boulder, Colo.: Lynne Rienner, Publishers, Inc.

Zublena, Héctor. 1996. Multiple interviews, May–June, Buenos Aires, Argentina.

Index